PIRATES

PIRATES

*Terror on the High Seas—
from the Caribbean to the
South China Sea*

CONSULTING EDITOR–DAVID CORDINGLY

TURNER PUBLISHING, INC.
ATLANTA

Library of Congress Cataloging-in-Publication Data
Pirates: terror on the high seas, from the Caribbean to the South
  China Sea/edited by David Cordingly.–1st ed.
     p. cm.
  Includes bibliographical references.
  ISBN 1-57036-285-8 (alk. paper)
  1. Pirates. I. Cordingly, David.
  G525.P53 1996
  910.4' 5–dc20   96-15273
                     CIP

Published by Turner Publishing, Inc.
A Subsidiary of Turner Broadcasting System, Inc.
1050 Techwood Drive, N.W.
Atlanta, Georgia 30318

Produced by Salamander Books Ltd.
129–137 York Way, London N7 9LG, United Kingdom

Distributed by Andrews and McMeel
A Universal Press Syndicate Company
4900 Main Street
Kansas City, Missouri 64112

First Edition 10 9 8 7 6 5 4 3 2 1

Printed in the United States of America

CREDITS
Executive Editor: Walton Rawls
Managing Editor: Christopher Westhorp
Designer: John Heritage
Copy Editors: Gerard M. F. Hill and Jim Davis
Picture Research: Christopher Westhorp and Rachel Boone
Maps: Janos Marffy (© Salamander Books Ltd.)
Cutaway Artwork: John Batchelor (© Salamander Books Ltd.)
Filmset: SX DTP Ltd., England
Color reproduction: P & W Graphics PTE, Singapore

CONSULTANT EDITOR
David Cordingly was on the staff of the National Maritime Museum, London, for twelve years where he was Keeper of Pictures and then Head of Exhibitions. He is an authority on maritime history, including piracy. A graduate of Oxford University, where he read Modern History, he has a doctorate from the University of Sussex, and lives by the sea at Brighton, England, with his wife and family, working as a freelance writer and historical consultant.

CONTRIBUTING AUTHORS
David F. Marley is a Canadian historian specializing in Spanish maritime history. His work *Pirates and Privateers of the Americas* was awarded the "Best Reference Source 1995" prize by America's *Library Journal*, and the Anderson Prize from the Society for Nautical Research in the United Kingdom.

Jenifer G. Marx studied history at the University of Florence in Italy. She has written *Pirates and Privateers of the Caribbean* and collaborated with her husband, underwater archaeologist Robert F. Marx, on *The History of Underwater Exploration and Ocean Treasures*. Both worked on the excavations of Port Royal.

Richard Platt is a full-time writer with a special interest in maritime themes. His contraband gazetteer *Smuggler's Britain* was published in 1991, and since then he has written two books on topics connected with the ocean: *Eyewitness Pirate* and *Cross-Section Man of War*. He lives in Kent, England.

Marcus Rediker is Associate Professor of History at the University of Pittsburgh. He is the author of *Between the Devil and the Deep Blue Sea*, which won the Merle Curti Social History Award of the Organization of American Historians, and the John Hope Franklin Prize of the American Studies Association.

James C. Bradford earned his Ph.D. in early American history at the University of Virginia. After teaching at the U.S. Naval Academy in Annapolis, Maryland, he moved to Texas A & M University where he teaches courses in naval and maritime history and in early American history.

John Falconer is a photographic historian and has written extensively on South and Southeast Asia. Formerly at the National Maritime Museum, Greenwich, he was a joint curator of their exhibition on pirates in 1992. He is presently researching and cataloging the photographic archives of the British Library's Oriental and India Office Collections.

Dian H. Murray is Professor of History and Associate Dean for the College of Arts and Letters at the University of Notre Dame, South Bend, Indiana, where she has been researching Chinese history since 1975. Her publications include *Pirates of the South China Coast 1790–1810* and *The Origins of* Tiandihui: *The Chinese Triads in Legend and History*.

Eric Ellen is the executive director of the International Maritime Bureau and advises governments and shipping companies on how to combat piracy.

Identification of Additional Illustrations
Page 1: A Malay kris.
Page 2: *The Buccaneer Was a Picturesque Fellow* by Howard Pyle.
Page 3: Chinese junk pennant.
Page 4/5: Ottoman muzzle-loading rifle.

CONTENTS

INTRODUCTION

~

Ye and each of you are adjudged and sentenced to be carried back to the place from whence you came, from thence to the place of execution without the gates of this castle, and there within the flood marks to be hanged by the neck till you are dead, dead, dead. And the Lord have mercy on your souls.

CAPTAIN HERDMAN, PRESIDENT OF THE VICE-ADMIRALTY COURT 1722[1]

THIS VERSION OF the time-honored death sentence for piracy was used at a trial that took place on the west coast of Africa in 1722. The words were spoken by Captain Herdman, who had been appointed president of the Vice-Admiralty Court, and on trial were 160 men. They had been captured after a running battle between HMS *Swallow* and two ships led by the notorious Welsh pirate Bartholomew Roberts. The battle had taken place in a thunderstorm off Cape Lopez and Roberts himself had been killed by one of the first broadsides fired by the British warship. His death took the heart out of his crew and they surrendered half an hour later.

The trial began on March 28 and was held at Cape Coast Castle, a massive stone fort overlooking the waters of the Bight of Benin. It was here that black slaves were assembled before being shipped across the Atlantic to the plantations in the West Indies. Within three weeks of the opening of the trial fifty-two men had been hanged, twenty men had been sentenced to seven years' servitude in the mines at Cape Coast, and seventeen had been condemned to imprisonment in London's Marshalsea Prison.

In Jamaica that same year fifty-seven pirates who had been captured off the island of Hispaniola were put on trial and forty-one men were subsequently hanged at Gallows Point alongside the harbor at Port Royal. In October five Spanish pirates were hanged at Nassau in the Bahamas. In the following year twenty-six pirates captured by Captain Solgard of HMS *Greyhound* were hanged at Newport, Rhode Island, and five men were hanged for piracy at Antigua and their bodies hung in chains on Rat Island in St. Johns harbor.

The number of pirates executed in the 1720s was unusually high, but the attitude of the authorities to piracy had always been harsh. Since medieval times the usual punishment in Britain and her overseas colonies was death by hanging. The traditional place for pirate executions in London was on the north bank of the River Thames at Wapping. A wooden gallows was set up between the low and high tide marks alongside the wharf that became known as Execution Dock. It was the custom to wait for three tides to wash over the dead body before it was taken away. The corpses of the more notorious pirates were covered with tar as a preservative, placed in a cage of iron hoops and chains, and then suspended from a gibbet in a prominent place along the waterfront at Deptford, Greenwich, or Woolwich, where they could be seen by all seamen using the port of London. Other European countries treated condemned pirates with equal severity. When the German pirate Klein Henszlein was captured in 1573 after years of plundering in the North Sea, he and his entire crew of thirty-three men were beheaded in the market place at Hamburg. Pirates captured by the French or the Spanish authorities were executed, imprisoned, or condemned to life as galley slaves. In China and many other countries in the Far East, captured pirates were usually beheaded.

In view of the almost universal condemnation of piracy, and the savage treatment of those caught and found guilty, it is perhaps surprising that it has flourished in so many parts of the world from the earliest times and that it continues to flourish today. What is equally surprising is that it has acquired a romance and a glamor that would have astonished the thousands of victims of pirate attacks, as well as the men who languished in the Marshalsea Prison

Left: *Samuel Scott's painting of the capture of the Spanish treasure galleon* Nuestra Señora de Cabadonga *by the English ship* Centurion *on June 20, 1743, epitomizes the fine and debatable line between renegade piracy and state-sponsored theft. Captain George Anson was sent by the Admiralty to harass Spanish colonies in South America. His squadron of eight ships was decimated by storms, shipwrecks, and scurvy, and only the* Centurion *completed the circumnavigation. The capture of the Manila galleon, with its fabulous cargo of treasure, saved the day.*

Below: *An Italian compass from about 1580, made of ivory. The compass was the most important of all navigational instruments for seafarers. Its use from early medieval times onward enabled charts to be compiled and, used together with the astrolabe, made long ocean voyages possible.*

awaiting execution. What exactly was the attraction of piracy and what were the underlying causes? Was it simply the lure of gold, or were there deeper motives that encouraged so many men to sign the pirate articles and embark on a life of robbery and plunder?

Causes of Piracy

In 1724 Lieutenant-Governor Hope reported from Bermuda that the Spanish were attacking ships and setting their crews ashore on deserted islands. He described the marooned seamen as "poor, abandoned wretches" and warned that they would "embrace the only thing left them to do, that is, to save their lives from starving they are obliged to rob the first they meet. This my lord is the reason and the source of piracy."[2]

Robbing ships simply to survive has always been the most basic form of piracy, and continues to this day in certain parts of the world. For many seamen and fishermen their only skill is handling a ship and their only means of earning a living is through the use of a fishing boat or larger vessel. When the fishing fails to bring in sufficient income to support the men and their families, or the seamen are unable to find employment in the navy or on a merchant ship, then piracy or smuggling provides an alternative livelihood, particularly if there are tempting targets in the vicinity or just over the horizon. In her chapter on the Chinese pirates, Dian Murray shows how piracy was for centuries a seasonal occupation among the fishermen from the southeast coast of China. When the fishing was poor in the summer months, the fishermen sailed north and plundered ships and coastal settlements. In the autumn they abandoned piracy, sailed south, and returned to their traditional fishing grounds.

On the coast of Central America in the bays of Campeche and Honduras a minor but flourishing logwood industry had developed during the seventeenth century. Mixed bands of seamen and adventurers labored in the sweltering heat and the swamps to cut down and export the logwood trees, which provided a valuable dye used in the textile industry in Britain and elsewhere. The Spanish, who claimed most of America by right of conquest, regarded the logwood cutters as foreign interlopers engaged in an illegal trade. Following the peace of Utrecht, they began driving them out and burning their ships. The result was noted by Jeremiah Dummer, a British official working in the American colonies:

> The Spaniards have at several times fallen upon our people whom they found cutting wood in the Bays before mentioned and seized their ships, whereby we have lost that trade, and the mariners who were employed in it to the number of 3,000, have since turned pirates and infested all our seas.[3]

The logwood cutters were a rough bunch of men, and many were former buccaneers and privateers, but by turning them out of a useful occupation the Spanish left them with little alternative but to starve or to join the growing numbers of pirates who were roaming the Caribbean.

The alternating pattern of war and peace was considered by many contemporary observers to be a prime cause of piracy. During a prolonged period of war many maritime nations recruited large numbers of men into their navies. A whole generation of young men abandoned other trades and professions and became adept at seamanship and shiphandling. This happened to a marked extent during the last two decades of Queen Elizabeth I's reign when England and Spain were locked in maritime conflict. When peace came with the accession to the English throne of King James I, nearly fifty thousand seamen had to find peaceful employment or starve. The mayor of Plymouth informed the Privy Council that his town was filled with sailors who had previously been at sea in men-o'-war. With nothing better to do "they steal and take away boats in the night out of the harbour and rob both English and French."[4] Other ports and harbors throughout southern England experienced similar problems. Sir Henry Mainwaring, a reformed pirate who became a pillar of the establishment, reckoned that by 1618 there were ten times more pirates than there ever were in Queen Elizabeth I's reign.[5]

There was another surge in the early eighteenth century when the Treaty of Utrecht brought an end to the War of the Spanish Succession, which had involved the navies of England, France, Holland, and Spain. The Royal Navy shrank from a wartime strength of some fifty-three thousand down to thirteen thousand, which put forty thousand seamen

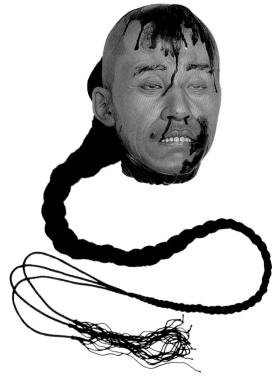

Above: *A graphic reminder of the punishment for piracy the world over: death. While hanging was the preferred method in the West, in the Far East it was beheading. The execution of the Namoa pirates in Kowloon, Hong Kong, in 1891 (above) was supervised by British officers from the Argyll and Sutherland Highlanders. This plaster head (above, right) is from a cast made of an executed Yangtse River pirate's head at the turn of this century. The pigtail attached is from the head of a different Chinese pirate executed in Java in 1898.*

Far left: *A Chinese two-handed sword or* dadao *from the Qing dynasty. This nineteenth-century sword has a slightly curved, single-edged blade and a wooden grip bound with coarse linen tape. Note the iron ring pommel and angular recurved guard with crudely carved quillons. The two-handed grip enabled a powerful decapitating stroke.*

out of work.[6] No doubt many of these men were happy to return to their homes and families and were able to find work locally, but many had difficulty in finding employment. Piracy was a tempting occupation for some of these redundant seamen, and it is no coincidence that the years between 1715 and 1725 witnessed a major outbreak of piracy around the shores of the Atlantic.

Many of the seamen onboard pirate ships, particularly the ships operating in the Caribbean and on the shores of the North Atlantic in the late seventeenth and early eighteenth centuries, were "forced men." That is to say, they were victims of pirate attacks who had been forced to join the pirates against their will. Particularly vulnerable were seamen with specialist skills, such as coopers, carpenters, and surgeons, but pirates were also on the lookout for experienced seamen who were strong and able-bodied. Some of these men adjusted to the new life, but many endured it for years before finding a suitable opportunity to escape.

Privateering

Privateering, which invariably flourished during a time of war, often degenerated into piracy when peace was declared. A privateer was an armed vessel, or the commander or crew of that vessel, authorized by a commis-sion (or letter of marque, as it was called) to capture the merchant vessels of a hostile nation. They were called privateers because they were private ships in private ownership as opposed to the naval ships belonging to the sovereign or government of a country. There were many times in history when privateering suited governments as well as private shipowners. For governments it was a cheap way of augmenting the standing navy during a time of war and, as James Bradford shows in chapter eight, privateering was frequently resorted to during the course of the seventeenth and eighteenth centuries. For shipowners who found trade disrupted during times of war, privateering enabled them to use their existing ships to capture enemy ships and their cargoes. The shipowners were expected to declare their prizes but could keep a proportion of their value.

Inevitably there was a fine line between privateering and piracy, and the definition of which was which often depended on whose side you were on. Many of Francis Drake's raids on Spanish shipping and coastal towns in the 1570s were acts of piracy because they were carried out when England was officially at peace with Spain. The same applied to Henry Morgan's raid on Panama a century later. To the Spanish both men were pirates, and the Spanish ambassadors in London lodged angry protests and demanded retribution, but because Spain was Britain's traditional rival and enemy, Drake and Morgan were treated as heroes by their countrymen. Drake received a knighthood and went on to lead naval expeditions as an admiral of the Royal Navy. Henry Morgan was also knighted and returned to the scene of his piracies in the Caribbean as lieutenant-governor of Jamaica.

Privateering was a double-edged sword as far as the authorities were concerned. It provided reinforcements to the navy in war, but when peace was declared the harbors were filled with armed private ships manned by crews who found that plundering merchant

ships provided a very good living. In August 1721 Sir Nicholas Lawes, the governor of Jamaica, wrote to the Council of Trade and Plantations in London:

> Since the calling in of our privateers, I find already a considerable number of seafaring men at the towns of Kingston and Port Royal that can't find employment, who I am very apprehensive, for want of occupation in their way, may in a short time desert us and turn pirates.[7]

This is exactly what happened.

The licensing of private ships to attack the ships of hostile nations in times of war was a form of government-sponsored piracy that was common to the maritime nations of western Europe and North America. A rather different form of officially sponsored piracy was practiced by the corsairs who terrorized merchant shipping in the Mediterranean. The Barbary corsairs operated out of Muslim ports such as Tunis and Salé along the North African coast, and their targets were the cargoes, passengers, and crews of ships of the Christian nations. Their Christian counterparts were the corsairs based on the island of Malta, who were sponsored by the Knights of the Order of St. John and attacked the ships and crews of Muslim nations. Since the targets of the corsairs were determined by religion rather than nationality, they were indifferent to the wars and peace treaties of other countries. Their oared galleys roamed and plundered without interruption for nearly three centuries. The most notorious feature of the corsair operations was the taking of captives who were either ransomed or sold to work as galley slaves. As Richard Platt shows in chapter four, the corsairs ran a highly organized business. The division of plunder was regulated: a certain proportion went to the state and to port officials as well as to the captains and crews of the corsair galleys, and the ransom and sale of captives was conducted as a commercial operation.

Treasure!
The most obvious cause of piracy was the lure of treasure. The discovery by the Spanish conquistadores of astonishing quantities of gold in the Aztec and Inca empires of Central and South America, and the subsequent discovery of rich silver mines in Bolivia, was responsible for two centuries of buccaneering and piracy on the Spanish Main. As David Marley and Jenifer Marx show in their chapters, the convoys of treasure ships traveling from Veracruz, Puerto Bello, and Havana across the Atlantic to Spain became irresistible targets for the ships of many nations.

On the other side of the world the riches of the East were a powerful magnet for privateers and pirates. The Manila galleons that sailed across the Pacific from the Philippines loaded with silks, spices, and gold were the main target, but they were so well armed that they rarely fell into the hands of pirates. Smaller merchant ships were less fortunate, and the many written accounts produced by William Dampier, Basil Ringrose, and Lionel Wafer are full of graphic descriptions of buccaneer attacks on the Pacific coast of South America. In the Indian Ocean, the annual voyages of the ships of the Great Mogul of India to and from Mecca became the target for generations of pirates, including Henry Avery and Captain Kidd.

A Life of Liberty
A less obvious cause of piracy is explored by Marcus Rediker in his chapter on Libertalia. It is what might be called the piracy of protest. Many merchant seamen suffered savage cruelties at the hands of brutal and sadistic captains. When the opportunity arose, they joined the crew of a pirate ship or took over their own ship and set up as pirates. For them piracy was not simply a means of escape to a better life. It was also a rebellion against authority and a protest against the harsh regimes they had suffered under. To safeguard their freedom they organized their ships along democratic lines. Captains were appointed by the majority vote of the crew and could be dismissed by a majority vote. A quartermaster was appointed to represent the crew and to settle minor disputes. He was expected to lead the attack when boarding a ship and he usually took command of a captured vessel.

Every member of the crew had to agree to a set of articles or rules of conduct. These varied from ship to ship but were designed to settle disputes, to regulate the fair distribution of plunder, and to ensure the safety of the ship. Today there seems nothing unusual about the regimes the pirates established, but it has to be remembered that in the

Above: *The French naval hero Jean Bart in action at the height of a sea battle. As leader of the much feared Dunkirk corsairs he was responsible for the capture of more than eighty merchant ships in the English Channel. He later took command of a French naval squadron and captured several English warships and an entire Dutch convoy. His success as a naval commander led to him being ennobled by King Louis XIV.*

seventeenth and eighteenth centuries most naval and merchant ships were run on autocratic lines. There was a strict hierarchy, and the captain and his officers demanded unquestioning obedience from the seamen under their command, and took a disproportionate share of any prize money. The pirates rejected this regime and anticipated by seventy or eighty years the ideals of liberty, equality, and fraternity that were to become the watchwords of the French Revolution.

Piracy, like highway robbery, provided an opportunity for ruthless men to make their fortune, but it also had other attractions. For young men it offered a means of escape from the drudgery and monotony of shore-based jobs and had the added spice of danger, violence, wine, and women, and a chance to see the world. In theory piracy should have been equally attractive for older men because pirate ships with their large crews and relaxed discipline offered an easier life than that to be found on board naval or merchant ships. However, the records show that most pirates operating in the Caribbean and along the shores of the Americas in the seventeenth and eighteenth centuries were young men in their twenties.

Very few pirate crews included men in their forties or fifties, and with good reason. The work of a deckhand in the days of sail was arduous and dangerous and demanded a knowledge of seamanship that was best learned when young. Life at sea involved hauling on wet ropes at all hours of the day and night, going aloft to handle heavy canvas sails, and often manning the pumps for hours on end. It meant living in cramped, damp quarters smelling of bilgewater, tar, and unwashed humanity in company with an assorted collection of pigs, goats, cattle, and chickens. The pirates did not have the pressures put on merchant seamen from shipowners to deliver their cargo as fast as possible with a minimum crew, but they had pressures of a different kind.

Unable to take on provisions in port and unable to use port facilities for carrying out repairs, they were always on the lookout for food, water, and basic equipment, and were often driven to raid coastal villages to obtain supplies of beef and flour and vegetables. Constantly on the move to avoid the attentions of warships sent to look for them, they sometimes spent weeks at sea, where they were at the mercy of storms, uncharted shoals, and rocks. A study of the lives of the buccaneers and pirates shows that few engaged in active piracy for more than ten years, and the careers of the more famous pirates like Blackbeard, Kidd, and Avery lasted no more than two or three years.[8] Sir

Henry Morgan, who retired to his estates in Jamaica, and the English pirate John Ward, who spent his last years in a Tunisian palace, were unusual examples of men who lived long enough to enjoy their plundered wealth.

Piracy Then and Now

Piracy has tended to flourish in places where trade routes funnel through narrow straits or pass through groups of islands. Merchant ships were not easy to track down in the vast open tracts of the oceans, but as they approached land they became easy targets for swift and well-armed pirate ships hiding among the offshore islands or in creeks and bays near a busy sea route. The Strait of Malacca and what are now the Indonesian islands have been hunting grounds for the pirates of the East for centuries, and the string of large and small islands in the Caribbean provided innumerable bases for the buccaneers and pirates in the seventeenth and eighteenth centuries. In Europe the constant procession of merchant ships up the English Channel and through the Dover Strait provided rich pickings for Dutch and French pirates, notably the Dunkirk pirates who were such a menace in the sixteenth and seventeenth centuries.

One of the earliest strongholds of pirates was the coastal strip alongside the Strait of Hormuz at the mouth of the Persian Gulf. Through the narrow strait came ships from India and the Far East laden with silks, spices, gold and silver, teak and copper. They were constantly at the mercy of the pirates who lurked among the coral shoals and sandbanks of the area, which became known as "the pirate coast." Several attempts were made to stamp out the pirates of the gulf, the most notable being an expedition ordered by the Assyrian king Sennacherib in 694 B.C., another led by the Roman emperor Trajan in the first century A.D., and a determined campaign by King Shapur of Persia in the fourth century A.D.[9]

In the Mediterranean there were pirates from time immemorial. They preyed on the ships of the Phoenician merchants and seized their cargoes of copper, silver, amber, and tin as the merchants headed to and from the trading centers of Tyre and Sidon. The numerous islands of the Aegean Sea were home to generations of pirates in ancient and classical Greek times: their exploits were recorded by Herodotus and Thucydides, and were woven into the stories and myths of the Epic poets. Alexander the Great attempted to stamp out piracy around 330 B.C., but the pirates were still going strong two centuries later during the height of the Roman Empire. The greatest threat came from the pirates of Cilicia, who operated from the rocky inlets and bays along the southern coast of what is now Turkey.[10] They had more than a thousand ships at their disposal. They defeated a Roman fleet, attacked Syracuse, and sacked some four hundred coastal towns and villages. The young Julius Caesar was among their victims and was held prisoner on the island of Pharmacusa for six weeks in 78 B.C. until a ransom could be raised for his release. By 69 B.C. the Cilician pirates had a stranglehold on trade throughout the eastern Mediterranean and were threatening Rome itself with starvation. Pompey was appointed to the office of proconsul with the prime task of stamping out the pirates. He assembled a fleet of 270 ships and swept the Mediterranean from one end to the other. His three-month campaign ended with a major sea battle off the coast of Cilicia and an attack on the pirate bases there. Ten thousand pirates were killed during the campaign, four hundred of their ships were captured, and the remainder were destroyed. To guard against further attacks, military outposts were set up at strategic points, and docks were built to accommodate galleys that could be used to patrol the coast. For a while the seas were relatively safe, and it was not till the rise of the Barbary corsairs in the sixteenth century that Mediterranean shipping was again under serious threat from pirate attack.

As Eric Ellen shows in his chapter, piracy continues to be a serious threat to shipping in many parts of the world today. The pirates may use assault rifles rather than muskets, and their vessels may be driven by powerful outboard engines rather than oars or sails, but their tactics are much the same as those used by pirates throughout the ages. They rely on surprise and terror, and employ the hit-and-run tactics that were favored by the buccaneers and Barbary corsairs as well as by generations of highwaymen and bank robbers. Sometimes a particularly vicious attack

Below: *Some examples of round shot of the Elizabethan period. The simple cannonball or round shot was the principal ammunition of all navies for several centuries. Early round shot was made of stone, which caused great damage because it shattered on impact. However, it was difficult to manufacture and by 1600 it had fallen into disuse and been replaced by shot cast from iron. The effect of such balls on impact could be highly destructive to masts and rigging, and internally the results could be quite horrific as the timbers shattered and deadly wooden splinters projected in all directions. Even more gruesome missiles were devised over the centuries with the introduction of bar and chain shot intended to cause maximum maiming of the men onboard.*

Beginning BLACKBEARD the BUCCANEER, By Ralph D. Paine
"Lost!" The True Story of the Tragedy at Fife Lake—"The Kidsnappers"—"Bighorn Battles"

Above: *In literary form, pirates attained a certain aura of glamor and romance. This cover illustration of Blackbeard was produced by Frank Schoonover, a former pupil of Howard Pyle, to illustrate an article entitled "Blackbeard the Buccaneer" in* American Boy *magazine in March 1922. Blackbeard is one of the few pirates of history whose appearance and dramatic life and death match up to the piratical heroes and villains depicted by writers and directors.*

resulting in the murder of the crew of a yacht in the Caribbean, or the captain of a cargo ship in the Malacca Strait, will hit the headlines, but many attacks go unreported. And yet each year there are numerous pirate attacks in different parts of the world.

Swashbuckling Heroes

In view of the continuing menace of piracy it is curious that the subject has acquired an aura of glamor and romance. What is more curious is that pirates are particularly associated with children. They are a regular feature of children's stories and cartoons, and are linked with treasure hunts and party games and dressing up. Much of this can be traced to the popularity of three works: *Treasure Island* by Robert Louis Stevenson, which was first published in book form in 1883 and introduced Long John Silver to the world; J. M. Barrie's play *Peter Pan*, which was first performed in 1904 and featured the alarming Captain Hook and an eccentric band of pirates; and Gilbert and Sullivan's light opera *The Pirates of Penzance*, which opened in London in 1880. Other influences on our perception of pirates have been swashbuckling films like *The Black Pirate*, which starred Douglas Fairbanks, Sr., and *Captain*

Blood, which made a star of Errol Flynn; the dramatic paintings and illustrations of the gifted American artist Howard Pyle; and the children's stories by Arthur Ransome—particularly *Swallows and Amazons*, an evocative account of children playing pirates during their summer holidays in the English Lake District.

The glamorizing of pirates is not a recent phenomenon. Lord Byron's epic poem *The Corsair* astonished his publisher in 1814 by selling ten thousand copies on the day of publication. It subsequently inspired an opera, an overture, a ballet, and numerous paintings. Sir Walter Scott wrote a weighty novel in 1821 entitled *The Pirate*, which was based on the life of the notorious Scottish pirate John Gow. The life of Blackbeard was celebrated in a melodrama entitled *Blackbeard or the Captive Princess* (1798), which was popular on into the Victorian era, and earlier in the eighteenth century, Henry Avery was the subject of a play entitled *The Successful Pirate* (1713) by the hack playwright Charles Johnson.

But more influential than any of these works were two histories of piracy that were closely based on the facts and made no attempt to disguise the brutality of the pirates. Indeed much of the popularity of the books was due to their bloodthirsty accounts of pirate attacks, torture, murder, and maroonings. The earliest of these was *Bucaniers of America*, which was first published in Amsterdam in 1678 and later in France and England. The author was Alexander Esquemelin or Exquemeling, a surgeon who traveled with the buccaneers and was present at some of the actions he recorded. The second was *A General History of the Robberies and Murders of the most notorious Pyrates* by Captain Charles Johnson, which was first published in London in 1724 and went into numerous later editions. For many years it was thought that Daniel Defoe was the real author, but serious doubt has been cast on this theory and the identity of Captain Johnson (no relation to the playwright of the same name) remains a mystery.

The combined effect of three centuries of books, plays, operas, films, cartoons, and children's games has been to create a popular image of pirates that is extraordinarily powerful. When we think of pirates today we think of buried treasure, and walking the plank, and distant tropical islands. Pirates are ready-made villains for adventure stories, or romantic heroes for escapist dramas. They have become mythical figures like giants, vampires, wizards, or witches. They are instantly recognizable and they come with an assortment of standard props. Just as witches are linked with black cats, broomsticks, and pointed hats, so pirates are associated with parrots, cutlasses, black eye patches, and wooden legs.

The problem is that they no longer seem real. And yet they *were* real and they bore little resemblance to the jovial fellows in *The Pirates of Penzance*. Most of them were rough-and-ready seamen who had a well-deserved reputation for hard drinking, foul language, and casual violence. They may have acquired a mysterious attraction over the years, but it is salutary to remember the definition of piracy that was laid down in a British court of 1696:

> Piracy is only the sea term for robbery within the jurisdiction of the Admiralty. . . . If the mariner of any ship shall violently dispossess the master and afterwards carry away the ship itself or any of the goods with a felonious intention in any place where the Lord Admiral hath jurisdiction this is robbery and piracy.[11]

Below: *Preserved in the Public Record Office in London, this is the account of the trial in April 1722 of Bartholomew Roberts's crew following their capture after a sea battle off the west coast of Africa in March 1722. The fascinating testimony reveals much about the lives of the pirates, as well as the attitude of the authorities. Ninety-one men were found guilty and fifty-two were hanged in batches between April 3 and April 20; the remainder were imprisoned or given sentences of servitude. Perhaps surprisingly, seventy-four were acquitted.*

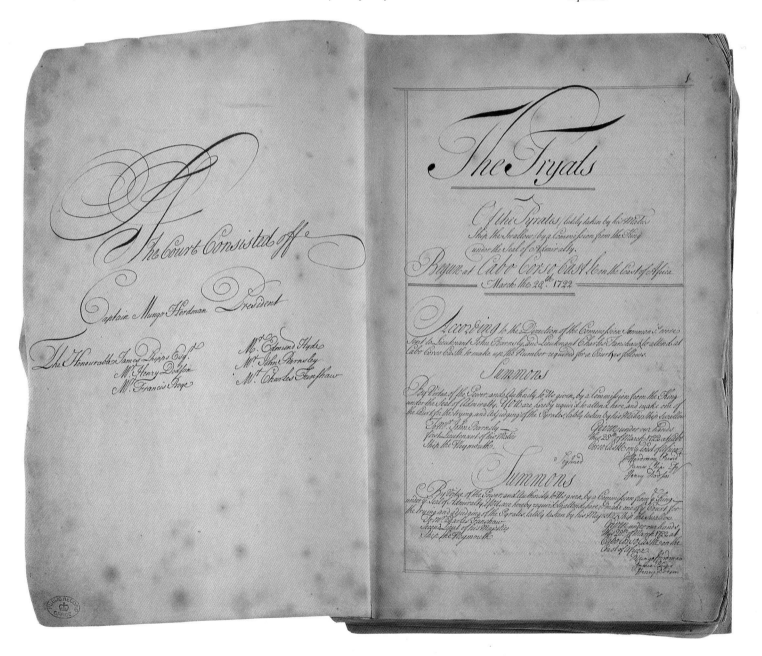

CHAPTER ONE

THE LURE OF
SPANISH GOLD

~

We entreat Your Majesty to remedy the grievous conditions prevailing today in the Indies; for every two ships that come hither from Spain, twenty corsairs appear. Because of this not a town on all this coast can be safe, for whenever they choose, they take and plunder our settlements. They even boast they are lords of the sea and of the land.

PLEA TO PHILIP II FROM THE CITIZENS OF RÍOHACHA, COLOMBIA, 1568[1]

IN AUGUST 1521, deep within the misty highlands of central Mexico, a small army of Spanish conquistadors stormed the Aztec capital of Tenochtitlán, climaxing a three-month siege in which perhaps 100 thousand people had perished. Once its last exhausted defender succumbed, the Spaniards spent several weeks recuperating, before dividing up into companies to occupy their vast new dominion. Hernán de Cortés dispatched three caravels with bulletins announcing his victory to the distant emperor, Charles V. These were accompanied by an exotic assortment of artifacts, as proof of the wealth and splendor of His Catholic Majesty's newest lands: gold and silver jewelry, "pearls the size of filberts,"[2] jade figurines, ceremonial costumes, feathered headdresses, mosaic masks, even three live jaguars.

But ironically most of this booty never reached its destination, for near the Azores this trio stumbled upon a half dozen French corsair vessels under Jean Fleury of Honfleur, who promptly took two of the caravels. Thus the spoils of Spain's greatest overseas triumph were not enjoyed by the imperial court at Madrid, but rather by Fleury's chieftain, the piratical Jean Ango of Dieppe.[3] Europe's sea rovers had gained their first taste of American gold. Five years later, a fête was celebrated at Ango's magnificent new *manoir* at Varengeville, just outside Dieppe. A masque entitled *Les biens* was performed, supposedly representing the riches of the New World, which people came from as far away as Paris to witness. A fantastic stream of players paraded before their eyes, garbed in all the finery of the vanished Aztec empire. One actor was carried past on a dais made by Indians, preceded by a half-naked page adorned with plumes, holding a two-handed Aztec sword.[4]

But although the Old World was to remain enthralled by the Americas for many decades to come, only a handful of its seamen would prove brave enough to attempt the daunting ocean that lay in between to visit its forbidden shores. Rugged individuals who recognized few laws but their own, they came to these verdant tropical shores to trade, to poach—to steal.

First Wave: Huguenot Corsairs

Fleury's interception of the Aztec treasure had been a legitimate act of war, although the Spaniards were loath to recognize this. To them, such roving did not constitute military prowess, but rather seagoing criminality. Certainly France's privateers—like those of virtually every other Western European nation around this time—operated very much to suit their own purposes, being far removed from the concerns of their weak central governments. Thus, when Fleury had the misfortune to be captured near Cadiz in October 1527 by Martín Pérez de Irizar, he was summarily executed as a pirate rather than being exchanged.[5] Such brutal treatment only hardened other privateers' resolve.

For the rulers of France and Spain had indeed been involved in open warfare during 1494–95, 1499–1505, 1508–14, 1515–16, and 1521–29, furnishing ample justification for licensed privateers such as Fleury. The accession of nineteen-year-old Charles V as Holy Roman Emperor in 1519 had further embittered this rivalry between the Hapsburg and Valois dynasties, as—already being king of Spain and duke of the Netherlands—his dominions now completely encircled France.[6]

It was during this latter conflict that French rovers began striking out across the Atlantic for the first time: in 1525 Sebastian Cabot

Left: *New World gold and silver enriched Spain, and her treasure ships became the focus of her enemies' attacks. This is part of the cargo that went down with the* flota *vessel* Nuestra Señora de las Maravillas.

Below: *Most gold was melted down from beautiful objects like this idol (below) looted from the Incas, which dates from the fifteenth century.*

encountered one such interloper off Santos, Brazil, while the next year the Spanish galleon *San Gabriel* of Rodrigo de Acuña—separated from Garci Jofre de Loaysa's expedition to the Strait of Magellan—was astonished to be attacked by three French vessels off Brazil. Similar formations were soon sighted prowling past Puerto Rico and Santo Domingo, their crews going ashore to refresh themselves on their lonely coastlines.[7]

Illicit Trade with the Useless Isles
Many of the lesser Caribbean isles had never been inhabited by the Spanish—being dismissed on their nautical charts as *Islas Inútiles*, or "Useless Isles"—while their few major settlements had been further depopulated by the lure of Mexico's enormous wealth. Early life on the islands had been hard, and those colonists who remained were too few, too isolated, and too impoverished to resist the French intruders, in fact welcoming their trade. "I am witness," wrote a disgusted Spanish observer, "how the residents give a better reception to Lutheran Frenchmen than to those [Spaniards] who go forth to colonize and conquer."[8]

Gradually these clandestine contacts began to blossom, especially after peace was restored between both powers in August 1529. For despite Madrid's repeated expressions of disapproval, French vessels visited the Americas in growing numbers, adding another ingredient to the resentment among Spanish officialdom: the charge of smuggling.

Within the next several decades the Spanish Crown came to regard any foreign vessel in the New World as guilty of trespassing, at best; if any American products were found aboard, this would be considered proof of poaching or smuggling; while resistance to the king's officials would be taken as piratical intent, punishable by death. Such sternness was scarcely shared by Spain's American colonists, thereby complicating matters: for an honest merchant might visit the West Indies and be made welcome in certain quarters, only to be attacked in others. Such inconsistency bred distrust—just as when European traders, in turn, used their knowledge of local geography to launch privateering strikes against Spanish-American towns during wartime. Under such circumstances, there could never be "peace beyond the line."

Above: *The Indians were treated barbarously by their Spanish conquerors —acts made famous by Bartolomé de Las Casas—whose thirst for gold was not easily quenched. This woodcut by de Bry shows Indians in rebellion, dismembering their Spanish oppressors, and making a point of providing them with the gold they wanted by pouring it down their throats in molten form.*

In 1535, relations between Paris and Madrid once again began to deteriorate, leading numerous French corsairs to take up station off the western approaches to Spain, threatening its returning ships—especially those bringing treasure from Peru, recently conquered by Pizarro. As a result, warfare erupted that following spring.

This conflict proved significant in that the effectiveness of French privateers brought Spain's transatlantic traffic to a complete standstill, obliging its leader to impose a convoy system for the protection of its overseas communications. On their outward-bound leg, galleons gathered at Seville and Cadiz to be escorted south past the Canaries by men-o'-war; on their return journey, they assembled at Santo Domingo to leave via the Windward Passage or the Strait of Florida, before gaining the Azores and being escorted home. While this method provided better security, it nonetheless inflated the cost of

all Spanish merchandise and starved their colonies of goods—much to the advantage of foreign smugglers.

Interlopers in Puerto Rico

The signing of the Truce of Nice by French and Spanish plenipotentiaries in June 1538 scarcely slowed these hostilities. Two years later, a band of French corsairs disembarked from a ship near San Germán de Puerto Rico, then sacked the town. Such depredations reinforced the Spaniards' notion that all foreign privateers were vicious pirates rather than honorable men of war, and that they conveniently ignored the strictures of their own commissions whenever possible.

Full-scale fighting resumed between France and Spain in 1542, and in February 1543 a rare Spanish victory was won over interlopers in the West Indies. Two French ships and a small auxiliary attacked San Germán de Puerto Rico again, making off with four car-

Below: Warships off Cadiz in 1674, *a painting attributed to Daniel Schellinks. Cadiz, an ancient and fortified port in southwest Spain, was one of the destinations, with Seville, of the treasure* flotas *crossing the Atlantic. One of the greatest coups of the English was a daring raid on its harbor ships in 1587 when a squadron led by Drake destroyed thirty-one Spanish ships. Earlier, in 1527, the French corsair Jean Florin from La Rochelle had been hanged in public in Cadiz, together with 150 of his men, for his attacks on Spain's treasure ships in the Cape St. Vincent area.*

Above: *A snaphance pistol, a common armament of the 1570s' period. Arms were traded widely in Europe during this era because national armaments factories had not yet been established. The snaphance lies midway between the wheel-lock and flintlock in terms of firearms development. It could be concealed and cocked, then drawn and fired; it was, however, only effective at close range—such as occurred when boarding a ship.*

Right: *This astronomical compendium was made in 1569 by Humphrey Cole, the finest English instrument-maker of his day. Designed for use at sea, it combines a number of navigational instruments, including a compass, a sun-dial, lunar and solar dials, and information for determining high water. It is made of brass-gilt and folds flat when not in use.*

avels. Two Spanish galleons and two lateen-rigged caravels were hastily manned by 250 volunteers on the neighboring island of Santo Domingo, setting forth in pursuit under Captain Ginés de Carrion, commander of the galleon *San Cristóbal*. Five days later he returned triumphantly, having captured the French flagship and forty of its crew members, plus sinking its smaller consort.[9]

Despite this victory, the inhabitants of San Germán remained too frightened to return to their dwellings, preferring to resettle inland at Guayanilla, far removed from invaders. And well they did so, for that June, five French corsair ships and an auxiliary, led by a Flemish Walloon named Robert Waal, assaulted the island of Margarita off Venezuela, burning the pearl-fishing town of Nuevo Cadiz on its adjoining island of Cubagua before withdrawing. One month later they appeared before Santa Marta, Colombia, landing four to five hundred men at noon next day to occupy this town. The marauders remained for seven days, destroying everything of value before retiring with four bronze cannons and other booty. The night of July 24–25, this same French naval squadron deposited 450 raiders near Cartagena, taking control with ease and forcing its populace to surrender 37,500 pesos in specie, plus another two thousand as ransom for its buildings to be spared.[10]

Raid and Trade

Such high-handedness persisted even after the Treaty of Crépy was signed in September 1544, marking an end to this latest round of Franco-Spanish hostilities. Cuba and Puerto Rico continued to be harassed, while five cor-

sair vessels and a smaller auxiliary surprised Ríohacha, Colombia, early the following year. After seizing five Spanish vessels in its roads, these raiders found themselves unable to disembark—so they called for a truce with its inhabitants, eventually selling them seventy slaves. This tactic of "forcing a trade" by occupying a position of strength, and then using it to barter, was to prove singularly popular among interlopers, as it ensured cooperation, prevented any sudden counter-

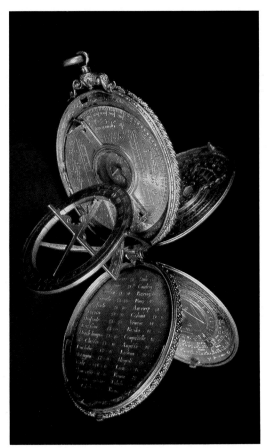

attacks, and provided the local Spanish-American bureaucrats with a pretext for negotiation with foreigners.

Revenge Attacks

The Spanish, too, resorted to extralegal measures in their frustration. When the French corsair Jean Alphonse de Saintonge carried a number of prizes into La Rochelle after the official cessation of hostilities, he was pursued into that very harbor by the flotilla of Pedro Menéndez de Aviles. In a stroke as bold as any pirate's, Menéndez recaptured five Spanish prizes under the very muzzles of the shore batteries, before boarding De Saintonge's flagship *Marie*, and massacring the French commander and most of his crew.[11]

For several years, the covert yet honest traffic in the Caribbean continued (attracting the first few English and Dutch adventurers as well), combining with the occasional piratical outburst. Such uncertainty obliged Spain's government to maintain its wartime convoys, notwithstanding the lack of a state of war;[12] thus by their very presence, the rovers had forced the Spaniards to adopt the plate-fleet system, a decision that would have far-reaching consequences for their empire.

Another war flared up in April 1552, prompting numerous new descents by French privateers. Antoine Alphonse de Saintonge, son of the deceased Jean Alphonse, sailed directly into the roadstead of Santa Cruz de Tenerife that November, determined to avenge his father. Instead, his flagship was struck and sunk by artillery fire, taking its captain and most of his crew down with him. Early the following year, cruel François Le Clerc—nicknamed "Jambe-de-Bois," literally "Wooden Leg" or "Peg-Leg"—rampaged throughout the Canaries, spreading terror.[13]

But the corsairs' greatest successes were on the far side of the ocean, amid Spain's vulnerable colonies. One major raid occurred on April 29, 1553, when five corsair vessels, a storeship, and three lesser craft deposited a landing force to sack Monte Cristi and La Yaguana, on the north coast of Santo Domingo. The Spanish-American settlers felt powerless to resist such invaders, who numbered eight hundred men, half of them harquebusiers. Such firepower was overwhelming in New World confrontations, because firearms continued to be expensive,

Right: *The long running rivalry at sea between Spain and England reached a climax in 1588 when the Spanish Armada attempted to land an army of invasion. Its failure meant that the balance of maritime power changed decisively in England's favor. Spain's power was reduced greatly and English maritime trade expanded, enabling England to project influence into new areas and to gain in power and strength as a result. From that, there grew a navy and an empire.*
This painting dates from 1590 and is by an unidentified English artist. It probably interprets the Battle of Gravelines, the only large fleet encounter. Flanked by two English vessels, the Spanish ship in the foreground flies the papal banner and is pointedly depicted carrying zealous monks and a jester.

Below: *The port of Havana was an assembly point for the treasure ships en route to Seville. Using a convoy system for protection, ships picked up gold in Nombre de Dios (later the transit point was Puerto Bello), proceeded to Cartagena to load further precious items, then met up in Havana with ships from Veracruz carrying Mexican gold. All then provisioned and headed for the Azores to join a protective escort.*

scarce commodities for the local inhabitants. A similar fate befell Santiago de Cuba the following summer.[14]

Frenchmen in Havana

Yet another important raid began at dawn on July 10, 1555, when strange sails were spotted near Havana, disgorging several score French corsairs a mile and a half from its dusty streets. The flamboyant Huguenot privateer Jacques de Sores of La Rochelle led this descent, advancing rapidly to take

HAVANA

Havana's lone twelve-gun battery from the rear. Its two dozen defenders surrendered by sunup of the twelfth. The French then occupied the town and brought four vessels in to careen.[15]

De Sores was a former subordinate to Le Clerc, having gained particular infamy by capturing the Portuguese galleon *Santiago* off Tenerife, then casting its thirty-eight Jesuit passengers into the waves to perish. While in possession of Havana, he demanded thirty thousand pesos to spare its buildings, five hundred for every Spanish captive, and 100 for each slave he held. Instead, the Spanish governor Dr. Angulo launched a surprise assault the night of the twelfth with thirty-five Spanish, 220 black, and eighty Indian volunteers, only to have his attack fail, and the startled French corsairs slaughter their Spanish prisoners.

The next morning, a wrathful De Sores hanged numerous slaves by their heels at prominent places along the town's outskirts, then used them for target practice in a brutal signal intended to discourage any further Spanish assaults. His men then leveled Havana and its surrounding countryside up to five miles (8km) inland, before retiring to the sea on August 5, carrying away the fort's twelve cannons.[16] Two months later, sixteen French ships arrived at Havana, coming to rest inside a harbor they knew to be unprotected since De Sores's raid. Foraging parties probed inland, securing some booty such as hides, before departing.

Early in 1559, a squadron of seven French corsair vessels appeared off Santa Marta, Colombia, under the famed commanders Jean-Martin Cotes and Jean Bontemps. These took a small amount of plunder, in the face of only token opposition from Indians armed with bows and arrows, before proceeding west-southwestward toward Cartagena. Arriving outside its harbor on April 11, they set three hundred harquebusiers ashore, easily brushing aside three dozen defenders. They pillaged and eventually spared the city for a ransom of four thousand pesos.[17]

Corsairs Don't Sign Treaties

But unknown to Cotes and Bontemps, the war had actually ended eight days prior to their assault, when the Treaty of Cateau-Cambrésis had been signed between Philip II of Spain and Henry II of France. Neither com-

Above: *Hundreds of soldiers and civilians died on the beaches and in the coastal towns of Florida, Mexico, the Caribbean, and Central America as the Spanish fought to defend their overseas empire from the predations of privateers, pirates, and adventurers from the seafaring countries of Europe.*

mander was unduly concerned, of course, and this agreement between two Catholic sovereigns did little to restrain the activities of Huguenot corsairs. Religious differences were already fracturing France's body politic, while its central authority was further weakened by the death of forty-year-old Henry just three months later in a jousting accident, leaving the rovers free to their own devices.

To the Spanish Crown, emerging as the European champion for Catholicism, the faith of many of these adventurers became an especially alarming cause of detestation: trespassers, smugglers, pirates, and now heretics too. In 1561, corsairs sacked Campeche, Mexico, and Puerto Cabellos and Trujillo on the north coast of Honduras. The Spaniards in turn captured a thirty-man French corsair vessel off Guanaja Island, summarily executing three of its crew members who were Huguenots, while conveying the remainder to Guatemala as prisoners.

Elsewhere, three other Spanish galleons were ransacked, one being the two hundred-ton merchantman *Santa María* of Captain Bartolomé Rodriguez, which had traveled to Honduras.[18] In July 1561, the mere presence of a French corsair vessel off Havana was suf-

ficient to force an arriving Spanish ship to offload its cargo on the nearby coast, rather than risk losing it in battle; a trio of small Huguenot vessels also materialized before Campeche, landing thirty men who were engaged by its local defenders and defeated.

The Florida Colony

However, at daybreak on April 30, 1562, a wholly different kind of threat emerged out of the sea mists, when an expedition from Le Havre sighted the Florida coast somewhere near present-day Saint Augustine. In a bid to establish a permanent foothold athwart Spain's American trade routes, two ships and a large sloop bearing 150 Huguenots under Jean Ribault of Dieppe explored as far north as modern-day South Carolina, before building a small fort near what is today Parris Island. Ribault then left two dozen volunteers behind under Captain Albert de la Pierria, before departing on June 11, and vowed to return within six months with some reinforcements.[19]

Upon his arrival in France, though, Ribault found the country wracked by religious strife, so he was not able to keep his promise. That April, civil war had erupted between a

Catholic faction led by François Duc de Guise, and the Huguenots under Louis de Bourbon, Prince de Condé. The thirty-six-year long French Wars of Religion would drain the Huguenot rovers of much of their expansional vigor.

It was not until June 1564 that Ribault's lieutenant, René de Laudonnière, was able to return to Florida with three hundred Huguenot settlers aboard three ships. Building a sizeable compound called Fort Caroline at the mouth of the Saint Johns River near present-day Jacksonville, this colony endured a year of disease, mutinies, and starvation. Two shallops were stolen by some members for a piratical cruise, while natives attacked foraging parties that ventured inland.[20]

Ribault himself did not reach his new settlement until August 28, 1565, when he brought six hundred more colonists aboard five vessels, plus two small Spanish prizes he had seized en route. But death also followed close astern; for at dusk one week later, a force that had been sent out from Spain to eradicate this intrusive outpost spotted Ribault's flotilla lying at anchor. The Spanish commander—Pedro Menéndez de Aviles, who had slain De Saintonge within La Rochelle twenty years earlier, and was now a knight of the Order of Santiago—put up his helm and stood directly toward shore, precipitating the French anchor watches to cut their cables and flee out to sea.[21]

These eventually succeeded in outrunning Menéndez's flagship *San Pelayo* and four other consorts, obliging the Spanish admiral to put into Saint Augustine's harbor, thirty-five miles (56km) due south, to land his troops and entrench ashore. Two of his shallops were also detached to fetch cavalry mounts from Santo Domingo, while Menéndez himself began an overland march on September 16 with four hundred men— two hundred of them harquebusiers—toward Fort Caroline. After being delayed by a hurricane, the Spaniards burst upon the French encampment before dawn four days later, sending its few residents fleeing through the marshes toward their ships anchored in the river.[22]

Ribault had earlier departed with the bulk of his forces aboard three vessels, hoping to circle around by sea and fall upon the Spaniards' base. What followed, therefore, was a massacre in which the Spaniards slew 112 inhabitants, and captured another seventy women and children, without suffering a single casualty. About sixty survivors managed to escape back to France; among these were Ribault's son, Jacques, and Laudonnière.[23]

Having secured the settlement, Pedro Menéndez renamed it Fort San Mateo ("Saint Matthew," on whose day this victory was won), then installed Captain Gonzalo de Villarroel as garrison commander with three hundred troops. Returning to Saint Augustine with the remainder of his force, the Spanish admiral subsequently learned that Ribault had been shipwrecked farther south by the same storm that had delayed his own advance northward. The Huguenot commander and six hundred of his men were left stranded ashore without food, water, or firearms, and were mercilessly hunted down and finished off by the Spaniards. Having drifted apart from the others, Ribault's own party of two hundred survivors finally surrendered on October 10. Their hands tied behind their backs, all the Huguenots—save

Below: A fine example of an English swept-hilt rapier (c. 1605) with an elaborate guard to protect the swordsman's hand. Rapiers, with their long, narrow blade, were designed for aristocrats and gentlemen, and were much used for duelling. Rapier fencing was a two-handed art; the other hand being used to parry and defend or to carry a dagger for attack. The Italians originated this form of swordsmanship that relied on speed and skill rather than force, but the Spanish refined it to an art with specialized schools that taught complex and precise movements to their pupils. While officers in the Caribbean would have used rapiers, many seamen preferred cutlasses or short hunting swords called hangers that were easier to wield in the confined spaces onboard a ship.

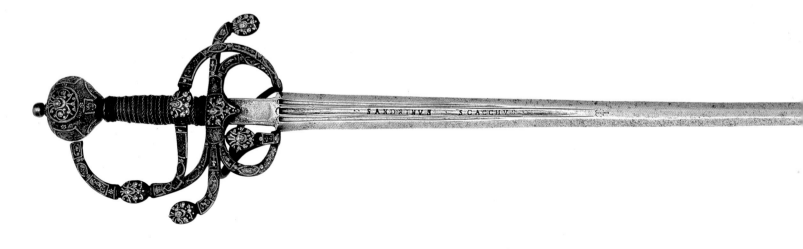

five youngsters—had their throats cut at a place later known as Matanzas—literally, the place of "killings" or "slaughter."[24]

Menéndez concluded his campaign by departing toward Havana on October 30 with three ships and the bulk of his men, leaving a small garrison behind in Florida. Near Cape Canaveral, he found another 150 French survivors, who surrendered on condition that their lives would be spared. These men were then shipped toward Havana aboard the *San Pelayo*. (Remarkably, they rose against the crew of Menéndez's flagship and carried it across the Atlantic to Denmark.)

The ferocity of Menéndez's conduct reflected more than half a century of bitter conflict during which rovers had become demonized as pirates and heretics to all Spaniards. Such callousness could cut both ways, as two-and-a-half years later the Gascon rover Dominique de Gourgues surprised the tiny Spanish force left guarding Fort San Mateo with three ships and 280 Huguenot followers. After being besieged within their keep, the outnumbered Spaniards under Captain Villarroel attempted to flee southward to Saint Augustine under the cover of darkness, only to suffer thirty killed and thirty-eight taken prisoner. In revenge for the massacre of Ribault's followers, De Gourgues put all his captives to death before sailing away over the horizon.

Second Wave: Elizabethan Sea-Dogs

French seamen would continue prowling the Caribbean for many decades to come, but their presence nonetheless underwent a noticeable decline because of the civil war raging at home. In their place came a gradual rise of English interventions in the New

World—an ironic development, given that throughout much of the first half of the sixteenth century, England had been one of Spain's staunchest allies in its struggles against France. This relationship soured as the century wore on, however, until by the late 1550s Anglo-Spanish cooperation had dwindled to almost nothing. The causes for this decline were many, including Spain's alarming growth in wealth and might, cou-

Above: *A stone carving of a two-masted sailing ship forms the dominant feature of this coat of arms displayed on the town hall at La Rochelle. The French were the first to challenge Spain's hegemony in the New World, and the predominantly Protestant port of La Rochelle provided a disproportionate number of adventurers to harass Spanish shipping in the Caribbean.*

Below: This watercolor detail from the Anthony Anthony Roll in Magdalen College, Cambridge, depicts John Hawkins's warship Jesus of Lübeck. Note the towering poop and forecastle to repel boarders. He used the royal vessel as his flagship during his second foray along the Spanish Main, but she was already an old ship by then and leaked badly in heavy weather. Hawkins eventually abandoned her when he and Drake were ambushed in the port of San Juan de Ulúa.

pled with its championing of the Catholic counter-Reformation, plus a steadfast refusal to open its American markets to foreign traders, however friendly. Following Elizabeth I's accession to the English throne in November 1558, such frictions inevitably began leading toward open conflict.

The period of the late 1550s and early 1560s also witnessed a dramatic rise in Spanish-American silver production, accelerating the pace of events elsewhere. In 1554, a new method for extracting silver from medium-grade ores had been perfected in Pachuca, Mexico: called the *patio* process, it proved simple yet effective enough to treat many ores heretofore deemed unprofitable by the older smelting methods, thus creating a boom in production as far south as Chile.[25]

Two major new strikes also occurred in Mexico around this same time, with vast deposits being uncovered at Guanajuato and Zacatecas, which promised enormous profits. The result was a steady yet spectacular rise in the wealth of Spain's American colonies, as well as an increasing need for reliable slave labor, both of which proved irresistible inducements for foreign traders.

Hawkins Realizes His Investment

One of the first Englishmen to brave the hazards was the Plymouth merchant John Hawkins, who made three voyages to the West Indies early in the new queen's reign. He departed on the first voyage in 1562, pausing at Guinea in West Africa to load his ships, the *Solomon* of 120 tons, the *Swallow* of

100 tons, and a Portuguese prize, with three hundred black slaves. He then traversed the Atlantic and arrived off Santo Domingo's north coast early that following year, disposing of his cargo ashore with the connivance of Lorenzo Bernáldez, commander of a 120-man cavalry patrol sent specifically to prevent this sale. Hawkins was so certain of his situation that he even shipped some of the goods he received by way of payment to Seville aboard Spanish vessels, where this clandestine transaction was later discovered and his merchandise impounded. Nevertheless, he realized a handsome profit with what he had conveyed back to England alone.[26]

The profits from this first venture proved so lucrative that they made Hawkins the richest man in Plymouth and attracted a host of investors for his second voyage—including his sovereign. In March 1565, Hawkins returned into the Caribbean with the queen's ship *Jesus of Lübeck*, of thirty guns and seven hundred tons, along with the smaller consorts *Solomon, Swallow,* and the fifty-ton *Tiger,* bearing another four hundred slaves from Sierra Leone. After watering at Dominica, he was refused trade by the Spaniards at Margarita island, but then enjoyed better fortune in mid-April at Borburata—a harbor a few miles east of modern-day Puerto Cabello, Venezuela—where he employed a brief show of force to overawe its local authorities. The Englishman then employed this same tactic at Ríohacha, Colombia, selling off the remainder of his cargo.[27]

Hawkins arrived back in England in September 1565 with even greater profits than from his first voyage. The Spanish ambassador in London complained heatedly to the queen, but Hawkins unabashedly assured her that his third crossing would be just as peaceable as the first two, it being his intent merely "to lade Negroes in Guinea and sell them in the West Indies in truck of gold, pearls and emeralds." However, after first experiencing considerable difficulty procuring slaves, Hawkins then underwent a series of hardships in the New World. Good fortune deserted him, and all the familiar obstacles to trading with Spanish America manifested themselves.[28]

Trading Insults

The problems began on June 4, 1568, when his twenty-eight-year-old kinsman Francis

Drake arrived opposite Ríohacha with the advance vessel, and sent a boat ashore to request watering privileges. The local Crown official, Miguel de Castellanos, ordered his three-gun battery to open fire, and, after a protracted exchange of shot, Drake retired out of range, instituting a close blockade. Hawkins's main squadron joined Drake five days later, and slipped two hundred men ashore on the tenth around noon, a mile from town. These men defeated a Spanish force drawn up to bar their path into Ríohacha, which was then occupied. On the fifteenth, led by a runaway Spanish slave, Hawkins sent a detachment on a nocturnal march deep into the jungle, which seized the Spaniards' hidden treasures and non-combatants, putting an end to all resistance and permitting some trade.[29]

Departing Ríohacha three weeks afterward, Hawkins's squadron came within sight of the port of Santa Marta at dusk. Hawkins sent a message ashore, and then met the next morning with its local governor, who agreed to trade after a mock battle had been arranged, in order to preserve appearances. The Englishmen remained in this harbor for another fortnight, before arriving outside the

Above: *The English triumvirate of sea-dogs that proved such a thorn in Spain's side, providing an ever-present danger to the security of their settlements and treasure fleets. From left to right: Sir John Hawkins who challenged the Spanish monopoly of trade to the New World with his three slaving voyages; Sir Francis Drake who raided the Spanish treasure ports, sailed around the world, attacked Cadiz, and became England's greatest naval hero prior to Nelson; and Sir Thomas Cavendish who circumnavigated the world in 1586–88 and seized the Manila galleon carrying twenty-two thousand gold pesos.*

Below: *This miniature by Nicholas Hilliard portrays George Clifford, Earl of Cumberland, as the queen's champion (Queen Elizabeth I's glove is pinned to his hat). An accomplished and elegant courtier, he was also a considerable seaman who commanded a ship in the Armada campaign and led a series of privateering expeditions against the Spanish that took him to the Azores, the Canaries, and the coast of Brazil.*

much larger port of Cartagena in late July. Again contacting the Spaniards, Hawkins's initial request for trade was rebuffed by Governor Martín de las Alas, prompting the English to bombard its outer defenses from long range with the vice-flagship *Minion*, while sending boats into the bay to forage for provisions. Hawkins scrupulously paid for everything that was taken with barter items, hoping to encourage further trade, yet he was forced to quit Cartagena empty-handed on the twenty-fourth.[30]

He then laid a course northward across the Caribbean, but after sighting Isla de Pinos off Cuba, his ships were engulfed in a hurricane while attempting to round the western tip of that island. Once this storm abated, Hawkins found himself on September 11 off the Triángulos Reef deep within the Gulf of Mexico. There he intercepted one of a pair of Spanish coasters passing by, whose master informed him that the only shelter to leeward where he could effect repairs was the port of San Juan de Ulúa, opposite the city of Veracruz. Hawkins's squadron limped toward this destination, capturing two other outward-bound Spanish vessels, so as to preclude any warning from reaching there ahead of his arrival.[31]

Fiasco off Veracruz

At dusk on the fifteenth, Hawkins's ten vessels anchored within sight of San Juan de Ulúa, whose lookouts mistook the vessels for advance elements of the annual plate fleet, which was daily expected from Spain. The following morning Hawkins got under way, flying false colors that allowed him to lure the welcoming pilot boat close enough to capture all the dignitaries onboard, after which he calmly passed the shore batteries—which were firing salutes—and moored within the roadstead before its defenders realized these were foreign intruders. Having thus secured the island without bloodshed, the Englishman sent a message across to Veracruz explaining his action, and promising to depart without further incident once his repairs were complete.[32]

At sunrise on the seventeenth, Admiral Francisco Luján's flagship *San Pedro* also appeared before the harbor, escorting a half dozen galleons of the real plate fleet. His second-in-command, Juan de Ubilla, soon brought up another five with his vice-flagship *Santa Clara*; moreover, aboard traveled the new viceroy-designate for New Spain, Martín Enríquez, who had been sent out to restore Crown rule in Mexico City following an attempted usurpation by Martín Cortés, son of the famous conquistador. A boat warned the galleons of Hawkins's occupation, and shortly thereafter the English commander offered to permit the plate fleet to enter, if its leaders would agree to let the English refit and depart in peace. Short of food and water, on a dangerously lee shore, the Spaniards

had no choice but to comply, although contrary winds then prevented their galleons from entering until September 21.[33]

It had never been Enríquez's intention to honor this extortionate agreement, however, from men he regarded as trespassers, smugglers, criminals, and heretics. Perhaps some minor coastal official might be bullied into such an arrangement, but not the king's direct representative in New Spain; the problems awaiting him in Mexico City alone would be sufficient to preclude any such beginning to his rule. Therefore, once the two fleets were moored side by side in their crowded berths, Spanish troops were slipped under cover of darkness aboard Diego Felipe's dismasted hulk *San Salvador*, which lay nearest the invaders. At ten o'clock on the morning of the twenty-third, a suspicious Hawkins opened fire upon this hulk, and most of his ships desperately attempted to get under way.[34]

Taken by surprise themselves—as they had not planned on attacking the English for another hour—the Spaniards nonetheless reacted well by quickly overrunning Hawkins's garrison upon the island, thus regaining control of their shore batteries. In a heated day-long exchange, all the English vessels were either destroyed or captured, except the vice-flagship *Minion* and Drake's tiny *Judith*, which managed to stagger out to sea via the perilous eastern channel. Behind them were left several dozen dead and captured comrades, as well as the sunken Spanish vice-flagship. During that night Drake parted company, sailing directly toward England while leaving Hawkins with more than two hundred survivors crammed aboard his *Minion*. Half this number later went ashore and surrendered to the Spaniards, while Hawkins resupplied as best he could, then set sail for Europe with the remainder. A nightmarish crossing ensued, with perhaps as few as fifteen of his men reaching England alive.[35]

Drake and the *Swan*

Although a relatively minor incident when set against other events occurring in the West Indies and Europe, Hawkins's defeat nevertheless proved somewhat of a watershed in Anglo-Spanish relations, so embittering feelings among English adventurers that

Above: *The final stages of the action at San Juan de Ulúa on September 23, 1568. A small island to the south of Veracruz, it had a sheltered harbor protected by a fort. Hawkins had succeeded in stealthily taking his ships into the harbor a few days before the arrival of the Spanish treasure fleet, intending only to refit and depart. But during the morning of September 23 the Spanish launched an attack and by nightfall five of Hawkins's ships had been captured or destroyed.*

Above: *Drake escaped the carnage at San Juan de Ulúa and wreaked his revenge against the Spanish at any opportunity thereafter. This engraving by Howard Pyle shows Drake's men at Santiago in the Cape Verde Islands. In September 1585 he had set sail from Plymouth in command of a fleet of twenty-nine warships. He headed first for the Canaries and then for the Cape Verde Islands where Santiago and Puerto Praya were sacked, thus letting the Spanish king know he was "mightily at sea again."*

future expeditions into the New World grew unmistakably more aggressive. Drake in particular sought to avenge San Juan de Ulúa by returning into the West Indies in 1570, commanding the small ships *Dragon* and *Swan*. Little is known about his activities during this voyage, yet it is assumed its tone was unabashedly piratical.[36]

Certainly this was the case the following year, when Drake again ventured into the Caribbean, this time with the *Swan* only. A contemporary Spanish document states that "upon the coast of Nombre de Dios [he] did rob diverse barques in the river of Chagres, and in the same river did rob diverse barques that were transporting of merchandise of forty thousand ducats and velvets and taffetas, besides other merchandise with gold and silver in other barques, and with the same came to Plymouth, where it was divided amongst his partners."[37] It appears Drake preferred operating off the Main in conjunction with French consorts. (This same year, the rover Jean Bontemps also died on the Spanish island of Curaçao, when he attempted to plunder it with seventy men. Confronted in a driving downpour by its principal landowner and numerous militiamen, the

invaders' temporary lack of firepower led to their stinging defeat. Bontemps succumbed of an arrow wound to the throat, his head later being carried into Santo Domingo as a grisly trophy.)[38]

Returning into the West Indies in the summer of 1572 with Hawkins's seventy-ton *Pascha* and the twenty-five-ton *Swan*, bearing a total of seventy-three crew members, Drake was joined by Captain James Raunce's ship, with an additional thirty men. Assembling a boat party between all three, Drake left Raunce in charge of the anchor watches, while he led a stealthy entry into the port of Nombre de Dios on the night of July 28–29. Discovered as they approached its beach at three o'clock that morning, the English had a sharp engagement with its hastily assembled town militia in the main square, during which Drake received a wound. Before Nombre de Dios could be fully secured, he fainted from loss of blood, and his men retreated back toward the boats. Upon rejoining the anchored ships, Raunce quit the enterprise, leaving Drake to establish a small base ashore in the Gulf of San Blas. From here, Drake harried the Spanish Main as far east as Curaçao, from September 1572 through January 1573.[39]

Good Queen Bess's Pirate

It was Drake's breathtakingly spectacular voyage of 1577, however, that truly elevated piracy to another plane. In a singularly audacious and fortunate cruise, Drake circumnavigated the globe, seizing a wealthy Peruvian galleon in the Pacific Ocean, and touching exotic new lands along the way. Unlike clandestine smuggling raids into the West Indies, such an effort could not be discreetly ignored, even by the queen. Over the Spanish ambassador's strenuous objections, Elizabeth granted Drake an audience upon his return in 1580, and questioned him for six hours regarding his epic cruise. She then bestowed a knighthood upon her paladin aboard the *Golden Hind* at Deptford, amid great public rejoicing and lavish ceremonies, henceforth referring to Drake jocularly as her "pirate."

Such support, during a period of supposedly peaceful diplomatic relations with Spain, could not but reinforce the outlaw appeal of any venture into the West Indies for the English, while at the same time hardening Madrid's resistance to foreign encroachments of any kind upon their empire. Fired by Drake's example, ever more rovers began taking to the sea. This change was clearly underscored when Drake next appeared in the New World, only five years later; for rather than the tiny craft of yesteryear, he now commanded a full-blown naval expedition of 2,300 soldiers aboard twenty-one warships, including two on loan from the queen—the flagship *Elizabeth Bonaventure* of six hundred tons, and the *Aid* of 250 tons—plus Martin Frobisher's private merchantman, the *Primrose*, which served as fleet vice-flagship, and the four hundred–ton galleon *Leicester*.

At eight o'clock on the morning of January 10, 1586, this huge force materialized off the coast of Hispaniola, capturing a Spanish bark with a Greek pilot on board, who informed

Left: *This fine portrait of Sir Francis Drake is attributed to Marcus Gheerhaerts the Younger and was painted in 1591, five years before Drake's death in the West Indies. The former privateer and pirate is shown with various symbols of his accomplishments. The globe represents his circumnavigation of the world, and the sword refers to his service to his country. Around his waist hangs the jewelled Drake pendant, and in the top left-hand corner is the coat of arms he was granted by Queen Elizabeth I when he received his knighthood. The motto reads "Sic parvus magna" (Greatness from small beginnings).*

Above: *This colored chart by Baptista Boazio dates from the sixteenth century and shows Drake's attack in January 1586 on Santo Domingo, then the capital of Hispaniola. Spain had founded the town in 1496, and when Drake arrived in the West Indies with a fleet of twenty-one warships he made it his first target. The English ships, flying flags of St. George, are shown at anchor off the town. Drake's flagship, the six hundred–ton Elizabeth Bonaventure, can be identified by her size and by the royal ensign flying at her stern. The local ships are gathered in the harbor alongside the town, and two have been sunk to block the entrance.*

Drake that the best disembarkation point lay at the mouth of the Jaina River, ten miles (16km) west of its capital city of Santo Domingo. Arriving there that evening, the English began landing eight hundred troops under the command of Christopher Carleill. Next day, Drake's fleet menaced Santo Domingo's seaward defenses, precipitating the Spaniards into scuttling two of their ships in a vain attempt to block its entrance; but when Carleill's small army unexpectedly approached from overland that noon, the Spanish will collapsed. The invaders remained in Santo Domingo for a month, during which time they ruthlessly pillaged the city, burning its buildings to extort ransom from the luckless inhabitants cowering inland. These unfortunates eventually raised twenty-five thousand ducats, with which sum

Drake grudgingly professed himself satisfied, and departed on February 11.[40]

Drake at Cartagena

Eight days later, Drake's fleet gathered before Cartagena, Spain's largest city facing on to the Caribbean Sea. Governor Pedro Fernández de Bustos had received ample warning of the Englishman's earlier assault on Santo Domingo, so had mustered a force of fifty-four riders, 450 harquebusiers, 100 spearmen, twenty armed black slaves, and four hundred Indian archers to resist Drake. Furthermore, out in the harbor lay two well-accoutered galleys, recently arrived from Spain under their veteran commander, Pedro Vique Manrique. Still, rumors as to the unprecedented size and armament of Drake's English fleet had already sapped the defenders' morale, even before any attack could be made.

Drake led his vessels directly into Cartagena's vast outer harbor, landing six hundred men under Carleill toward the evening of February 19. While these circled around to the north, Frobisher probed the Boquerón fortress with some pinnaces in the dark, until being obliged to withdraw. Next morning, Carleill's column brushed aside a shaky line of entrenched defenders, thus spreading fear throughout the rest of Cartagena's ranks. Vique's galleys were run ashore, their panic-stricken crews abandoning them by splashing ashore through the surf, while behind them the galley slaves rose in revolt. By the twenty-first, all Spanish resistance had ceased and the city fell; a mere seven or eight Spaniards had lost their lives during this fighting, as opposed to about thirty Englishmen. Cartagena was then ransacked, its vacant buildings being ransomed by the Spaniards for 107,000 ducats—against which amount Drake even extended a receipt. He remained until late April, then set sail for England via Florida and Virginia.[41]

The sheer scale of this expedition dwarfed previous efforts, marking another significant departure from piracy into the realm of naval strategy. The rovers had become much more than mere seagoing brigands—they were now a force to be reckoned with, capable of major conquests. Europe's royal navies were still extremely small establishments at this time, only a few dozen men-o'-war being owned outright by any government. The numbers of skilled privateers that any nation could muster during wartime would henceforth have a significant impact upon history. Elizabeth's reign had witnessed the evolution of a gifted new generation of rover, well schooled in prize-hunting and raiding around the world. It is estimated that during the subsequent fifteen years of conflict with Spain (1588–1603), 100 to two hundred privateering enterprises set out from England every year, averaging £150,000 to £300,000 per annum in Spanish booty.[42]

Third Wave: Dutch Sea-Beggars

When the Elizabethan wars ended early in the seventeenth century, a new maritime power emerged from across the cold, gray, choppy waters of the North Sea: the Dutch. Like their English coreligionists, the Dutch had once enjoyed good relations with the Spaniards, being fellow subjects under the Hapsburg emperor, Charles V. But the two peoples had gradually drifted apart over questions of faith and liberty, culminating in a protracted struggle for independence by the Dutch.[43]

However, the Low Countries remained so rich in manufacturing, shipping, and finance, that they maintained extensive commercial ties with Spain, even at the height of these difficulties. When the newly crowned Philip III, for example, ordered all Dutch shipping detained in Iberian ports in 1598, more than five hundred vessels were seized: obviously thirty years of cruel fighting and religious bigotry had scarcely blunted the needs on either side. Almost half these Dutch ships eventually regained their freedom through flight or bribery, and their clandestine trade resumed. Neither country could actually survive without it.

Soon Dutch seamen began looking beyond Spain as well, having gained newfound confidence and skill during their struggle for independence. The Canary Islands, Africa, Brazil, Asia, and the Caribbean all beckoned—the "Far Countries," as the Dutch called them. Their experiences mirrored those of the French and English adventurers who had gone before them: slavers and smugglers were made welcome in out-of-the-way estuaries by Spanish-American intermediaries known as

Below: *Another beautiful colored chart by Boazio, this time graphically depicting Drake's attack on Cartagena in February 1586. The English fleet is shown at three stages in the action as it moved from anchorage to anchorage toward the town. Drake's flagship is positioned at the lower left. Note the exotic creatures, particularly the large iguana much prized by the English sailors for its meat. The seizure of Cartagena, the principal city of the Spanish Main, was a great blow for Spain.*

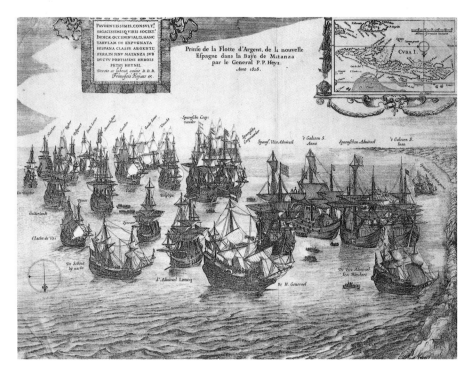

Above: *Piet Heyn commanded the thirty-one ship Dutch fleet that carried out the most spectacular and successful attack on a Spanish treasure fleet. Heyn's squadron captured part of the annual Spanish treasure fleet assembled in 1628 (top) at Matanzas Bay, Cuba, for the journey to Spain. The booty provided the economic means for the Dutch republic to continue its struggle against Spain for control of the southern Netherlands. Heyn was killed less than a year later suppressing the North Sea's Dunkirk pirates.*

rescatadores, and the volume of this traffic became quite remarkable, it being recorded in one particularly well-documented case that between 1599 and 1605, no fewer that 768 foreign vessels called at Araya, on the northern coast of present-day Venezeuela, either to gather salt from its pans or buy tobacco and pearls from the local inhabitants. The northern coasts of Hispaniola and southeastern Cuba also became highly popular destinations, where a brisk trade developed in hides.[44]

How Spain Discouraged Trading

On the other hand, the Spanish Crown continued to regard all such interlopers as pirates and heretics. When Admiral Francisco Coloma captured ten Dutch merchantmen off the coast of Nueva Andulucía in 1593, he summarily hanged their masters and condemned the crews as galley slaves. Nor was Madrid's wrath confined to foreigners: for on August 2, 1605, the governor of Santo Domingo suddenly appeared with 150 soldiers at the town of Bayahá, on the northwestern shores of that island, to read aloud a proclamation from the king complaining of the "inveterate and pernicious traffic" between smugglers and the Spanish residents. This concluded by directing that all households be transferred to the south coast forthwith, where such activities might be more

closely monitored. The troops then put every building in Bayahá to the torch, along with those of nearby Puerto Plata, Monte Cristi, and La Yaguana, in spite of the inhabitants' impassioned pleas. A Spanish battle fleet under Admiral Luis Fajardo called upon this coast in January of the following year, to ensure the complete evacuation of all its Spanish settlers.

But this "scorched-earth" policy not only failed to discourage foreign interlopers, it actually provided them with a better foothold. Certainly Holland's seamen were not dissuaded; when hostilities resumed between these two powers in 1621, after a hiatus known as the Twelve-Year Truce, numerous Dutch expeditions entered the Caribbean and showed their taste for booty.

Thus the old familiar tales were told, only the names having been changed: Pieter Schouten, for example, led a three-ship reconnaissance force through the West Indies in 1624, ransacking the towns of Zilam and Sisal on the northern coast of Yucatán, as well as capturing one of the rich Spanish galleons trafficking with Honduras. The following September, Boudewijn Hendricksz attacked San Juan de Puerto Rico with fourteen sail, landing between seven and eight hundred soldiers and besieging its citadel, only to be repulsed with heavy losses.[45]

It was in September 1628, though, that the pirate dream at last came true. For it was in this month that a fifty-one-year-old Dutch commander named Pieter Pieterszoon Heyn —better known to history as Piet Heyn— stealthily approached the north coast of Cuba with an expedition comprised of thirty-one ships mounting a total of 679 cannon, manned by 2,300 sailors and one thousand soldiers. At the port of Matanzas they cornered an entire Mexican treasure convoy, capturing it in its entirety. Notwithstanding the enormous expense of financing this expedition, there still remained a profit of more than seven million guilders following Heyn's return to Holland with this haul. It took five days for the thousands of chests of bullion and coins to be loaded onto more than a thousand mule carts that followed Heyn's coach on a triumphal march through the city of Amsterdam. Privateers everywhere must have exulted, as the lure of Spanish gold shone brighter than before.

Below: *This painting by Adam Willaerts shows a Dutch squadron (sailing in from the right) attacking a Spanish port. Although peace was reached in 1609, Spain and the United Provinces remained in a state of war until the Treaty of Münster in 1648. Fighting in the Netherlands was sporadic but the colonial interests of the two often clashed in Brazil and the East. This picture records a naval attack on a Spanish colonial fort. The defending Spanish galley in the foreground flies the Burgundian flag, carried by all ships of the Spanish-occupied Netherlands, and the man-o'-war just beyond it flies a flag showing the Virgin Mary upon a crescent moon.*

CHAPTER TWO

BRETHREN
OF THE COAST

~

A. DEBELLE DEL

A. CATEL SC

In France it is said that a rolling stone gathers no moss. The contrary is true in America. Fortune is to be found on the sea, where one must go to collect it. . . . I spoke highly of the attractions of a life in which no day is like that which precedes or follows it, in which freedom is the rule and great riches can be quickly acquired.

LOUIS LE GOLIF, FRENCH BUCCANEER 1734[1]

THE INK WAS scarcely dry on the Treaty of Tordesillas in 1494 before pirates and privateers began poaching on Spain's New World preserve. The maritime nations of Europe rejected the pact by which Spanish-born Pope Alexander divided the New World and its riches between Spain and Portugal. "The sun shines for me as for others," declared King Francis I, who had imperial designs of his own. In 1522 French corsairs intercepted two Spanish ships coming from Mexico. They were crammed with spectacular Aztec treasures that Cortés was sending to dazzle King Charles I (Emperor Charles V). Instead, the shipment of "wondrously wrought gold works," brilliant feathered mantles, a huge amount of bar gold, three hundred pounds (136kg) of pearls, and an emerald "as large as a man's fist" awed the French court and ignited the spark that soon burst into flame as the rest of Europe determined to share in the riches of the Indies. "I should like to see the clause in Adam's will that excludes me from a share in the world!" King Francis I exclaimed, and he encouraged the corsairs of Dieppe, La Rochelle, and St. Malo to cross the Atlantic and take what they could.

Over the next two-and-a-half centuries Europe's Wild West was the West Indies and the American coast. The frontiersmen and cowboys were the swashbuckling pirates and privateers whose exploits live on in song and story. It is not widely recognized that pirates played leading roles in a geopolitical drama of many acts that pitted expansionist forces against one another in the Caribbean, around the Spanish Main, and even along the Pacific coast of the Americas.

From Privateer to Buccaneer

Outright pirates in time of peace, and de facto pirates when sailing as privateers, they were all *piratas* to the Spanish. Avid for gold and glory the interlopers sailed "beyond the line" of Papal demarcation to prey on treasure-laden ships, merchantmen, and slavers. No one was safe. Buccaneer armies descended like locusts on settlements along the coast and even ventured inland to pillage and burn settlements and cities. The buccaneers tortured, raped, and slaughtered inhabitants. Some towns were battered and held for ransom *(rescate)* over and over.

For all their brutality and crudeness, pirates and privateers made signal contributions in a variety of areas. They destabilized the Spanish colonial system and made it possible for other nations to gain a foothold in the Western Hemisphere. They threatened the economic security of several other maritime nations. They also stimulated developments in naval architecture and were a catalyst in the transformation of small defense-oriented naval fleets into powerful navies that spearheaded global imperial expansion.

The buccaneers were as colorful a group of characters as ever went to sea. Held together in an amorphous confederation by a common spirit of adventure, greed, and intense hatred of the Spanish, they made an organized and generally profitable business of piracy. They were fearless, inventive, and dramatic, creating their own mythology. Our romantic vision of the buccaneer as a weather-beaten swashbuckler is confirmed by contemporary descriptions of the buccaneers.

A French buccaneer named Louis le Golif, better known as "Borgne-Fesse" or "Half-Ass," reminisced in his memoirs about a raid on Caracas in Venezuela: "I marched in front, as was right, with my pistols in my

Left: *The buccaneers were popularly depicted—not inaccurately—as leading an adventurous but dissolute lifestyle, and this nineteenth-century French illustration of Henry Morgan and his crew celebrating the looting of a Spanish ship is of that ilk. It is one of a series of illustrations by a French artist for P. Christian's* Histoire des Pirates.

Below: *The bowl of a clay smoking pipe excavated from Port Royal, Jamaica. One of thousands of domestic items found, the clay pipe was one of the distinguishing characteristic accessories —together with the long-barreled musket—of the original* boucaniers. *Smoking a pipe was, of course, strictly an onshore activity; because of the risk of fire, tobacco was only chewed at sea.*

belt, my fine high boots and plumed hat, and a sword at my side." Quite a stirring picture, but he may have had a rather peculiar strut, since a cannon shot had blown away one of his buttocks.

The buccaneers were key players in the struggle for New World supremacy. They produced a vivid record of their exploits. The richest source of buccaneer lore was written by a French Huguenot, Alexandre Oliver Esquemelin, or Exquemeling, who sailed to the West Indies as an indentured servant and then lived on Tortuga and sailed with the buccaneers as a barber-surgeon for several years. *The Buccaneers of America,* published in Amsterdam in 1678 and in London in 1684, became an immediate best-seller and has been printed in many languages since.

A Golden Opportunity

The combination of Spain's inability to defend her "Golden Empire" and the lack of honest opportunity for the masses of men flooding into the Caribbean favored the development of buccaneering. The Spanish Crown was obsessed with wringing the maximum amount of treasure from the Americas. Her severely limited defense forces concentrated on such vital ports as Havana, Puerto Bello, Veracruz, and Cartagena, leaving peripheral settlements vulnerable to pirate attack. These settlements, struggling in commercial isolation and chafing under neglect and trade restrictions, welcomed contraband goods from any nation. Spanish settlers actually joined with Dutch privateers to successfully plunder a Spanish fleet off the Mexican coast. The Council of the Indies, alarmed at the flourishing illicit trade between colonial settlements and the *piratas,* ordered the evacuation of a number of remote towns.

An edict in 1603 ordered the evacuation of towns along the Banda del Norte, the northwest coast of the great island of Hispaniola. For two years local authorities procrastinated, fearing the vacuum would be filled by pirates. In 1605 Governor Osorio accompanied troops to enforce the edict and compel people to move. His report of the actions taken is chilling, and no wonder there were those who fled aboard French, English, or Dutch ships to Cuba or hid from the governor's hunting parties in the area's densely forested hills.

As predicted, the evacuated areas became

a haven for foreign interlopers. They were the first of the buccaneers, the old guard of the fabled "Brethren of the Coast," whose bold and often bloody deeds brought plundering in the Caribbean and along the Spanish Main to outrageous new levels. Buccaneering was a peculiar blend of piracy and privateering in which the two elements were often indistinguishable. As long as pirates were furthering French interests, France cared little whether a pirate had a letter of marque officially permitting him to attack her enemies. The English felt much the same way. In any case it was never very difficult to procure some kind of paper. Buccaneering evolved from small-scale operations in the West Indies to massive land raids—the buccaneer hallmark in which motley buccaneer armies, thousands strong, ravaged settlements along the Spanish Main, holding cities for ransom and leaving behind such a residue of terror that mothers still threaten naughty children with buccaneer bogeymen.

Les Boucaniers

Buccaneering had a very modest beginning, when French hunters were attracted to what is now northwest Haiti by vast herds of wild cattle and swine that roamed the rolling grasslands and were descended from Spanish stock abandoned in 1605. The rough hunters, scarcely less wild than the animals they hunted, took to the bush, remaining for up to a year at a time, camping in the wilds and sleeping on the ground. The few remaining native Arawaks taught them how to smoke strips of meat on a wooden grill called a *boucan.* The *boucaniers,* or buccaneers, smoked beef and pork jerky, which, along with hides, they bartered for guns, powder, shot, liquor, and tobacco with ships that put in at harbors on the Banda del Norte.

They were savages in dress and habits. No amount of bathing could eradicate the stink of guts and grease that clung to them. Their rough homespun garments were stiff with the blood of slaughtered animals. They made their round brimless hats, boots, and belts of untanned hides, and smeared their faces with tallow to repel insects. On the coast they lived in shacks covered with palm leaves and slept in sleeping bags next to smoking fires to ward off mosquitoes.

Each man generally carried a six-foot-long

Above: *The Spanish acquired far more silver than gold from the New World (only about 10 percent of the new wealth derived from gold), and much of that which was sent back to Spain was fashioned by craftsmen into fine silverware for the use of the church and the state—just as, ironically, the indigenous Americans had done with the precious metals. This parcel-gilt pyx (top) is from Burgos and dates from about 1500. The oblong chrismatory (top) dates from about 1585 and has a high-pitched cover and scroll finial, the sides ornately chased with panels of strapwork.*

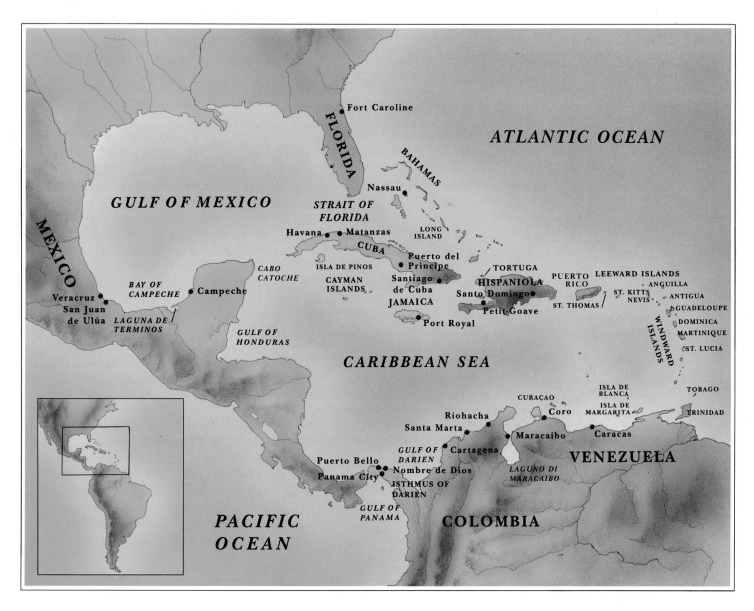

The map shows locations including:

Fort Caroline, FLORIDA, ATLANTIC OCEAN, BAHAMAS, Nassau, STRAIT OF FLORIDA, GULF OF MEXICO, Havana, Matanzas, LONG ISLAND, CUBA, MEXICO, CABO CATOCHE, ISLA DE PINOS, Puerto del Principe, TORTUGA, PUERTO RICO, LEEWARD ISLANDS, BAY OF CAMPECHE, Campeche, CAYMAN ISLANDS, Santiago de Cuba, HISPANIOLA, ANGUILLA, ST. KITTS, Veracruz, JAMAICA, Santo Domingo, NEVIS, ANTIGUA, San Juan de Ulúa, LAGUNA DE TERMINOS, ST. THOMAS, GUADELOUPE, Petit Goave, Port Royal, DOMINICA, MARTINIQUE, GULF OF HONDURAS, WINDWARD ISLANDS, ST. LUCIA, CARIBBEAN SEA, ISLA DE BLANCA, TOBAGO, CURAÇAO, Coro, ISLA DE MARGARITA, TRINIDAD, Ríohacha, Santa Marta, Maracaibo, Caracas, GULF OF DARIEN, Cartagena, VENEZUELA, Puerto Bello, Nombre de Dios, LAGUNO DI MARACAIBO, Panama City, ISTHMUS OF DARIEN, GULF OF PANAMA, COLOMBIA, PACIFIC OCEAN

Above: *A map of Central America and the Caribbean during the time of the privateers, buccaneers, and pirates—approximately 1500 to 1730. Spanish ships traveling from the treasure ports of Veracruz, Puerto Bello, Cartagena, and Havana made irresistible targets for generations of pirates who operated from the numerous islands of the West Indies. There were, however, even greater natural dangers in the narrow Florida Strait: ships headed north from Havana until reaching the latitude of Cape Canaveral, then turned east for Bermuda and onward to the Azores. It was a highly dangerous route and many ships were lost due to storms and faulty navigation.*

(2m) firelock gun and had an ax and a cutlass or two stuck in his belt. Marrow, which they ate straight from the bones of freshly slain beasts, was their favorite food, and drinking and gambling their favorite pastimes.

The early buccaneers typically lived in groups of six to eight, sharing all they had and abiding by mutual agreements. Some lived in a kind of homosexual union known as *matelotage* (from the French for "sailor" and the possible origin of the word "mate" meaning companion). The two *matelots* held their meager possessions in common, with the survivor inheriting. Even after women joined the buccaneers on Tortuga, *matelotage* continued with a partner sharing his wife with his *matelot*. In mid-century the French governor on Tortuga imported hundreds of prosti-tutes, hoping to regularize the lives of the unruly pirates.

Spanish authorities in Santo Domingo, on the island's south coast, became alarmed at the increasing numbers of poaching buccaneers and sent hunters to exterminate the animals. The mass slaughter backfired. By depriving the *boucaniers* of their livelihood, the representatives of the Spanish government unleashed a wave of piracy that lasted almost a century and did as much as any nation to further erode Spain's golden monopoly. Previously the *boucaniers* had sometimes turned to piracy in the rainy season, making stealthy nocturnal attacks on passing ships from small, oared sailboats. Now, deprived of cattle and hogs, they went after new quarry—the ships and settlements of the mortally ill Spanish colossus.

Above: *French buccaneer Pierre François and his men boarding one of the Spanish men-o'-war guarding the pearling fleet. Alexander Esquemelin described in his book how François sailed to Rancherias on the coast of Venezuela: "In this place lies a rich bank of pearls, to the fishery whereof they yearly send from Cartagena a fleet of a dozen vessels, with a man-of-war for their defence. Every vessel has at least a couple of negroes in it, who are very dexterous in diving, even to the depths of six fathoms within the sea, whereabouts they find good store of pearls."*

Tortuga: "Seminary of Pirates"

In 1630 the buccaneers settled on Tortuga, lying off the north coast of Hispaniola. The small turtle-shaped island offered fresh water and fertile ground. Best of all it offered good anchorages, defensible harbors, and an ideal position on the Windward Passage between Hispaniola and Cuba. It became "the common place of refuge of all sorts of wickedness, the seminary . . . of pirates and thieves." Spanish troops tried periodically to exterminate this pirate nest, but the buccaneers, like weeds, defied their efforts.

One of the first successes for the Tortuga-based buccaneers was the capture of a straggling vice-admiral's ship, part of a Spanish treasure fleet, by Pierre le Grand and a crew of twenty-eight. The buccaneers were cruising off the western coast of Hispaniola in a small pirogue when they first sighted the galleon. The buccaneers were near starvation and weak from thirst and exposure and voted to attack during the night. To bolster their determination they agreed that the ship's surgeon should bore holes in the hull of their little boat. Thus motivated, they stealthily approached and boarded, surprising the captain, who was playing cards with several of his officers. The buccaneers sailed straight for the French corsair port of Dieppe, and Le Grand, content with his rich prize, never sallied forth again.

Another French buccaneer, Pierre François, wasn't as lucky. Like many pirates he was undone by his insatiable greed. Cruising in an open boat with twenty-six men, he headed south to raid the pearl fisheries off the coast of Venezuela. The buccaneers came upon the pearling fleet, a dozen large canoes protected by two men-o'-war. To deceive the Spaniards into thinking they were a local craft from Maracaibo, they lowered their sails and rowed directly alongside the smaller escort ship, which, with sixty armed men and eight cannons, was still a formidable opponent.

François demanded surrender, and a fight followed. Amazingly, the buccaneers prevailed. Had they been content with the fortune of pearls they found aboard, all would have gone well. However, they tempted fate by assaulting the larger man-o'-war and were themselves captured.

Le Grand's success arose from a relatively low level of Spanish vigilance. News of this "happy event" precipitated a rush to the sea among the hunters and planters of Tortuga. Esquemelin wrote that men were so eager to emulate the pirates that they left whatever work they had and sought boats "wherein to exercise piracy." In the first couple of years they took a lot of Spanish ships, some of them with exceptional cargoes like two richly laden galleons sailing from Campeche to Caracas.

Before random buccaneering activities matured into the trademark large-scale orgies of pillaging led by several great captains, L'Olonnois, De Grammont, De Graaf, Morgan, and Mansfield, the buccaneers of the old guard favored small, easily maneuvered cedar sloops holding as many as fifty men and eleven to fourteen guns. Equipped with oar and sail, they were swift and could operate in extremely shallow water. Bermuda-built boats were considered the best. The English liked cannons, while French buccaneers preferred small arms and knives. The buccaneers, particularly the veteran *boucaniers* who had been hunters, were superb marksmen. Their extraordinary boldness tilted the scales in their favor as they sailed right up to a crowded merchant vessel and aimed their fire at the helmsman and any mariners in the rigging. They followed up by lowering the mast and triangular sail, and closed in on the stern to incapacitate the rudder before swarming aboard with pistols ready and knives clenched between their teeth. After fierce hand-to-hand combat, victory was often theirs.

Outbound vessels were preferred as prey because their crews and passengers were fewer and their cargoes more valuable. The periods before dawn or after dusk were favored for their attacks because it was during those hours that ships tended to sail past Tortuga, taking advantage of the winds that blew them toward the Atlantic by night but reversed by day. The buccaneers seldom left any Spaniards alive.

Brethren of the Coast

The Tortuga buccaneers began to call themselves the Brethren of the Coast about 1640. To become a member of this democratic confraternity a man vowed to subscribe to a strict code called the Custom of the Coast. Among the fiercely independent buccaneers it took precedence over any national code of law. By crossing the Tropic of Cancer they had, according to superstition, drowned their former lives. Last names were taboo, generally known only if a man was married. Before setting out on an expedition the buccaneers agreed to the *chasse-partie,* or articles describing the conditions under which they were to sail. In the days of the early *boucaniers,* before the huge expeditions organized by Mansfield or Morgan, the men generally selected their leader from among themselves.

Before sailing, the participants assembled in a council held aboard ship and decided where to head for provisions, "especially of flesh, seeing they scarce eat anything else," wrote Esquemelin, who gives us fascinating details of buccaneer preparations. They obtained pork by raiding Spanish hog ranches. Turtle meat, eaten fresh or salted, was a favorite, and when they could they ate manatees, the gentle sea cows that are now an endangered species.

The buccaneer council decided where to go to "seek their desperate fortunes" and precisely what share of the booty each man was to receive. Esquemelin's account of these negotiations records that like all pirates the buccaneers adhered to the law of "no prey, no pay":

In the first place, therefore, they mention how much the Captain ought to have for his ship. Next the salary of the carpenter, or shipwright, who careened, mended and rigged the vessel. . . . Afterwards for provisions and victualling they draw out of the same common stock. . . . Also a competent salary for the surgeon and his chest of medicaments. . . . Lastly, they stipulate in writing what recompense or reward each one ought to have, that is either wounded or maimed in his body, suffering the loss of any limb, by that voyage. Thus they order for the loss of a right arm 600 pieces of eight, or six slaves; for the loss of a left arm 500 pieces of eight, or five slaves; for a right leg 500 pieces of eight, or five slaves; for the left

Below: An Attack on a Galleon, *by Howard Pyle. This is one of the evocative oil paintings of buccaneers in action that Pyle produced to illustrate his story "The Fate of a Treasure-Town." The story was published in* Harper's Monthly Magazine *in December 1905.*

SLOOP, 1700–1730

ALTHOUGH SOME famous pirates sailed three-masted ships, most pirate attacks on the American seaboard and in the Caribbean in the early eighteenth century were made in sloops. The majority were rigged as gaff cutters, which meant that they had a single mast with a large gaff-rigged mainsail, and two foresails. In addition they could hoist one or two squaresails when running before the wind. They were between thirty-five and sixty-five feet (11-20m) in length, and carried anything from six to twelve guns on their broad decks. The crews were often very large, with as many as 150 men on the bigger vessels.

The sloops built in Bermuda and Jamaica were renowned for their speed and were ideal for piracy. Apart from being fast, they were extremely seaworthy and their relatively shallow draft enabled them to navigate in shallow waters out of reach of naval warships. When Calico Jack was captured off Jamaica in 1720 he was sailing a twelve-ton sloop that he had stolen from the harbor at Nassau a few months before.

Key

1 Mainsail wrapped around the boom.
2 Sternlight to cabin.
3 The captain's cabin.
4 Hatch to captain's cabin.
5 The tiller for steering the vessel.
6 Skylight for lighting and ventilating below deck.
7 Spare or looted gun

barrels stowed as ballast.
8 Pumps for pumping water out of the hold.
9 Four-pounder gun on carriage.
10 The boom for extending the mainsail.
11 The hold for storage of barrels of food and drink, sails, spare cordage and cables, and

looted stores and valuables.
12 Water barrels.
13 Main hatch.
14 Gun port: when the vessel went into action the gun ports were raised so the guns could be run out.
15 The windlass for raising the anchor.
16 The anchor.

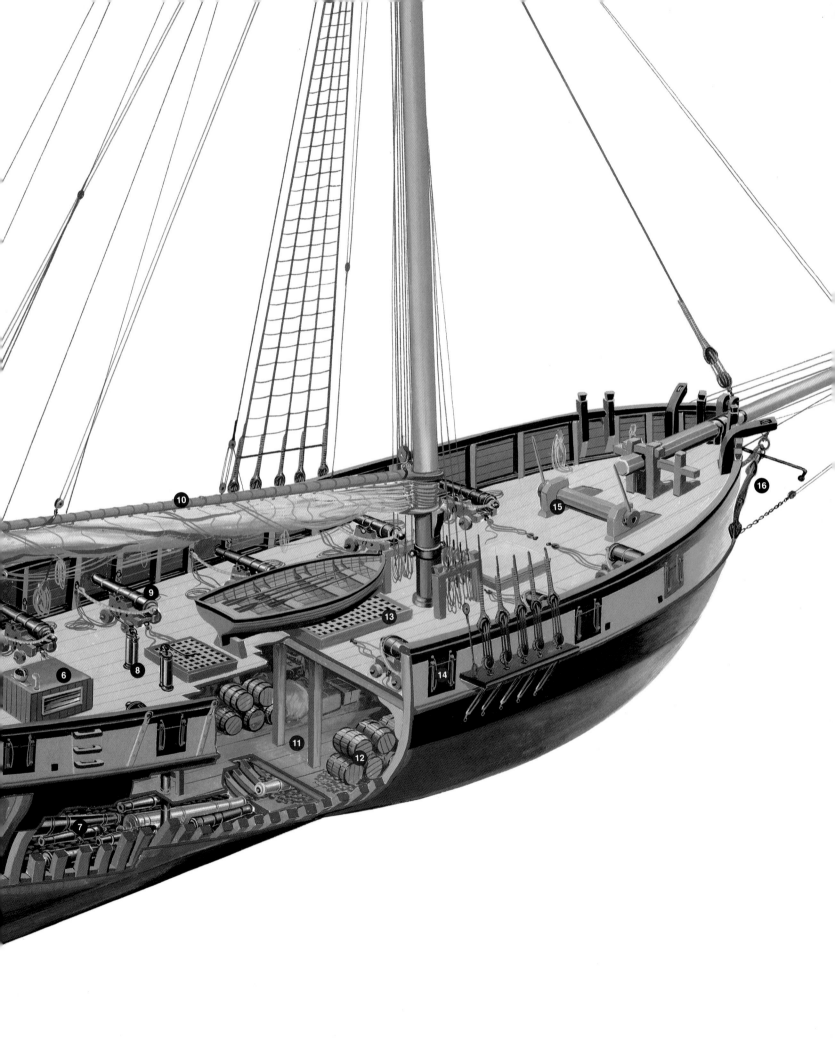

leg 400 pieces of eight, or four slaves; for an eye 100 pieces of eight or one slave; for a finger of the hand, the same reward as for the eye.[2]

Whatever remained in the pot after paying out the above was divided into shares. The buccaneer leader got five or six times what the ordinary crewmen received. The officers received an amount proportionate to their position, and the lowest-ranked boys were awarded a half share "by reason that, when they happen to take a better vessel than their own, it is the duty of the boys to set fire to the ship or boat wherein they are, and then retire to the prize which they have taken." The first to sight a prize won an extra share. The buc-

caneers swore not to steal from one another nor conceal any plunder. No locks or keys were allowed onboard. Any man found stealing from a brother had his nose and ears sliced off. Following a second offense, a man was marooned on a deserted shore with nothing more than one jug of water, a musket, and shot.[3]

El Portugués

From Bartholomew El Portugués, who with thirty men and four cannons in a leaking boat captured a large Spanish brig with a crew of seventy and twenty cannons, to the arch-buccaneer Henry Morgan, who traded piracy for politics, the buccaneers shared quick wits, astonishing courage, and an insatiable hunger for gold. El Portugués's wits saved his life. Not long after El Portugués captured a prize cargo of seventy thousand pieces of eight and a fortune in cacao pods, three passing galleons seized it. El Portugués was taken to Campeche, on the Yucatán coast, and held prisoner aboard a ship in the harbor.

On the eve of his execution El Portugués made a novel escape. Like most buccaneers he was unable to swim, but one night he managed to stab his guard and jump overboard, making his way to shore using two earthenware wine jugs as flotation devices. He escaped into the jungle, trekking 140 miles (225km) to the Cape of Golfo Triste, where a buccaneer ship picked him up and took him to the buccaneer haven of Port Royal.

L'Olonnois Terrorizes the Main

The most notorious of the Tortuga buccaneers was Jean-David Nau, called L'Olonnois after his birthplace in Brittany. Born at the bottom of the social ladder, he was transported to the West Indies, escaped to Hispaniola, and eventually joined the Brethren of the Coast on Tortuga. He was a psychopath by any century's measurement.

"It was the custom of L'Olonnois that, having tormented any persons and they not confessing, he would instantly cut them in pieces with his hanger [cutlass], and pull out their tongues,"[4] wrote Esquemelin, who also described other of his fiendish tortures, including "burning with matches and such-like torments, to cut a man to pieces, first some flesh, then a hand, an arm, a leg, sometimes tying a cord about his head and with a stick twisting it till his eyes shoot out, which

Below: *A portrait of Jean-David Nau, better known as François L'Olonnois. The engraving is from an early edition of Esquemelin's* Buccaneers of America. *L'Olonnois's savage cruelty was legendary, but he was also a remarkably successful buccaneer and his raids on Spanish colonial towns rivalled those of Henry Morgan.*

FRANCIS LOLONOIS.

Part. 2. Page. 1.

is called woolding." Once, when a prisoner refused to answer questions, L'Olonnois ripped open the man's chest with his cutlass and began gnawing on the still-beating heart, threatening to do the same to whoever refused to speak. Not surprisingly a number of his men, brutal as they were, thought this was too much and split off from him.

When L'Olonnois tired of preying on ships he turned his barbarous attention on the towns along the Spanish Main. In partnership with Michel le Basque he equipped a fleet, crewing it with seven hundred Tortuga ruffians. En route to Maracaibo, the buccaneers captured a Spanish vessel carrying forty thousand pieces of eight, chests of gems, and a valuable cargo of cacao. The buccaneers spent two weeks sacking Maracaibo, torturing prisoners over and over to discover every bit of hidden treasure. They moved on to the wealthy town of Gibraltar, which surrendered after five hundred Spanish troops

had been killed. The pirates remained a month, repeating their orgy of pillaging and carnage, and coming away with a total of 260,000 pieces of eight, jewels, plate, silk, and many slaves.

Not content with all that booty, the buccaneers returned to Maracaibo, extracting a further ransom of twenty thousand pieces of eight and five hundred cows. Three days after the buccaneers had weighed anchor, people were terrified to see their ships again at the port entrance. A boat came ashore with a message from L'Olonnois requesting a pilot to guide his largest ship over the treacherous bank at Lake Maracaibo's entrance. Needless to say, one was dispatched at once.

Tales of L'Olonnois's daring and the dazzle of booty that his men spread around Tortuga's taverns and brothels had men clamoring to sign on with him in spite of his sadistic behavior. He easily raised a thousand ruffians for a buccaneer army that descended

Above: *Captain Johnson's* History of the Pirates *describes how pirates who deserted their quarters in battle, or defrauded their shipmates of money or treasure, were punished by marooning: "This was a barbarous custom of putting the offender on shore, on some desolate or uninhabited cape or island, with a gun, a few shot, a bottle of water, and a bottle of powder, to subsist with or starve." The custom is vividly illustrated here in Howard Pyle's painting,* Marooned.

on the coast of Nicaragua, destroying the villages of Spaniards and Indians alike. L'Olonnois met a fitting end. He was captured by Indians who killed him by cutting him into pieces, which they then burned, throwing the ashes to the winds to ensure he would never return.

Spain is Mortally Wounded

Buccaneer prey was not always Spanish. Greed, not patriotism, motivated the buccaneers. Operating "beyond the line," they tended to ignore European peace treaties and could always find a colonial governor willing to issue a dubious license or letter of marque in return for a "gift." Tortuga buccaneers, for example, played a prominent role in attacks on Dutch settlements and shipping and helped years later to precipitate the bankruptcy of the Dutch West India Company. Ironically, the company had been enormously enriched when the privateer Piet Heyn realized the dream of every pirate and privateer: he was the first to capture an entire home-bound Spanish treasure fleet. In command of thirty-one Dutch West India Company vessels, Heyn lay in wait off Matanzas, Cuba, in 1628 and ensnared the fleet with scarcely a shot fired.

The capture of the treasure fleet was a triumph that was never repeated. The unmatched haul of treasure and goods returned a 50 percent dividend to company shareholders and financed further plundering expeditions. Since Spain had unwisely based its national economy on the mineral wealth of the New World, this singular achievement dealt a near fatal blow to Spain's already weak credit. The psychological effect of the capture, so close to Havana, was stunning. Fewer Spanish ships sailed, and they watched with impotent rage as more and more foreign vessels turned the Caribbean into an international sea.

In 1629 the Spanish empire was at its lowest ebb. For the first time since the introduction of the convoy system, no treasure fleets sailed. Fewer floating prizes, coupled with the growing numbers of the dreaded *piratas,* meant an increase in land raids with yet more horror for battered towns throughout the Indies and the Caribbean.

The Spanish Crown was alarmed at more than the mounting tempo of piratical attacks in the region. A major concern was the growing numbers of interlopers, especially English and French, who were settling in the islands as planters. There had been a population explosion in the West Indies, resulting in a corresponding surge in the pirate population. Buccaneering prospered as more and more men, most of them fugitives, escaped slaves, or former indentured servants, gravitated to the islands. France, England, Holland, and Denmark planted flags on a number of islands and encouraged immigration by selling patents to joint-stock ventures for agricultural companies.

The Buccaneer Labor Pool

Spain was wealthy but weak. She was unable to dislodge permanently the new plantation colonies that filled with European paupers working out terms of indenture and with transported laborers; there were also convicted felons, vagrants, and prostitutes who were sold by the government and forbidden to return to their native countries at the end of their term of bondage. After Cromwell's victory in the English Civil War, the English islands became a dumping ground for political and religious dissenters and prisoners of war, mainly Irish and Scottish. By mid-century, English colonists made St. Kitts and Barbados among the most densely populated places on earth.

The most piteous indentured servants were children and youths lured from back streets and alleys. One Englishman claimed to have kidnapped five hundred children a year over a twelve-year period. In 1640, two hundred French youths were kidnapped by their own countrymen and then carried to Barbados, where each was sold for a term of at least five years. The going price was nine hundred pounds (408kg) of cotton per person. Life as an indentured worker was grim. Often contracts were extended on flimsy grounds and workers were bought and sold; some never managed to gain their freedom. Slaves, a lifetime investment, were often treated better than indentured laborers.

Even when a laborer was free to start an independent life, he found there was little hope of employment. By mid-century sugar was king and African slaves had replaced indentured or free white laborers. Small farmers who had been growing tobacco or produce were squeezed out by expanding plantations with wealthy owners.

Above: *A buccaneer, armed with a blunderbuss and boarding ax, waiting to ambush some unsuspecting victims. The blunderbuss or musketoon was designed to fire a spray of lead pellets like a shotgun. It was in use by 1600, but the most popular weapon among the buccaneers of the West Indies was the long-barrelled musket, which offered range and accuracy. The buccaneers were noted for their high degree of skill with such muskets.*

More than once, indentured laborers helped the Spanish to spite their masters. In 1629 the treasure *flota* sailing from Spain was instructed to call at the infant English settlements on St. Kitts and Nevis and drive out the "trespassers." Admiral Fabrique de Toledo took Nevis easily when the island's indentured servants, many of them Irish Catholics, refused to fight alongside their planter-masters. John Hilton, a storekeeper, said that "our servants proved treacherous, running away from us and swimed aboard and told them where we hid our provisions and in what case our islands stood."

St. Kitts, which had both French and English settlers, surrendered too. Most of the French had escaped, but the English were taken prisoner. Their homes and crops were destroyed, although de Toledo treated them humanely, sending the majority back to England and taking only a few to Spain as hostages. Some of the former settlers of Nevis and St. Kitts despaired of restoring their plantations and drifted to Tortuga, where most took up the buccaneering life.

International Buccaneering

The Brethren of the Coast formed a roving sea republic made up of a shifting confederation of English, Irish, French, Dutch, and Flemish buccaneers, and with a sprinkling of other nationalities. Both able-bodied seamen and slaves on a prize were strongly encouraged to sign articles joining the buccaneer crew. The alternative was to labor without enjoying a share of plunder. Passengers of means were allowed to pay ransom, but feeble or sick men were abandoned or slain. Runaway slaves and fugitive indentured servants, as well as a few Caribbean natives also joined the fraternity of marauders.

Several prominent Tortuga buccaneers came from the highest reaches of the social scale. The most successful nobleman was the Chevalier de Grammont. Following a scandalous duel in Paris, he joined the French Royal Marines and sailed to the West Indies. In command of a privateer he captured a rich Dutch merchantman near Martinique and realized the equivalent of four hundred thousand livres for his prize at Hispaniola, where, according to the Jesuit historian Charlevoix, he proceeded to disgrace himself gambling, wenching, and drinking until not a penny remained.[5]

De Grammont couldn't return to France, so he chose to join the Brethren of the Coast. Pirates were a superstitious lot, but they overlooked De Grammont's atheism and flocked to sign on with him because he was a courageous leader, generous, and fair. In 1678 De Grammont and seven hundred men established a base on Lake Maracaibo. For six months they sallied forth to ravage coastal settlements and seize Spanish vessels, but the spoils were disappointing.

In 1683 De Grammont joined an international buccaneering expedition against Veracruz that made up for past disappointments. With De Grammont were an English captain and five Dutch captains, including the leaders Laurens de Graaf and a pirate named Vanhorn, who had come to the Caribbean to sell a cargo of slaves seized on Africa's Guinea Coast. De Graaf's reputation as a successful leader had been boosted by his seizure of a ship laden with 120,000 pieces of eight en route from Havana to pay off the garrison at Puerto Rico. Each of his crew had received seven hundred pieces of eight, and the French governor of Petit-Goave, who had supplied a license, was in for a share as well.

De Graaf, a veteran of many expeditions, was an interesting man who pioneered the French claim to Louisiana. He had been a Dutch gunner in the Spanish navy, working his way up to commander. On his first tour in the Caribbean he was captured by buccaneers and became one of them. His name made Spanish colonists tremble, and prayers were offered at masses begging God to spare towns from his savagery.

The seven captains of the international expedition made their rendezvous off Cabo Catoche, Yucatán. Aware that the city was awaiting the arrival of two ships from Caracas, the buccaneers crammed about eight hundred of the one thousand men on two of the ships. The ships, with the buccaneers lying out of sight, hoisted the Spanish flag and calmly sailed into the harbor guided by welcoming bonfire beacons. What followed was the familiar litany of rapine and pillage, which went on for four days. The governor was found hiding in a hayloft and ransomed for seventy thousand pieces of eight. The expedition yielded 1,300 slaves and enough booty for each of the one thousand participants to receive a share of eight hundred pieces of eight.

Vanhorn, whose two ships had been used for transporting all the buccaneers to shore, demanded thirty shares. He and De Graaf got in a fight over the division, and Vanhorn was wounded on the wrist. What seemed like a mere scratch turned septic, and two weeks later he died of gangrene.

The governor of Veracruz was beheaded for allowing the *piratas* to take the city with such ease. The raid forced the cancellation of the annual Veracruz Fair, with the result that the

Cadiz-bound Mexican treasure fleet was less than half normal size. In spite of Spanish objections, both Governor Lynch of Jamaica and the French governor on Hispaniola courted De Graaf to make his headquarters with them. By this time the French king had ordered a halt to buccaneering on his islands, and at least one governor tried valiantly to comply. De Franquesnay, while temporary governor of Hispaniola, really cracked down on the buccaneers, who threatened to rise up in arms. He was replaced by De Cussy, who dispensed commissions freely until forced by the king to repress the buccaneers.

Port Royal: Buccaneer Boom Town

In mid-century, England wrested control of Jamaica from Spain, and Port Royal became the leading buccaneer base. The island fell into English hands in a roundabout way when Lord Protector Oliver Cromwell's grandiose Western Design misfired. His plan to seize Hispaniola was nothing more than a piratical expedition, launched with no declaration of war while English and Spanish diplomats were discussing a possible alliance. Cromwell had grossly underestimated the Spanish force and overestimated his own. The attack on Hispaniola was a debacle. Returning to England without some kind of territorial acquisition was unthinkable, so the expedition set its sights on Jamaica, which lay at the very core of the Spanish Caribbean. In 1655

Below: A nineteenth-century engraving entitled The Retreat of the Pirates *shows a band of men heading back to the coast after attacking and looting a coastal settlement. Because of increased security with the better protected* flotas, *the pickings from Spanish shipping became thinner, and land raids became a staple of buccaneer life. In the space of just a few years in the mid-seventeenth century, Port Royal buccaneers ransacked more than fifty such*

ROCK BRASILIANO
Part 1 Chi 6 pa 561

new licenses for taverns were granted in July 1661 alone. The drink of choice was a potent rum punch called "kill-devil" about which Governor Modyford wrote that "the Spaniards wondered much at the sickness of our people, until they knew the strength of their drinks, but then wondered more that they were not all dead."

A clergyman arriving to minister to Port Royal returned to England on the same ship that had brought him, declaring "since the majority of its population consists of pirates, cutthroats, whores and some of the vilest persons in the whole of the world, I felt my permanence there was of no use."

Buccaneer raids were so frequent and so brutal that Spanish colonists took to the hills in reflex action at the mere sight of an unexpected sail on the horizon. In the six years following the English occupation of Jamaica, Port Royal buccaneers ravaged eighteen cities, four towns, and some three dozen smaller settlements. Some villages were assaulted again and again, including a number far inland where sea robbers would hardly seem likely to venture.

Christopher Myngs brought the first spectacular haul back to Port Royal. He and a band of three hundred ruffians descended on the southern Caribbean like a plague that devastated many settlements on the coast of the Spanish Main. At Coro, the major city on Venezuela's Lake Maracaibo, the buccaneers pursued fleeing inhabitants into the forest and discovered a cache of plate, pearls, cocoa, and twenty-two chests of royal treasure, each crammed with four hundred pounds (180kg) of silver coins, some £500,000 worth. When English authorities discovered Myngs had not only skimmed twelve thousand pieces of eight before he shared out with his crew but also pillaged six Dutch ships, they banished him to England. Like so many of his fellows, he was soon back in Port Royal and engaging in buccaneering.

In 1692 the apocalyptic destruction of Port Royal in an earthquake and tidal wave was widely regarded as God's judgment on the "Sodom of the New World." But the heyday of the buccaneers was over. The city had outgrown its need for the buccaneers.

Roche Brasiliano

Port Royal's buccaneers ran the gamut from unstable sociopaths to brilliant leaders like

Left: *An engraved portrait of the particularly brutal Dutch buccaneer Roche Brasiliano. Originally from the Netherlands, he emigrated to the Dutch colony of Bahia in Brazil, later finding his way to Jamaica where the English buccaneers called him "Rock the Brazilian." He participated in Morgan's attacks on Puerto Bello and Panama and provides one of the few documented examples of a pirate who buried his treasure.*

the expedition managed to wrest the sparsely settled island from the Spaniards despite one of the most inept military campaigns in British history.

English buccaneers, driven from Tortuga by the French, found an ideal base at Port Royal, "a citadel over all the Spanish West Indies." The early governors welcomed Dutch, Portuguese, and French buccaneers too, freely issuing letters of marque to anyone who would aid the vulnerable new colony by harassing the Spaniards. As early as 1662, so much plundered gold and silver was flowing into Port Royal that the government proposed establishing a mint. It was said that in Port Royal there was "more plenty of running cash [proportionately to the population] than in London."

With a vast harbor capable of sheltering five hundred ships, an ideal location at the center of Caribbean shipping routes, a ready market, and sympathetic officials, Port Royal was pirate heaven. The town rapidly filled with buccaneers and their loot: "gold and silver in bullion and coins, Bars and cakes of gold, wedges and pigs of silver, Pistoles, Pieces of Eight and several other coins of both metals, with store of wrought Plate, jewels, rich pearl necklaces, and of Pearl unsorted and drilled . . . bushels."[6]

Brothels, gaming houses, taverns, and grog shops sprang up like mushrooms to accommodate the free-spending buccaneers; forty

Below: Shipping off Port Royal, Jamaica, c. 1760, by Richard Paton. In its heyday in the 1670s and 1680s, Port Royal was one of the richest and busiest trading ports in the West Indies. It was hit by a devastating earthquake in 1692 that killed two thousand people and sank much of the town beneath the sea. One eyewitness reported the horror of people whom the earth had swallowed up to their necks and then closed upon them again, squeezing them to death with just their heads above the ground—which dogs then ate. Here, the remains of the town can be seen at the end of the spit of land in the middle distance. Beyond it is the town of Kingston with the Blue Mountains rising up behind.

Henry Morgan. One of the least savory was a squat, barrel-chested Hollander with a truly terrible temper who had lived in Brazil and was called Roche Brasiliano. He was noted for running through the streets in a drunken rage, beating every person he saw. He once roasted Spanish captives alive on wooden spits when they refused to provide him with information.

Brasiliano led a buccaneer band recruited from waterfront taverns. One of its early prizes was a treasure galleon sailing from Mexico. According to Esquemelin, the men returned to Port Royal after each expedition and "wasted in a few days . . . all they had gained, by giving themselves over to every manner of debauchery." This was typical pirate behavior. Contrary to popular belief, pirates rarely buried their treasure. Brasiliano was one of the few who did. When he fell into Spanish hands he was tortured by the Inquisition in Campeche and admitted to having hidden treasure on the Isla de Pinos, off Cuba. Spanish soldiers sent to search for it dug up more than 100,000 pieces of eight.[7]

Sir Henry Morgan

The most celebrated of all the buccaneers was the ruthless and clever Welshman Henry Morgan. He was born in 1635, but little else is known of Morgan's boyhood, although he most likely came to the Caribbean as an indentured servant.

Morgan's fame rests on his skill as a tactician, his courage, the scale of his expeditions, and their phenomenal success. In 1668 he led seven hundred buccaneers in a dozen ships to Puerto del Principe (now Camaguey), Cuba, where torture of captive citizens produced an abundance of valuables. Later the same year Morgan led an outnumbered band to attack Puerto Bello, third largest city in the New

Below: *Henry Morgan at the storming of Panama City in 1671, "the greatest mart for silver and gold in the whole world." A tough and ruthless buccaneer, he led 1,400 of his men on a gruelling march across the Isthmus of Panama. This illustration from Captain Johnson's book offers a somewhat fanciful portrayal of the cunning and ferocious Welshman.*

World, urging the men on as Drake had done a century before: "If our number is small, our hearts are great; and the fewer persons we are, the more union, and the better shares we shall have in the spoil!"

Puerto Bello was so heavily fortified that the only hope of taking it lay in complete surprise. Morgan, accordingly, landed 460 men 100 miles (160km) up the coast. They transferred to large canoes, approaching the city before dawn. Morgan's men captured a sentry and forced him to call upon the defenders of the fort to surrender or die. The answering fire of Spanish muskets sent the intrepid buccaneers over the walls to overwhelm the still sleepy enemy. True to his word, Morgan locked all the Spanish soldiers into a single building that he blew up with gunpowder. The second of the three forts was taken with ease, but the third, which the governor commanded, proved another story. Vowing to die rather than give in to the *piratas ingleses*, the governor organized a staunch defense, all but forcing Morgan to retreat.

The battle raged from dawn until noon. The population took advantage of the fighting to bolt for the woods with their valuables. This sight inspired Morgan to redouble his efforts. He employed a novel, and terrible, stratagem. He had his men construct siege ladders. Then he corralled all the priests, friars, and nuns who could be found. Relying on the Spaniards' reputation for reverence, he forced the servants of God to carry the ladders to the ramparts and set them up against the walls. To Morgan's consternation the governor, torn between duty and piety, ordered his troops to keep up their barrage of fire. Despite the governor's decision, the fort soon surrendered.

Once the city surrendered, the butchery began. The buccaneers, in a perpetual state of drunkenness, indulged in an orgy of torture, rape, and murder. Esquemelin, who was among the buccaneers on this expedition, wrote that Morgan had citizens stretched on the rack to reveal where their valuables were hidden. From gardens, cisterns, and caves a stream of gold, silver, plate, and jewels poured into the buccaneer headquarters. Valuable merchandise was systematically collected from waterfront warehouses, and the buccaneers returned to a rousing welcome at Port Royal with five hundred thousand pieces of eight, a mountain of loot, and three hundred slaves. For a month the great event was celebrated in the taverns and brothels of the pirate port.

The Capture of Panama

An expedition the following year yielded more plunder in spite of an inauspicious start. In January 1669 Morgan held a wild bon voyage party aboard his flagship, the *Oxford,* at Cow Island (Île à Vache) off the south coast of Hispaniola, where the force of

English and French buccaneers made their rendezvous. When drunken gunners shot off muskets, a spark ignited a powder barrel, blowing up the *Oxford* and killing 350 men, including those across the table from Morgan. The sea turned red with blood from the dismembered corpses. Buccaneers from the other ships rowed among the bodies in small boats, stripping them of all valuables, even hacking off fingers to salvage the gold rings that buccaneers liked so much.

Morgan already enjoyed considerable fame when he organized the greatest expedition of his career. In late 1670 he easily raised a fleet of some forty ships and two thousand buccaneers. His objective was Panama City, the golden warehouse of the Indies. The Pacific port would have to be reached overland and taken by surprise from the rear, a challenge even for the toughest adventurers.

Morgan captured Fort San Lorenzo, on the Caribbean side of Panama, where he left a contingent of men to hold it and guard the anchored fleet. He constructed thirty-six huge canoes to carry 1,400 of his best men up the

Chagres River. They embarked with no provisions, expecting to procure them from villages along the route to Venta Cruz. After seven days with little or no food the buccaneers were in poor condition for the next stage of Morgan's plan: the grueling march through hostile jungle. Weakened by hunger and dysentery and ravaged by fever, they set out, falling prey several times to ambushes.

Again they found no food. Some men resorted to eating their leather satchels and their boiled shoes. After more than a week the treasure hunters sighted Panama City from a hilltop. In the distant bay they spied the billowing sails of a great galleon headed toward the open sea. Later, to their great sorrow, they learned it was on its way to safety with nearly five million pieces of eight. Another ship carried away gold and jewels.

By afternoon, the buccaneers made camp on the outskirts of the city. They slaughtered and roasted some cattle and slept well with full stomachs. In the morning as they prepared to march on the city, 2,100 Spanish infantrymen and six hundred cavalry troops

Above: *Howard Pyle's potentially more accurate portrayal is entitled* Henry Morgan at Portobello. *Here, Morgan is interrogating the inhabitants of the town to find out where they have hidden their valuables. The careful application of torture quickly achieved the desired information, and the buccaneers took great riches from the town after having indulged in a month-long victory orgy. Giving in to such desires for excess did not stop Morgan and his men from defeating a Spanish force sent during that time to relieve the town. Tipped off by Indians, Morgan took 100 men into the jungle to ambush the advancing Spanish force of several thousand. He chose his site—a narrow pass—well and sent the Spanish retreating in terror.*

appeared in battle formation on the plain in front of the city. Outnumbered but undaunted, Morgan didn't hesitate. He ordered an advance, judging that the rising sun shining in enemy eyes would offset their great advantage. The entire Spanish cavalry then charged the buccaneers, who held their ground and repelled the charge with deadly accurate volleys of musket fire. The Spanish infantry massed for another advance. At the same time they had Indians stampede two thousand head of cattle at Morgan's rear guard. Again buccaneer fire dispersed the

charge. The Spanish infantrymen, now within range of the buccaneers, fired once, then flung their heavy, cumbersome muskets to the ground and ran for the city, where fresh troops waited to defend the barricaded streets.

Rather than have Panama fall into the clutches of the buccaneers, the Spanish destroyed it. The principal buildings were set on fire. The fort was blown up in such haste that forty soldiers inside went with it. The populace escaped to the woods so that Morgan and his men met little resistance as they came through the city gates. By the time

Below: *Howard Pyle's illustration of the sacking of Panama—a potentially rich prize that had eluded Drake—produced for a story, "Buccaneers and Marooners of the Spanish Main" in* Harper's Monthly Magazine *in August 1887, shows the buccaneers leaving the city that had been burned to the ground. In the days that followed their capture of the town, Morgan's men put out the flames and repeated their earlier patterns of behavior with debauchery and torture.*

they extinguished the holocaust, three-quarters of the city had been leveled, including the majority of the more than two hundred richly stocked warehouses and the homes of the wealthiest citizens.

Morgan's Booty

The buccaneers spent a month entrenched in the ruins, sending out parties to hunt down Spaniards whom they tortured to find out where valuables had been cached. Ironically, the buccaneers overlooked the greatest treasure of all, which was right in their midst. They had been outfoxed by a resourceful friar who had hastily slapped a coat of whitewash on the great golden altar of the cathedral.

The booty, although less than hoped for, was substantial. Most of it came from *rescate*, or ransom of prisoners. It included 750,000 pieces of eight, some gold doubloons, silver bars, gold ingots, pearls, jewelry, silks, and spices. It was carried across the isthmus by 175 mules and then divided up. During the expedition there had been constant friction between the predominantly Catholic French group and the Protestant English. When Morgan got wind of a separatist faction that had secretly provisioned a ship to be used on an independent plundering cruise in the South Seas, he scuttled the ship.

When the treasure haul was divided up at Fort San Lorenzo, rebellion flared into mutiny. The mutineers claimed Morgan had kept the lion's share of the spoils and the best jewels for himself. The two hundred pieces of eight each man received seemed far too little reward for the privation and suffering. Morgan refused to listen to complaints and then managed to weigh anchor and sail off, leaving his buccaneer force without a word of good-bye. Faced with a lack of provisions, the remaining buccaneers split up and went their various ways. Esquemelin, who was on the expedition, was one of those left on the shore in Panama. His ship cruised for plunder along the coasts of Costa Rica and Cuba before returning to Jamaica.

Officially Disowned

All of Jamaica celebrated Morgan's return. Jubilation reigned at Port Royal, and the Colonial Council issued a vote of thanks to Morgan. However, when word reached King Charles II he was not at all pleased, because, as Morgan well knew, Spain and England were officially at peace. The king of Spain threatened to declare war on England if the pirates who destroyed Panama were not punished immediately. Charles II was anxious to preserve the peace and ordered Morgan and Governor Modyford, who had countenanced his venture, transported to England in chains.

Modyford was held in the Tower of London until 1674, when tensions with Spain had eased. Morgan, however, with a talent for turning a disaster into a triumph, not only avoided a trial and prison but was lionized by the English public and knighted by the king. Setting a thief to catch a thief, King Charles sent Sir Henry back to Jamaica, where he sat as judge of Jamaica's Vice-Admiralty Court, which tried pirates.

Morgan publicly espoused the official anti-buccaneering line, boasting "I have put to death, imprisoned and transported to the Spaniard for execution all English and Spanish pirates I could get." However, his many detractors complained that at the same time he was secretly operating a private employment agency for former Port Royal buccaneers, collecting 10 percent of the prizes taken under clandestine commissions issued by his old ally Governor d'Ogeron in French Hispaniola. So many English buccaneers carried commissions from the French that King Charles II angrily declared that he was determined Jamaica be a plantation and not "a Christian Algiers."

Autres Temps, Autres Moeurs

From 1674 onward, Lieutenant-Governor Morgan clashed repeatedly with Governor Vaughn, a fastidious nobleman who didn't hide his distaste for the rough-edged ex-buccaneer. Vaughn brought Morgan before the Jamaica Council on various charges, which Sir Henry's popularity repeatedly overcame. The old sea rover, his allegiance torn, spent more and more time in Port Royal's taverns, and in 1683 Vaughn succeeded in having him suspended from office for disloyalty and drunken disorder.

Governments, which had used the buccaneers for their own ends, discovered that they were not easily persuaded to desist once national interests dictated a change in tactics. The rough-and-ready buccaneers cared little for newly forged alliances and even less for the commercial opportunities they made possible, which were far more valuable to

Above: *Until the Treaty of Ryswick in 1697, the principal European powers were in an ever-shifting set of alliances of convenience during the seventeenth century that saw almost constant warfare being waged between the parties in different combinations. The Spanish towns and settlements in Central and South America came under frequent attack from the ships of Europe's major maritime powers. In this engraving, a large fleet of Dutch and French ships is depicted attacking and entering a Spanish harbor in the New World.*

national interests than piracy. French buccaneers claimed that the 1688 Treaty of Aix-la-Chapelle, making peace between France and Spain, didn't apply to them, since they had neither negotiated it nor signed it. Several governors of Jamaica succumbed to the temptation to allow outlawed activities. But corrupt officials in the Bermudas, the Bahamas, St. Thomas, Petit-Goave, and Tortuga (whose governor sent to Portugal for commissions when France and Spain were officially at peace) didn't scruple to issue permits of dubious validity.

Toward the end of the seventeenth century, having established their own territorial claims, the very maritime nations that once had encouraged buccaneering as a weapon against Spain—England and France—shut

down the buccaneers' bases, dispersing the unruly predators all over the globe, from Massachusetts to Madagascar.

Throughout the 1670s and 1680s buccaneering verged increasingly on piracy. Morgan was correct in calling it a drain on Jamaica, which depended on residents for defense. Between 1668 and 1671 some 2,600 Jamaicans went off "on the account." In 1673 a buccaneer force sacked Trinidad, and in 1683 a joint French, Dutch, and English buccaneer expedition plundered Veracruz, carrying off $6,000,000. Attacks on non-Spanish ships proliferated. Suppressing the buccaneers was no easy task: a plan to turn pirate swords into plowshares offered each man who had "followed the Course" a free pardon and thirty-five acres of Jamaican land, but this failed to lure many buccaneers into the agricultural life.

As the sun set on Caribbean buccaneering some unrepentant buccaneers set up at Petit-Goave on the Hispaniola coast, ignoring French authority. Some sought haven in Bermuda or the Bahamas. A few joined in the challenging Pirate Round between the Indian Ocean and the North American colonies, and a number of the most audacious buccaneer veterans prowled the Pacific coasts of Central and South America, where neither French nor English governments would harass them.

Between 1675 and 1742, at least twenty-five expeditions slogged on foot across the Isthmus of Panama or made the bruising voyage around Cape Horn to the Pacific. The "merry boys of the South Sea," as they called themselves, were lured by tales of Drake's capture off Peru of the *Cacafuego,* one of the richest Spanish galleons ever to sail, and by Cavendish's 1587 haul of gold and porcelain from a Manila galleon seized off the coast of California.

Morgan: the End

In 1688 Sir Hans Sloane, whose West Indian journals form part of the foundation of the British Museum library, was a young physician at Port Royal. He had occasion to examine Sir Henry Morgan, who by that time was a debauched alcoholic bearing little resemblance to the dashing buccaneer leader he had been. Sloane described him as "lean, sallow colored, his eyes a little yellowish and belly jutting out or prominent." The doctor prescribed various purges and diuretics, including scorpion oil, but Morgan preferred to be treated by a black obeah man who gave him "clysters of urine, and plastered him all over with clay and water, and by it augmented his cough."[8] Morgan died soon after and was buried in the churchyard at Port Royal. On June 7, 1692, the earth quaked and the sea rushed in, claiming the bones of the greatest buccaneer of them all and obliterating the pirate port to which he brought immortal fame.

A contemporary verse mourned the passing of the man and the era:

> You was a flyer, Morgan,
> You was the lad to crowd
> When you was in your flagship,
> But now you're in your shroud.[9]

Left: *A seated Morgan watches from the deck of his ship as the Spanish galleon* Magdalen *burns in the Gulf of Venezuela following Morgan's assault on Gibraltar in 1669. It was a brilliant escape by Morgan, further enhancing his reputation.*

Below: *An oil painting of Sir Christopher Myngs by Sir Peter Lely. This portrait was painted after the Battle of Lowestoft when Vice-Admiral Myngs led the victorious English fleet against the Dutch in the second Anglo-Dutch war. He first made his name, however, carrying out highly profitable raids on Spanish towns in the West Indies. Both Morgan—a "pupil" of Myngs—and Myngs moved to and fro as both official and unofficial practitioners of piracy.*

CHAPTER THREE

BUCCANEER EXPLORERS

~

On 6 December in the morning, being off the volcano of Colima, we saw a sail, and soon came up with her. She proved to be the Manila ship. So we, being all provided, gave her several broadsides, before she could get any of her guns clear.

WILLIAM FUNNELL, 1704.[1]

DURING THE course of the seventeenth century small bands of seafarers roamed the Caribbean in search of plunder. Their prime targets were the Spanish treasure galleons. These included the Manila ships that traveled across the Pacific with rich cargoes from the Orient, and other ships that brought the treasure from the New World across the Atlantic back to Spain. Coastal settlements, ports, and merchant ships voyaging around the coasts of South and Central America were also attacked. Some of these marauding seafarers were licensed privateers with authority from their sovereigns to attack Spanish ships, but many were freelance adventurers, or pirates. They came from Britain, France, the Netherlands, and the other maritime nations of Europe, and they were described as buccaneers or sea-rovers by Esquemelin, who traveled with them and wrote their history.

Among the buccaneers were a number of educated men who kept journals of their exploits. Many of these journals were published and proved immensely popular in England and on the Continent. What is fascinating about these published accounts is that they are not simply tales of sea battles and storms. They also include descriptions of new lands and new peoples, and often describe in meticulous detail the exotic fauna and flora encountered en route. They provide a vivid insight into the hardship and perils suffered by the buccaneers, but they are also records of plundering expeditions that turned into voyages of exploration.

These buccaneer explorers were an intrepid bunch of men. Among their number were Captain Bartholomew Sharp, whose voyage around South America was recorded by Basil Ringrose and published in the 1684 edition of Esquemelin's famous history of the buccaneers, *The Buccaneers of America*; William Dick,[2] whose account of the same voyage was also published in Esquemelin's book; John Cox, who traveled with Sharp and Ringrose and wrote a journal of their exploits; the surgeon Lionel Wafer, who described his adventures among the Cuna Indians and a voyage around Cape Horn in the *Batchelor's Delight*; Captain Swan, commander of the *Cygnet*, who traveled extensively in the Pacific; and William Dampier, who achieved lasting fame through his writings and his travels.

Dampier: The Circumnavigator

Dampier has some claim to being the most remarkable of all the seamen of the seventeenth century. He went around the world three times. He took part in numerous pirate attacks, but he also led an official voyage of exploration to the South Seas in a naval warship. He traveled with the expedition that marooned the Scottish seaman Alexander Selkirk, the inspiration for Daniel Defoe's Robinson Crusoe. He was also present when Captain Woodes Rogers rescued Selkirk from his four years as a castaway. He wrote a discourse on the tides, winds, and weather systems of the world that was admired by generations of sailors, while his reports on the hitherto unexplored lands that he visited were a revelation to people back in Europe.

Dampier was a complex and not altogether likable character. "He was always a man so much self-conceited that he would never hear any reason," was the opinion of one man who sailed with him,[3] and others condemned him for his foul language, his drunkenness, and his lack of leadership in battle. Most damning were the findings of a court-martial that was set up in 1702 following the loss

Left: *This drawing of shipping anchored off Bantam in Java is by Edward Barlow and is taken from his famous work,* Journal of His Life at Sea, 1659–1703. *He served in East and West Indiamen between 1659 and 1703, recording along the way the ships, coastal views, and animals he saw on his voyages.*

Below: *A mariner's astrolabe from about 1588. Such instruments were in use between about 1500 and 1700 and were a means of determining latitude by measuring the altitude of the sun or the Pole Star. For several generations of seamen, this and the compass were their principal navigational instruments.*

Above: The Battle of the Texel *by Willem van de Velde the Younger. The encounter took place on August 11, 1673, and was witnessed by William Dampier who served with the Royal Navy during the Anglo-Dutch wars. Both strong maritime powers, England and the Netherlands became fierce competitors for dominance of long-distance trading routes. This rivalry caused the first three Anglo-Dutch wars between 1652 and 1674. They were a stalemate militarily but the Royal Navy emerged from them as a permanent force with professional officers. A fourth war that broke out in 1780 marked the end of Dutch power and prestige.*

of HMS *Roebuck* on her return journey from Australia. Dampier was condemned for his harsh treatment of one of his officers and was found not fit to be employed as commander of any of Her Majesty's ships.

And yet in spite of his shortcomings as a leader of men, Dampier was a resolute explorer, a gifted navigator, and a wonderful observer and commentator on the people and the places he visited. His first book, which included his adventures with Captain Swan and other buccaneers, was entitled *A New Voyage Round the World* and was first published in 1697. This was followed in 1699 by *Voyages and Descriptions*, which was in three parts: *A Supplement of the Voyage Round the World, The Campeachy Voyages,* and *A Discourse of Winds.* His third book, which appeared in 1703, was *A Voyage to New Holland* and was a record of the ill-fated expedition to Australia. Dampier's books are remarkable for their immensely detailed descriptions of trees and plants, birds, animals, and fish. Like Gilbert White of Selborne, he had an intense curiosity about everything he saw and was able to write with a freshness and a cool detachment that was admired by generations of readers. Unlike Gilbert White, who confined his meticulous observations to a few square miles of English countryside, Dampier crossed three oceans and visited four continents.

William Dampier was born in the west of England, at East Coker, near Yeovil in Somerset, where his family were farmers. His date of birth is not known, but he was baptized on September 5, 1651. Following a good education at local schools, he was apprenticed to a shipmaster at Weymouth. At the age of eighteen he sailed on a merchant ship to Newfoundland. Although the voyage was made in the summer months, Dampier did not like the bitter cold of the northern latitudes, and on his return he joined the crew of an East Indiaman bound for the warmer waters of the Far East. He was away a year and visited Java before returning to England via Ascension Island. With the outbreak of war against the Dutch, Dampier decided to join the Royal Navy. He was on board Sir Edward Spragge's flagship, the *Prince*, at the two battles of Schooneveld that were fought off the mouth of the River Scheldt. He fell ill and was put aboard a hospital ship, which sailed north with the fleet. On August 11, 1673, he witnessed at a distance the Battle of the Texel, the last major action of the Anglo-Dutch wars.

The Logwood Cutters of Campeche
Invalided out of the Royal Navy, Dampier went home to his brother in Somerset, and there he received an offer from Colonel

Hellier, one of his neighbors, to go out to Jamaica and assist in the management of his sugar plantation. Dampier worked his passage out to the West Indies, and spent several months on plantations in different parts of the island. He had no talent for the work and decided to sail to Central America where he joined a small company of logwood cutters on the island of Carmen in Campeche Bay.

Many of the logwood cutters were former seamen and buccaneers. When the opportunity arose they would join the crew of a privateer or pirate ship and raid a local village or attack a passing merchant ship. They were a notoriously tough bunch of men, and they needed to be so. The logwood trees (*Haematoxylon campechianum*), which would produce the valuable red dye used in Europe for dyeing cloth, grew on the edges of swamps and rivers in one of the most inhospitable regions of the world. Mosquitoes abounded in the steamy heat and alligators infested the waterways. During the rainy season much of the area was submerged. The men slept in flimsy huts on crude wooden beds that were raised above the water. In the morning they stepped from

their beds into the water, and they spent most of the day wading ankle deep through the swamps. They were constantly at the mercy of a variety of unpleasant worms that burrowed into their feet and legs with possibly fatal results unless extracted and treated. The men cut down the trees, sawed them into logs, and then carried or dragged them to a place where they could be loaded onto ships. According to Dampier, some of the men were capable of carrying logs weighing three or four hundred pounds (136–181kg).

In June 1676 the Bay of Campeche was hit by a hurricane that raged for two days. The logwood cutters managed to save their canoe and one of their huts; the rest blew away. The winds tore through the forests and were accompanied by torrential rain and a tidal surge that flooded the region. Most of the trees in the path of the hurricane were torn up by their roots and hurled down in such a tangled state that it was almost impossible to find a pathway through them. Dampier and his fellow logwood cutters were forced to find alternative employment. They joined a company of buccaneers and spent several months

Below: *The extensive voyages and explorations undertaken by the buccaneers and their contemporaries is quite remarkable. The range was vast, covering Central and South America and the Pacific and Indian oceans. The information they accumulated in their journals—descriptive, illustrative, and navigational—contributed to our knowledge of the world, its peoples, and animal life. Although generally not the first to visit many of the places, the buccaneers' achievement is nevertheless impressive for having been undertaken with poor equipment, unpredictable supplies, and for overcoming very daunting natural obstacles.*

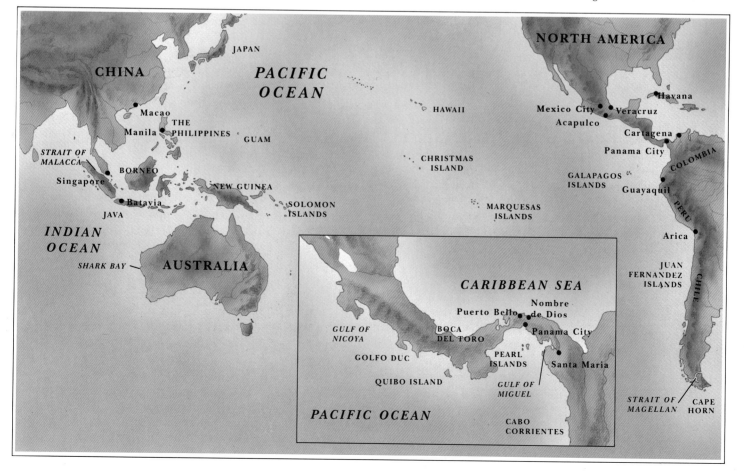

Above: *A portrait of William Dampier by Thomas Murray painted around 1702, just a few years after he had made his name with the publication of his best-selling book* A New Voyage Round the World. *In it he described his voyages in the West Indies and the coasts and islands of the Pacific, in particular "their Soil, Rivers, Harbours, Plants, Fruits, Animals, and Inhabitants."*

making piratical raids along the coast and up the rivers of Tabasco.

In August 1678 Dampier went back to England. Before sailing away on his travels again he was wed to Judith, who worked at Arlington House and seems to have been a maid to Isabella, Duchess of Grafton.

Dampier Joins the Buccaneers

Early in 1679 Dampier set sail for Jamaica in the ship *Loyal Merchant* of London. He was twenty-eight years old, and the next phase of his life was spent as a pirate. He did not, of course, describe himself or his fellow seamen as pirates (in his later accounts of his travels he usually referred to his companions as privateers), but the fact is that the captains he served under were prepared to make indiscriminate raids on ships and coastal settlements in their search for plunder. Although some of them appeared to have purchased commissions that gave them authority to attack Spanish ships,[4] they also captured the ships of neutral nations on many occasions and left a trail of murder and burned-out villages in their wake as they cruised up and down the coasts of America.

Dampier joined a company of buccaneers on the west coast of Jamaica. Their five ships were anchored in Long Bay at Negril and their leaders included Captain John Coxon, Captain Richard Sawkins, and Captain Bartholomew Sharp. The buccaneer fleet set sail at the end of December 1679 and headed for the Spanish treasure ports on the coast of Central America. They ransacked Puerto Bello and then marched across the Isthmus of Darien till they were in sight of Panama. From there they headed south, traveling in boats they acquired from the local Indians. During October and November of 1680 they carried out some raids on coastal towns.

Dampier gives very little detail about this period of his life because a full account was published by Basil Ringrose.[5] However, it was not too long after this that Dampier parted company with Ringrose and Captain Sharp. When these buccaneers sailed to the Juan Fernandez Islands, off the coast of Chile, to refit and provision their ship, there was a mutiny that resulted in the men voting Sharp out of his command and replacing him with an old privateer called Watling.

Under their new commander they sailed back to the mainland, and in January 1681 they launched a bold but ill-advised attack on the town of Arica. Watling was killed during the attack and Sharp was restored as commander of the captured ship *Trinity*. On April 17 near the Isle of Plate there was another mutiny among the crew of the *Trinity*, many of whom were unhappy about Sharp's style of command. The matter was put to a vote. The majority cast votes for Sharp, including Basil Ringrose, who remained with him during his subsequent adventures. But then a group of around fifty men voted against him. They were determined to leave the *Trinity* and to return to Panama. This group included John Cook, later to lead an expedition round Cape Horn, the ship's surgeon Lionel Wafer, and Dampier himself. It took them twenty-three days to march back across the mountains and valleys to the Caribbean.

Soon after their arrival on the coast Dampier and his companions joined the crew of a French buccaneer vessel commanded by Captain Tristian. They went aboard his ship on May 24 and for the next several months they cruised with him. They then transferred to an English ship commanded by Captain Wright and cruised up and down the Caribbean, capturing several small ships. Proceeding south, they survived by raiding coastal villages and trading vessels. After a year spent with Captain Wright, Dampier and twenty of the buccaneers took their share of the plunder and journeyed to Virginia. He remained in the colony for a year.

In August 1683 John Cook announced that he was planning a voyage around South America to the treasure ports of the Pacific. Dampier joined his crew, and Lionel Wafer went as surgeon. To take advantage of the Atlantic trade winds they sailed first across to the Cape Verde Islands off Africa. Just a few days out from the American coast they encountered the worst storm that Dampier was ever to experience, and his description suggests that they were hit by a hurricane. For three days they ran before mountainous seas under bare poles. On one fearful occasion the ship broached to, turning broadside to the waves, and was in imminent danger of capsizing. The wind was too fierce to hoist any sail, so an experienced seaman volunteered to go aloft and see whether he could turn the ship's head back into the wind. Dampier was persuaded to go with him. They climbed up the shrouds till they were halfway up the mast, "and there we spread abroad the flaps of our coats, and presently the ship wore. I think we did not stay there above three minutes before we gained our point and came down again."[6]

The *Batchelor's Delight*

They survived the storm and eventually reached the mouth of what they called the Sierra Leone River, where they captured a Danish ship of thirty-six guns. They took her over, renamed her the *Batchelor's Delight*, and sailed in her from Africa across the Atlantic toward Cape Horn. They passed the Falkland Islands, weathered Cape Horn, and headed northward to the Juan Fernandez Islands.

From Juan Fernandez, the *Batchelor's Delight* headed 2,800 miles (4,500km) north to the Galapagos Islands. Dampier described

the trees, shrubs, turtles, tortoises, and iguanas. During their stay among the islands John Cook became seriously ill. A few weeks later, as they were approaching the American coast near Cabo Blanco, he died. His body was carried ashore and buried. He was succeeded by Edward Davis, who took them northward up the coast of South America until they joined forces with other buccaneers. They captured the town of Paita in northern Peru and, after waiting five days for a ransom, burned it to the ground. They captured a ship whose cargo amounted to no more than a few boxes of marmalade and three or four jars of brandy.

Compared to the spectacular raids of Drake and Henry Morgan, these buccaneers were not having much luck. It was time to go for a bigger prize. In May 1685 Davis joined a fleet of buccaneers anchored at Pacheca Island some forty miles (64km) from Panama City. Their objective was nothing less than the Spanish treasure fleet from Lima. What they did not realize until afterward was the strength of the opposition. The Spanish had six warships, two fireships, six smaller vessels, and several large canoes and a total of more than three thousand men. The bucca-

Left: *An engraving from* The Pirates' Own Book, *published in 1837, that shows Captain William Lewis giving a lock of his hair to the Devil in return for speed while chasing a vessel in the Gulf of Guinea, his main mast having been disabled by gunfire. This desperate remedy for overcoming an unfavorable situation at sea—the observing of "superstitions" among seamen was by no means rare—is reminiscent of William Dampier's experience in a storm when he and a shipmate climbed the mast and spread out the flaps of their coats in order to try to get the ship back into the wind.*

neers had only 960 men scattered among ten small ships, only two of which were armed with cannons. The pirates attacked in the afternoon of May 28, but the Spanish kept their distance and, although shots had been fired, the two fleets had failed to engage by nightfall. During the night the Spanish cleverly misled the pirates with false lights and in the morning the pirates were dismayed to find the enemy bearing down on them under full sail with the wind behind them. The pirates fled. After a running fight with few casualties on either side the pirates escaped, having failed to capture a single ship.

Dampier's First Circumnavigation

Learning that Captain Swan, one of the buccaneer leaders, was planning an extended voyage to the Orient, Dampier left Captain Davis and joined the crew of Swan's ship, appropriately named the *Cygnet*. They set sail from Cabo Corrientes on the west coast of Mexico on March 31, 1686. The *Cygnet* was a ship of twelve guns with a crew of 100 men, and she was accompanied by a smaller vessel rigged as a bark with a crew of fifty. Fresh winds took them swiftly westward, away from the South American coast, and fine weather with clear skies enabled them to make good observations of the sun.

According to the English charts, the distance from the South American coast to Guam was 1,900 leagues (about six thousand miles/9,600km), and when the buccaneers' calculations showed they had passed this point with no land in sight, there were signs of mutiny among the crew. It was later discovered that the men were planning to eat Captain Swan if the food ran out. Fortunately for the captain it was not long before some motionless clouds were observed on the horizon. The two ships then changed course and headed north, and within a few hours they saw the island of Guam ahead of them. When they dropped anchor that evening they had food for only three days more. They had been at sea for fifty-two days and had traveled 7,323 miles (11,785km).

Below: *The writings of Esquemelin, Dampier, and others who lived among the buccaneers confirm their fondness for wine, women, and riotous living. These French buccaneers are enjoying life ashore at Guayaquil on the coast of Ecuador. Established by the Spanish in the 1530s, the town was a frequent target for buccaneers.*

From Guam they sailed to the island of Mindanao, where Captain Swan abandoned himself to a life of pleasure, reveling in the feasts and dancing girls that were provided for his entertainment. After six months his crew decided to move on without him. They elected a new captain and set sail in the *Cygnet*, leaving Swan behind. They sailed across the South China Sea to the Mekong River, and then cruised up the coast of China. From there they threaded their way through the islands of the East Indies (now Indonesia) and continued south until on January 4, 1688, they sighted Australia, or New Holland, as it was then called. They anchored in a sheltered bay, which was probably King Sound on the northwest coast. Dampier and his fellow buccaneers thus became the first Englishmen to set foot on Australian soil. The observations he made were the first extended descriptions of the Australian landscape and the aborigines to be published in Europe.

Dampier remained with the buccaneers for a few months more, but when they reached the Nicobar Islands he decided to desert the ship. Together with two English and four Malay members of the crew he went ashore one night. They purchased a canoe from one of the islanders and made their escape. After many adventures Dampier joined the crew of a trading vessel and spent the next two years sailing in the East Indies and along the coast of India. In January 1691 he decided to join an English ship and sailed for home. The ship sailed via Cape Town and St. Helena and reached England on September 16, 1691. Dampier was forty years old and had been away for twelve-and-a-half years.

A New Voyage
During his travels Dampier had managed to preserve his journal and drawings through storms and battles and shipwrecks. He had kept his journal in a length of bamboo sealed at the ends with wax. Working from his sea-stained notes Dampier wrote up his travels, and five years after his return *A New Voyage Round the World* was finally published. It was an immediate success and four editions were published within two years. Soon after its publication, Dampier was approached by the Admiralty and invited to lead an expedition to the South Seas. On January 14, 1699, he once again set off on his travels, this time as

captain of HMS *Roebuck*, a twelve-gun ship with a crew of fifty men and boys and provisions for a twenty-month voyage. Apart from the wonderful descriptions he later published of the places he visited, the expedition was a dismal failure. They sailed via Tenerife and the Cape of Good Hope to Australia, where they spent about five weeks exploring the west coast in the vicinity of Shark Bay. No new lands were found or discoveries made, and on the return journey the ship developed a serious leak and sank in twelve fathoms (seventy feet/22m) of water off Ascension Island. Dampier and his crew managed to get ashore on a makeshift raft and were eventually picked up by a naval ship and returned home to England.

In spite of the damning findings of the court-martial into his conduct, Dampier's reputation survived, and within a few months he was approached by a group of merchants from London and Bristol and asked to take charge of a privateering voyage. Dampier took command of the *St. George*, a twenty-six-gun ship, and he was joined in Ireland by the *Cinque Ports*, another privateer commanded by Charles Pickering.

They sailed from the Irish port of Kinsale in May 1703 and headed for South America, where they planned to attack and plunder

Above: *According to Dampier's journal, the buccaneer Captain Swan abandoned himself to a life of pleasure after crossing the Pacific and encountering the women of the Philippines. On the island of Mindanao he was entertained by a continuous round of feasts and dancing girls. A similar scene—and the dream of most buccaneers—is conjured up in this mural by Frank Schoonover.*

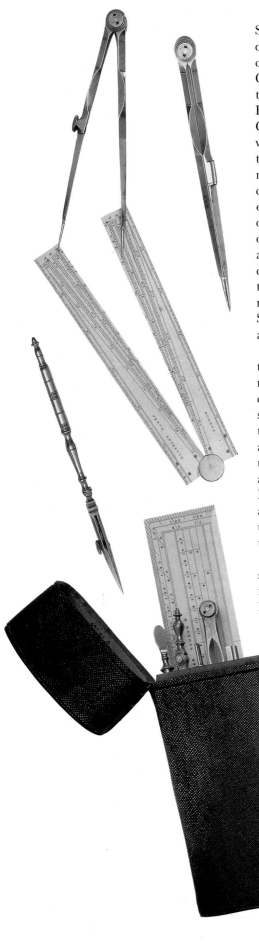

Spanish ships. The expedition was almost as disastrous as the *Roebuck* venture. Dampier continued to quarrel with his men and at the Cape Verde Islands he turned his first lieutenant off the ship. When they arrived at Brazil he put a further nine men ashore. Captain Pickering died soon after this and was replaced by Thomas Stradling, first lieutenant of the *Cinque Ports*. Stradling was even more ineffective than Dampier as a privateer commander. Between them they lost every encounter with every ship they met, and in one encounter with a French ship nine of Dampier's crew were killed. When they anchored at the Juan Fernandez Islands to careen and refit, forty-two seamen deserted the ships. They were eventually persuaded to rejoin their vessels, but Alexander Selkirk, a Scottish seaman, demanded to be left ashore, and Stradling left him there.

The rifts between the commanders and their crew became so bad that when they reached Panama Bay the two ships parted company. Stradling sailed north, wrecked his ship on a deserted island, was captured by the Spaniards, and spent five years chained to a wall in a dungeon in Lima. Dampier roved up and down the coast of the Gulf of Panama, attacking coastal craft and raiding villages. He captured a few small vessels, but all his attempts to take larger vessels ended in failure. The final straw was his abortive attempt to capture the Manila galleon. In December 1704, Dampier intercepted the galleon and succeeded in coming alongside without alerting the Spanish captain of his intentions, but he failed to follow up his advantage. His indecision gave the galleon's crew time to run out their guns and fire a broadside that forced the smaller English ship to withdraw. Dampier's crew were so bitter at the loss of the hoped-for riches that half of them deserted the ship at the next port. After some desultory raids off the coast of Ecuador, Dampier found that the hull of the *St. George* had become so rotten that he had to abandon her. With the remnants of his crew he set off westward across the Pacific in a small Spanish ship he had captured. He eventually reached England toward the end of 1707 and thus completed his second circum-

navigation. The merchants who had sponsored the voyage were faced with a complete loss on their investment and prepared to take Dampier to court for committing fraud.

Woodes Rogers: Honest Privateering

Fortunately for Dampier, his reputation as an explorer and his unrivaled knowledge of the coasts and islands of the South Seas outweighed his obvious incompetence as a commander. Shortly after his return to London he was asked to join another round-the-world voyage, this time as the pilot and navigator. Unlike most of Dampier's previous ventures, this one was an entirely legal undertaking. A Bristol syndicate had put up the money to purchase and equip two powerful ships: the *Duke*, which was a vessel of 320 tons and armed with thirty guns, and the *Dutchess*, a 260-ton ship with twenty-six guns. They had assembled a crew of 330 men and had appointed Woodes Rogers as leader of the expedition. Although a relatively young man of twenty-nine, Captain Rogers was a tough and experienced seaman who was to prove himself a formidable leader.[7]

The expedition set sail from Bristol on August 2, 1708. After calling in at Cork, the two ships headed for the Canary Islands, where they captured their first prize, a small Spanish merchantman. They crossed the Atlantic and reached the coast of Brazil on November 19. After heading south, the ships encountered weeks of gales, but by mid-January they had rounded Cape Horn, and then two weeks later they sighted the Juan Fernandez Islands off the west coast of Chile. They sailed into a bay on the leeward side of the largest of the islands and on February 2, 1709, they sent a pinnace ashore to investigate a light that they had seen during the night. The pinnace returned with a wild-looking man who was clothed in a coat and cap of goatskins. It was the marooned Scottish seaman Alexander Selkirk, who had made a fire to attract their attention. He had been alone on the island for four years and four months, surviving on crawfish, goat meat, and fruit.

"At his first coming on board us," Woodes Rogers noted, "he had so much forgot his language for want of use, that we could scarce understand him, for he seemed to speak his words by halves."[8] Dampier confirmed that Selkirk had been master of the *Cinque Ports* and had been the best seaman onboard her.

On his recommendation Rogers agreed to appoint Selkirk as a mate onboard the *Duke*. They spent two weeks at Juan Fernandez, carrying out repairs to sails and refitting the ships. When the ships were ready and they had stocked up with wood, water, goats, and vegetables, they sailed away to the north. Off the coast of Peru they captured their second prize, a small vessel of sixteen tons that they decided to keep. They took her to the island of Lobos, where they fitted her with four swivel guns, put a crew of thirty-two seamen aboard, and named her the *Beginning*.

On April 15 they attacked a Spanish ship from Lima, but on this occasion they met with fierce resistance and Woodes Rogers's brother was killed. The following day they launched a second attack and captured the ship. They followed this by a successful raid on the town of Guayaquil, and then sailed out into the Pacific again. By the time they had reached the Galapagos Islands in mid-May, nearly half of the ships' crews were ill with fever. Rogers decided to head back to the island of Gorgona near the South American mainland. There the sick were put ashore in tents to recover.

The Manila Galleons

They stayed two months to recuperate and to careen their ships and then set off westward to intercept the Manila galleon. For weeks they searched for the Spanish treasure ship. The men were getting mutinous and Rogers had almost abandoned the search when a Spanish galleon was sighted near the island of Guam. The *Duke* and *Dutchess* launched a furious attack on the ship with several broadsides and a fusillade of small arms fire. The Spanish ship fought back, but her rate of fire could not match that from the English ships

and eventually she surrendered with the loss of nine men killed and ten wounded. The only injury on the English side was Captain Rogers himself, who was shot through the jaw. In spite of spitting blood and teeth onto the deck, he continued to direct the action until the Spanish hauled down their colors.

The Spanish galleon was the *Nuestra Señora de la Incarnacion Disengaño*. She was a vessel of four hundred tons and she was armed with twenty mounted guns, twenty swivel guns, and had a crew of 193. They took her into Port Segura on the coast of California, where they learned from her crew that she had set off from Manila in company with a much larger galleon, the *Nuestra Señora de Begoña* of nine hundred tons, but had lost contact with her some weeks back. Although the captured ship was loaded with treasure, Rogers was determined to go for the bigger prize as well.

They intercepted the ship *Nuestra Señora de Begoña* a few days later. She proved to be a formidable adversary. She was commanded by the admiral of Manila, was armed with forty mounted guns and as many swivel guns, and had 450 men aboard, including a number of former pirates who defended her fiercely. They fought for seven hours. Rogers's ships were badly damaged in the encounter and twenty men on the *Dutchess* were killed or wounded, and eleven men wounded aboard the *Duke*, including Rogers himself, who was struck in the foot. They were forced to call off the action, and the Manila galleon sailed on her way.

On January 10, the privateers, now heavily laden, set off across the Pacific. The passage to Guam took them two months. From Guam they sailed to the Moluccas, Java, and the town of Batavia. They sailed from Batavia on October 12 and headed directly for the Cape

Above: *An engraving of navigators, or "sea artists," at work. Most of the tools of the trade are visible, including globes, pilot books and charts, and a range of instrumentation, including a compass, an hourglass, astrolabes, and a cross-staff. In an age when accurate printed maps were not yet available, such charts as existed were the keys to finding the wealth of the new territories; then, of course, one helped oneself to it. Those men who could compile or read such charts were highly prized members of the crew.*

Far left: *A case containing dividers, protractor, ruling pens, and other instruments used by navigators when carrying out chartwork. The navigational achievements of the seventeenth-century privateers and explorers are astonishing considering the inaccuracy of the contemporary charts and the vast areas of uncharted oceans that they covered in their various travels.*

Above: *Captain Woodes Rogers and his crew frisking Spanish ladies for hidden jewels and gold at Guayaquil in April 1709. Woodes Rogers's voyage around the world was one of the most successful of all privateering expeditions: according to contemporary accounts he brought back treasure valued at £800,000. Just two decades later Rogers was governor in Nassau and sufficiently highly respected to have his portrait painted by Hogarth.*

of Good Hope, which they reached on December 28, 1710. There they repaired and provisioned their three ships, the *Duke*, the *Dutchess*, and their prize, which they had named the *Batchelor*. To protect their valuable cargo, Rogers delayed their departure until they could sail in convoy with a fleet of Dutch warships and merchant ships. They eventually set sail on April 6, 1711. Rogers himself was very ill and his ship was leaking badly, but they pressed onward, through thunder, lightning, rain, and squall of winds.

On the morning of July 23 the convoy sighted Holland and they dropped anchor in the Texel. Rogers went ashore and traveled to Amsterdam to secure orders from the owners of his ship. After some problems with the Dutch Customs and the East India Company, he returned to his ship and set sail for England. They anchored in the Downs to wait for a favorable wind and then sailed round the Kent coast and up the Thames estuary. They reached their destination on October 14, 1711. In the words of Captain Woodes Rogers, "This day at 11 of the clock, we and our consort and prize got up to Erith, where we came to an anchor, which ends our long and fatiguing voyage."[9]

The total value of the treasure captured during the voyage was stated in a contemporary petition to be £800,000. For Dampier it was the end of his travels. His share of the expedition's net profits came to £1,500 which would be worth around £100,000 today.[10] He

took a house in Coleman Street near Moorgate and died three years later, at the age of sixty-three.

Ringrose: "An Exact and Curious Journal"

Apart from Esquemelin's earlier *History of the Buccaneers*, the only buccaneer writings that can be compared with Dampier's are those of Basil Ringrose, an intelligent and educated Englishman who spent most of his short life among pirates. Ringrose was a member of the crew led by Captain Bartholomew Sharp that made a plundering voyage around the coast of South America. During the course of the voyage the buccaneers destroyed twenty-five ships, killed several hundred people, and caused damage estimated at more than four million pesos by the Spanish authorities. The expedition was typical of many piratical voyages, but it achieved lasting fame because several members of the ship's company recorded their own observations and published them. The account by Ringrose was the most extensive and the most detailed. In the words of his old companion William Dick, "This Gentleman kept an exact and very curious Journal of all our Voyage, from our first setting out to the very last day, took also all the observations we made, and likewise an accurate description of all the Ports, Towns and Lands we came to."[11]

Basil Ringrose was born in London and baptized on January 28, 1653, at the church of St. Martin-in-the-Fields. His parents, Richard and Mary Ringrose, lived on a street close to the present site of Charing Cross Station. There is no record of his attending any of the major London schools, but we know that he acquired a working knowledge of French and Latin, and during his travels in South America he had no problem in learning Spanish and was able to act as interpreter for the buccaneers. There is no information in his later writings about his upbringing or his early life; nor is there any explanation of how he came to be in Central America with the buccaneers. He seems to have been liked and respected by his shipmates, although on one occasion he fought a duel with the ship's quartermaster. Dampier, who knew him well and shared many of his travels, called him "my ingenious friend Mr. Ringrose."

His journal begins in March 1679 and launches straight into a description of the buccaneers meeting for a general rendezvous at Boca del Tora near Puerto Bello, the Spanish treasure port. Having sacked Puerto Bello, they were now determined to attack the town of Santa Maria, which was situated up a great river and was an assembly point for gold from the surrounding region. Leaving a party of seamen to guard their ships, the buccaneers landed on the coast of Darien near Golden Island and marched inland. There were 327 of them and they were divided into seven companies. They were heavily armed with muskets, pistols, and short swords, and each company marched behind a colored flag. It took them ten days to tramp over the mountains, down through the wooded valleys, and along the banks of the river. During the journey they were joined by fifty local Indians, who hated the Spanish conquerors of their country.

On April 15, 1680, they emerged from the woods and had their first disappointment. Instead of an impressive Spanish town, Santa Maria proved to be a rough collection of huts beside a large fort on the muddy banks of a wide, shallow river. The fort was protected by a twelve-foot-high (3.6m) palisade. Warned of the buccaneers' advance, the governor, the priest, and many others had fled, leaving some two hundred men to defend the town. The buccaneers charged directly at the fort, pulled down a section of the palisade, and after a short fight overcame all resistance. Twenty-six Spaniards were killed and sixteen wounded. The only casualties among the buccaneers were two men wounded in the first assault. The next disappointment was to find that they had arrived too late. Twice a year a ship called in to collect the gold stored in the town. It had sailed for Panama only three days before their arrival, with three hundred-weight (150kg) of gold on board.

The Attack on Panama

Having failed to make their fortunes at Santa Maria, the buccaneers resolved to attack Panama itself. They set off downstream in thirty-five canoes, and at dawn on April 23, 1680, the buccaneers' motley fleet of canoes arrived within sight of the city of Panama. The Spanish were expecting them, and when their canoes were sighted the alarm was given and three warships weighed anchor and got under sail. The Spanish commanders had orders to give no quarter to the pirates and must have expected an easy victory. The

Spanish admiral had 228 men on his three ships, and these included experienced seamen and first-class soldiers. They faced sixty-eight buccaneers in five canoes, who were weary after rowing and paddling through the night. The action that followed revealed the remarkable fighting qualities of the buccaneers. They proved to be utterly fearless in the face of apparently overwhelming odds. They had extraordinary reserves of stamina, and their marksmen proved to be astonishingly accurate at hitting moving targets from the unstable platform of their dugout canoes.

Below: *A map of the island of Juan Fernandez from William Hack's* Waggoner of the South Sea, *published in 1685, that was accompanied by notes on the island from Basil Ringrose's journal. This uninhabited island was a frequent port of call for privateers and buccaneers voyaging along the west coast of South America and was visited by Ringrose on Christmas Day 1680.*

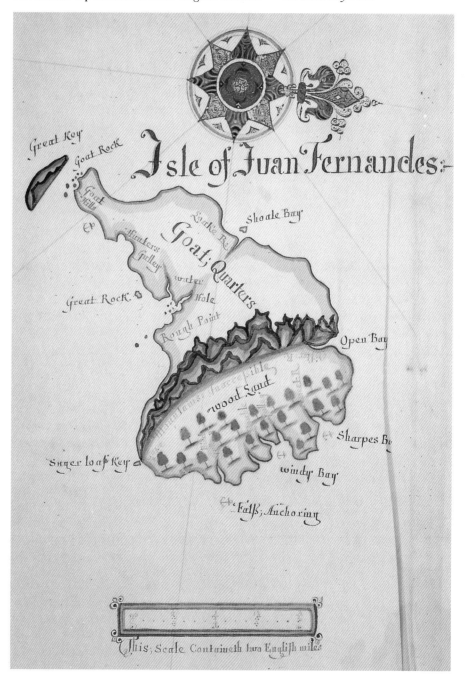

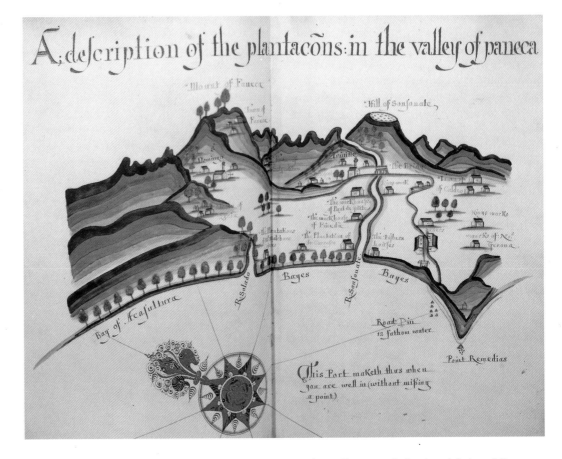

A description of the plantacōns in the valley of paneca

Above: *William Hack's version of the plantations in the valley of Paneca on the coast of El Salvador. It was produced from a map made on the spot by Basil Ringrose in 1681. Ringrose described the area as having "spacious walks and gardens of pleasure, all very artificial."*

As the Spanish ships swept down on them, the buccaneers took advantage of the maneuverability of their canoes and paddled out of range and upwind. They then picked off the ships one by one. Their technique was to shoot the helmsman and any of the crew on deck who were working the sails. Coming up under the stern, they shot away the braces controlling the sails, disabled the rudder, and clambered aboard. The fusillade of deadly fire from their long-barreled muskets killed two-thirds of the crew of one ship, and when they went aboard the second ship they found the blood of the dead and wounded running down the deck in whole streams.

After several hours of fierce fighting the buccaneers captured two of the ships and forced the third to flee. They then turned their attention to the other shipping anchored nearby. The most imposing of these was the *Santissima Trinidad*, a fine ship of four hundred tons that was laden with a rich cargo of wine, sugar, sweetmeats, and skins. It was seized by the buccaneers and henceforth became their flagship; they anglicized her name to the *Trinity*. Two other ships were also commandeered. Various merchant ships and smaller vessels in the vicinity of Panama were plundered of their cargoes and then burned. No attempt was made to sack the city itself, and after ten days the buccaneers weighed anchor and sailed to the nearby island of Tavoga.

Sharp Takes Over

In May 1680 they left the Gulf of Panama in search of other prizes. On May 22 Captain Sawkins was killed while leading an attack on the town of Puebla Nueva. Captain Sharp took over as chief commander and called a council of all the men. He told them that he intended to make a voyage around South America via the Strait of Magellan, and he promised that everyone who stayed with him would be worth £1,000. Sixty-three men decided to leave and set sail in an old ship for the Gulf of San Miguel. The original company of three hundred buccaneers was now down to 146 men in two ships. After careening their vessels at the island of Gorgona, they sailed south past the Cape of San Francisco toward Arica. They weathered storms, captured a ship off Guayaquil, and plundered and set fire to the city of La

Serena. By November, Ringrose was writing in his journal, "We were now about this time many of us very much troubled and diseased with the scurvy. It proceeded, as we judged, from the great hardship and want of provisions which we had endured for several months past, as having had only bread and water . . ."[12]

On Christmas Day 1680 they reached the Juan Fernandez Islands and dropped anchor off a steep section of coast. This was the occasion, already noted, when the men deposed Sharp from his command and replaced him with John Watling, an experienced seaman who had spent many years as a privateer. Forced to put out to sea again by the approach of Spanish warships, the buccaneers headed back to the mainland. Watling decided to attack the coastal town of Arica, which was used by the Spanish as a collection point for silver from the outlying regions. The subsequent action was a disaster. The buccaneers suffered very heavy losses and Watling was among those killed. Captain Sharp resumed command, organized an orderly retreat, and the buccaneers sailed away. For the next three months they hugged the coast and made occasional forays inland to raid villages and steal sheep, goats, corn, and wine from the inhabitants. On April 17 there was another mutiny among the crew of the *Trinity*. This was the point at which Dampier and fifty other members of the crew parted company from Sharp and Ringrose and headed back to the Caribbean.

This left sixty-five men under the command of Captain Sharp. With the weather deteriorating they decided to head north, and in the Gulf of Nicoya they carried out repairs and improvements to the ship and careened her. When they put to sea again their fortunes improved dramatically. On July 8 they captured the *San Pedro*, a large merchant ship that was so deeply laden that she seemed almost to be buried in the water. Her main cargo was coconuts, but she also carried wine, gunpowder, and no less than thirty-seven thousand pieces of eight, stored in chests and bags. Three weeks later they sighted another Spanish merchantman, *El Santo Rosario*, which fired three or four guns at them as they approached. The buccaneers waited until they were alongside and then swept the decks with a volley of small arms fire that killed the captain and a seaman and wounded the boatswain. The remaining forty men onboard surrendered. The buccaneers looted the ship of silver in the form of coins and plate, as well as 620 jars of wine and brandy.

Round the Horn

But the most important item onboard was not treasure but a volume of sea charts that was later to be instrumental in saving the lives of those who survived the voyage. The volume described all the ports and anchorages, rivers and creeks, bays and headlands between Acapulco and Cape Horn. It also included instructions on how to navigate a ship into any of the harbors along this vast stretch of coast. It was of immense value from a strategic point of view, and according to the journals of Sharp and Ringrose the Spanish were intending to throw the book overboard to prevent its falling into enemy hands. Having plundered the Spanish ship, the buccaneers cut down her masts, leaving only the foremast, and set her adrift.

By the end of August the buccaneers decided to end their plundering and to head for home. Taking advantage of the southeast trade winds, they set their course for the Strait of Magellan. By the end of October they were encountering harsh gales and snowstorms, and two weeks later they were sighting whales and icebergs. The worsening

Below: *Like Jamaica and Hispaniola, the West Indian island of Puerto Rico was a regular pirate haunt during the seventeenth century. This engraving shows shipping at anchor in the harbor of San Juan in 1671. A popular target of French corsairs in the 1560s, the Spanish fortified it. Ironically, by the early eighteenth century it was a base of Spanish pirates in the Caribbean and remained so for a century.*

weather drove them farther and farther south. On November 10 their mainsail and mizzen were blown to pieces "so that all the rest of this day we lay a-hull in very dark weather, foggy and windy, with a huge sea, which oftentimes rolled over us."[13] They failed to locate the Pacific entrance to the strait and found themselves in the desolate seas beyond. They thus became the first Englishmen to round Cape Horn itself and appear to have gone farther south at that point than any seamen before them. In the words of William Dick:

> Neither could we make any Land, but came round about such a way, as peradventure never any Mortals came before us, yet nothing remarkable did we see or meet withal, except hard Weather, and here and there some floats of Ice, of two or three Leagues long.[14]

The weather continued to be appalling. As the *Trinity* headed northeast into the Atlantic she was battered by gales, a whirlwind, and a storm of large hailstones. But slowly the weather improved. Instead of whales there were dolphins and flying fish, and the temperature became warmer. By December 25

they were baking in hot weather in the latitude of Rio de Janeiro and celebrated Christmas by killing a pig that they had brought with them from the Gulf of Nicoya.

Mixed Fortunes

Toward the end of January 1682 they began to see so many birds that they knew they must be getting close to land. At dawn on January 28 the buccaneers sighted the island of Barbados. There were several ships at anchor in Spikes Road, and as they drew closer a small boat passed them that proved to be the barge of the English warship HMS *Richmond*, which was anchored in Bridgetown harbor. From the crew of the barge they learned that there was peace at home, but the buccaneers dared not proceed into the harbor in case the captain of the frigate arrested them for piracy. As Ringrose put it, "we feared lest the said frigate should seize us for privateers and for having acted in all our voyages without commission."[15]

But they were heartened by the contact with their countrymen and set sail with high hopes. On January 30 they came to the island of Antigua, where they sent a canoe ashore to ask permission to enter the port. The local people were kind and welcoming but Colonel

Right: *The magnificent title page of William Hack's* Waggoner of the South Sea. *The London chartmaker was commissioned to make manuscript copies of the volume of Spanish charts captured from the* El Santo Rosario *by Bartholomew Sharp, who wrote, "I took a manuscript of a prodigious value —it describes all the ports, roads, harbours, bays, sands, rocks and rising of the land, and instructions how to work a ship into any port or harbour. They were going to throw it overboard but by good luck I saved it."*

Far right: *A cross-staff and a back-staff used for finding latitude at sea by measuring the altitude of the sun at midday. To use the cross-staff meant staring at the sun to measure its angle above the horizon—a far from easy task. The back-staff was invented by Captain John Davis in about 1594; it enabled the observer to take sights with his back to the sun and avoid its glare.*

Codrington, the governor, refused to allow their ship entry. They therefore decided to leave the ship to seven of the buccaneers who had lost all their money in gambling. The remainder took passage in two ships that were bound for England. Ringrose and thirteen others sailed on the *Lisbon Merchant*, commanded by Captain Robert Porteen. They departed from Antigua in February and landed at Dartmouth on March 26, 1682.

When Don Pedro Ronquillo, the Spanish ambassador in London, learned that the buccaneers had arrived in England, he insisted that they be brought to trial for piracy and murder. The landlord of the Anchor Inn, in London's East End, reported that ten of Sharp's crew were in town and that Sharp himself had been boasting of his piratical exploits. On May 18, the Admiralty issued a warrant for the arrest of Sharp, Dick, and Scott, and in due course the three men were committed to the Marshalsea Prison in Southwark, the traditional holding place for debtors and pirates. Meanwhile, the valuable book of sea charts and sailing directions, which Sharp had seized from the Spanish ship *El Santo Rosario*, had been brought to the attention of King Charles II. A great deal of intrigue seems to have taken place, and there is some evidence that the influence of the king and his advisers affected the outcome of the trial of the buccaneers.[16] In any case the jury acquitted the three men when they came before the High Court of Admiralty on June 10, 1682. The Spanish ambassador was outraged and complained to Charles II, but the king replied that he did not meddle in matters relating to the law.

Piracy, Prison, and Poverty

The volume of charts was translated into English and several copies were made by the London mapmaker William Hack. One of these handsome volumes, with beautifully drawn and hand-colored charts, was dedicated to the king by Sharp himself and joined the other maritime publications in the royal library. This was a shrewd move by Sharp, and must have helped toward his being given a captain's commission in the Royal Navy. Another factor in restoring the former pirate to favor was no doubt traditional British hostility toward Spain and the recognition that Sharp, like Sir Henry Morgan before him, had been remarkably effective in challenging

Spanish supremacy in the Americas. For some reason Sharp never took up his commission in the Royal Navy but went off to the Caribbean. The governor of Nevis and Bermuda employed him on antipiracy duties, but he soon fell back into his old ways and by 1686 he was brought before a court in Nevis for committing acts of piracy in Jamaica and at Campeche. He was acquitted for lack of evidence. The last record of him comes from the Danish governor of St. Thomas in the Virgin Islands, who told Admiral Benbow in 1699 that the only English subject on his island was the noted pirate Captain Sharp, who was in prison for his misdemeanors. Sharp would have been around fifty-one years old at this time.

Basil Ringrose stayed in England for no more than a year and a half before setting off on his travels again. In October 1683 he sailed for the South Sea onboard the ship *Cygnet* under the command of Captain Swan. According to Dampier, who joined Swan's crew a few months later, "He had no mind for this voyage, but was necessitated to engage in it or starve."[17] After a fruitless year attempting to undertake legitimate trading on the coast near Costa Rica, Swan joined company with a number of French and English buccaneer ships and turned his attention to raiding Spanish settlements. It was during one of these raids that Ringrose lost his life. Swan had dropped anchor at the mouth of a river not far from the town of Mazatlán on the Mexican coast. He marched his men inland and captured the small town of Santa Pecaque. While they were looting the town they learned that the Spanish had assembled an armed force of nearly one thousand men and were only a few miles away. Swan sent half his men back to the anchorage with fifty-four heavily laden horses. The remainder stayed behind to continue with their looting.

Shortly after the party of buccaneers had disappeared down the track, there was the sound of distant gunfire. Swan gathered together the men in the town and set off to investigate. They had traveled about a mile when they came across a scene that must have shocked the most hardened of the buccaneers. Fifty bodies lay scattered along the track. Most of the corpses had been stripped and they were so cut about that they were almost unrecognizable. The Spanish had set

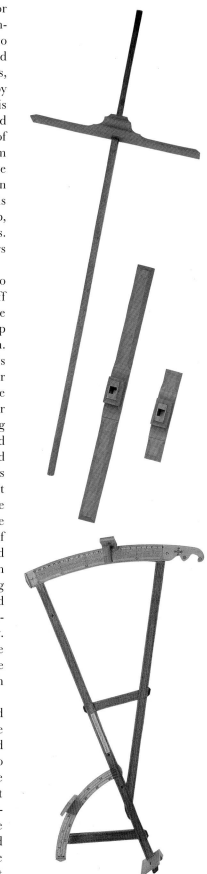

up an ambush and had massacred all the men accompanying the train of horses. Basil Ringrose was found among the dead. He was no more than thirty-two or thirty-three years old.

Wafer and the Legacy of the Buccaneers

The published accounts of Esquemelin, Dampier, Woodes Rogers, and Ringrose provide a vivid picture of the lives and travels of the buccaneers. But there was another eyewitness of their exploits whose work is less well known. Although he took part in several of the adventures described by Dampier and Ringrose, the buccaneer surgeon Lionel Wafer devoted much of his published writings to descriptions of the Cuna Indians and the fauna and flora of Central America. He had been badly injured in the leg during a march across the Isthmus of Panama and had spent four months recuperating among the Indians. He learned their language, studied their customs, and later wrote a wonderful account of their way of life.[18]

Lionel Wafer was raised in the Scottish Highlands and was probably the son of a Scottish soldier. He went to sea in 1677 as a surgeon's assistant, or what seamen used to call a loblolly boy. His first voyage was to Java in an East Indiaman, and his second voyage took him to Jamaica, where he had a brother who was employed on a sugar plantation. At Port Royal in Jamaica he met Captain Edmund Cook and decided to join his ship. Cook sailed to Central America to join the fleet of buccaneer ships that had assembled in Almirante Bay. For the next three years Wafer traveled with Cook, Sharp, Sawkins, and the other buccaneers whose exploits have already been described. He was surgeon onboard the *Batchelor's Delight* between 1683 and 1684 and sailed in her from the coast of Africa across to Cape Horn and north to Panama. In October 1684 his ship joined company with Captain Swan and the *Cygnet*, and Wafer spent the next two years traveling in the Pacific. In the autumn of 1687 the *Batchelor's Delight*, now under the command of Captain Edmund Davis, headed once again for Cape Horn. They encountered fierce gales as they rounded the cape but survived the storms and made their next landfall close to Montevideo.

When Captain Davis, Wafer, and a seaman named John Hincent arrived in Virginia in June 1688, they were arrested for piracy and thrown into jail in Jamestown. During the course of their voyages they had plundered considerable quantities of treasure from Spanish ships. Wafer himself had in his sea chest 1,158 pieces of eight, 162 pounds (74kg) of silver plate, one and a half ounces (45g) of gold, and silks and cloth to the value of forty pounds sterling. In 1689, after a year in prison, they were set free. Wafer returned to England and seems to have spent the remainder of his life in London. In 1699 he published *A New Voyage & Description of the Isthmus of America* and dedicated it to the earl of Romney. The book was well received and in 1704 a second edition was published, this time dedicated to the duke of Marlborough. Wafer is believed to have died in London soon after this, probably in 1705.

No Small Achievements

The buccaneers of the seventeenth century were followed by the men of the great age of piracy, freelance adventurers who had little loyalty toward their own countries and were prepared to attack the ships of any nation. They too made extensive voyages in search of victims. Bartholomew Roberts traveled from the Caribbean north to Newfoundland and made two voyages across the Atlantic to plunder on the west coast of Africa. Edward Low roamed from the West Indies to the Azores, traveled back to Rhode Island, and made a second crossing of the Atlantic to the Cape Verde Islands and then on to Sierra Leone. Thomas Tew and Edward England were among the numerous known pirates who sailed from New York and Boston to India via Madagascar and Mauritius. None of these men left any personal records or journals, so we are dependent on the depositions of seamen, the reports of colonial governors, trial documents, and newspapers for first-hand accounts of their travels.

What was significantly different about Sharp, Ringrose, Cox, Dampier, and the other buccaneers of the 1670s and 1680s is the information they published about their voyages and the new lands and native peoples they encountered. It would be foolish to pretend that they made a massive contribution to the exploration of the coast of America or the charting of the Pacific. The Spanish had already charted most of the harbors and

Below: An octant made by Benjamin Cole in 1761. The octant was invented by John Hadley in 1731 and was an improvement on the earlier cross-staff and back-staff. It helped to overcome the problem of taking sights from a moving ship by the use of two mirrors that enabled the observer to view the horizon and the sun simultaneously. By the latter part of the eighteenth century it had been replaced by the sextant, which became the standard navigational instrument for measuring the altitude of heavenly bodies.

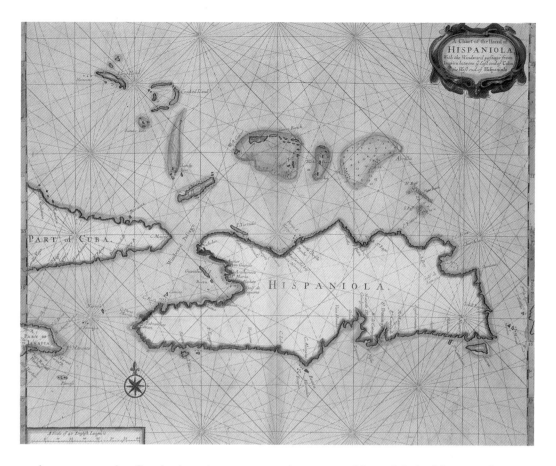

anchorages on the South American coast before the buccaneers made their plundering voyages along the coasts of Peru, Chile, and Brazil. The volume of charts captured by Sharp's men, brought to England, and copied by William Hack seems never to have been used by later seamen.[19] Dampier was the first Englishman to explore the northwest coast of Australia, but it was the Dutch who were largely responsible for mapping the continent's outline. Captain Swan and Captain Woodes Rogers were preceded across the Pacific by Magellan, Drake, and Cavendish, and by the Dutchmen Olivier van Noort and Abel Tasman. All the previous voyages of exploration in the Pacific were eclipsed by the discoveries of Captain James Cook. His three voyages between 1768 and 1780 opened up and charted the length and breadth of the ocean, its islands and coasts, in a systematic way that was entirely alien to the haphazard ramblings of the buccaneers.

While the buccaneers' contribution to the history of exploration may have been modest, their seafaring skills were astonishing. Their navigational instruments were primitive and the few charts available were notoriously inaccurate. Most of their ships were between two hundred and three hundred tons and would have been no more than 100 feet (30m) in length. For food and ships' gear they were entirely dependent on what they could plunder from other vessels and from coastal raids. Like the vikings many centuries earlier, their voyages of plunder took them thousands of miles across uncharted waters. In the Caribbean they were at the mercy of hurricanes and in the southern ocean they had to face mountainous waves and weeks of gales. Yet a surprising number of them lived through storms, battles, tropical diseases, and scurvy, and survived to tell the tale. Some idea of their achievement can be glimpsed in this extract from the writings of Lionel Wafer:

> In all our passage round Terra del Fuego the weather was so stormy for the 3 weeks that we lay to the southward of Cape Horn, and the sun and stars so obscured, that we could take no observation of our latitude, yet by our reckoning we were in very near 63 degrees south which is the farthest to the south that any European probably ever yet was, and perhaps any man.[20]

Above: *A map of the island of Hispaniola, the original island of settlement for the groups of hunters who became the earliest buccaneers. After being driven out of their hunting grounds by the Spanish, many of them turned to buccaneering. Some settled on the island of Tortuga, which became a pirate base for attacks on Spanish shipping; others subsequently moved to Saona and Île à Vache just off Hispaniola's shore.*

CHAPTER FOUR

CORSAIRS OF
THE MEDITERRANEAN

~

Sometimes the galley slaves row ten, twelve or even twenty hours at a stretch, without the slightest rest or break. . . . if one of the slaves falls exhausted over his oar (which is quite a common occurrence) he is flogged until he appears to be dead, and is thrown overboard without ceremony.

JEAN MARTELLEILLE DE BERGERAC[1]

THIS HORRIFIC description might be thought to report treatment of galley slaves in ancient Greece. But it does not; it comes instead from a much more recent and largely forgotten period in the history of Mediterranean piracy, when maritime plunder and pillage masqueraded as religious war at sea.

On one side were the Barbary corsairs. These were slave galleys of the Barbary states —semi-autonomous city-states on the North African coast. There the Muslim fiefdoms had been building and equipping rowed galleys to raid Mediterranean shipping from the early sixteenth century onward. Captured Christians worked the oars in a punishing ritual that has been used in succeeding centuries as a touchstone of Muslim cruelty.

But the story from the other side of the religious divide is less well known. Christian forces based in Malta also sponsored piracy, in actions that precisely mirrored those of the Barbary corsairs. Furthermore, the organization that equipped and organized these counteroffensives is still with us. Though changed beyond all recognition, the Knights Hospitaler of St. John of Jerusalem are, ironically, now represented by a charity organization better known as the St. John's Ambulance Brigade.

Pirates and Popes

Piracy in the Mediterranean is an ancient calling. When tiny merchant ships made their first halting voyages on the sea's calm waters, pirates were never far behind. Early mariners made easy targets because (lacking compass or charts) they sailed "coastwise," never straying out of sight of land. Pirates had just to wait behind a convenient headland overlooking a busy sea route, and sooner or later a prize would stray into their clutches.

When trade in the Mediterranean expanded, so too did piracy. As early as the seventh century B.C., Phoenician ships suffered regular attacks by pirates. The Greek and Roman civilizations also experienced the pirates' unwanted attentions.

It was the Crusades, though, that established the pattern for later piracy in the region. The nominal aim of these military pilgrimages was to recapture the Holy Land from "the infidel," who had controlled the region since the seventh century A.D. Launched by the pope in 1096, the first Crusade was a huge success. Christian warriors captured the coastal region of the Holy Land and created Crusader kingdoms there; but this decisive victory proved hard to repeat in later campaigns, and after two centuries of bloody warfare, the real achievements of the Crusades must have seemed slim to their Christian advocates.

One tangible advance, though, was that the Crusades secured the Mediterranean for European shipping. Equally important, from the point of view of later piracy in the Mediterranean, was the establishment of military-religious orders. Their aristocratic members initially aimed to nurse sick pilgrims and Christian warriors, and to defend the roads that they followed on their path to the Holy Land. The Knights Hospitaler of St. John formed in Jerusalem, taking their name from the hospital dedicated to the saint in the Holy City. The pope gave the group his approval in 1113. The wealth and influence of the Hospitalers

Left: A Spanish Engagement with the Barbary Corsairs *by Andries van Eertvelt. Although the Spanish warship is surrounded by oared corsair galleys, the rough seas put the corsairs at a disadvantage because of the difficulty of rowing and maneuvering their long, narrow vessels.*

Below: *A rare example of an original nineteenth-century pirate flag. It was brought back from North Africa by Finnish seafarers and is now in the collections of the maritime museum at Mariehamn. The black flag with white skull and crossbones (itself a common representation of death) seems to have come into general use in the Caribbean in the early eighteenth century and spread rapidly among pirates worldwide. It seems likely that it was a symbol chosen to reflect the pirates' godless, cynical, and defiant challenge to the society of their time.*

grew rapidly, and they soon acquired vast estates in Europe and in the Crusader kingdoms. The Hospitalers were among the most single-minded of the crusading warriors, and were to continue the Holy War long after the Crusades had ended.

The Ottoman Empire

The Hospitalers' wrath would eventually be directed against the Ottoman Empire. However, at the time of the last Crusade in 1270, the Ottomans were relatively unimportant warlords based in a small state in northwest Turkey. Ottoman expansion began slowly, but rapidly accelerated. In 1453, the Ottomans captured Constantinople; early in the following century the ruthless Sultan Selim the Grim (1470–1520) conquered Persia, Syria, and Egypt. By the time of his death, the Islamic world was united under Ottoman rule.

When the fortunes of the Crusaders declined, those of the Hospitalers naturally fell, also. With the defeat of Acre (the last Crusader stronghold in the Holy Land) by Muslim forces in 1291, the Hospitalers retreated to Cyprus, and soon to Rhodes. This island was the home of the order for more than two hundred years.

Ottoman expansion evicted the Hospitalers from Rhodes in 1522, leading to a few years of feckless wandering in search of a permanent base. Eventually Charles V (1500–1558), the king of Spain and Holy Roman emperor, granted the Hospitalers the rocky island of Malta as a base. There they consolidated their forces, and eventually became known as the Knights of Malta, or simply "The Religion."

With this turbulent history, perhaps it is not surprising that religious fanaticism runs through early accounts of the war against the pirates of the Barbary coast. As late as 1980, a popular writer on piracy felt able to describe "the corsair menace to sea trade" that "remained a scourge until 1700, when their activities were curtailed by an English admiral"[2] without once mentioning that Maltese corsairs continued a corresponding business from their island base.

The Barbary Corsairs

Since the earliest times Christians had used the name "Barbary" to describe the southern coast of the Mediterranean, from Egypt to the Atlantic, and on beyond Gibraltar. The origins of the name are unclear: the usual explanation is that it is a corruption of Berber, which is derived from a derogatory ancient Greek word for anything non-Greek; this became the root of the word "barbarian."

The Phoenicians and Greeks established colonies in Barbary, and the Romans conquered and subdued the region. The Byzantine Empire briefly controlled the coast in the sixth century, but by 711 most of the North African shoreline was under Arab rule,[3] and the Muslim world additionally took control of the Iberian peninsula soon after. Muslim domination of the North African coast was to continue virtually unchallenged until the early sixteenth century. However, in Spain, Christian power grew, and by 1248 only Granada, in the extreme south, remained in Muslim hands. The expulsion in 1492 of the Moorish rulers of Granada by Ferdinand V (1452–1516) marked an intensification of the religious feud between the Christian and Muslim worlds that faced each other across the great sea.

Attacks by Spanish and Portuguese privateers in the early years of the sixteenth century gave the Europeans a brief and uncertain foothold on the North African shore. The most important conquests were Algiers, Tunis, and Tripoli.

Spanish forces took the first of these towns in 1510 and fortified the island of Peñon that overlooked the harbor area. After a revolt six years later, the Algerians appointed an Arab leader and laid siege to Peñon. The stalemate continued for an amazing thirteen years, but the Spanish were finally expelled in 1529. The capture of Tunis followed in 1535, and the Spanish controlled it for more than three decades. They again took the port in 1573, before finally relinquishing it the following year. Tripoli was a Norman possession from the twelfth century to 1510, when the Spanish took the town. With the fall of Tripoli to Ottoman forces in 1551, the major ports of the Barbary coast were in Muslim hands. Prior to their capture by the Spanish, the towns had been used to supply and

Below: *A map of the Mediterranean Sea region showing Europe, North Africa, and the Levant. Piracy existed around the British Isles and in the Baltic, but the principal zone of activity was the Mediterranean Sea. As the center of the Ancient World, seaborne trade was long established in the area and piracy had existed for millennia; a young Julius Caesar had been held captive and the Cilicians had posed a threat to Rome. Later, the growth of Moorish power was held in check by the Crusades and the Spanish Reconquista. This religious conflict was the backdrop for a variety of piratical practices lasting centuries.*

Above: *The corsair warrior Dragut Reis preparing for a boarding. He was a lieutenant of Barbarossa and had once been a slave on a Christian galley. He defeated a Spanish fleet near Jerba in 1560 but was killed during the siege of Malta in 1565.*

Right: *The Barbarossa brothers, Aruj and Kheir-ed-din, who became the most feared of the Barbary pirates. Through their efforts Spain's attempts to conquer and expand Christian influence in the western parts of North Africa were checked and the foundations laid for a stong Muslim power. The brothers controlled a powerful fleet and acquired the name because of their red beards.*

shelter pirate ships. On their return to Muslim control, corsair activities expanded and became more institutionalized.

The Great Corsair Leader, Barbarossa

Two brothers were largely responsible for building the ports into bases for corsairs. Maritime adventurers Aruj (c. 1474–1518) and Kheir-ed-din ("Defender of the Faith") came from a Greek family that had converted to Islam. The older brother, Aruj, was the first to rise to prominence. As a young man he served in the Turkish navy, but eventually took command of a privateering vessel. By 1504 he had begun to cruise off the Barbary coast. He called at Tunis and struck a deal with the king there. In exchange for harbor facilities, the pirate would pay him one-fifth of everything he captured. The arrangement quickly bore fruit: commanding a small

galleot off the coast of Elba, Aruj captured two of the pope's grand galleys. It was an extraordinary achievement, and it earned Aruj fame throughout Barbary. Within five years he had eight ships under his command. News of the corsair's skills also spread among European sailors, who dubbed him Barbarossa on account of his red beard.

Barbarossa's career was not entirely without setbacks: he lost an arm while trying to seize Bougie from the Spanish in 1514, and, while he was recovering, his brother Kheir-ed-din took control. Further setbacks followed, but the fortunes of the pair were transformed when they responded to the call to wrest Algiers from Spanish hands. Barbarossa and his followers rapidly took control of the town, put down a rebellion, and repelled a flotilla of Spanish ships. By 1517, he controlled most of what is now Algeria, with the exception of Peñon and a handful of isolated Spanish garrisons.

Kheir-ed-din and Dragut

Barbarossa's reign over Algiers ended with his death in a land battle against Spanish forces and their local supporters. His place was taken by his younger brother, Kheir-ed-din. Like Barbarossa, Kheir-ed-din was a superb seaman, but not from the salty-sea-dog mold. He was cultured and sophisticated, and fluent in six languages.

By 1525 Kheir-ed-din had reinforced his hold over Algiers, building it into a powerful

corsair base and strengthening Ottoman power on the waves. His formidable successor, Dragut, recovered Tripoli for Islam.

However, by the end of the sixteenth century, the role of the Barbary states was starting to change. As regencies, the Barbary ports had enjoyed a certain degree of independence, and this continued after their recapture from the Spanish. The coastal towns were, in principle, outposts of the Ottoman Empire, but in practice they grew into self-governing fiefdoms. In the early years of Ottoman rule a pasha, nominated by the sultan, controlled the ports. His authority was guaranteed by a corp of janissaries—the elite fighters of the Ottoman army.

Throughout the later sixteenth century, the balance of power shifted away from the pasha, and toward a council of janissary officers called the Divan. The Divan appointed a bey or dey, and it was these figures who actually controlled the Barbary kingdoms. The system bordered on the anarchic, and corruption, assassination, and political intrigue were commonplace. But despite their sometimes chaotic political life, the Barbary states blossomed into military powers with the capability to prey on Christian shipping over wide areas of the Mediterranean.

The Corsair Ships

The principal weapon of the Barbary states was the slave galley. This narrow, sleek ship was the traditional fighting machine of the Mediterranean. To the casual eye it was little different from the trireme of ancient Greece. However, closer inspection would reveal many differences; for example, the oars of the Barbary galley were arranged in a single bank, rather than the superimposed rows of the Greek craft. And whereas the sixteenth-century North African slave ship had a pointed prow, this was above the waterline; the ship's Aegean ancestor had its ram at water level, to hole and sink its victims.

The Barbary slave ship was enclosed at the stern, to provide shelter for a company of janissaries. But, forward to the bows, the rest of the vessel was open to the elements. There was a fixed cannon, but on a low deck area rather than in the raised forecastle that is such a characteristic element of northern European "round ships" of the period. Further swivel guns were mounted amidships. A single lateen (triangular) sail pro-

pelled the galley when there was enough wind, but it was the oarsmen who provided the power in a chase, when sailing into the wind, or on a calm day.

Galleys were the largest Barbary vessels: the table[4] summarizes the key features.

Corsair ships

Vessel	Benches	Men
	(2 oars per bench)	per oar
galley	24-28	4-5
galleot	17-23	2-3
brigantine	6-16	1
frigate	6-12	1
fellucca	3-5	1

From the early seventeenth century, the Barbary corsairs began to supplement their galley fleets with the round ships that, by then, dominated Atlantic warfare.

Above: *A plan of Algiers produced by Robert Norton in 1620. During the era of the Barbarossas, Algiers became a base for the pirates and remained one of the principal ports for such operations for the next three hundred years. Initially, many of those most active there were Western seamen made unemployed by the end of the Spanish War in 1603 who found a ready market for their skills in the protection of the Barbary states, which remained at war with the Spanish.*

A CORSAIR VESSEL, 1770

THE OAR-POWERED galley was a formidable fighting machine and was developed in the Mediterranean from the vessels of Ancient Greece and Rome. The oars, which were manned by eighty or ninety galley slaves, provided rapid acceleration and speed, and enabled the vessel to run rings round a sailing vessel in calms or light winds. The galley slaves sat on wooden benches, usually four or six men to an oar, and were chained by their feet. Although most cruises were short, the slaves were expected to row for many hours at a time. Some men endured the life for years, but not surprisingly it was considered the worst fate that could befall anyone who was captured alive by the corsairs.

In fresh or strong winds the galley was able to set one, two, or three lateen sails, and these would have driven her long, narrow hull at a considerable rate. Big guns were mounted in the bows and a few swivel guns along the rails, but what made the galley so alarming was the large force of armed fighting men that was carried onboard. These men, who were renowned for their discipline and courage, took no part in the rowing or sailing of the ship. The usual tactic was to come sweeping alongside a merchant ship and to board her. The fighting men then scrambled across with spears, muskets, and scimitars and overpowered the opposition in hand-to-hand fighting.

Key

1 Bronze ram.
2 Anchor cat supporting the anchor.
3 Swivel gun.
4 Heavy thirty-pounder gun mounted on sliding carriage on the center line.
5 Forecastle for men working swivel guns.
6 Twenty-four-pounder gun on sliding carriage.

7 Captured European eighteen-pounder gun on wheeled carriage.
8 Chains for securing the ankles of galley slaves.
9 Benches for seating four men to each sweep.
10 Sweeps for propelling the galley in calms and light airs.
11 Center line walkway for the overseeing men in

charge of the galley slaves.
12 Outboard walkway for swivel gun crews, and boarding crews of fighting men.
13 Covered area for the captain and the commander of the fighting men.
14 Sterncastle for swivel gun crews.

Galley Slaves

The slaves sat naked on benches, four or five of them pulling on each oar. They were encouraged by the crew of the vessel, who would not hesitate to apply the whip to the shoulders of any slave who was (quite literally) not pulling his weight. This description, written by a Frenchman who had felt the lash upon his own back, vividly evokes the privations that slaves endured:

> They are chained six to a bench; these are four foot wide covered with sacking stuffed with wool, over which are laid sheepskins. . . . When the captain gives the order to row, the officer gives the signal with a silver whistle which hangs on a cord around his neck; the signal is repeated by the under-officers, and very soon all fifty oars strike the water as one. . . . Sometimes the galley slaves row ten, twelve or even twenty hours at a stretch, without the slightest rest or break. On these occasions the officer will go round and put pieces of bread soaked in wine into the mouths of the wretched rowers, to prevent them from fainting. . . .[5]

It is not easy to judge exactly how fast the slaves could drive the ship forward. Five miles (8km) during the first hour of rowing[6] seems a reasonable guess, but some naval historians[7] have suggested speeds as high as twelve knots (fourteen miles per hour/22kph) in short bursts.

The Ship's Complement

Command of the ship was the responsibility of the *raïs* or captain. He controlled all aspects of sailing and navigation. His crew was often a mixture of captured Christian and Muslim sailors; European "sea artists" were highly valued, and their skills secured them a more comfortable position than the slave's bench.

The Christian seamen needed freedom to work the ship, and, unlike the slaves, they were shackled only when attack was imminent. The threat of demotion to the oars was presumably enough to ensure their loyalty at other times. By contrast, the slaves, who greatly outnumbered the Turks onboard, had almost nothing to lose by mutiny, and they were controlled only by their constant confinement in chains.

In addition to the oarsmen and crew, every Barbary galley carried a complement of janissaries—between 100 and 140 on a large vessel. The janissaries played no part in sailing the ship, and were there simply to fight. This they evidently did with considerable courage and tenacity, attacking with musket, arrow, and scimitar.

Though the agha—the commander of the janissaries—had no say over the sailing of the ship, he was the superior officer and made decisions about whether or not to engage a vessel. In this respect, the agha was in overall charge of the cruise.

A quick sum will reveal that a Barbary gal-

Below: *An eighteenth-century Arabian sword or* Nimcha, *typical of those used in Morocco and elsewhere along the North African coast. It is richly mounted with chased and embossed silver and parcel-gilt. The blade is multifullered, possibly Ottoman but made in the European style. Curved blades originated in Asia where their cutting advantages had long been recognized. They reached Europe via the Turks whose scimitar-type weapons, such as this, provided the model for cavalry sabers and the like.*

ley carried an enormous number of people, and with so many mouths to feed, cruises were necessarily short. A typical trip might last six to eight weeks, perhaps less if the galley was quick to find a prize. There was another compelling reason to return to port at regular intervals. The Barbary galleys relied on speed for their success, and this was impossible without frequent careening. The galley would be beached and laboriously scraped to remove the coating of barnacles and weeds that adhered below the waterline. A coating of wax helped it to slip smoothly through the water. Careening took about ten days, and had to be repeated every two months or so.

Where They Hunted

Until the late sixteenth century, the galleys of the Barbary states were more or less integrated into the fleet of the Ottoman Empire, but by the end of the century, Barbary vessels were operating independently. Ships of the three states had their own hunting grounds, but inevitably there was some overlap. Algiers galleys cruised between Sicily and Gibraltar—and beyond, out into the Atlantic. Those from Tripoli harassed shipping to the east of Sicily. Tunis, roughly midway between the other two Barbary states, operated vessels in the central and eastern Mediterranean.

The practices of all three fleets were essentially opportunistic. If their quarry made seasonal voyages—perhaps transporting a new harvest—then the galleys would change their

routes and timings to take fullest advantage of the increase in maritime traffic.

The Chase and Capture

The tactics of the Barbary pirates naturally varied with time and circumstances, but in the era of the galley there seems to have been a fairly consistent approach to pursuit and capture. As the pirates closed in on their victims, they would fire the cannon placed forward, but more by way of a warning than for the destructive power of the ball. Firing the smaller swivel guns amidships might use-

Above: *Violence and torture were common features of pirate attacks, and this 1807 illustration gives some idea of the terrifying scene on the deck of a ship under assault. Mr. Sharp, the chief mate of the brig* Admiral Trowbridge, *has been wounded, put in irons, and spiked to the deck.*

fully clear the decks of opponents, but gunnery generally was not a priority.

The janissaries did the real work of attacking and boarding the ship. The corsair captain would aim to ram the victim, so that the fighters could swarm aboard from the raised prow. Not many vessels put up a fight, and indeed most were so lightly armed that they were incapable of doing so. The crews of those ships that carried sufficient cannons to fight back, or enough sail to flee, were often so frightened that they surrendered anyway. To encourage submission, the janissaries made themselves as terrifying as possible, shouting, screaming, and hurling abuse, and hammering on the sides of the other vessel. A few crews resisted, or scuppered their vessels rather than surrender. The Dutch in particular had a reputation for going out with a

bang, setting fire to the ship's powder magazine when it was clear that further resistance was pointless.

Once aboard, the pirates set about releasing any Muslim slaves, and put Christians in their places at the oars. The vessel was plundered for anything of value in the cargo or in the personal possessions of those onboard, but the main object of the attack was to take slaves, which were as good as money on return to Barbary. Furthermore, much of the value of the slaves lay in their social status. An English nobleman was a very worthwhile prize, because his family could be relied upon to redeem him with the payment of a considerable ransom. A servant or laborer, on the other hand, had a far lesser value.

The anticipation of imminent capture occasionally produced some tragicomic

Below: An English Ship in Action Against Barbary Corsairs, *by Willem van de Velde the Younger, c. 1675. This fine painting by the great Dutch marine artist shows a furious battle in the Mediterranean between a large English warship and a number of galleys. The warship is firing broadsides to port and starboard with devastating effect. A galley on the left is dismasted and on fire with most of the corsairs having taken to the boats.*

effects onboard Christian ships. Wealthy passengers did their utmost to conceal valuable jewelry: some went so far as to swallow heavy gold coins or precious stones; others threw their valuables overboard rather than surrender them to the hated Turk. Aristocrats tried to reduce the inevitable ransom demand by swapping clothes with their servants.

The corsairs had answers to most of these ruses. The mere threat of *bastinado* (beating on the soles of the feet) was often enough to extract the location of hidden treasures. Some pirate crews administered a powerful emetic mixture to outwit the swallowers. The crafty change of clothes was perhaps the simplest of tricks to see through—for merely by examining the hands of captives, the corsairs could quickly sort out the smooth-skinned noblemen from the callused, rough laborers.

The treatment of women has been widely misrepresented in the past, especially by those campaigning for the suppression of piracy. Far from suffering a "fate worse than death," women seem generally to have been treated reasonably well. One account, written in 1719, describes the consideration with which a corsair treated his female captives—though it hints at a sinister threat. A group of women onboard the ship seized by the pirate captain is advised to remain in their own vessel, rather than entering the galley that took them in tow:

> That she was at her own option, whether she would remove into the cruiser, or continue in the tartan, where indeed she might be much quieter and more at liberty than on board his ship, wherein were nearly two hundred, between Turks and Moors, among whom there was no very safe trusting either herself or the young females she had with her.[8]

Other sources suggest that janissaries or crew who molested women passengers were themselves severely punished.[9] Christian captives and their belongings were not the only reward for a successful attack: if the ship itself was suitable for use in the Barbary fleet, the corsairs would put a crew onboard and sail it home.

Subterfuge and False Colors

The speed advantage of the corsair ships was so great that capture, or at least engage-

ment, was almost inevitable once the prey was in sight. However, the corsairs were not above subterfuge if a change of wind came to the aid of their target. Flying false colors was an age-old pirate trick, and it was as effective in the Mediterranean as it would later prove to be on the Spanish Main.

Seventeenth-century traveler Le Sieur du Chastelet des Boys described his relief when six Dutch ships appeared, just as a Barbary corsair was closing in for the kill. However, his relief turned to horror when:

> the Dutch flags disappeared and the masts and poop were simultaneously shaded by flags of taffeta of all colors, enriched and embroidered with stars, crescents, suns, crossed swords and other devices.[10]

The similarities between Christian and Muslim ships were so great that the true identity of the attackers often did not become clear until the ship was alongside. To make the disguise complete, the janissaries hid from view; perhaps renegade Christian members of the crew stood at the deck rail with a welcoming wave. Since the victims expected turbaned Turks, they were easily taken in.

Ransacking the Ship

Those taken captive by the Barbary corsairs often commented on how disciplined the crews and janissaries were about the division of the spoils. There were well-established rules about who was entitled to what: the ship's equipment and cargo, for example, were part of the prize, and had to be accounted for. But the possessions of passengers and crew could be pillaged with impunity. Those who broke the rules and cheated their comrades could expect swift retribution.

The Conditions of Slaves

Those whom the corsairs captured eventually found their way back to the Barbary states, facing, at worst, indefinite slavery, or, at best, a long wait for a ransom to arrive. First, though, they had to endure the humiliation of the slave auction. In an initial sorting procedure, the bey selected the very best captives; the remainder were taken to a slave market:

> There are ready the *dilaleen* or auctioneers, who walk them up and down the street, pub-

Above: Dutch Ships off Tripoli, *by Reinier Nooms. In 1551 the Ottoman forces captured Tripoli from the Spanish, and thereafter it became another base for the Barbary pirates. Protected by a fortified harbor, it was well positioned for attacks on merchant ships traveling from the eastern Mediterranean to Venice, Genoa, and other westerly points.*

after each has answered to his name, and all have been exactly counted. They are by day employed in different services of the public . . . in the vilest offices and drudgeries at the Dey's house; in public works, which consist chiefly in demolishing walls, hewing rocks, drawing carriages laden with materials for building &c.[12]

This description was written by a traveler aiming to whip up support for the redemption or ransoming of bagnio slaves.

Not all were worked to death in quarries or on building sites, though. Slaves earned a small amount of money and could rest on the Muslim sabbath, as well as daily for three hours before sunset. Arguably they lived better than many in England at the time, where enclosure had created a class of landless, rootless poor. A few enterprising slaves even borrowed money and set up bars in the bagnios, eventually earning enough to buy their freedom; "but still they are slaves, always hated on account of their religion; incessantly overburdened with labor."[13]

Christians in Turbans

There was one other route to freedom open to slaves. By apostatizing—renouncing the Christian religion—slaves could throw off their chains and theoretically become the social equals of their jailers. In the eyes of Christendom they were exchanging discomfort and imprisonment on earth for eternal torment in the afterlife, but this prospect does not seem to have had much of a deterrent effect.

On the contrary, many slaves apostatized. Christian sailors captured by the Barbary corsairs often seemed casual about "changing sides," and would as happily crew a galley as serve on a European merchant ship. Furthermore, the Barbary states even acted as a magnet to Christian freemen eager to "take the turban."

However, it would be misleading to represent this change of allegiance as a Pauline conversion, taken after many months of silent contemplation and prayer. Navy chaplains from every century have complained that the religion of most British seamen was at best token, and many of those who apostatized probably did so for practical rather than religious reasons: to escape the harsh conditions prevalent in British vessels.

lishing the quality, profession &c. of each, specifying the last price has been offered, 'till no higher bidder appears.[11]

This sale, though, was just a preliminary to the main event that took place later in the bey's courtyard. There the bey was entitled to buy any slave at the price originally bid, and a second auction followed, at which the prices generally rose much higher. The difference between the winning bids at the first and second auctions went into the public purse, and the first, lower bid was divided up according to a time-honored formula.

Islamic law reserved a portion of the goods seized "for God." In practice this share—usually one-seventh or one-eighth—also went to the state, as the embodiment of God on earth. Port fees and payments to officials took a share, and the expenses of the ship had to be paid. What remained was divided equally between the ship's owners, often a consortium of investors, and the crew. Those seamen who had distinguished themselves during the engagement in which the vessel was seized got a bonus, and the remainder of the crew's share was divided in proportion to seniority. The captain received twelve times more than a sailor, and a janissary could expect half the sailor's share.

In Algiers, those slaves who did not join the bey's retinue ended up in one of three bagnios, or slave prisons:

> wherein they are every evening locked up

The ranks of the renegade Christian sailors were swelled by those from bagnios seeking a way out of punishing labor and a life of servitude. Some were under relentless pressure to embrace Islam, but many were undoubtedly seduced by the exoticism and the lush, leisurely lifestyle of the narrow green fringe where Africa meets the Mediterranean. A redemptionist observed that slaves in the bagnios were "everlastingly in danger of renouncing their faith; either through debauchery,[14] if they have a little liberty, which is but too frequently in the Cafe, or through despair, if their treatment is too rigid."[15]

Life of a Renegade in Barbary

The influence of the Christian renegades reached a climax during the late sixteenth century, when up to two-thirds of the galleys and galleots operating out of Algiers were commanded by them. Of course, not all were masters, but even those with little ambition could live well: the climate was relatively mild; food abundant and varied; and the city environment clean and pleasant.

The Western European renegades seem to have got away with some appalling behavior that would, at the very least, have raised eyebrows back in their homelands: "They carry swords at their side, they run drunk through the town . . . they sleep with the wives of the Moors . . . every kind of debauchery and unchecked license is permitted to them."[16]

Indeed, even before embarking for Barbary, one renegade corsair made no secret of his hankering for such a life, harking back to an earlier, happier pirate era: "Where are the days that have been, and the seasons that we have seen, when we might sing, swear, drink, drab[17] and kill men as freely as your cakemakers do flies. . . ."[18] The Barbary regimes tolerated these snakes in their African Eden because they brought back valuable prizes and shared the booty with their hosts. But some of them were clearly extremely difficult guests who overstayed their welcome.

Below: *Another Christian-Muslim confrontation at sea, this time between a Dutch fleet and Barbary corsairs, painted by Lieve Pietersz Verschuir. The constant attacks on, and harassment of, Mediterranean shipping —not to mention the hostage-taking— provoked counterattacks by Europe's major maritime powers. The swift galleys were, however, an elusive prey and large fleet actions by warships were few and far between.*

Below: *Christian slaves in chains in the streets of one of the Barbary towns. Captives were either held until a ransom was paid for their release or condemned to become slaves; at worst this meant working in the quarries or as a galley slave. The hostage issue was an important one in its day and in England villages sent contributions to a central fund for redemptions—goodwill very often exploited by unscrupulous middlemen. In 1624 letters patent were granted for a nationwide appeal that raised £70,000, but most of it was taken by the Admiralty for defense funding.*

An eyewitness description of renegade corsair John Ward suggests that he epitomized the loutish European pirate in Barbary: "Speaks little, always swearing. Drunk from morn till night. Most prodigal and plucky. Sleeps a good deal. A fool and an idiot out of his trade." He is certainly among the most famous renegades. Born in Faversham, Kent, in 1553, Ward went to sea as a fisherman, and later enlisted in the navy. Before long, though, he and like-minded tars set off on their own account. They seized a French merchant ship and sailed it to Tunis, where Ward began his career as a corsair. By 1606 he commanded a small fleet, employing five hundred seamen.

A pamphlet of the time detailed more than twenty English ships captured by Ward, and the Venetians complained constantly of his attentions. In fact, it was the capture of a Venetian galeass that dramatically increased Ward's notoriety. The *Reinera e Soderina* was valued at £100,000, and though direct comparisons with present-day values are difficult to make, a craftsman of the time earned a pound for three weeks' work,[19] so the prize might have been worth £90 million in modern money. Ward may have realized that he had overstepped the mark with this seizure—or perhaps he was simply homesick—for in 1609 he tried unsuccessfully to obtain a pardon from the English king, James I.

He lived out his life in Tunis, under the protection of successive beys. Ward converted a castle there into "a fair palace, beautified with rich marble and alabaster stones," where he lived in some luxury with fifteen of his crew. He died of the plague in 1622.

Ransoming Slaves

Penniless Christian slaves in Barbary who refused to apostatize had little hope of release from their yoke unless they were fortunate enough to be bought out of slavery by a religious redemptionist organization. These charities collected money in European countries on the premise that the funds would be used to buy the freedom of slaves in Barbary. Indeed, when the fathers eventually reached the Barbary coast, they occasionally had sufficient funds to redeem a handful of captives. However, more often, the expenses of collecting funds and traveling to their destination consumed the vast bulk of donations.

So once they arrived in Barbary and had spent what little remained of their funds, the redemptionist fathers played the role of intermediaries, passing messages between the enslaved and their families, making credit arrangements, ensuring that the release took place as planned, and finally securing a passage for the ransomed slaves on ships home. The most well-known redemptionist figure is Father Pierre Dan, a priest who visited the Barbary coast in the early seventeenth century. His 1637 book, *Histoire de Barbarie & de ses Corsaires*, is the most comprehensive surviving description of the conditions for Christian slaves in Barbary; naturally, though, it can hardly be described as a balanced view.

Above: *The crucifixion of a Christian captive, a typically lurid contemporary illustration—this one from Father Dan. Such horror stories of torture and murder meted out in the Barbary states were widespread in the seventeenth and eighteenth centuries and served to harden the suspicion and hostility between the Christian and Muslim worlds. While some prisoners were no doubt treated with savage cruelty, most were condemned to a life of hard labor, with a few eking out a tolerable existence as domestic servants.*

Controlling the Corsairs

The major European maritime nations always had a duplicitous attitude to Barbary. In public, they deplored the corsairs and demanded concerted action to suppress them. Privately, though, they conceded that the corsairs were acting to their commercial advantage by harming the maritime interests of smaller nations. So, inevitably, moves to suppress the corsairs smacked of sham and half-hearted saber rattling. France and Britain periodically sent fleets of varying strength to harass the Barbary coast and give the beys bloody noses, but until the nineteenth century they stopped short of decisive military action.

What we might now term gunboat diplomacy began around 1650 when Holland and England launched expeditions against the Barbary states to gain immunity for their own shipping; France soon joined them. Algiers replied to a 1683 French bombardment by firing from a cannon some thirty French residents, including the French consul. By 1750 many of the smaller Christian nations had additionally succeeded in negotiating immunity for their merchant fleets. However, lacking the naval power of the bigger states, they had to pay for the privilege in cash or in kind. The rulers of the Barbary states were the main beneficiaries and, since the treaties progressively whittled away at the livelihood of the corsair ships, the agreements were frequently breached.

By the end of the century the Barbary corsairs had begun to harass the shipping of the fledgling United States in the Atlantic. The Americans appealed to the British for help, but were rebuffed, and instead had to pay tribute to the regencies. In 1801 an American squadron visited the Mediterranean to try to resolve the corsair threat to the country's shipping there. This was repeated for the next two years, but the third visit turned to disaster when the fleet lost a warship and many of the crew were held for ransom.

With the end of the Napoleonic Wars in 1815, it became clear that the Barbary corsairs served nobody's interests but their own. Additionally, the tide of opinion was turning against slavery, whether on land or at sea. The Americans again sent a fleet to the Mediterranean, this time with more success, extracting indemnities from the three main corsair states. The beginning of the end came in 1816, when a British fleet pounded Algiers, forcing the bey to release 1,600 slaves. Finally, in 1830, a French fleet occupied Algiers, putting a decisive stop to the activities of the Barbary corsairs.

The Christian Corsairs

Close to Sicily the Mediterranean is less than ninety-five miles (150km) wide, and all eastbound and westbound shipping passes a succession of islands, ranging from the small to the very tiny. Apart from Sicily, Malta is the biggest. Roughly the size of Martha's Vine-

Above: *The defeat of Napoleon and decisions taken at the Congress of Vienna led to a renewed effort to suppress North African piracy. When the bey had foreigners rounded up in order to pre-empt this, the Western powers reacted. On August 27, 1816, an Anglo-Dutch naval squadron under the command of Lord Exmouth attacked and bombarded the Barbary stronghold of Algiers—events depicted here by George Chambers. Subsequent negotiations resulted in the freeing of more than one thousand Christians and the bey vowing that the practice of piracy was finally at an end.*

yard, its only real asset is a sheltered deep-water harbor. Gozo, three miles (5km) to the northwest, is less than half the size, and tiny Comino guards the channel between the two bigger islands.

It was to Malta that the Knights Hospitaler eventually decamped after their long spell on Rhodes. The Knights arrived on Malta at a time when the island's fortunes were in decline. It was ruled from Sicily, and was a neglected and impoverished fiefdom of the Spanish kingdom of Aragon.

For the Knights, Malta was not an ideal base. The island had to import from Sicily at least half the food its people needed, and its fortifications were dilapidated. Nor were the Maltese particularly pleased with their new landlords, but they were given no choice in the matter, and could do little but accept the liveried and arrogant aristocratic cuckoos who had settled among them.

At first, the Knights looked upon Malta as a temporary home, hoping for something better. But eventually it became obvious to all but the most gung-ho of the order that hot, arid Malta was the end of the line. While they still regarded Malta as a waiting room, the Knights did very little to develop its undoubted military potential. But a bruising Ottoman attack in 1551 forced them to fortify Sceberras, the peninsula overlooking the harbor. An even greater blow followed fifteen years later, when a huge Ottoman force besieged the island.

The Knights suffered terrible losses during the protracted battles of the 1565 siege, but in the long run it was a turning point, forcing them to make a wholehearted commitment to the island. They constructed an elaborate system of defenses; and under their benevolent oligarchy, Malta began to flourish once more. Much of the expansion that followed was centered on Malta's magnificent harbor.

The Navy of the Religion

In Malta's shipyards the Knights built and repaired a remarkable navy. Their former island home of Rhodes had obliged them to master warfare on sea as well as on land, and they had learned how to build and equip war galleys. When they came to Malta, the Knights brought three galleys with them, but their fleet was eventually expanded to more.

The Knight's galleys had a legendary reputation: they could sail very close to the wind, and their three-foot (1m) draft allowed them to pursue their quarry in the shallowest water. They were well armed, too. The *Santa Anna*, completed in 1524, was the most powerful warship in the Mediterranean. She carried fifty heavy cannons, and could transport six hundred armed Christian warriors.

Until 1576, the Knights' navy effectively sailed as part of the Spanish fleet. Later, the role of the galleys changed to corsair-chasers, harassing the galleys of Barbary and guarding Christian merchant shipping. Their effectiveness can be judged from the fact that Algiers became the principal base for the Barbary corsairs: it was three times as far from Malta as Tunis and Tripoli.

Not all the ships of the order's navy were galleys. From 1478 the Knights had been using carracks as supply vessels, to extend the range of the galley fleet. In the early eighteenth century the order began to replace some galleys with ships of the line, and it was with a combination of galleys and round ships, roughly half-and-half, that the order's navy waged war on the Barbary corsairs in the late eighteenth century.

The Knights and the Corsairs

In addition to building up a powerful naval presence on Malta, the Knights also encouraged and systematically organized the island's corsairs. A small corsair fleet predated the Knights' arrival; indeed, Malta's excellent harbor had often acted as a magnet for privateers and near-pirates, just as it had for legitimate mariners. In the pre-Hospitaler period, the corsairs were licensed by Sicily to raid Turkish shipping; after 1530 they fell under the Knights' jurisdiction.

Initially, the system continued almost unchanged but, cultivated by the order, the *corso* grew rapidly. In 1605 the grand master (the head of the order) set up a commission, the *Tribunale degli Armamenti*, to control and regulate the booming trade. Under the commission's rules, corsairs using the islands were to fly the flag of the order; they could attack only Muslim shipping; and they had to respect safe-conduct passes issued by Christian monarchs. The *Tribunale* also set out the procedures to be followed if any of the corsairs broke the rules. These provided for injured parties to bring a case in specially convened Maltese courts, with the Vatican as the final court of appeal. Corsairs that were judged to have overstepped the mark sacrificed the cash surety that they were obliged to lodge before setting sail.

The Maltese Galleys

The galleys of the Maltese corsairs were similar to the Barbary ships in many ways, but the differences between the two types of vessels highlight the different skills of the mariners in each fleet, and how they deployed them. The Maltese were more reliant on gunnery than their Barbary counterparts, so their ships were better armed. This in turn meant that the ships had to be more heavily constructed, for gunfire would "shiver the timbers" of a lightly built craft.

Both the corsair galleys and those of the order's navy were rowed principally by slaves.

Below: *A dramatic engraving showing British sailors boarding an Algerian corsair vessel. Although stylized and replete with melodramatic poses, the image serves to give a vivid impression of the type of hand-to-hand fighting that took place when a ship was boarded. It was not, of course, neccessarily always so dramatic and bloody; when an American party led by Stephen Decatur boarded Rais Hamidou's ship in 1815 after a running fight, they were taken aback to find the janissaries seated and quietly smoking their pipes.*

Most were Muslims, but Christian riffraff took a few of the seats on the benches. Some were serving sentences for crimes committed in Italian city-states. There was also a sprinkling of oarsmen who were nominally free, though debt-slavery might be a better description of their condition. These wretches were called *buonavoglie*. The word literally means "free-willer" or volunteer, but in the Maltese language it still connotes a rascal.[20] They received similar treatment to that of the slaves, but they had a few extra privileges. *Buonavoglie* could wear mustaches, and were chained by only one shackle!

Generally, though, the conditions for slaves onboard the Maltese galleys were worse than those of their counterparts on Barbary vessels, as this description makes clear:

Many of the galley slaves have not the room to sleep at full length, for they put seven men on one bench; that is to say, on a space about ten feet long by four broad. . . . The captain and officers who live on the poop are scarcely better lodged . . . the creaking of the blocks and cordage, the loud cries of the sailors, the horrible maledictions of the galley slaves, the groaning of the timbers are mingled with the clank of chains. Calm itself has its inconveniences as the evil smells which arise from the galley are then so strong that one cannot get away from them in spite of the tobacco with which one is obliged to plug one's nostrils.[21]

The Knights themselves sailed onboard the galleys. Some captained corsair ships, and there would be as many as thirty knights on the largest naval vessels. These Maltese vessels also carried a group of mercenary soldiers, the Christian equivalent of the janissaries.

Where They Hunted

The Knights licensed corsairs to patrol specific regions of ocean: they were supposed to concentrate on either the Barbary coast or the Levant, the eastern Mediterranean. However, after reprisals against pilgrims in Palestine, seizures close to the country's

Below: *The galleys of the Christian forces differed little from those of their Muslim enemies, although they were usually more heavily armed and therefore of stronger construction. This model of a 1770 galley has a mizzen sail behind the triangular lateen sail at the center, a feature not prevalent until the eighteenth century. The sleek, narrow hull enabled quick movement through the water, and the ram provided one means of smashing an enemy vessel prior to boarding her from the raised forecastle platform.*

Above: The Siege of Malta, *painted by Matteo Perez d' Aleccio. The Knights of Malta withstood a lengthy siege by the Ottoman forces in the summer of 1565, fighting back from within their fortified positions for long enough to enable Spanish forces to arrive and prompt an Ottoman withdrawal. The Ottomans had been fully confident of quick success, but luck and good leadership, combined with strategic blunders by the Turks, saved the Hospitalers.*

coast were progressively forbidden to Maltese corsairs. The exclusion zone eventually extended to all waters within fifty miles (80km) of the coast.

Even with these restrictions, the corsairs were free to roam over vast stretches of the Mediterranean. In practice they hunted in the few areas where shipping traffic was at its densest. The most lucrative of these crossed the sea's eastern end, connecting Constantinople and Egypt. Heavily laden Ottoman merchant ships traveled in convoy on this route, and their substantial protection made them invulnerable to attack by all but the most powerful of the Knights' galleys. A few of the more intrepid corsairs tried to cut out ships from the convoy, but it was generally safer to pick on smaller fry around the more important islands in the region: Rhodes, Crete, and Cyprus.

The Chase and Capture

The tactics of the Maltese corsairs differed substantially from their Barbary counterparts. As the Maltese corsairs closed on what was seen to be legitimate prey, they attempted first to shoot down the rigging. When the victim was comprehensively crippled, they would come alongside to take the prize, perhaps peppering those on deck with small-arms fire first to discourage resistance to

boarding. In a prolonged battle, the Maltese sailing ships used their height advantage to drop primitive grenades onto the decks of their adversaries.

More often than not, though, such desperate tactics were not needed. The corsairs generally targeted small vessels that were unlikely to resist. They would hail the ship, then come alongside and question the crew about their destination, the ownership of the cargo, and the nationality of the vessel, crew, and passengers. If there was any suggestion at all that the ship was carrying Turkish goods or passengers, the Maltese would board and carry out an inspection.

The corsairs staunchly defended their right to carry out this procedure, which was called a *visità*. Their justification, as ever, was that it was simply a continuation of the war against the infidel. In an era when the Cross and the Crescent were bitterly opposed, this argument had some merit. But as the memory of the Crusades faded, it seemed more and more like a feeble excuse for piracy.

The *visità* was a cause of considerable friction between the Maltese and the other maritime nations of the Mediterranean. Even if the ransacking caused no real damage or injury to the crew and passengers (and it often did), a *visità* would nevertheless delay the voyage. The Maltese corsairs knew that

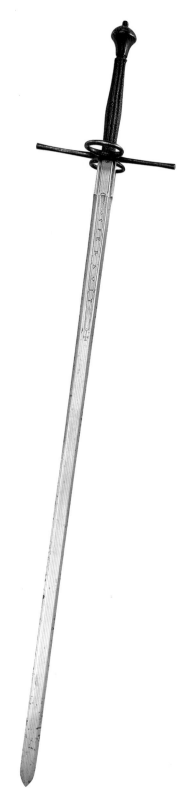

Above: *A two-handed sword, c. 1540, one of a series once kept in the arsenal of the Knights of St. John in their palace fortress in Valetta, Malta. The Latin inscription reads "He trusted in Thee, O Lord."*

the captain of any merchant vessel would be keen to discharge his cargo and load another, and the delay imposed by a *visità* was a potent bargaining chip. The very threat was sometimes sufficient to extract a ransom—effectively a bribe—from a master in a hurry.

The Fate of Those They Captured

The corsairs revealed the true nature of their calling in the way they dealt with passengers and crew of the ships they "visited." Muslims, of course, did not expect to be well treated by those who claimed a holy mission against the infidel, but there were often unpleasant surprises for Christians, too. French traveler Jean Thévenot[22] described how he was stripped naked by the corsairs, then left shivering in a shirt. Only the monks on his ship were spared the same treatment. Thévenot was prudent enough to hand over his gold ring as soon as it was spotted—the threat of a flogging was usually all the corsairs needed to discover the hiding places of other valuable items.

Thévenot was eventually dumped on the Palestine coast, and must have counted himself lucky to escape with his life. It was not uncommon for corsair masters to set Christian captives adrift in a small boat, leaving them to find their own way to land.

Muslims who were unfortunate enough to be taken back to Malta faced an experience that closely mirrored that of Christian captives in Barbary. The thriving slave market on Malta was the second largest in the Christian world, and captives auctioned there found themselves at work for the order, or for private individuals on the islands. A few were sold on the international slave market, perhaps to pull on the oars of a Venetian galley.

The Conditions of Slaves in Malta

Those slaves who were not chained to a galley oar or sold abroad slept under lock and key in three large slave prisons built in the area surrounding the Grand Harbor. By day they worked outside the prisons, doing all manner of heavy labor and menial work. Some slaves had domestic roles in households on the island. Others worked in quarries or on building sites. The badges of rank of Maltese slaves were their Arab clothing (Christian clothes were forbidden to them), cropped hair, and an iron ring on one leg.

Just as in Algiers, Maltese slaves were per-

mitted to run businesses in an attempt to raise enough money to buy their freedom. In Malta, though, the scale of such activities was more limited. Slaves worked as barbers or kept bars; others sold goods from stalls. All had to return to the bagnios at night. The Knights granted exceptions only for those working on the other side of the island, and for small groups on galleys in the harbor.

The similarity between the conditions of captivity of slaves in Malta and Barbary seems uncanny, but there is a mundane explanation. If conditions worsened for one group, the captors of the other were quick to exact vengeance. These tit-for-tat reprisals maintained a kind of parity between the bagnios of Barbary and Malta.

Buying Freedom

For Muslim slaves on Malta, ransoming was a possibility, just as it was for Christians in Barbary. The process was easier for slaves employed on the island than for those chained to the oars of galleys. Wettinger[23] traced the fate of 1,336 captives taken in 1685 when the Knights besieged the small Greek town of Coron on the southwest of the peninsula of Morea. After sharing the human booty with their allies, the Knights retained 223 slaves. Though a few were ransomed and left the island within a year, half were still there two decades later.

Galley slaves were such a scarce commodity that many were forced to stay at the oars until they were too sick or too weak to row any longer. Then they would be released without ransom. One Egyptian slave who had rowed a Maltese galley for half a century petitioned to be released at the age of eighty. Promised freedom for his services on two occasions, he had been twice cheated! Galley slaves who hoped to secure their freedom had to find not only the ransom, but a substitute—or even two—to take their place at the oars. Naturally, this was an insurmountable obstacle for many.

On balance, though, the system of ransoming slaves in Malta was probably no more harsh than in Barbary. Agents existed in Malta to lubricate the ransoming process, and some slaves were even allowed to return to their homes to collect the ransom payment. More often, though, one or two individuals would travel to Barbary to collect ransoms on behalf of a much larger group, who stayed in Maltese prisons to ensure that the bargain was honored.

How the Booty was Divided

Profit from the sale of slaves was added to the value of other seizures recorded in a ledger by the purser on the corsair ship. At the end of the cruise, the purser's books were used to determine the profit that had accrued, so the various parties that had a stake in the voyage could claim their due.

As in Barbary, the state (in this case, the order) had first claim. The grand master took one-tenth of the profits. Next in line was a group called the *Cinque Lancie*, mostly officials who had responsibilities associated with the voyage. The captain then claimed 11 percent of the profit, and what remained was divided into three. The crew received one-third, and the balance went to pay off those who had financed the building, fitting out, and supply of the ship.

Of these people, the first to be paid off were the bondholders, who received their initial investment plus an agreed percentage. The many bondholders came from every social class, so the success or failure of a corsair voyage potentially affected the whole island. The remaining money went to equity holders (principally businessmen), in proportion to their stake in the voyage.

This simplified description conceals many perks and complications. The ship's master, for example, had to supplement the pay of senior officers from his share, but was entitled to any loose money found in ransacking the ship. Tradesmen such as the cook could keep equipment relevant to their craft.

Clearly a corsair captain stood to make a handsome profit from a successful cruise. Equally, though, he needed a lucky streak, for capture by a Barbary vessel would inevitably lead to a somewhat less comfortable job onboard ship. This combination of risk and reward attracted characters who aimed to live fast and, if need be, die young. Anecdotal evidence suggests that the corsairs spent much of the profit of their cruises in the brothels and bars of Valletta, but reliable details of their lives are very hard to find.

The Development of the *Corso*

Reorganized and regularized after 1605, the Maltese corsair trade developed and expanded throughout the seventeenth century. The fleet probably reached its zenith in the 1660s, when there were thirty corsair vessels operating. They directly employed four thousand men, roughly one-fifth of the adult male population of Malta.[24]

This growth exacted a price. The corsairs licensed by the Knights were running commercial enterprises, and given the undoubted importance of their operations to the economy of the islands, there was clearly considerable pressure on every corsair crew to make a financial success of their voyage. Inevitably, many found it difficult to stick to the rules, particularly when pickings were slim. Just as English privateers were tempted to interpret their letters of marque with considerable discretion, so too the urge to raid Christian shipping was sometimes too great for the Maltese corsairs to resist.

In the early seventeenth century it was the ships of Venice that suffered from the unsolicited attentions of the Maltese corsair fleet. But merchants from the *Serenissima* won compensation in the Maltese courts, and the corsairs were forced to toe the line after the seizure in 1645 of the Knights' estates on Venetian territory.[25] Later in the century, the corsairs turned their attentions to Greek ships. Some Maltese doubtless felt that Christian Greeks were legitimate victims because they owed their allegiance to the Eastern Church, rather than to Rome. It was also easy for a Greek Muslim captain to pretend to be Christian when his ship was raided. Greek ships often carried Turkish cargoes, and this too made them vulnerable to attack. However, it is clear that there were many Maltese corsairs who simply used these arguments as a cover for piracy. Like the Venetians, the Greeks were initially widely successful with their litigation in the Knights' courts, though achieving satisfaction sometimes took years of legal action.

But the corsairs created problems in the Mediterranean, even when they raided shipping that was unambiguously Muslim. Most of the Knights of St. John came from France, and with the passing of time the Maltese corsair ships came to be identified as French privateers. Muslim merchants who lost ships and cargoes to the corsairs could not demand compensation, so instead they took reprisals against French nationals elsewhere.

The French naturally resented such actions against their citizens and brought

Above: *An illustration from Abbé Thiron's* Ordres Religeaux *showing a Grand Master of the Order of Malta (St. John of Jerusalem). In 1605 the grand master set up a commission to control the activities of the ships based in Malta; they had to fly the Order's flag and were only authorized to attack Muslim shipping.*

Below: *A Chevalier Grand-Croix of the Order of Malta (St. John of Jerusalem). The Order's original hospital, established in 1099 near the Church of St. John the Baptist, could care for two thousand patients.*

pressure to bear on the Knights to control the worst excesses of their corsair captains. Gradually this pressure from the French and the Vatican whittled away at the freedom of operation of the Maltese fleet.

During the latter half of the seventeenth century, French merchants had a further reason to resent the Maltese corsairs. The French were actively wooing the huge Ottoman market, and French shipping was carrying an increasing proportion of the Muslim trade. When these ships were raided by the Maltese, there was an inevitable diplomatic backlash.

Eventually it was clear that the Knights would have to submit to French pressure; most of the land that provided the Knights' income was in France, and they risked confiscation of their assets if they continued to defy the French king. French shipping was thus off limits; English and Dutch ships were generally too well defended to be vulnerable to corsair attacks; so the Maltese concentrated once more on the Greek vessels, using every kind of legal chicanery to justify their continuing harassment of the Greeks. But eventually political pressure put virtually all the corsairs' traditional victims beyond reach.

The corsairs were thus ironically defeated not by their nominal "infidel" adversary, but by the diplomacy of their Christian allies, and by 1740 the *corso* was effectively extinct.

The Knights' Decline

The events that brought about the decline of the Maltese corsairs were eventually to destroy the organization that had nurtured and built up the fleet. However, the Knights' sojourn on Malta continued for another sixty years or so. By then they had changed the island's economy beyond all recognition. They had fortified the peninsula jutting into the island's deep-water harbor and created a city, Valletta, within the walls. They built shipyards, churches, a theater, factories, warehouses, and docks. They encouraged agriculture and provided employment.

Inevitably, though, this patronage caused resentment on the island, and the Knights' dissolute lifestyle did not help. Though the order was a religious one, all its members lived well, and a few became notorious for drinking and whoring. One grand master, La Cassière (c. 1572–81), made the foolish mistake of trying to rid Valletta of prostitutes; the Knights jailed him.[26]

Above: *An engraving showing Turks boarding a Greek corsair. While the French conquest of much of North Africa ended most piracy, the Rif pirates in Morocco remained active until the 1860s, and farther east piracy remained a problem. Lord Byron's celebrated poem* The Corsair *was based on his knowledge of the activities of the Greek corsairs. Struggling for independence, Greek buccaneers were very active in the Aegean islands; few vessels were safe from their predations, most particularly Turkish ones.*

Right: *A Turkish* miquelet-*lock muzzle-loading rifle, c. 1800. The lock is decorated with coral and the maplewood stock is richly inlaid with roundels, bands, and other typically Islamic geometric shapes in ebony, brass, and ivory—some of the ivory is stained green. The rifled barrel is of fine "Damascus twist" watered steel inlaid, like the lock, in gold.*

The lifestyle and haughty manner of the Knights led in 1775 to a botched rebellion in which they temporarily lost control of the fort of St. Elmo. But it was changes in the wider world, rather than pressure from within Malta, that destroyed the Hospitalers. By the eighteenth century the crusading religious zeal that gave birth to the order had faded. The Knights looked increasingly anachronistic in a mercantile world where Christian and Muslim traded freely.

The final blow was the French Revolution. The order was openly aristocratic, and noble refugees from the guillotine sought sanctuary on Malta. The seizure of the Knights' huge French estates was therefore inevitable, and when this happened in 1792, it crippled the order financially. The Knights struggled on for another six years, until Napoleon's fleet anchored off the island en route for Egypt in 1798. When the Knights refused a request for fresh water, French troops landed. The Knights put up no resistance, and within a few days most had been unceremoniously bundled off the island.[27]

The Wider Picture
Pirate, privateer, missionary, businessman, slaver—a corsair was a mixture of all these. But as in any famous dish, the quantities varied from recipe to recipe. In many respects, the fight for supremacy in the Mediterranean was as much about commerce and politics as it was about religion.

Both Barbary and Maltese corsairs were privateers; their licenses were little different from the letters of marque and reprisal carried by the captains of privateer vessels from the maritime nations of northern Europe. Their privateering activities raked in huge amounts of capital, and on both sides of the Mediterranean investors took a stake in the trips, in the hope of reaping rich rewards. In this respect, it is fair to consider the corsair trade as simply a seedy aspect of maritime commerce. Corsair warfare also, however, admirably served the purposes of the great maritime powers.

The ships of Holland, France, and Britain are conspicuous by their absence from descriptions of corsair raids. This is no mere coincidence: being Christian nations, the British, French, and Dutch were safe from the crusading corsairs of Malta. And by negotiating treaties with the Barbary regencies, they were also able to secure immunity from attack by the Muslim corsairs.

The result was a cozy cartel. British, French, and Dutch ships could sail the waters of the Mediterranean with impunity, while relying on corsairs of both complexions to harass the shipping of their competitors. This cunning arrangement allowed British and French merchantmen to take a substantial proportion of the Mediterranean carrying trade. In France there was clear and sometimes explicit understanding that the raids of the Barbary corsairs had advantages: "We are certain that it is not in our interest that all the Barbary corsairs be destroyed," ran one anonymous French memo, "since then we would be on a par with all the Italians and the peoples of the North Sea."[28]

The Legacy of the Corsairs
The memory of the Barbary corsairs lingered on long after they had ceased to pose any real threat. They came to symbolize all that was dark, cruel, and unpleasant about piracy, and their religious fanaticism made them seem especially dangerous. But even as the Barbary galleys were being burned or broken up in the early nineteenth century, the image of the corsair was beginning to be embroidered with a romance and mystery that would have appalled those who had the misfortune to pull on their oars.

Lord Byron's epic 1814 poem *The Corsair* depicted the eponymous pirate as a swarthy, inspiring hero. However, notwithstanding Byron's (perhaps unintentional) efforts to rehabilitate the Barbary corsairs, their long-term legacy has been one of hatred and mistrust. As a result, the Western image of the Islamic people is today a negative and essentially racist one.

The West's underlying distrust of the Islamic world remains, along with the hypocrisy that characterized French and English dealings with the corsairs of Barbary and Malta. The Western nations that allied against Iraq in the Gulf War were precisely those who provided the arms the country had used to attack its neighbors.

Despite the passage of more than seven centuries, echoes of the Crusades still ring through. Arguably the battle between the corsairs of Barbary and Malta served to prolong and nurture mutual hostility between Christian and Muslim, sustaining it from the Middle Ages to the modern world.

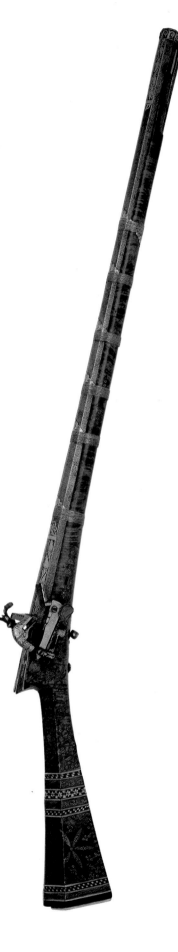

CHAPTER FIVE

THE GOLDEN AGE OF PIRACY

~

Roberts himself made a gallant figure at the time of the engagement, being dressed in a rich crimson damask waistcoat and breeches, a red feather in his hat, a gold chain around his neck, with a diamond cross hanging to it, a sword in his hand and two pair of pistols, hanging at the end of a silk sling, flung over his shoulders.

CAPTAIN CHARLES JOHNSON, 1724.[1]

SEVERAL CHAPTERS stand out in the bloody annals of seaborne villainy, but none boasts more fascinating exploits than the brief but brilliant period around the beginning of the eighteenth century known as the Golden Age of Piracy. For thirty years or so, pirates in record numbers sallied forth from nerve centers in the Caribbean and North American ports to prey on the burgeoning mercantile traffic sailing between Europe and America and traffic from Africa and the East.

The great flare-up of maritime lawlessness that convulsed the Caribbean and the North American coast involved pirates of various nationalities. The Virgin Islands harbored outlaws from many countries and New Providence in the Bahamas was the nest of a swarm of British and American pirates. Spanish pirates operated out of Cuba, Puerto Rico, and St. Augustine. French pirates continued to use Martinique as their main base.

The Golden Age furnished the classic pirate images immortalized by painters, writers, and film makers. Most of the pirates we are familiar with today were members of this international fraternity who prowled the seas until the Admiralty trials in 1722, when the hanging of fifty-two of Captain Roberts's men at Cape Coast Castle on the African coast brought the curtain down on one of history's greatest outbreaks of sea robbery. Pirates continued to plunder shipping for another century but without the devastating effects of previous eras and certainly without providing such flamboyant characters.

The pirates were a motley lot: men of many nations, several races, varied abilities, and widely ranging temperaments. The following description fits the typical pirate of the age: "his parentage was but meane, his estate lowe, and his hope less." Some, however, like Major Stede Bonnet, the runaway planter, were well born. Others were well educated: Dr. John Hincher, a graduate of the University of Edinburgh, was tried for piracy in Newport, Rhode Island, in 1723. He was acquitted when he testified that he had been forced against his will to act as ship's surgeon by the infamous Captain Low.[2]

Pirates were the darlings of the eighteenth-century media and the public avidly followed their exploits. Their many feats and foibles, recorded in contemporary chronicles and trial proceedings, were embellished upon in broadsides and handbills that the public lapped up. A pirate trial was always mobbed with spectators, but what they loved best was a good hanging. Many of the rogues went to the gallows displaying the dash that had marked their careers. Finely dressed in silk and velvet, a condemned man might sprinkle the mob with gold coins or pearls before he swung off.

The spectators waited with bated breath to hear the "last words" the condemned addressed to the crowd before mounting the gallows. They applauded the pirates who "died well," jeered those who didn't, and generally enjoyed themselves.

War Brings Privateers

England and Spain were inevitably drawn into the wars of the eighteenth century, which were primarily concerned with maintaining the balance of power in Europe. Just as inevitably, these conflicts spread to the Spanish Indies. At intervals throughout the century, Anglo-French controversy over control of Spain's New World dominions and over the monopoly of trade erupted in naval warfare, which was played out in the Caribbean and the western Atlantic. During wars pirates enjoyed the sanction of privateering licenses. As soon

Left: Blackbeard in Smoke and Flame, *a painting by Frank Schoonover commissioned to illustrate an article in* American Boy *magazine in September 1922. All the descriptions of Blackbeard suggest that he was as terrifying as he appears here, and that he deliberately cultivated a fearsome image in order to keep his crew in their place and to encourage his victims to surrender without a fight.*

Below: *A double-headed shot for cutting through the rigging of an enemy ship. This particular example was fired during the Battle of Trafalgar and killed eight men onboard Admiral Nelson's* Victory.

Above: *A final fling of the officially tolerated French buccaneers—and perhaps the greatest—was their attack on the Spanish treasure port of Cartagena in April 1697. A fleet of warships led by Baron de Pointis joined forces with French buccaneers under the command of Jean Baptise du Casse and launched a massive attack on the heavily fortified city. While the ships bombarded the forts, the troops laid siege to them. On May 6 the governor surrendered after securing terms that would permit the citizens to keep their possessions. Even so, the French ships were able to sail away on May 31 with their holds filled with treasure. They did so hastily, fearing that Spanish and English forces were en route.*

as peace treaties were signed far across the Atlantic, "the West Indies always swarm with pirates," a colonial official in the Bahamas complained in 1706.[3]

As early as 1695 the governor of Jamaica had written the king of England that so many men were involved in piracy that it was impossible to find crews for merchant ships anywhere in the West Indies. A few years later, following the Treaty of Ryswick, which ended war between England and France, thousands of seamen and privateers were out of work and eager to go "on the account."

Peace Brings Pirates

Times were hard after the Treaty of Utrecht ended the War of Spanish Succession in 1713, bringing a quarter century of peace to Europe but unleashing a horde of hungry seamen in tarred breeches and canvas jackets who couldn't find honest employment. During the war they had pillaged and plundered with official sanction. After the war many turned pirate, continuing hostilities "beyond the line" as both France and England vied to fill the vacuum left by the erosion of Spanish domination, turning a blind eye to the pirates as long as they furthered their geopolitical objectives. Hollander pirates were notably absent from the action because the Dutch government

wisely paid their skilled troops to work in the herring fleet so they could be marshaled for the next inevitable conflict.

The surge in piracy was predictable. Veterans' prospects were far from rosy in the West Indies where slave labor had severely restricted opportunity for the average white man. Navies and mercantile shipping never had enough berths in peacetime to absorb great numbers of men. What places there were in peacetime offered low wages and harsh conditions.

The colonies in the West Indies and along the American seaboard prospered after the war. At the peace, England wrested from Spain the *asiento*, or monopoly for supplying slaves to the Spanish colonies, along with their other commercial privileges. Increasing volumes of English, French, and Dutch colonial trade provided attractive piratical opportunities. Spain resumed scheduled sailings of the treasure fleet, making the area a more rewarding "cruising ground" than it had been for over a century. Consequently, in 1717 James Logan, colonial secretary of Pennsylvania, estimated there were at least 1,500 pirates lying in wait off the North American coast. The same year the governor of Bermuda lamented that "North and South America are infested with the rogues."

An Infestation of Rogues

Who were these "rogues"? Judging from records, including trial records, the majority were lower-class men with roots in England's West Country and Wales, where piracy was in the blood. Nearly half of the fifty-two members of Black Bart Roberts's crew hanged at Cape Coast Castle on Africa's Gold Coast in 1722 were Welsh or West Countrymen. Others were former indentured servants or poor colonial whites. Then there were the Catholics. National ambitions pitted Protestant countries against Catholic Europe, so Catholic Irish and Scots pirates often signed on with Spanish and French expeditions rather than with British crews. Protestant Frenchmen served aboard English pirate ships.

On many ships there were runaway slaves and mulattos. There is even a record of a Native American from Martha's Vineyard who sailed with the pirate Captain Charles Harris.[4] Pirates might invite slaves to join them if there were only a few aboard a prize. However, in the case of a slave ship, the entire cargo was generally marketed to unscrupulous dealers. For twenty years a band of Scots, English, Spaniards, Portuguese, blacks, and mulattos was headquartered in the Bahamas under the leadership of Spaniard Agostino Blanco. Other nationalities included Dutch, Scandinavians, Greeks, and East Indians. Most pirates were single and not particularly tied to any one place. Pirate crews often excluded married men to avoid potential domestic entanglements.

Golden Age pirate captains might be in their thirties or forties but the average pirate was about twenty-five, young by today's standards but not in the eighteenth century, when a man of thirty was regarded as relatively old. Sailors were generally able-bodied seamen by age seventeen. An arrest warrant duly issued in December 1699 by Governor Nicholson of Virginia, one of the few colonial authorities genuinely committed to suppressing piracy, gives a vivid glimpse of a pirate crew. Among the outlaws at large in Virginia, and wanted for plundering in the Red Sea on the *Adventure*, were: "Tee Wetherlly, short, very small, blind in one eye, about eighteen; Thomas Jameson, cooper, Scot, tall, meagre, sickly look, large black eyes, twenty; William Griffith, short, well set, broad face, darkest hair, about thirty." There was another thirty-year-old, John Loyd, "of ordinary stature, rawboned, very pale, dark hair, remarkably deformed in the lower eyelid," as well as two children, one aged fifteen and the other "Thomas Simpson, short and small, much squint-eyed, about ten of age."

A Seaman's Lot

Almost all English-speaking pirates were recruited from the ranks of the British navy or had served as merchant seamen or priva-

Below: Extorting Tribute from the Citizens, *by Howard Pyle, painted to illustrate his article "The Fate of a Treasure-Town" published in* Harper's Monthly Magazine *in December 1905. Du Casse's buccaneers had felt cheated at the reward distributed to them by de Pointis. A renegade group of them returned and managed to extract further riches by torture and threats.*

teers. In comparison, life as member of a pirate crew was tantamount to a holiday cruise. It is hard to imagine how truly horrible the conditions for ordinary seamen were aboard navy and merchant vessels. Many of the men had been unwillingly seized, or pressed, and at times when vessels were in port the men were shackled to keep them from abandoning ship. "So much disabled by sickness, death, and desertion of their sea-

men"[5] were His Majesty's ships, noted an officer, that they could scarcely combat the pirates. According to some estimates, 50 percent of all British and American men pressed between 1600 and 1800 died at sea.

A Pirate's Perks

Piracy offered immediate escape. When a merchant vessel was seized, the pirates often gave seamen the option to join them. Most

Below: Action off Cartagena, May 28, 1708, *by Samuel Scott. Just a few years after the French sacking, a British squadron attacked the Spanish treasure fleet in the vicinity of the town. One ship was captured and another was driven ashore, but the* San Jose, *carrying the bulk of the treasure, blew up and sank due to the detonation of her powder magazine.*

did so willingly. The pirates questioned the men about their officers, especially the captain and the quartermaster. Officers deemed unusually cruel or otherwise despicable were usually killed, frequently after torture. Otherwise they might be marooned, set afloat in a small boat, left in a burning ship, or even ransomed.

Piracy offered more than release from a floating hell. A rover's life wasn't easy, but at least as part of a pirate crew he was an equal among equals, a member of an organized egalitarian community in which decisions were made collectively. Pirates were risk-sharing partners enjoying a kind of freedom unthinkable ashore or in lawful sea service. Before setting out on a voyage, or upon election of a new captain, crew members subscribed to a set of written articles that forged a strong esprit de corps. They were derived from privateering articles and sworn to over a Bible or boarding ax and governed life aboard ship. They defined responsibilities, specified disciplinary measures, and dictated terms of the share-out of plunder.

Pirates of this era also established an early welfare system similar to that pioneered by the buccaneers. A portion of plunder was set aside in a fund to compensate men who were disabled during an engagement.

One For All and All For One
Pirates gloried in turning the rigid stratification and tyrannical organization of the navy and merchant service upside down. The pirate captain was elected by the crew and served at their pleasure. He was commander only "in fighting, chasing, being chased," and could be deposed by a vote for cruelty, cowardice, refusal to go after a potential prize, or any other reason. The men elected a quartermaster who was their representative and who distributed food and cash and acted as ombudsman, adjudicating any disputes between them. The quartermaster often became captain of any prize vessel deemed worth keeping.

Perhaps one of the things pirates most appreciated was the Pirate Council, which was the highest authority for each pirate voyage, deciding where to go, what to do, and how to deal with problems. It paralleled the traditional council of war on naval vessels, in which only the highest-ranking officers participated, but with one huge difference: every man was a member.

Pirate Articles
Articles varied only slightly from captain to captain. The articles sworn to by the pirates signing on with Bartholomew Roberts are typical and appear in Johnson's book. They reveal democracy, equality, and discipline.[6]

Captain Johnson wrote that the original signed articles had been thrown overboard when Roberts was captured, hinting that there were clauses that contained "something too horrid to be disclosed to any except such as were willing to be sharers in the iniquity of them."

One of the articles on Captain George Lowther's ship stipulated that the man who first spied a sail should have the best pistol or small arm on her. Fire was an ever-present danger often addressed in a set of articles. Article VI aboard Captain John Phillips's *Revenge* stated: "That man that shall snap his arms, or smoke tobacco in the hold without a cap to his pipe, or carry a candle lighted without a lanthorn, shall suffer the same punishment as in the former article." The punishment referred to was "Moses's Law" or thirty-nine stripes on a man's bare back.

The captain had few special privileges, receiving the same rations as his mates, and having to share his cabin with whoever walked in. Men ate where they wished and slept wherever they wanted. The captain, quartermaster, and skilled "sea artists" including surgeons, carpenters, and boatswains received a greater share of plunder than the common pirates. So did musicians, whose loud (and often cacophonous) renderings served to urge the outlaws on and unnerve the enemy.

Prisoners
Pirates were vengeful and often vented feelings of rage at the injustice of life on captives of higher birth and particularly on officers who represented the arbitrary authority they had been subject to on men-o'-war and merchant ships. When Philip Lyne was caught in 1726, he boasted that he had killed thirty-seven "Masters of Vessels" during "the time of his Piracy."

Some pirates were particularly sadistic. One of the worst was Captain Edward Low. When the captain of a Portuguese merchantman dropped a large bag filled with gold *moidores* (coins) overboard, he had the man's lips cut off and broiled in front of him and

Above: *An eighteenth-century gravestone from Skipness in Kintyre, Scotland. The skull and crossed bones were often used to symbolize death—an image adopted by pirates for their flags. The hourglass and other symbols represent the passing of time and the limited span of our lives on earth; it was also incorporated into pirate flags to warn that the time for surrendering was limited.*

then forced the Portuguese mate to eat them before slaughtering the entire crew. Although pirates kept many prize vessels, generally modifying them to fit their needs, they rifled unsuitable vessels and then often set them ablaze to drift, sometimes with captives tied to the mast. The psychopathic Captain Low once took everyone off of a captured French prize except the cook, whom he strapped to the mast before setting the vessel on fire, because "being a greasy fellow" he would fry well.

Women often received some protection; however, the cost might mean accepting the amorous advances of a particular pirate, and there are records of women suffering barbarous atrocities. Prisoners were tortured for a variety of reasons: chief among them, to make them reveal hidden valuables or because there was no valuable cargo. Prisoners were sometimes hauled up in the rigging by block and tackle and then dropped to their death on the deck. Naked captives might be used as target practice.

A rather nasty pirate game was called "sweating." It involved arranging a circle of lighted candles on deck and forcing one captive after another to run around and around between the candles and the mast while each pirate, armed with a knife, fork, or sword, ran "his Instrument into his Posteriors" until the prisoner collapsed; all to the accompaniment of horn, drum, and violin.

On occasion pirates showed clemency and even kindness to officers who were well spoken of by their men. But it wouldn't do to be too nice; after all, pirates relied on their ability to inspire terror to hasten the capitulation of a vessel. In addition to pirates' fearsome reputation for torture, they employed the icon of piracy, the grisly Jolly Roger; still *jolie* (to the pirates) but no longer *rouge* or red, as the buccaneers' had been. The mere glimpse of a pirate pennant on the mast of an approaching ship was notice that "no quarter will be given" and paralyzed many a vessel.

The Jolly Roger

The banner of "King Death" was also a potent symbol of pirate solidarity. In an age when children could be hanged for stealing a loaf of bread, the specter of the noose was hardly a deterrent to men who scorned society and all its laws, and thumbed their noses at death.

Flags during the Golden Age varied but generally had in common a black ground with symbols representing death, violence, and time running out for pirates' prey. The skull and crossbones image appeared on seventeenth-century English tombstones, and at sea when a man died the ship's captain drew a skull next to the man's name in the vessel's log. A number of pirate standards featured a skeleton toasting death with a raised rum glass. The glass, called a rummer, was popular in English taverns during the period when elaborate rum drinks were popular, but pirates in the Caribbean drank almost exclusively from pewter mugs or coconut shell cups.

Beware and Take Care

The pennant of Captain Low, a blood-red skeleton on a black ground, was especially feared. Low and George Lowther, with whom he sailed early in his career, represent the acme of senseless pirate cruelty. Low was born in Westminster, England, and from his childhood was a bully and a thief. After a stint as a merchant seaman he worked briefly in a Boston shipyard before being fired for antisocial behavior. Like so many others who couldn't make a go of it elsewhere, Low found his way to the Bay of Honduras to cut logwood. During a violent argument with his boss, Low shot a bystander and fled the camp. He and a dozen companions seized a small vessel and set out to "make a black Flag and declare War against all the World."

Lowther began as a second mate on a Royal Africa Company ship carrying slaves. Sailors loathed voyages to the pestilential heat of the African coast. To prevent mutinies, slaving captains tried to mix slaves from a variety of tribes and languages, so ships often lay at anchor for months while human cargo was assembled:

> Beware and take care
> Of the Bight of Benin;
> For one that comes out,
> There are forty go in.[7]

This bit of doggerel exaggerates a bit but many men died of tropical diseases while waiting off the coast. Lowther, frustrated by a long layover, led a mutiny aboard the *Gambia Castle* and was elected captain of the ship, which later appeared in the Caribbean in search of plunder. Records show that almost 72 percent of the 110 *Gambia Castle* crewmen who refused to turn pirate and remained behind died within a year. Despite large numbers of rovers who died on the gallows of "hempen fever," more pirates died of drink and disease than ever were hanged; and more perished in shipwrecks than were killed in battle.

Lowther and Low, Two of a Nasty Kind

The Cayman Islands, where the buccaneers had once gone for turtles, became something of a pirate sanctuary, and it was there that Lowther met up with Low, whom he made his lieutenant. They were two of a kind and together cruised the West Indies and the Virginia capes, plundering ships and "barbarously using" their captives. Lowther's specialty was putting slow-burning matches between a man's fingers, letting them burn

through to the bone if his victim didn't divulge where his valuables were hidden.

In May 1722, after Low split off, taking forty-four pirates to form his own company, Lowther's luck took a turn for the worse. His ship was all but destroyed when an English merchantman put up a surprisingly strong defense when attacked off South Carolina. Lowther was forced to hole up for the winter in a remote North Carolina inlet, living off the land while the ship was repaired.

In the spring he headed north and spent the summer plundering vessels with modest cargoes on the Newfoundland Banks. Following the traditional pattern of wintering in a more hospitable climate, Lowther made for the West Indies in August 1723. He seized a few prizes among the islands, but most of the time his men were on half rations for lack of provisions. When it was time for the periodic

Below: *A painting by an unknown artist showing a British warship chasing a pirate lugger in the English Channel. The three-masted lugger is flying the black pirate flag or Jolly Roger at her mizzen mast. Pirate ships often carried a range of flags, and it was common practice to fly a friendly or neutral flag when approaching a victim, and to replace the flag with the Jolly Roger at the last moment in order to take the victim by surprise.*

Below: *George Lowther and his men with a tent made of ship's sails to serve as a temporary shelter. They have beached their ship,* Happy Delivery, *for careening, a process involving hauling the ship onto its side in order to burn and scrape the weeds and barnacles from the ship's bottom, recaulk the seams, and replace rotten or infested planking. The task left pirates temporarily vulnerable.*

careening of his sloop, Lowther headed for the small island of Blanquilla, northeast of Tortuga. As their ship lay careened on its side, masts and rigging spread on the beach, Lowther and his company were surprised by the *Eagle*, a sloop out of Barbados belonging to the South Sea Company.

In the warm waters of the Caribbean, marine growth quickly fouled a ship's hull, making it necessary to frequently careen a vessel, and pirates shared their knowledge of many secluded coves that were safe. This was one of the surprisingly few cases where pirates were attacked while most vulnerable, while careening their vessel. The *Eagle*'s crew engaged the pirates, killing several and capturing all the rest save Lowther, three others, and a small drummer boy. George Lowther was found dead on the beach next to his gun after the *Eagle* had sailed away with his ship and captive men, most of whom were condemned to death by a Vice-Admiralty Court at St. Kitts and executed. He appears to have committed suicide, an act exceedingly rare among pirates.

His former partner fared better, leading his company of sadists on many daring attacks, sometimes cutting rich prizes right out of guarded harbors. He swept over the seas, from the West Indies to Newfoundland and across to the Azores, the Canaries, and Cape Verde. Sailors' blood curdled at the sight of his ensign. Low's appearance was equally bloodcurdling: his face had been disfigured when one of his drunken men missed a prisoner with his cutlass and slashed the side of Low's face open.

Low and his barbaric gang lopped heads off with abandon. They cut off a New England whaling captain's ears and made him eat them seasoned with pepper and salt. They ripped men open for sport, and strung two Portuguese friars to a yardarm and left them dangling. Captain Johnson wrote that they "almost as often murdered a man from the excess of good humour as out of passion and resentment. . . . for danger lurked in their very smiles."[8]

Whether the lunatic Low ever got his just desserts is unclear. Accounts vary. Some say he perished with all hands when his ship, the *Merry Christmas*, went down, but he may have sailed to Brazil. Many believed that he killed his quartermaster during one of his violent rages and was cast adrift in an open unprovisioned boat with three companions.

New Providence: "Nest of Pyrates"

The pirates of this extraordinary period could not have operated without their bases. None was as important as the Bahamas, particularly the island of New Providence, which by 1716 had become the "Nest of Pyrates" that Virginia's Governor Spotswood was so concerned about.[9] The sparsely settled Bahamas had been a pirate rendezvous since the 1680s, when the obliging Governor Robert Clarke issued privateering commissions, giving them a veneer of legality.

New Providence boasted a perfect pirate harbor, spacious enough for five hundred pirate craft, yet too shallow for pursuing warships; an abundance of provisions; and a good location. Rude taverns sprang up along the beach. Whores and outcasts, mangy dogs, and multiplying rats added to the fluctuating population. Merchants and traders were drawn to the settlement. They catered to the outlaws' needs and purchased their plunder, much of which was then smuggled to the colonies for resale. By 1700 it was reported from Virginia that "all the news of America is the swarming of pirates not only on these coasts but all the West Indies over, which doth ruin trade ten times worse than a war."

A Pirate Republic

A number of administrators were sent to New Providence, but the burgeoning pirate forces sent them packing. English pirate chieftains Thomas Barrow and Benjamin Hornigold proclaimed a pirate republic, with themselves as governors of New Providence. They were joined by leading captains such as Charles Vane, Thomas Burgess, Calico Jack Rackham, and Blackbeard. Ex-privateers and outlaws from all over the New World swelled the population of the pirate sanctuary. Logwood cutters from the Central American coast, who had been chased away by the Spanish, came. Escaped indentured servants, male and female, also found their way to the squalid tent city that grew up around Nassau harbor.

After a cruise, pirates looked forward to shore leave on New Providence, which met the recreational requirements of women and wine. It was said every pirate's wish was to find himself not in heaven after death but back on that island paradise where the resting rovers could laze in their hammocks beneath the palms, swinging gently in the fanning breezes. There were whores aplenty, continuous gambling, the camaraderie of fellow rovers, and unlimited drink.

Pirate Fare and Pirate Fashion

Pirate drinks were hearty and spicy. Popular bombo or bumboo, for instance, was a concoction of rum, water, sugar, and nutmeg. Another favorite was a blend of raw eggs,

sugar, sherry, gin, and beer called Rumfustian, although it contained no rum. The rovers also greatly appreciated brandy, sherry, and port, which they looted from prizes. Alcoholism was an occupational hazard and led to many untimely deaths.

Pirates liked their victuals hearty and spicy too. The shanty taverns of New Providence offered palate-pleasing dishes of "Solomon Grundy" or *salamagundi*, a sort of spicy chef's salad that included whatever was handy. Bits of meat, fish, turtle, and shellfish were marinated in a mixture of herbs, palm hearts, garlic, spiced wine, and oil, and then served with hard-boiled eggs and pickled onions, cabbage, grapes, and olives.

Pirates generally wore trousers and jerkins of rough sailcloth at sea, except during an engagement when most donned garments coated with pitch (which could deflect sword thrusts), or doublets of thick leather. On shore many pirates made up for their drab work garb by affecting the colorful dress of gentlemen and exaggerating their mannerisms if not their hygiene. They minced along in silver-buckled high heels, tricorn hats under their arms, clad in plundered combinations of rich-hued and often mismatched garments of embroidered silks and satins,

Above: *Captain Edward Low, onetime partner of Lowther, stands at the shore in stormy weather while a ship founders in the heavy seas. Low acquired an evil reputation because of the savage cruelty with which he and his men treated their victims.*

velvets and lace, which often verged on the ludicrous. Some even wore powdered wigs and powdered their stubbled faces like London dandies. Pirates loved gaudy jewelry, wearing rings, elaborate ear pendants, pearls, ornate heavy gold chains, and diamond and emerald crosses stolen from Catholic ships.

Sunken Treasure

In 1715 all twelve galleons of the annual Spanish plate fleet sailing from Havana to Spain sank off the coast of Florida in a hurricane with more than fourteen million pesos worth of treasure.[10] The viceroy of Havana immediately dispatched salvage ships with divers and soldiers to protect them. Working from a camp on shore, they recovered much of the sunken treasure.

Before long every would-be treasure hunter in the Caribbean had heard of the disaster. Henry Jennings, an ex-privateer, raised a contingent of three hundred pirates from New Providence to raid the salvage camp. Their numbers panicked the guards, who fled into the bush, abandoning 350,000 pieces of eight plus assorted other treasure. The pirates then seized a Spanish cargo ship, plundering her rich cargo of cash, cochineal, and indigo, and, based at New Providence, went on to wreak havoc throughout the West Indies.

By 1716 the "Flying Gang," as the New Providence exponents of sea robbery called themselves, had such a stranglehold on the sea lanes from Nova Scotia to the Spanish Main that the governor of Antigua wrote, "I do not think it advisable to go from hence except upon an extraordinary occasion, not knowing but that I may be intercepted by the pirates." Merchant ships traveled in convoys protected by navy warships that charged as much as 12½ percent of a cargo's value for their services.

Bellamy, "the Orator"

Among the New Providence sea vultures who cruised off the North American coast during this period was Captain Samuel Bellamy, whose ship the *Whydah Galley* was wrecked in stormy seas off Cape Cod while the drunken crew were sampling some prize Madeira wine. In 1984 the remains of the wreck were located in about twenty feet (6m) of water. Salvors brought up several thousand gold and silver coins, as well as gold bars and jewelry, and the ship's bell.

Bellamy left a wife and children near Canterbury in order to cut his teeth in the West Indies as a "wracker," one of those who set out false beacons to lure unwary vessels to their shores and plunder their cargoes. Before cruising the east coast in 1717 Bellamy had "fished" on the 1715 galleons and made a name for himself in the islands as a pirate. His flagship, the *Whydah Galley*, mounted twenty-eight guns. His motley crew of two hundred was predominantly English and Irish with a sprinkling of other nationalities, including twenty-five slaves stolen from a Guinea ship. He was accompanied on his North American cruise by a twelve-gun sloop with a crew of forty, captained by Paul Williams, a mulatto in a periwig. They took prize after prize. One of his crew later testified they had taken fifty vessels. Some ships they scuttled and burned, others were plundered and let go after a certain number of their men had signed articles.

Bellamy epitomized the anarchic spirit of the classic pirate who was at odds with restrictive society, and was dubbed "the Orator" because he enjoyed delivering impassioned speeches. He harangued the captain of a Boston merchant ship taken off South Carolina: "I am a free prince and I have as much authority to make war on the whole World as he who has a hundred sail of ships at sea and 100,000 men in the field."[11]

Woodes Rogers Sails In

Growing alarm about the havoc the pirates were wreaking caused King George I to act. In July 1718 Woodes Rogers, ex-privateer and circumnavigator, arrived at Nassau harbor, where more than two hundred ships rode at anchor and where an estimated thousand pirates were ashore. He brought with him a royal commission as "Captain-General and Governor-in-Chief in and over Our Bahama Islands." He also had with him an Act of Grace, a royal pardon for all pirates who turned themselves in before September 5, 1718, and were willing to swear an oath to abstain from further piracies. After that date all were to be hunted down and hanged.

Many of the pirates elected to retire from "the sweet trade." A few decamped rather than forswear their seaborne profession, and a small group of dissenters vowed to resist the governor's authority. Charles Vane, their ringleader, turned a French prize into a fire ship fully loaded with ignited explosives. Cut adrift, it bore down on the newly arrived English vessels. The fire's heat set off round after round of cannonballs, musketballs, and bits and pieces of assorted metal scrap. As the powder magazines ignited, the French ship went up like a dazzling, deafening fireworks display, lighting the tropic night for miles around.

In the general confusion Vane, with a number of his men, slipped out to the open sea in a sloop piled high with booty and vanished into the night. For the next three years he remained at large, poaching for silver bullion on the 1715 wrecks off Florida and cruising up the American coast, where he

Above: *A romanticized engraving by the French artist Auguste-François Biard showing pirates cunningly dressed up as women and harmless civilians in order to deceive an American ship of their intentions as they come alongside.*

Below: *A famous engraving of Edward Teach, better known as Blackbeard, from an early edition of Captain Johnson's famous work. Heavily armed, he sports smoking fuses stuck under his hat. Anchored in the bay behind him is his forty-gun ship,* Queen Anne's Revenge, *in which he cruised the Caribbean and eastern seaboard of the United States.*

terrorized shipping off the Carolinas. He met Blackbeard offshore one time and the two crews retired to an inlet for a drunken orgy.

Eventually his luck ran out. He was shipwrecked and picked up by an English vessel, identified, taken to Port Royal, tried, and then hanged.

Woodes Rogers succeeded in wiping out the pirate nest and even turned some of the men into farmers. Many of New Providence's former denizens found life under the new regime far too disciplined and dull for "men o' spirit" who preferred bumboo to Bible tracts, and they left to return to their old ways. Several former pirates, including Captain Benjamin Hornigold, became Rogers's most trusted agents and went after the backsliders.

Blackbeard

One New Providence alumnus who never for a moment considered accepting a pardon was Blackbeard. In the *Queen Anne's Revenge*, he prowled the West Indies with a crew of three hundred men. Engagements like the one in which he bested a British warship made Blackbeard the most talked-about man in the Caribbean. Even the reformed Hornigold had boasted of his role as the great pirate's tutor, and former rovers talked wistfully in the taverns of New Providence of their former comrade's raw courage in taking on and beating a Royal Navy ship. Even in absentia, Blackbeard made life difficult for Rogers, whose hold on his domesticated pirates was tenuous at best.

Blackbeard, a protégé of Hornigold, was not as savage as some pirates but none surpassed him at self-promotion, so that his name lives on as the pirate "whose name was a Terror" and "the Spawn of the Devil." Like so many of his kind, his origins are obscure. His name has been rendered a dozen ways from Teach to Tash to Thatch. He was a native of Bristol, England, and had come to Jamaica first as a deckhand aboard a privateer during the war.

He served his pirate apprenticeship on Hornigold's brigantine *Ranger* and proved so capable and fearless that his mentor put him in charge of a six-gun sloop with a crew of seventy. The two cruised together, taking prizes off Cuba and elsewhere along the way to the American coast, where they careened their ships on the Virginia shore. After the vessels had been scraped, sealed with tallow, and repaired, they set out again along the coast before heading to the West Indies with their holds brimming with prize goods.

Off St. Vincent they took a French guineaman en route from Africa to Martinique. The cargo of slaves, gold dust, bullion, plate, jewels, and other choice goods was beyond their dreams. Hornigold rewarded Teach's ability by giving him command of the prize.

Right: *This evocative picture—entitled* This, Lean Straight Rover Looked the Part of a Competent Soldier—*was painted by Frank Schoonover and shows Blackbeard's men marching through Charleston, South Carolina. The most remarkable feat in Blackbeard's pirate career was his blockade of Charleston in 1718. He sailed into the harbor with a warship and three smaller vessels and held the town to ransom. Tired of his depredations, Governor Spotswood sent two Royal Navy vessels into Ocracoke Inlet to put an end to his activities.*

She was a big Dutch-built ship, strong, and well armed. Blackbeard converted her to his use and patriotically renamed her the *Queen Anne's Revenge.*

During an eighteen-month rampage Blackbeard ranged from Virginia to Honduras, terrorizing shipping and taking at least twenty prizes. He burned some ships but added others to his growing fleet. Most of the American colonies had turned their backs on the pirates, but struggling North Carolina, lacking the lucrative trade in rice and indigo that made neighboring colonies strong

enough to shun traffic with smugglers and pirates, still welcomed them.

Blackbeard was a man of imposing stature and frightening aspect. A mane of thick black hair and a long beard, both plaited with colored ribbons, framed his naturally scowling face with its wild-looking deep-set eyes. In battle, armed with three brace of pistols slung in bandoleers, he appeared to be a fury from hell, with smoldering gunner's matches sticking out from under his hat. Blackbeard's awesome figure was matched by his extravagant and impetuous temperament. Even his

Left: Blackbeard's Last Fight, *by Howard Pyle. As befitted the image he had created for himself, Blackbeard died in an epic manner. Tracked down and cornered in Ocracoke Inlet by a two-ship naval expeditionary force led by Lieutenant Maynard of HMS* Pearl, *Blackbeard met them head-on in a violent frenzy that culminated in the boarding of Maynard's sloop, and a vicious hand-to-hand encounter ensued. Blackbeard picked out Maynard and shot at him, but missed. Maynard returned fire and hit his quarry, then the two closed with swords. Maynard's sword broke and the fatal blow that came for him missed when another sailor slashed Blackbeard's throat and thus ruined his thrust. Suffering five gunshot wounds and twenty sword wounds, Blackbeard fought on, gurgling blood, until he sank slowly to the deck, unable to function as the life oozed from him.*

own men were subjected to terrifying displays calculated to cow the observers.

One time he was drinking a rousing concoction of rum and gunpowder with his men aboard ship. He was smitten with the idea of creating a hell of their own to see what it was like. He took two or three obliging crewmen into the hold, where they sat on ballast rocks. Blackbeard had lit pots of brimstone handed down. Then the hatches were closed and the pirates sat in the pitch-black hold breathing the suffocating fumes until one by one they begged for release from the sulfurous prison. Blackbeard finally opened the hatches, delighted that he had held out the longest.

One night he was drinking with his gunner, Israel Hands (the prototype for Stevenson's Israel Hands in *Treasure Island*) and another pirate in his cabin. Suddenly, without a word of warning, he drew and cocked a pair of his pistols under the table. One man, wary of his captain's unpredictable temper, went on deck, while Hands stayed to drink. Blackbeard snuffed the candle and fired both pistols. One slug ripped through the gunner's knee, crippling him for life. When his crew asked why he had done such a thing, Blackbeard cursed them and replied that if he didn't kill one of his men now and then they would forget who he was.

In January 1718 Blackbeard and his crew surrendered to Governor Charles Eden at the town of Bath, on the Pamlico River in North Carolina, under the latest Act of Grace. Eden took a percentage of Blackbeard's booty and made no move to stop him from brazenly careening in the vicinity while he prepared for another cruise. Tobias Knight, the colony's secretary and collector of customs, openly aided Blackbeard before he sailed off for another foray to the Gulf of Honduras.

Stede Bonnet: the Amateur Pirate

On his first voyage to Honduras, Blackbeard had met up with one of the Golden Age's least likely pirate captains, Major Stede Bonnet from Barbados. Bonnet was a middle-aged, upper-class Englishman who had retired from the army to run a large sugar plantation. It came as a shock to Barbados society when the major deserted his comfortable life for an outlaw career at sea. Discord with his shrewish wife may have spurred him on. In any case he outfitted his sloop the *Revenge* with ten guns, breaking pirate precedent by buying the ship instead of seizing it. He crewed her with seventy men, only some of them seasoned rovers, and took off.

By the time he met Blackbeard, Bonnet had managed to capture a few prizes without being very capable or inspiring confidence in his crew. An odder couple would be hard to imagine: the flamboyant Blackbeard, larger than life with his wild mane and blazing eyes, and the pudgy little dandy with his satin waistcoat, snow-white breeches, and powdered wig. Despite their differences they got on famously and decided to cruise together. Almost immediately Blackbeard realized that Bonnet was a bungling amateur.

The crew of the *Revenge* was pleased when Blackbeard placed his second-in-command, Lieutenant Richards, in charge of Bonnet's ship. He showed uncharacteristic tact in suggesting to Bonnet that "as he had not been used to the fatigues and care of such a post, it would be better for him to decline it and live easy, at his pleasure, in such a ship as his, where he should not be obliged to perform duty, but follow his own inclinations." In effect, Bonnet was Blackbeard's prisoner.

His crew was dead set against him and he had begun to wonder if he wouldn't rather settle ashore in a Spanish colony. There was no getting away, however, as Blackbeard's fleet beat the seas between the Carolinas and the West Indies, taking a dozen prizes.

Bonnet had sought a privateer's commission from the governor while the pirate fleet put in at Topsail Inlet. During his absence, Blackbeard stripped his sloop clean and sailed off, marooning twenty-five of the crew on a sand spit. Bonnet started after Blackbeard, but when he realized he couldn't catch up with him, he cruised up the coast of Virginia into Delaware Bay. He had become more adept during his sojourn with Blackbeard and seized several prizes, including a large ship that he took ashore near the Cape Fear River for modifications.

It was there that he was captured by Colonel William Rhett of South Carolina. A bribe of gold bought him escape from the Charleston jail, but Rhett caught the portly pirate again and he was brought to trial in Charleston with thirty-three other pirates. Bonnet was found guilty despite his pleas that he had never taken a ship save in the company of "Captain Thatch" (Blackbeard). His ineptitude cost the lives of twenty-eight

of his men, many of them young, who were hanged on November 8, 1718.

The gentleman pirate thought he would be spared and wrote a groveling letter begging for mercy from the governor. If reprieved he would separate all his limbs from his body, he promised, "only reserving the Use of my Tongue to call continually on, and pray to the Lord."[12] But South Carolina had had its fill of pirates and he was hanged on December 10 at White Point, near Charleston, the traditional bouquet clutched in his chained hands.

Blackbeard's Nemesis

Unhindered maritime commerce was vital to Virginia, and Blackbeard's continued haunting of the sea-lanes between the West Indies and the mainland was intolerable. When Governor Eden took no action against the pirate, the traders and plantation owners of Virginia implored Governor Spotswood, implacable pirate foe, to do something. When the Virginia legislature quibbled over how to fund a naval expedition, Spotswood paid the cost himself.

Blackbeard's reign of terror ended a month before Bonnet's execution, when Governor Spotswood sent Lieutenant Robert Maynard of the HMS *Pearl* to beard the pirate in his den. The pirates' sloop *Adventure* and a merchantman prize were at anchor up

the Ocracoke Inlet, North Carolina, where word had it Blackbeard planned to carve out a pirate stronghold. He had been smitten by a sixteen-year-old planter's daughter in nearby Bath. He had a wench in every port and is credited with fourteen wives, although the first thirteen were probably amours of the moment who went through mock weddings conducted by one of the pirate officers. The fourteenth marriage was the real thing performed by Governor Eden himself.

Lieutenant Maynard set out in command of two hired sloops, both shallow draft vessels able to navigate the shoals and channels around Ocracoke. He located the pirate ships at dusk of November 21, 1718. Blackbeard and the eighteen men who were with him spent the night getting drunk instead of preparing for battle. Next morning the pirates, still drinking, met the Royal Navy in one of history's great pirate engagements, which ended with a miraculous British victory after the pirates had all but won, having slain the captain of one of the navy sloops and wounded most of the sixty-two sailors.

Blackbeard shot at Maynard from almost point-blank range and missed. The lieutenant's answering shot found its mark. Wounded, Blackbeard fought on like a zombie amid the smoke and stench. The howling pirate attacked Maynard with his cutlass. Their blades clanged and flashed on the blood-slicked deck until Maynard's broke off near the hilt. Just as Blackbeard went to finish Maynard, a navy man slashed his throat open so that Blackbeard's thrust was deflected, barely grazing Maynard's hand. The dying giant fought on like a cornered wild beast. Drenched in blood that bubbled out of his neck, Blackbeard fired his pistols until the repeated sword thrusts of the sailors who closed in on him finally took their toll.

Blackbeard's grisly head was hung below Maynard's bowsprit as proof of his death and taken to Bath and then back to Virginia, where it was stripped of flesh and hung from a pole at the mouth of the Hampton River. Thirteen of the surviving fifteen pirates from the pirate band were tried and condemned to death at a trial in Williamsburg.

Harsh Measures

A spate of executions in Virginia and South Carolina, where forty-four pirates were hanged in one month, broke the pirates' stranglehold on the American coast, but ships in the West Indies were still not safe from rebellious New Providencers. Although he had no legal powers to do so, Rogers held a swift trial for ten pirates Hornigold had brought back to Nassau. Their mutiny threatened to undermine the fragile structure of his authority. Nine were found guilty and one spared because he proved he had been forced to pirate.

On December 12, 1718, two days after they were sentenced, a single gallows was erected with nine nooses dangling over a scaffold resting on three barrels. The pirates were led out and unshackled; after their hands had been tied in front of them, they mounted the gallows. Each of the condemned men was allowed to address the crowd of about three hundred former and potential pirates. The militia of 100 soldiers and irregulars was present to maintain order because feelings ran high in favor of the pirates, who met their end with the courage that had been the hallmark of their careers.

Rogers took a risk executing the pirates, but it paid off. When one member of the sullen mob jumped on a barrel to exhort the others to riot, Rogers calmly shot him dead. After that, although there were mutters of rebellion, Rogers never again had a mutiny. In fact, he had the colonists staunchly behind him when 1,300 Spanish troops poured off four warships to attack the colony in late February of 1720. One British infantry division and five hundred rum-soaked ex-rovers beat off the Spanish.

Anne Bonny and Mary Read

Surely the most unusual pirates ever to have set foot on the pirates' island were Anne Bonny and Mary Read, who sailed with Vane's former quartermaster John Rackham, the man whose striped pants earned him the nickname of "Calico Jack." The eighteenth-century press had a field day when the two were brought to trial in Port Royal. They were the subject of numerous ballads.

Anne Bonny was the bastard daughter of William Cormac, a prominent Cork attorney, and a housemaid. The trio settled in Charleston, South Carolina, where Cormac prospered as a businessman and planter. Anne had a wild temper. When she was thirteen she allegedly stabbed a servant girl in the belly with a table knife. When her mother died she took on the duties of housekeeper

for her father, whose wealth made her an attractive catch despite her temper.

She eloped with a feckless sailor named James Bonny and Cormac disinherited her. The couple found their way to New Providence, where Anne tired of her husband, who had turned spy for Woodes Rogers. She fell for dashing "Calico Jack." She and Jack stole a sloop at anchor in the harbor and set off "on the account," putting together a crew and taking several prizes.

They captured a Dutch vessel and pressed a number of its crew to sign articles with them. One of the new pirates was a delicately handsome young boy to whom Anne took a fancy. Disappointment may have equaled shock when she discovered her favorite to be a young Englishwoman named Mary Read. Unlike Anne, Mary had spent most of her life in men's clothing. She was the illegitimate

Below: *Having fought and fatally wounded a fellow pirate in a duel, Mary Read pulls open her shirt to reveal that she is a woman. There were very few female pirates, but the lives of Mary Read and Ann Bonny are well documented. Witnesses at their trial in Jamaica said that they cursed and put up more of a fight than the other members of Calico Jack's crew.*

child of a London woman whose husband had been at sea for more than a year when she delivered. Mary was apprenticed as footboy to a French lady, but her nature demanded more excitement and she ran away to sea, signing on as a cabin boy on a warship.

Later she served as an infantryman and then in the mounted cavalry in Flanders, where the English and French were fighting the War of the Spanish Succession. Mary married but was soon widowed and returned to the life she preferred, signing on a Dutch merchantman bound for the West Indies, which was the same ship Rackham took. Mary shared her secret with Anne, who told Jack. He invited her to join the crew as a full-fledged member. The two women were first-rate pirates, never shirking battle. None among the crew "were more resolute, or ready to Board or undertake any Thing that was hazardous," Captain Johnson asserts.

Their ship was anchored off Jamaica's north coast in late October 1720 when they were challenged by a privateer sloop, whose captain had a commission from the governor of Jamaica to take pirates. There was a short, sharp action that ended with the pirates' surrender. Captain Jonathan Barnett, the sloop's commander, testified in court at

Spanishtown, Jamaica, that only two of the pirates had put up any fight and they had fought like wildcats, using pistols, cutlasses, and boarding axes before being overpowered. One of the two had fired into the hold where the men were hiding, screaming like a banshee that they should come up and fight like men. When it was discovered that these two pirates were women, it was arranged that they be tried separately from the men.

Anne and Mary were sentenced to hang along with Rackham and the rest of those who had been convicted. The courtroom was astounded at the women's answer to the judge's routine inquiry as to whether any of the condemned had anything further to say. "Milord," came the reply, "we plead our bellies." By law the court could not take the life of an unborn child by executing the mother. An examination revealed that the two pirates were indeed both pregnant. Mary died of fever in prison before her baby was born. Anne disappeared, perhaps paroled through her father's influence. She fades from history in a fury, for as Jack Rackham was going to be hanged (at a place near Port Royal still known as Rackham's Cay), he asked to see her. She gave him a scornful look and spat out that, "Had you fought like a man, you need not have been hang'd like a dog."

The End of an Era

A number of factors brought the Golden Age of Piracy to a gradual conclusion. By the end of the 1720s the naval abuses mentioned earlier had ended, and as the Crown ceased issuing proprietary charters the quality of government officials improved. Corrupt officials were replaced with better men, and the threat of revocation encouraged administrators to suppress piracy in those colonies that retained their charters.

The expanded Piracy Act of 1721 came down hard on those who "shall trade with, by truck, barter, or exchange," with a pirate, making them equally guilty of piracy. This legislation greatly aided officials like Governor Spotswood, who had been frustrated by the extent to which the community was involved with pirates. With time local economies were strong enough to shun trafficking in pirated goods.

In addition, the barbarous behavior of so many of the sea outlaws sickened people, outweighing their romantic appeal. Lowther and

Below: *Ann Bonny as depicted in an engraving from an early edition of Captain Johnson's book. After an adventurous early life, Bonny ended up on a pirate ship with Mary Read. With John Rackham they cruised the West Indies until captured off the west coast of Jamaica. They were put on trial at the Admiralty Court in Spanishtown presided over by Sir Nicholas Lawes, the governor of the island, and were only saved from the gallows by revealing that they were both pregnant.*

Low were the epitome of pirate savagery, but atrocities were commonplace and escalated as suppression and hanging of pirates increased. The New England–based John Roberts, for example, invariably tortured captives, urging his men on to the most sadistic acts. They whipped men to death, used them as target practice, and sliced off ears and noses. Captured pirates faced torture themselves. In 1725 Scots pirate Captain John Gow refused to plead at his trial at Newgate and was ordered pressed to death. Faced with the prospect of being crushed to death, the only torture then allowed by law, Gow decided to plead not guilty. Found guilty, he was hanged and his body taken to the shore of the Thames at Greenwich to hang in chains as a warning to others.

The "Great Pyrate Roberts"

Bartholomew Roberts, the last of the Golden Age pirate captains, was also the greatest. In his own day he was the "Great Pyrate Roberts," undisputed king of rovers; fearless, original, and a superlative seaman. He was born in Pembrokeshire and, according to Captain Johnson, had the dark complexion common among Welshmen. "Black Bart" was a handsome, commanding figure with a taste for elegant dress. He died during a battle wearing a rich crimson damask waistcoat and breeches, a scarlet plumed hat, and a massive gold chain attached to a jeweled cross.

During engagements he sported two brace of pistols tucked in a silk sling over his shoulder in addition to the razor-sharp cutlass that was his preferred weapon. He kept a tight rein on his crew, forbidding gambling for money and encouraging prayer. Roberts was piracy's only recorded teetotaler, but the fact he preferred tea to rum didn't mean he was a namby-pamby.

Roberts's amazing boldness inspired his men to the most daring acts. He crisscrossed the globe with a fleet so formidable that naval squadrons in the West Indies sent out to capture him turned away at the mere sight of his flag rather than risk confrontation. Even with a single ship, Roberts performed amazing feats. In June 1720, for example, with a single ten-gun sloop and a crew of sixty, he took twenty-two ships lying at anchor in Newfoundland's Trepassey Bay. More than 1,200 men were aboard the vessels when he appeared. With drums beating and

trumpets blaring, the pirates proceeded to take every one as the terror-stricken crews piled into launches and pulled for shore. The pirates plundered and sank all but a brigantine, which was needed to carry the booty. Roberts wasn't fazed a bit by a large French flotilla he encountered not far from the harbor. He attacked and destroyed the entire flotilla, keeping only a large brigantine that he renamed the *Royal Fortune* and made his flagship.

According to Captain Johnson, he embarked on a piratical career not because he had no other way of making a living, but "to get rid of the disagreeable Superiority of some Masters he was acquainted with . . . and the Love of Novelty and Change."[13] He turned pirate at the unusually advanced age of thirty-six. Born in 1682, he began his career in the merchant service and in 1719 he shipped as second mate on the *Princess* bound from London to the Guinea Coast to load slaves. Off the West African coast the *Princess* was seized by the famed Welsh pirate, Captain Howell Davis.

Howell Davis, Black Bart's Tutor

Davis's pirate career began when the slaver on which he was a mate was captured by Edward England, the Irish pirate, who was en route from Nassau to Madagascar. After prowling the West Indies, Davis headed for the eastern seas like so many of the West Indies rovers.

By the time Davis met Roberts he had taken many prize cargoes of gold dust, gold bars, coins, ivory, and slaves. Davis took pride in never having to force a seaman and was delighted when his compatriot Roberts was willing to sail with him.

Six weeks later, after taking several prizes, including a Holland-bound ship with a rich cargo and the governor of Accra aboard, Davis was killed in an ambush at the Portuguese settlement on Prince's Island in the Guinea Gulf.

Roberts Takes Charge

Despite his brief tenure, Bart Roberts's valor and intelligence had impressed his pirate mates so much that they elected him their new captain. Roberts retaliated for Davis's death by leveling the Portuguese settlement. Still in a vengeful mood, he then crossed the Atlantic to Bahia, the Bay of All Saints in

Above: *A silver-mounted presentation pistol, c. 1730, made in London and presented to Captain Reed of the privateer* Oliver Cromwell *by the Council of the West Indian island of St. Christophers. This is typical of the sort of weapon that would have been used by pirates in the Caribbean during the Golden Age. The butt was designed to be used as a club in hand-to-hand fighting.*

Above: *Bartholomew Roberts at Whydah on the Guinea Coast of Africa in 1722 with two of his ships in the background, the* Royal Fortune *and the* Great Ranger. *His flagship is flying the distinctive pirate flags he designed: he is depicted standing with each foot on a skull, one labeled ABH, the other AMH. These stood for "A Barbadian's Head" and "A Martinican's Head," respectively—a comment on the efforts of the governors of these islands to put an end to his Caribbean activities. At Whydah, Roberts held eleven ships to ransom (visible here) until they paid in gold for safe passage. Shortly after this incident, Roberts was tracked down and killed during a sea battle off Cape Lopez, as a result of which all his crew were captured.*

Brazil. There he found forty-two Portuguese ships at anchor loaded for the passage to Lisbon. He singled out the biggest, the vice-admiral's forty-gun vessel, and sailed up to her so brazenly that the pirates were aboard before the Portuguese realized what was happening. Before the two warships assigned to guard the Portuguese convoy could reach him, Roberts had sailed off with his prize containing sugar, hides, and tobacco, as well as forty thousand gold coins valued at about £80,000, gold trinkets, plate, and the diamond-studded cross that afterwards reposed on *his* chest rather than the king of Portugal's, for whom it had been designed.

The pirates sailed north to the cheerless little Spanish colony at Devil's Island off Guiana, where the señoritas proved especially eager to trade for the Portuguese loot. There is a legend that the treasure taken at Bahia is still buried deep inside a cave on Little Cayman Island. But it is unlikely the

pirates had much left after a couple of weeks of carousing, gambling, and wenching at Devil's Island.

A Nightmare Voyage

Roberts took his men into the Caribbean in the spring of 1720 and then north. He spent the summer rampaging around Newfoundland and the New England coast with a complement of about 100 men, including recruited cod-splitters who had been only too happy to leave their back-breaking work for piracy. After a spell in the Caribbean, where naval patrols were numerous, Roberts set sail for West Africa via the Cape Verde Islands. It turned into a nightmare voyage. Once across the Atlantic the prevailing southerly wind forced his ship too far north to reach the Cape Verdes. He had to recross the ocean and then head south into the Caribbean, taking advantage of the western Atlantic's prevailing northeasterly trade winds.

The ship didn't touch land for two thousand miles (3,200km). The days became weeks. Roberts doled out one swallow of water a day from the only remaining barrel of water until it was empty. The pirates were so crazed with thirst that some drank seawater or their own urine. Dysentery and fevers flashed through the crew, killing quite a few. Roberts with his unshakable faith in God's providence was the only man with a spark of hope. Most of the men were beyond caring whether they lived or died when they found themselves suddenly in shallow water, indicating land was not far off. The following day they sighted land and by evening were toasting one another with fresh water from the Maroni River in Suriname on the coast of South America.

Dazzling Feats

After this almost fatal episode Roberts ignored the threat of naval patrols and unleashed his lethal forces on the Caribbean in a desperate and dazzlingly successful campaign. The governor of the French Leewards reported that in a four-day period at the end of October 1720, the pirates had "seized, burned or sunk fifteen French and English vessels and one Dutch interloper of forty-two guns at Dominica." Sailing right under shore batteries at the Basseterre Road on St. Kitts, Roberts plundered and burned a number of vessels at anchor. Word spread that the pirates were slicing off the ears of prisoners, lashing them to the mast or yardarm for target practice, whipping them to death, and committing other atrocities.

By the spring of 1721 there was little left to plunder. The holds of Roberts's ships were solidly packed with booty that could be traded at a premium for Guinea gold. So in April he made for Africa, landing on the coast of Senegal and then proceeding to Sierra Leone, where his men careened their ships and relaxed in the company of independent English traders who operated in defiance of the Royal Africa Company's monopoly.

During the summer and early fall the arch-pirate plundered up and down the Guinea coast, sometimes attempting to trade with local tribes and battling them when they refused. One attack around Old Calabar was still a part of the orally transmitted history of the natives as late as the 1920s. At Whydah Roads, where Captain Johnson wrote that

there was "commonly the best booty," Roberts took eleven French, English, and Portuguese ships in a single day, releasing each for a ransom of eight pounds' worth of gold dust. One of the receipts he wrote for the gold refers to the pirates as "we Gentlemen of Fortune." No pirate captain ever had complete command of his crew and, when one captain refused to pay the ransom, his ship with its cargo of chained slaves still aboard was set afire against Roberts's orders.

Luck Runs Out for Roberts

Captain Roberts seemed invincible, but in February of 1722 the *Swallow*, a fifty-gun Royal Navy warship commanded by Captain Chaloner Ogle, caught sight of the pirate

Below: *A portrait of Captain Chaloner Ogle, knighted for his action against Roberts and ultimately to become Admiral of the Fleet. Ogle, in command of HMS* Swallow, *was sent in pursuit of Roberts after the Whydah incident. He found him at anchor under the lee of Cape Lopez. Roberts's crew had just previously taken a prize well stocked with liquor and most of his men were drunk, save Roberts himself. At the onset of the action, Roberts led from the front but was struck by a grapeshot in the throat. His death took the fight out of his men and they surrendered after throwing their leader overboard, according to his request.*

squadron at anchor in the lee of Parrot Island off Cape Lopez on the Guinea coast. HMS *Swallow* and HMS *Weymouth* had been hunting for Roberts for six months, frustrated by the coastline's interminable maze of tangled jungle, corkscrew rivers, and hot swampy lagoons. The pirates at first thought the *Swallow* was a Portuguese merchantman and Roberts sent the *Ranger* after her. Ogle lured the *Ranger* out of sight and then turned on her, slaying ten pirates and taking more than 100 others prisoner, many of whom were hideously wounded by an explosion.

When Ogle returned to Parrot Island at dawn five days later, the pirates' ships still rode at anchor. Captain Roberts was breakfasting on *salamagundi* and tea while most of his men slept off prodigious hangovers from liquor taken from a prize the previous day. The *Swallow*, flying the French flag, hove into view without causing alarm, but as it made straight for the *Royal Fortune* one of Roberts's crew, a navy deserter, recognized her as his old ship and raised a cry.

The pirate captain determined to cut cables and run since his crew was not in fighting trim. Then he made a fateful change in plan, ordering the helmsman to steer right for the *Swallow*. As the two ships drew closer, Roberts jumped onto a gun carriage to direct his ship's fire. The *Swallow* launched a broadside that toppled the pirate ship's mizzen topmast. The pirates returned fire. When the smoke cleared they saw Roberts's great body slumped on the the deck, his throat ripped open by a blast of grapeshot. His men, many of them sobbing, respected his last wishes and heaved his bleeding corpse overboard in all its finery—jewels, weapons, and all.

Thus ended the stunning career of the "Great Pyrate" Roberts, who in less than four years had captured over four hundred sail. His men fought on, but without their charismatic captain they lost their will. At two in the afternoon 152 survivors, many too drunk to stand, surrendered to a navy boarding party. One befuddled pirate who had spent the entire engagement in a drunken stupor suddenly came to and seeing the *Swallow* nearby shouted: "A prize! A prize!" urging

Below: *Cape Coast Castle on the Gold Coast of West Africa provided a fortified base of operations from which British trade and colonial control could be administered from 1664 onward. It became the overseas headquarters of the Royal Africa Company and a center for the trading of ivory and slaves. The castle also served as a military post from which antipiracy activities could be directed. It was at Cape Coast in 1722 that the largest ever trial of pirates was held, involving Bartholomew Roberts's surviving crew.*

the others to take her. A large quantity of plunder was found aboard the pirate ship, and Captain Ogle, who is the only naval officer ever knighted for capturing pirates, eventually became admiral of the fleet and acquired a fortune from the prizes he had taken off the African coast.

The Trials at Cape Coast Castle

A total of 264 pirates from the *Ranger* and the *Royal Fortune* were carried to Cape Coast Castle for the largest pirate trial ever held. Nineteen died of their wounds before the trial; some were released. Only eight of the 165 men tried were grizzled veterans. Two had previously sailed with Blackbeard and six were with Davis when he died. The rest were recruits. Seventy-four men including the musicians were acquitted. Fifty-four men were sentenced to death, two of whom were reprieved. Another seventeen were sentenced to prison in London, of whom all but four died en route to England. Not one of the twenty sentenced to seven years' hard labor in the Gold Coast mines of the Royal Africa Company outlived his sentence.

Fifty-two unrepentant pirates ranging in age from nineteen to forty-five were hanged "like dogs" in batches over a two-week period in April 1722. As he was led to the gallows erected outside the castle ramparts, one of Roberts's original crew, "Lord" Symson, saw a woman he knew in the crowd that had gathered to watch the show. She was Elizabeth Trengrove, an Englishwoman who had been a passenger on a ship Roberts had captured. "I have lain with that bitch three times," he shouted, "and now she has come to see me hanged."[14]

With the mass hangings on the African coast, the curtain came down on the Golden Age of Piracy. The bodies of eighteen of the pirates, coated in tar and wrapped with metal bands, were strung from gibbets on the hills overlooking the harbor. The macabre spectacle of the rotting cadavers twisting in the wind gave notice that there was no longer any place for the pirates in a world dominated by global European imperialism—a world that, ironically, piracy had helped make possible.

Sporadic episodes of piracy continued to flare up, and even today pirates plague shipping in several far-flung areas; for as Roman historian Dio Cassius noted in the first century A.D., "There was never a time when piracy was not practiced. Nor may it cease to be as long as the nature of mankind remains the same." But never again has piracy been a significant factor in shaping international political and economic policy. Nor has any pirate since captivated the public as did the antiheroes of the Golden Age, whose long shadows reach across the centuries.

Above: *One of the actual death sentences passed against nineteen of the accused at Cape Coast in 1722. The men were hanged outside the gates and some were left in chains as a warning to others. Ninety-one men were found guilty in total, with fifty-four sentenced to death, fifty-two of whom were hanged.*

CHAPTER SIX

LIBERTALIA:
THE PIRATE'S UTOPIA

~

In an honest Service, there is thin Commons, low Wages, and hard Labour; in this, Plenty and Satiety, Pleasure and Ease, Liberty and Power; and who would not ballance Creditor on this Side, when all the Hazard that is run for it, at worst, is only a sower Look or two at choaking. No, a **merry Life and a short one** *shall be my Motto.*

BARTHOLOMEW ROBERTS[1]

IN 1728 IN THE second volume of *A General History of the Pyrates*, Captain Charles Johnson told the tale of a Captain Misson and his fellow pirates. They had in recent years established a utopian republic on the island of Madagascar, and they had proudly called it "Libertalia." The settlement looked backward to the ancient prophecy that paradise would be found on the east coast of Africa; it looked forward, as prophecy in its own right, to societies that would in the future be based on the revolutionary ideals of liberty, equality, and fraternity. Those pirates who settled in Libertalia would be "vigilant Guardians of the People's Rights and Liberties"; they would stand as "Barriers against the Rich and Powerful" of their day. By waging war on behalf of "the Oppressed" against the "Oppressors," they would see that "Justice was equally distributed." Misson and his comrades had serious intentions.[2]

When it came to self-rule, Misson's pirates "look'd upon a Democratical Form, where the People themselves were the Makers and Judges of their own Laws, [as] the most agreeable." They sought to institutionalize their commitment to "a Life of Liberty," which they took for their natural right. They stood against monarchy, which was then dominant throughout Europe and much of the rest of the world, preferring to elect and rotate their leaders: "Power . . . should not be for Life, not hereditary, but determinate at the end of three Years." They limited the power of their principal leader, who was never to "think himself other than their Comrade" and was to use his power "for the publick Good only." They chose their council, their highest authority, "of the ablest among them, without Distinction of Nation or Colour."[3]

Misson's pirates were anticapitalist, opposed to the dispossession that necessarily accompanied the historic ascent of wage labor and capitalism. They insisted that "every Man was born free, and had as much Right to what would support him, as to the Air he respired." They resented the "encroachments" by which "Villains" and "unmerciful Creditors" grew "immensely rich" as others became "wretchedly miserable." They spoke of the "Natural right" to "a Share of the Earth as is necessary for our Support." They saw piracy as a war of self-preservation.[4]

Men who had been "ignorant of their Birth-Right, and the Sweets of Liberty" would recapture lost freedoms and guarantees of well-being in Libertalia, and they would do so by redefining fundamental relations of property and power. They had no need for money "where every Thing was in common, and no Hedge bounded any particular Man's Property," and they decreed that "the Treasure and Cattle they were Masters of should be equally divided." Formerly seamen, wage laborers, and perhaps even victims of dispossession themselves, these pirates would finally have "some Place to call their own," where "the Air was wholesome, the Soil fruitful, the Sea abounding with Fish," where they would enjoy "all the Necessaries of Life." "[W]hen Age or Wounds had render'd them incapable of Hardship," Libertalia would be a place "where they might enjoy the Fruits of their Labour, and go to their Graves in Peace."[5]

Concerns about "Birth-rights," "the Sweets of Liberty," and the "Fruits of Labor" were broad enough to sanction the abolition of slavery. Misson observed that "Trading for those of our own Species, cou'd never be agreeable to the Eyes of divine Justice: That no

Above: Portsmouth Point, *an engraving by Thomas Rowlandson in 1811. Dockside districts were notoriously rowdy, violent, and dangerous places, attracting a variety of malcontents and criminals, some of whom actually ended up serving onboard the vessels. This particular area of Portsmouth was well known for its taverns, prostitutes, and drunken seamen. Among the crowds in this picture are naval officers and seamen bidding farewell to their wives and sweethearts before boarding their ships anchored in the harbor.*

Man had power of Liberty of another." He "had not exempted his Neck from the Galling Yoak of Slavery, and asserted his own Liberty, to enslave others." Misson and his men thus took slaves from captured slave ships and incorporated them into their own social order as "Freemen." The result was literally a motley crew, half black and half white on some of their vessels, made up of African, Dutch, Portuguese, English, and French (Catholic *and* Huguenot) seamen. Misson "gave the Name of *Liberi* to his People, desiring in that might be drown'd the distinguish'd Names of French, English, Dutch, Africans, &c." Libertalia made room for many cultures, races, and nations.[6]

Misson and his men thus created a radical-democratic utopia that condemned dispossession, capitalist property relations, slavery, and nationalism, as it affirmed justice, democracy, liberty, and popular rights. Of course it was all a fiction, or so we have been told by scholars who have for many years insisted that the author of *A General History of the Pyrates* was in fact Daniel Defoe, who wrote under the pen name Captain Charles Johnson.[7] But was it a fiction? Since a man named Misson and a place named Libertalia apparently never existed, the literal answer must be yes. But in a deeper historical and political sense Misson and Libertalia were not just simply fictions. Christopher Hill has recently detected in Misson's utopia the lingering influence of the popular radicalism of the English Revolution. A group of pirates had, after all, settled at Madagascar in a place they had "given the name of Ranter Bay," named, it would seem, for the most radical of the Protestant sects of the English Revolution.[8]

This chapter carries Hill's argument further by suggesting that Libertalia was a literary expression of the living traditions, practices, and dreams of an Atlantic working

class, many of which were observed, synthesized, and translated into discourse by the author of *A General History of the Pyrates*. A mosaic assembled from the specific, almost utopian practices of the early eighteenth century pirate ship, Libertalia had objective bases in historical fact.[9] We can, by studying Libertalia and its actual historical sources, now comprehend the forces that shaped the common sailor's difficult life in the early eighteenth century, and we can explain why piracy was considered by many to be such an attractive alternative. In Libertalia and its antecedents we can see how common sailors imagined and in practice created a counterculture to the dominant ways of organizing maritime life and labor.

The Origins of Libertalia

The appearance of the maritime utopia of Libertalia in the early eighteenth century was unusual in the annals of piracy (though not, as suggested below, in the annals of the working class). It took a long time for seamen to get, as one man put it, "the choice in themselves"—that is, the autonomous power to organize the ship and its miniature society as they wanted.[10] Anglo-Atlantic piracy had long

served the needs of the state and the merchant community. But there was a long-term tendency for the control of piracy to devolve from the top of society to the bottom, from the highest functionaries of the state (late sixteenth century), to big merchants (early seventeenth century), to smaller, usually colonial merchants (late seventeenth century), and finally to the common men of the deep (early eighteenth century). When this devolution reached bottom, when seamen—as pirates—organized a social world apart from the dictates of mercantile and imperial authority and used it to attack merchants' property (as they had begun to do in the 1690s), then those who controlled the state resorted to massive violence, both military (the navy) and penal (the gallows), to eradicate piracy. Libertalia symbolized the process by which the maritime working class had seized control of piracy; its separatism was in many ways a response to the state's campaign of terror against this development.[11]

The sources of the pirate social order summarized in Libertalia were many and old, stretching from the traditional peasant utopia called "The Land of Cockaygne," where work had been abolished, property redistributed,

Below: Crime was no stranger to the dockside, whether it was the trading of illicit goods or more direct and violent sorts of exchange. This picture shows thieves attacking and robbing these genteel-looking passengers on a ferry.

social distinctions leveled, health restored, and food made abundant, to international custom of ancient and medieval maritime life, in which sailors had divided their money and goods into shares, consulted collectively and democratically on matters of moment, and elected "consuls" to adjudicate differences between captain and crew.[12] Even as piracy was of benefit to the upper classes of England, France, and the Netherlands in their New World struggles against their common enemy, Spain, common sailors were building their very own traditions, one of which was called the "Jamaica Discipline" or the "Law of the Privateers," the body of custom bequeathed by the buccaneers, a particular generation of pirates who haunted the Caribbean from roughly 1630 to 1680. This custom boasted a distinctive conception of justice and "a kind of class consciousness" against "the great"— shipmasters, shipowners, "gentlemen adventurers." It also featured democratic controls on authority and provision for the injured.[13]

The buccaneers were "the outcasts of all nations," drawn from the convicts, prostitutes, debtors, vagabonds, escaped slaves and indentured servants, religious radicals, and political prisoners who had migrated or been exiled to the Caribbean. According to one official, they were made up of "white servants and all men of unfortunate and desperate condition." Many French buccaneers, like Alexander Esquemelin (or Exquemeling), had been indentured servants (engagés) and before that, textile workers and day laborers. Most of the buccaneers were English or French, but Dutch, Irish, Scottish, Scandinavian, West Indian, and African men also joined up.[14]

The buccaneers had originated as a kind of multiracial maroon society based on hunting and gathering, formed by laborers free and unfree who had escaped the brutalities of a nascent plantation system. They hunted wild cattle and gathered the king of Spain's gold. They combined the diverse experiences of peasant rebels, demobilized soldiers, dispossessed small farmers, unemployed workers, and others from several nations and cultures, including the Carib and Cuna Indians.[15] One of the most potent memories and experiences that underlay the buccaneer culture, writes Christopher Hill, was the English Revolution: "A surprising number of English radicals emigrated to the West Indies either just before or just after 1660," including Ranters, Quakers, Familists, Anabaptists, radical soldiers, and others who "no doubt carried with them the ideas which had originated in revolutionary England." A number of buccaneers, we know, hunted and gathered while dressed in the "faded red coats of the New Model Army." In the New World they insisted upon the democratic election of their officers just as they had done in a revolutionary army on the other side of the Atlantic.[16]

According to the late J. S. Bromley, another source of buccaneering culture was a wave of peasant revolts that shook early seventeenth century France. Many French freebooters came, as engagés, "from areas affected by peasant risings against the royal fisc and the proliferating crown agents" in the 1630s. In these regions protesters "had shown a capacity for self-organization, the constitution of 'communes,' election of deputies and promulgation of Ordonnances," all in the name of the "Common people."[17] Such experiences, once carried to the Americas, informed the social code of the buccaneering "Brethren of the Coast." Evidence from the Old World and the New suggests that the pirates' social order in the early eighteenth century had many sources, some of them deeply rooted in past popular struggles from both sides of the Atlantic.

And yet the most immediate and powerful sources of that order lay closer at hand, in the experience of work, wages, culture, and authority accumulated in the normal, rugged course of maritime life and labor in the late seventeenth and early eighteenth centuries. The social world of the pirates cannot, in short, be comprehended apart from the social worlds of the merchant, naval, and privateering vessels in which the overwhelming majority of pirates had lived, often for many years. The preeminent source of Libertalia lay in the culture and experiences of the common seaman, to which we now turn.

The Sailor's Lot

The vast majority of the Atlantic's five thousand pirates came from merchant ships, joining as volunteers when their vessels were captured. The reasons why they joined are not difficult to discern. Dr. Samuel Johnson put the matter succinctly when he said, "no man will be a sailor who has contrivance enough to get himself into a jail; for being in

Below: Life Onboard a Ship at Sea, by Augustus Earle. Accurate depictions of the seaman's life below decks are rare, and this one gives a vivid impression of the scene in the midshipman's berth of a British frigate in the 1820s. Note a few exotic creatures depicted here, the products of a call ashore. Life onboard most merchant ships was much more cramped, with most of the space being occupied by cargo.

a ship is being in jail with the chance of being drowned . . . A man in jail has more room, better food, and commonly better company." Many sailors, of course, had made the comparison themselves, waking up punch drunk or just plain drunk in the jails of the port cities or in the holds of outward-bound merchant ships. Johnson's crucial point, however, was that the lot of merchant seamen in the early eighteenth century was a difficult one. Sailors suffered cramped, claustrophobic quarters, "food" that was often as rotten as it was meager, and worse.

They experienced, as a matter of course, devastating disease, disabling accidents, shipwreck, and premature death. They faced discipline from their officers that was brutal at best, and often murderous. And they got but small return for their death-defying labors, for peacetime wages were low and fraud in payment frequent. Seamen could expect little relief from the law, for its purpose on both sides of the eighteenth-century Atlantic was, according to Jesse Lemisch, "to assure a ready supply of cheap, docile labor." Merchant seamen also had to contend with

impressment as still practiced by the Royal Navy.[18]

In the navy, where many pirates had experience, shipboard conditions were equally harsh, if not in certain respects even worse. Wages, especially during wartime, were lower than in the merchant service, while the quantity and quality of food aboard the ship were consistently undermined by corrupt pursers and officers. Organizing cooperation and maintaining order among the often huge number of maritime workers on naval vessels required violent discipline, replete with intentionally spectacular executions, that was considerably more severe than on merchant ships. Another consequence of the numbers of sailors crowded onto ill-ventilated naval ships was the omnipresence of disease, often of epidemic proportions. In an irony that pirates would have savored, one official claimed that the navy could not effectively suppress piracy because its ships were "so much disabled by sickness, death, and desertion of their seamen." The naval ship in this era, concludes one scholar, was "a machine from which there was no escape, bar desertion, incapacitation, or death."[19]

Life was a little better on a privateering vessel: the food was better, the pay was higher, the work shifts shorter, the power of the crew in decision-making greater. But privateers were not always happy ships. Some captains ran their ships like naval vessels, imposing rigid discipline and other unpopular measures that occasionally generated grievances, protests, and even outright

Below: Manning the Navy, *by Collings. Here, a press gang led by a naval officer is rounding up men on Tower Hill near the port of London, before leading them off to become unwilling members of a ship's crew. The navy preferred fishermen and merchant seamen who could offer seafaring skills, but when short of manpower in time of war—a common state of affairs for long periods—the press gangs recruited any able-bodied men they could get their hands on.*

mutinies. Woodes Rogers, gentleman captain of a hugely successful privateering voyage in 1708, and later scourge of the pirates of the West Indies as royal governor of the Bahama Islands, clapped into irons a man named Peter Clark, who had wished himself "aboard a Pirate" and said that "he should be glad that an Enemy, who could over-power us, was a-long side of us."[20]

What would men like Peter Clark do once they got off a merchant, naval, or privateering vessel and "aboard a Pirate?" How would they organize their own sustenance? How would they organize their own labor, their access to money, to power? Had they internalized the dominant ideas of the age about how to run a ship? Or could these poor, uneducated men imagine better? Let us turn now to the actual experience of running a pirate ship as a means to understand the "fiction" called Libertalia.

The World Turned Upside-down

The early eighteenth century pirate ship, like Libertalia, was a "world turned upside down," made so by the articles of agreement that established the rules and customs of the pirates' social order. Pirates "distributed justice," elected their officers, divided their loot equally, and established a different discipline. They limited the authority of the captain, resisted many of the practices of capitalist merchant shipping, and maintained a multicultural, multiracial, multinational social order. They demonstrated quite clearly—and subversively—that ships did not have to be run in the brutal and oppressive ways of the merchant service and the Royal Navy.[21]

On the high seas, as in Libertalia—and in an age when political rights for working people were nearly unheard of—pirates elected their leaders democratically. They gave their captain unquestioned authority in chase and battle, but otherwise insisted that he be "governed by a Majority." As one observer noted, "They permit him to be Captain, on Condition, that they may be Captain over him."[22] They gave him few privileges: no extra food, no private mess, no special accommodation. Moreover, as the majority gave, so did it take away, deposing captains for cowardice, cruelty, refusing "to take and plunder English Vessels," or even for being "too Gentleman-like."[23] Captains

who dared to exceed their authority were sometimes executed. Most pirates, "having suffered formerly from the ill-treatment of their officers, provided carefully against any such evil" once free to organize the ship after their own hearts.[24] Further limitations on the captain's power appeared in the person of the quartermaster, who was elected to represent and protect "the interest of the Crew," and in the institution of the council, the democratic gathering that usually involved every man on the ship and always constituted its highest authority.[25]

The "equal division" of property in Libertalia had its basis in the pirates' shipboard distribution of plunder, which largely leveled the usual elaborate hierarchy of ranks and pay, and which dramatically reduced the gap between officers and common men. Captain and quartermaster received one and a half to two shares; minor officers and craftsmen, one and a quarter shares or one and a half; all others got one share each. Such egalitarianism flowed from crucial, material facts. By expropriating a merchant ship (after a mutiny or a capture), pirates seized the means of maritime production and declared

Above: *Alcohol was a widely berated social evil in times gone by and sailors in particular were well known for going ashore and spending all their money on a riotious orgy of drinking, womanizing, and gambling. Indeed, it was the prospect of more frequent bouts that lured many a man into piracy. In this engraving two drunken sailors have been put in irons under the watchful eye of a red-coated marine who will march them back to their ship as soon as they are sober enough to manage the journey.*

it to be the common property of those who did its work. They also abolished the wage relation central to the process of capitalist accumulation. So rather than work for wages using the tools and larger machine (the ship) owned by a merchant capitalist, pirates now commanded the ship as their own property, and shared equally in the risks of their common adventure.[26]

Pirates acted as "vigilant Guardians of the Peoples Rights and Liberties" and as "Barriers against the Rich and Powerful" when they took revenge against merchant captains who tyrannized the common seaman and against royal officials who upheld their bloody prerogative to do so. The comment about overseeing "the Distribution of Justice" in Libertalia referred to a specific practice among pirates known by the same name. After capturing a prize vessel, pirates "distributed justice" by inquiring about "the Commander's Behaviour to their Men." They "whipp'd and pickled" those "against whom Complaint was made."[27] Bartholomew Roberts's crew considered the matter so important that they formally designated one of their men—George Wilson, no doubt a fierce and lusty man—as the "Dispencer of Justice." Pirates "barbarously used" and occasionally executed some captured captains; a few even bragged of their avenging justice upon the gallows.[28] Pirate captain Howell Davis claimed that "their reasons for going a pirating were to revenge themselves on base Merchants and cruel commanders of Ships."[29] Still, pirates did not punish captains indiscriminately. They often rewarded the "honest Fellow that never abused any Sailors" and even offered to let one decent captain "return with a large sum of Money to London, and bid the Merchants defiance."[30] Pirates thus stood against the harsh injustices of the merchant shipping industry, one crew claiming to be "Robbin Hoods Men."[31]

Like their comrades in Libertalia, pirates reveled in their "Share of the Earth" that came in the form of food and drink, for these very items had, for many, figured crucially in the decision to "go upon the account" in the first place. A mutinous sailor aboard the *George Galley* in 1724 responded to his captain's orders to furl the mizzen-top by saying, "in a surly Tone, and with a kind of Disdain, 'So as we Eat so shall we work'." Other mutineers simply insisted that "it was not their business to starve," and that if a captain was making it so, hanging could be little worse.[32]

Many observers of pirate life noted the carnivalesque quality of their occasions—the eating, drinking, fiddling, dancing, and merriment—and some considered such "infinite Disorders" inimical to good discipline at sea.[33] Men who had suffered short or rotten provisions in other maritime employments now ate and drank "in a wanton and riotous Way," which was indeed their "Custom." They conducted so much business "over a Large Bowl of Punch" that sobriety sometimes brought "a Man under a suspicion of being in a Plot against the Commonwealth." The very first item in Bartholomew Roberts's articles guaranteed every man "a Vote in Affairs of Moment" and "equal Title" to "fresh provisions" and "strong Liquors." For some who joined, drink "had been a greater motive . . . than Gold." Most would have agreed with the motto: "No Adventures to be made without Belly-Timber."[34]

The real pirates of the Atlantic, like the settlers at Libertalia, struggled to assure their health and security, their own "self-preservation." The popular image of the freebooter as a man with a patched eye, a peg leg, and a hook for a hand is not wholly accurate, but still it speaks an essential truth: sailoring was dangerous work. Pirates therefore put a portion of all booty into a "common fund" to provide for those who sustained injuries of lasting effect, whether the loss of eyesight or any appendage. They tried to provide for those rendered "incapable of Hardship" by "Age or Wounds."[35]

Slavery

One of the most distinctive features of Misson's utopia was its attack on slavery. Did it have any basis in historical fact? The answer to this question—and indeed the entire record of relations between pirates and people of African descent—is ambiguous, even contradictory. A substantial minority of pirates had worked in the slave trade and had therefore been part of the machinery of enslavement and transportation. And when pirates took prize vessels, as they did near African and New World ports, slaves were sometimes part of the captured "cargo," and were in turn treated as such, traded or sold as commodities like any other. Pirates occasionally committed atrocities against the slaves they took.[36]

Below: So the Treasure Was Divided, *one of Howard Pyle's paintings for his article "The Fate of a Treasure-Town." Here, the unkempt, hungry-eyed pirates divide the spoils on a lonely island as the pirate chief watches over them and their booty. The treasure is laid out on a sailcloth they have placed on the sand.*

But it must also be noted that people of African descent figured prominently in pirate crews. A few of these men ended up "dancing to the four winds," like the mulatto who sailed with Black Bart Roberts and was hanged for it in Virginia in 1720.[37] Another "resolute Fellow, a Negroe" named Caesar, stood ready to blow up Blackbeard's ship rather than submit to the Royal Navy in 1718; he too was hanged. Black pirates also made up part of the pirates' vanguard, the most trusted and fearsome members of the crew designated to board all prospective prizes. The boarding party of the *Morning Star* had "a Negro Cook doubly arm'd"; more than half of Edward Condent's boarding party on the *Dragon* was black.[38]

These were not exceptional cases, for "Negroes and Molattoes" were present on almost every pirate ship, and only rarely did the many merchants and captains who commented on their presence call them "slaves."[39] Black pirates sailed with Captains Bellamy, Taylor, Williams, Harris, Winter,

Above: *Pirates very often took revenge on captains they considered to have been cruel, in much the same way as they took pleasure in torturing captives and enemies. This illustration is entitled* The Pirates Striking Off the Arm of Captain Babcock. *It refers to an incident that occurred after two English brigs en route from Bombay were intercepted by pirates and some of the crew took the opportunity to join the pirates, turn against their own captain, and inflict injury upon him.*

Shipton, Lyne, Skyrm, Roberts, Spriggs, Bonnet, Bellamy, Phillips, Baptist, Cooper, and others. In 1718, sixty of Blackbeard's crew of 100 were black, while Captain William Lewis boasted "40 able Negroe Sailors" among his crew of eighty. In 1719, Oliver la Bouche had a ship that was, like Misson's, "half French, half Negroes."[40] Black pirates were common enough—and considered nightmare enough —to move one newspaper to report that an all-mulatto band of sea robbers was marauding the Caribbean, eating the hearts of captured white men![41]

Some of the black pirates were free men, like the experienced "free Negro" seaman from Deptford who in 1721 led "a Mutiny that we had too many Officers, and that the work was too hard, and what not." Others were often escaped slaves. In 1716 the slaves of Antigua had grown "very impudent and insulting," causing their masters to fear an insurrection. Hugh Rankin writes that a substantial number of the unruly "went off to join those pirates who did not seem too concerned about color differences."[42] The "Negroes" captured with the rest of Black Bart's crew in 1722 grew mutinous over the

poor conditions and "thin Commons" they suffered at the hands of the Royal Navy, especially since "many of them" had "lived a long time" in the "pyratical Way." "The pyratical way" must have meant, to them as to others, more food and greater freedom.[43]

Such material and cultural contacts were not uncommon. A gang of pirates settled in West Africa in the early 1720s, joining and intermixing with the Kru, who were themselves known for their skill in things maritime (and also, when enslaved, for their leadership of revolts in the New World).[44] And of course pirates had for many years mixed with the native population of Madagascar, helping to produce "a dark Mulatto Race there."[45] Cultural exchanges among pirates, seamen, and Africans were extensive, resulting, for example, in the well-known similarities of form between African songs and sea shanties. In 1743 some seamen were court-martialed for singing a "negro song" in defiance of discipline.[46] There are also intriguing instances in which mutineers engaged in the same totemistic rites performed by slaves before a revolt. In 1731 a band of mutineers drank "rum and gunpowder," while on another occasion a sailor signaled his rebellious intentions by "Drinking Water out of a Musket barrel."[47] The direction of influence here is not clear, but influence itself seems likely.

Although little is known about black pirates, we may nonetheless conclude that if pirates did not self-consciously attack slavery as was done in Misson's utopia, neither did they adhere to the strict racial logic that governed a great many of the societies around the Atlantic. Some slaves and free blacks seem to have found relative freedom aboard the pirate ship, which was no easy thing to find in the pirates' main theater of operations, the Caribbean. The very existence of black pirates, contradictory though their lives probably were, may have moved the author of *A General History of the Pyrates* to imagine the critique of slavery that appeared in Libertalia.

A Motley Crew

Africans and African-Americans were but one part of a motley crew, in Libertalia and aboard most pirate ships. Governor Nicholas Lawes of Jamaica echoed the thoughts of royal officials everywhere when he called pirates "banditti of all nations." Black Sam Bellamy's crew was "a mix't multitude of all Country's," as were the principal mutineers aboard the *George Galley* in 1724: an Englishman, a Welshman, an Irishman, two Scots, two Swedes, and a Dane, all of whom became pirates. Benjamin Evans's crew consisted of men of English, French, Irish, Spanish, and African descent. Such mixing had its effects, as when pirate James Barrow sat at supper "prophanely singing . . . Spanish and French Songs out of a Dutch prayer book." When Barrow and his like hailed other vessels at sea, they emphasized their rejection of nationality by announcing that they came "From the Seas." And as a mutineer had muttered in 1699, "it signified nothing what part of the World a man liv'd in, so he Liv'd well."[48] Such was the separatist logic that led to the imaginative founding of Libertalia.

Two women named Anne Bonny and Mary Read, sword and pistol in hand, announced another utopian aspect of life beneath the Jolly Roger: the many freedoms of the pirates' life might be seized by women. Of course women were few aboard ships of any kind in the eighteenth century, but they were common enough to inspire ballads—about these cross-dressing "warrior women"—that proved extremely popular among the workers of the Atlantic world. Bonny and Read, whose exploits were announced on the cover page of *A General History of the Pyrates* and no doubt in many a wicked yarn in their own day and after, cursed and swore like any good sailor, carried their weapons like those well trained in the ways of war, and boarded prize vessels as only the most daring and well-respected members of the pirate crew were permitted to do. Operating beyond the reach of the traditional powers of family, state, and capital, and sharing in the rough solidarity of life among maritime outlaws, they added another dimension altogether to the subversive appeal of piracy by seizing the liberties usually reserved to men.[49]

The War Against Libertalia

The utopian features of the pirate ship were crucial to both the recruitment and replication of the pirate band, and eventually to its suppression, for both pirates and the English ruling class recognized the power of Libertalia and its alternative social order. Some worried that pirates might "set up a sort of Commonwealth" in areas where "no Power" would be "able to dispute it with them." Colonial and

Below: *A group of pirates, among them Gibbs and Wansley, burying their treasure on Barron Island. Charles Gibbs was born in Rhode Island and was notorious for piracy along the eastern seaboard and Caribbean. He was convicted of murder and piracy by a New York court in 1831 and hanged. The engraving is notable for its depiction of an African-American pirate, although ships' crews were quite international in nationality and race.*

metropolitan merchants and officials feared the incipient separatism of Libertalia in Madagascar, Sierra Leone, Bermuda, the Bay of Campeche, and even in other regions.[50] If Libertalia was a working-class dream, it was equally (and necessarily) a nightmare for the ruling class.

Colonel Benjamin Bennet wrote of pirates to the Council of Trade and Plantations in 1718: "I fear they will soon multiply for so many are willing to joyn with them when taken." Multiply they did: after the War of Spanish Succession, as working conditions in the merchant shipping industry rapidly deteriorated, seamen turned to the black flag by the thousands. Edward England's crew took nine vessels off the coast of Africa in the spring of 1719, and found fifty-five of the 143 seamen ready to sign their articles. Such desertion to floating Libertalias was common between roughly 1716 and 1722, when, as one pirate told a merchant captain, "People were generally glad of an opportunity of entring with them."[51] It is not hard to understand why. The prospect of plunder and "ready money," the food and the drink, the camaraderie, the democracy, equality, and justice, the promise of care for the injured—all of these must have been appealing. A pirate's life, as Bartholomew Roberts explained, was short but merry.

The English ruling class was less than keen about the merriment, but more than happy to oblige in making the lives of pirates short ones. Not so long ago such rulers had set pirates loose on the riches of other realms, but now they and their former national enemies discovered common interests in an orderly Atlantic system of capitalism, around and through which trade would flow and capital accumulate without attack and disruption. The thousands of pirates who haunted the sea-lanes of the Atlantic had made a great deal of "Noise in the World"—they had ignored nationalism by attacking English vessels and they had done deep damage to world shipping. English rulers, Whig and Tory alike, responded by drawing upon and continuing the reforms of the 1690s, hanging sea robbers by the hundreds. Merchants petitioned Parliament, whose members obliged with deadly new legislation; meanwhile, Prime Minister Robert Walpole took an active, personal interest in putting an end to piracy, as did scores of officials, newspaper correspondents, and clergymen who wrote reports, articles, and sermons all about the bloodthirsty monsters and vicious beasts who attacked property by sea. Their violent rhetoric demanded and legitimated the use of the gallows. Although many historians have claimed that the hangman was not

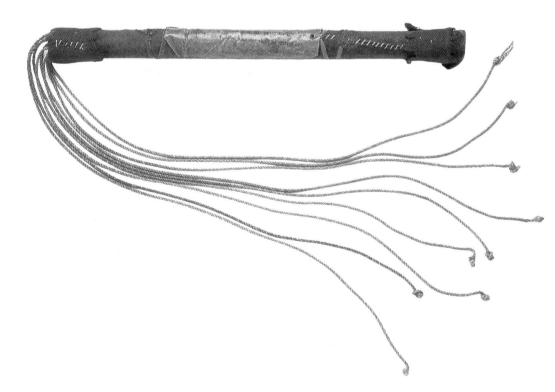

Left: *The cat-o'-nine tails was used to give a flogging, the most common form of punishment on Royal Navy ships until the practice was suspended in 1879. The cat was a whip with nine lengths of cord with a knot at the end of each. It could inflict awful injuries. Each time, the sailor to be whipped made the cat. He did so by unwinding a rope into its three strands; then he unwound each strand to make three further strands, which he knotted. Naval regulations laid down that no more than twelve lashes be given without a court-martial, but this rule was flouted by many captains and helped feed grievances held by crews.*

nearly as busy as he might have been in this age of rapidly expanding capital punishments, the point cannot be proved by pirates. They—and their dreams of Libertalia—were clearly marked for extinction.[52]

Libertalia Lives

And yet the dream proved resilient. The traditions expressed in Libertalia sometimes lived on because a few hearty souls survived the odds against longevity in seafaring work. Some of these old buccaneers themselves served on Jamaican privateers during the War of Spanish Succession, then took part in the new piracies in peacetime. The "Jamaica Discipline" and the exploits it made possible also lived on in folktale, song, ballad, and popular memory, not to mention the popular published (and frequently translated) accounts of Alexander Esquemelin, Père Labat, and others.[53]

Another kind of resiliency appeared in the mutiny aboard HMS *Chesterfield* in October,

1748, off the west coast of Africa, not far from Cape Coast Castle. One of the ringleaders of the mutiny, John Place, had been there before. He had sailed with the pirate Bartholomew Roberts and had been captured off Cape Coast Castle by Captain Chaloner Ogle in HMS *Swallow* in 1722. When the time came, a quarter of a century later, for the know-how of mutiny and an alternative social order, Place was the man of the moment, the one to help the mutineers do as Misson had done, "to settle a colony." Place embodied a tenacious tradition that had lived in tales, in action, in sullenly silent memory, on the lower deck of the *Chesterfield* and, no doubt, countless other vessels. He was obviously a patient man, but still victory would not be his. The authorities hanged Place, but they could not hang the subversive idea of Libertalia for which he was an abiding vessel.[54]

During the American Revolution, many thousands of captured American seamen were charged as "pirates" and "traitors" and

Above: *A flogging about to be carried out onboard a British man-o'-war, engraved by George Cruickshank in 1825. All hands are turned out to witness the exemplary flogging of the seaman who has been tied to one of the gratings. The guard of royal marines stand to attention above him, and on the left can be seen the officers and midshipmen. Entitled* Point of Honour, *the real offender is stepping forward to save his shipmate from unjust punishment.*

Left: *Until the reforms of the penal code in the nineteenth century, punishment of even the most minor offenses was extremely harsh on both sides of the Atlantic. Hangings were public spectacles and the execution of famous criminals invariably attracted huge crowds. This picture, by Howard Pyle, shows a condemned man being drawn in a cart to the gallows at Tyburn in London, the site now occupied by Marble Arch, a place for executions from 1300 until 1783.*

herded into British prisons and prison ships, where they quickly organized themselves in the ways of Libertalia. According to Jesse Lemisch, these seamen, now autonomous because their officers had asked for separate quarters, "governed themselves in accord with abstract notions of liberty, justice, and right" and created a social world characterized by "egalitarianism," "collectivism," and commitment to revolutionary ideals. What had functioned as "articles" among seamen and pirates now became a constitution of sorts, "a Code of By-Laws . . . for their own regulation and government." As always they used democratic practices, worked "to assure the equitable distribution of food and clothing," concerned themselves with questions of health, and established their own discipline. A captain who looked back with surprise on the Libertalia that had developed, oddly enough, within the walls of the prison remarked that seamen were "of that class . . . who are not easily controlled, and usually not the most ardent supporters of good order." What he and others like him failed to understand was that seamen had no trouble supporting an "order" of their own making.[55]

The same order appeared in a maritime utopia conceived and discussed by the English radical Thomas Spence. Spence's brave new world had its origins in a dying man's gift of a ship to his sons. It was, the man specified, to be "COMMON PROPERTY. You all will be EQUAL OWNERS, and shall share the profits of every voyage equally among you." Like pirates before him, the man insisted that the division of resources should heed no office. His injunctions were drawn up as a constitution (much like the pirates' articles), his plan soon implemented. But the marine republicans grew weary of the larger, oppressive government in their own land and they decided to "set sail for America, where they expected to see government administered more agreeably to their notions of equality and equity." When their ship was wrecked on an uninhabited island, they used their principles to establish the Republic of Spensonia, which according to A. L. Morton, "looks backward to the medieval commune and forward to the withering away of the state."[56]

Libertalia appeared in another, more material form only a few years later, in the world-shaking mutinies of English (and Irish and African and other) sailors at Spithead and the Nore in 1797. Sailors had been restless and more than normally mutinous since the American Revolution, and finally matters exploded. In 1797 they removed bad officers, elected their own delegates and set up their own "council," imposed their own discipline, and established their own "shipboard democracy." They also made demands for food, health, and liberty (the last of which, after all, had a special meaning for seamen). They drew on the radical practices of America's revolutionary seamen and some even spoke of some day settling a "New Colony," perhaps in America, perhaps even in Madagascar.[57]

The dream of Libertalia lived on, but only because common sailors-turned-pirates had risked the gallows in order to imagine and build a better world than those they had found on the merchant, naval, and privateering ships of the early modern Atlantic. They had transformed inflexibly harsh discipline into a looser, more libertarian way of running a ship that depended on "what Punishment the Captain and Majority of the Company shall think fit." They had transformed the realities of chronically meager rations into riotous (though not necessarily regular) feasting, an exploitative wage relation into collective risk-bearing, and injury and premature death into active care for health and security. Their democratic selection of officers had stood in stark, telling contrast to the near-dictatorial arrangement of command in the merchant service and Royal Navy. The pirates' social order had realized tendencies that had been dialectically generated and in turn suppressed in the course of work and life at sea. Many of the pirates themselves may have died upon the gallows, defeated, but Libertalia had many victories yet to claim.

Below: Mutiny, *by Howard Pyle. The captain is facing it off as events hang in the balance while discontent is aired. Mutiny onboard Royal Navy ships was comparatively rare, possibly because when it did take place the authorities acted very swiftly and the ringleaders, if caught, were invariably hanged. A ship was sent halfway around the world to track down the* Bounty *mutineers, three of whom were subsequently hanged at Spithead.*

CHAPTER SEVEN

THE
PIRATE ROUND

~

You must know that I am captain of this ship now, and this is my cabin, therefore you must walk out. I am bound to Madagascar, with the design of making my own fortune, and that of all the brave fellows joined with me.

THOMAS TEW[1]

DURING THE years when European pirates were poaching gold and silver on Spain's New World preserve, ships on the other side of the globe were transporting even more tempting cargoes. They were Mogul and Arab treasure ships plying ancient trade routes in the Indian Ocean. Many were pilgrim ships ferrying the faithful and their offerings, as well as merchants, from India to the Red Sea ports leading to Mecca.

From the early sixteenth century there were the East Indiamen of the Portuguese, and later those of England, Holland, and France, carrying the wealth of the East Indies, India, and the Orient. The most opulent cargoes of all were carried by the Great Mogul's fleet belonging to the ruler of India. The Mogul trading ships were laden with gold, silver, precious gems, pearls, spices, damasks, and silks—treasures with no equal in Christendom.

In contrast, in the closing decades of the seventeenth century, the pirates based in the Caribbean found the harvest leaner with each passing year. For almost two centuries sea rovers had "plucked the golden apples" from the king of Spain's New World orchard at will, plundering shipping, raiding coastal settlements, and ransoming towns throughout the West Indies and all around the Spanish Main. By the 1680s the king's formidably armed plate fleets sailed at infrequent intervals, and the settlements that had formerly yielded so much treasure were all but impregnable.

As England's agricultural colonies prospered, they began to export produce to the motherland so that most of the vessels in New World waters carried agricultural products, salt fish, cloth, sugar, timber, and other staples. Many sea robbers, for whom piracy was an occupation of last resort, were content to rifle such prosaic cargoes. But the price of capture remained high since penal codes did not recognize degrees of wickedness. In 1692, the same year that Port Royal disappeared beneath the waters, a Caribbean pirate was sentenced to hang for taking five hundred salted fish, forty bushels of corn, and four hundred pieces of eight—a typical inter-island cargo that an old buccaneer would have sneered at.

New Opportunities

At the turn of the century the routes between India and the Red Sea carried far more valuable shipping than the atrophying treasure lanes between the New World and Europe. Ambitious sea outlaws began to leave for the East on what became known as the Pirate Round: a route that, for some thirty years beginning in 1690, linked ports in the Caribbean and the North American colonies with Madagascar. Daring souls who would rather hang for a sheep than a lamb set sail for the Indian Ocean and Red Sea, a dazzling new El Dorado. Many of them were ex-buccaneers. The Round, in its first phase, lasted scarcely more than a decade, but what a decade it was. A wind-driven brotherhood of pirates roamed the globe taking from the very rich and selling smuggled cargoes of luxury goods to the Anglo-American colonists, who were hungering for contraband following passage of the protectionist Navigation Acts, which caused great hardship in the colonies.

At a time when Anglo-American seamen on a trading voyage to Madagascar were collecting less than twelve pounds sterling a year and a first mate would earn three pounds ten shillings as well as a slave,[2] the deep-water pirates could realize a hundred or even a thousand times more, if

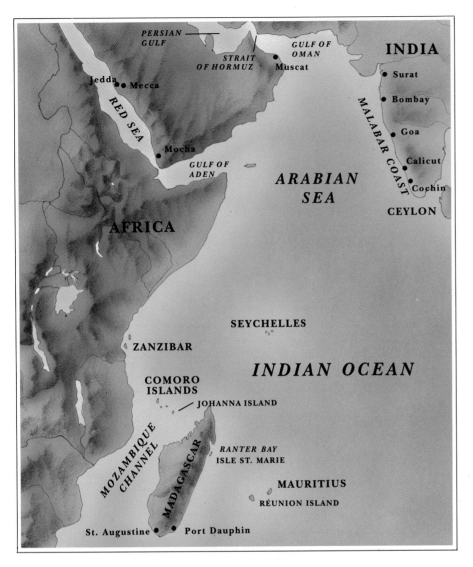

those with the most experience in long-range navigation and deep-water pirating. The typical plate ship was Anglo-American or English built with a short hull and tall masts, compared to the large hull and shorter masts of Spanish vessels.

It was a long, dangerous voyage but the stakes were incredibly high. A pirate could make more at one stroke than a leading English financier or a great landowner earned in two or three years. Not all did, of course, but many expeditions netted their

Above: *A map of the Indian Ocean region showing the islands and harbors visited by the men of the Pirate Round who made Madagascar the principal base for their raids on merchant shipping. The trading routes in this area—as in the Mediterranean—were ancient ones and there were indigenous pirates of longstanding, particularly in the Arabian Gulf and along the Malabar Coast of India. However, from the sixteenth century onward the opening up of trade routes to the East and the transportation of its exotic riches attracted pirates from further afield—men, furthermore, who had a willing market for such produce in the growing colonies of the Americas.*

they were lucky, and if they survived the battles, scurvy, and tropical fevers that decimated so many ships' crews.

Notorious names like Black Bart Roberts, Long Ben Avery, Thomas Tew, and Captain Kidd were among those who pirated not only Arab and Mogul vessels sailing between India's Malabar Coast and the Red Sea ports of Mocha and Jedda, but also richly laden East Indiamen and even ships coming from the west coast of Africa carrying slaves, gold dust, and ivory. They enjoyed the encouragement of North American colonists and developed pirate havens on Madagascar, Mauritius, and the Isle de Bourbon (Réunion).

High Stakes

Adventurers begged to sign on the tall ships in such numbers that the commanders could pick and choose the most "seaworthy artists," members as much as £2,000, while at one astounding share-out each pirate received some £4,000 worth of loot.

In 1688 two of the first Roundsmen, John Ireland and Thomas Hickman, old West Indies hands, went to the gallows for pirating two ships in the Indian Ocean. After taking a richly laden Muslim ship near Ceylon, they had plundered and sunk her, forcing the English captain to serve as pilot of their ship, the *Charming Mary*. Two weeks later, the pirates took a Portuguese prize that carried

fourteen bales of silk "richly flowered with gold" worth £6,000, sixty-four pounds (29kg) of "China gold all in Lumps and divers other Goods to a great Value." The description of their plunder indicates why the Eastern seas became a pirate lodestone.

Native Pirates

Indian Ocean trade routes are among the oldest in the world, and throughout history, wherever there have been ships laden with valuable cargoes, there have been sea rob-

Below: The Return of the Dutch East India Fleet, *by Andries van Eertvelt. This was the scene in Amsterdam when the inhabitants turned out to welcome home one of the first trading expeditions to return from the Far East in the early seventeenth century. The company was founded in 1602 to protect Dutch trade in the Indian Ocean and it prospered throughout the century as their monopolistic commercial empire in the region.*

Below: *The Great Mogul of India receiving Sir John Mildenhall in 1599. At this time rival European powers controlled the East India trade and thus the price of valuable spices. At the behest of a group of London merchants who formed an association in order to trade directly with India, Queen Elizabeth I sent a delegation led by Mildenhall to negotiate with the Great Mogul in an attempt to try and obtain privileges for the venture. The result was the establishment by royal charter of the East India Company on December 31, 1600.*

bers; so piracy was nothing new when the Roundsmen began their forays.[3] Pirates menaced voyagers in the Arabian Gulf as early as 1600 B.C. and the ancient Persians maintained an antipirate blockade at the mouth of the Tigris until the time of Alexander the Great. Pirates operating from many inconspicuous landing places along the Arabian coast harassed ancient shipping lanes in the Red Sea to such a degree that the Romans established marine patrols with archers aboard to counter them. And in the second century A.D. the Greek geographer Ptolemy wrote of the "Pirate Coast," referring to the west coast of India. In 1290 Marco Polo described the hazards of sailing along India's west coast, where pirates positioned block-

ades of up to 100 ships to trap richly laden vessels, often forcing captive merchants to drink a strong purgative so that not one pearl or gem eluded them.

The Angrian Pirates

Piracy was thus already well organized when the British East India Company established its first trading post in India at Surat in 1612. For over a century the company's ships were plagued by pirates, particularly the fierce Angrian pirates based along the coast south of Bombay, where the company set up a base in 1662.[4] The Angrians employed a number of European captains, just as the Barbary pirates, also Muslims, welcomed Christians among their ranks as long as they were committed to the enterprise. They sailed primarily in shallow draft, light, two-masted ships that the Europeans called grabs, from the Arabic *ghorab* for "raven." Typically several grabs worked together, darting out from protected inlets at night when they could move silently on the lightest of breezes. In 1707 brazen Angrian pirates managed to blow up the British East India Company's antipirate frigate, which had been put on station to curb native pirates and the Roundsmen.

The Great Mogul's Treasure

The Pirate Round prospered because of two important factors: the growing vulnerability of the Great Mogul's fleets and the insatiable appetite of English colonies for contraband goods. The Mogul dynasty, which had ruled uninterrupted since 1526, brought India to a zenith of unity and prosperity. A French jeweler and trader who visited the opulent court of Aurangzeb, the sixth Mogul emperor, described his richly canopied Peacock Throne. Worth £6,000,000, it was a magnificent golden affair ornately encrusted with precious stones and pearls.

The jeweler marveled at the annual tribute in "diamonds, rubies, emeralds, richly colored brocades intertwined with threads of gold and silver, and other stuffs" presented by the Mogul's subjects. They gave unwillingly, for he was a very brutal tyrant and India's Hindu majority, and even faithful Muslims, loathed his harsh rule and onerous taxes. Years of Hindu uprisings and perennial attacks from the Maratha pirates had weakened his fleets and disrupted his shipments, making it possible for the Roundsmen to prey on them.

The Navigation Acts

On the other side of the world, the pirates who returned from the Indian Ocean were each "received and caressed" in the North American colonies, much to England's fury. The mother country's cavalier attitude, which led eventually to the American Revolution, was responsible for the colonies' tolerance of the pirates. The chief goad was the series of Navigation Acts that England enacted, despite Spain's ruinous example, to exclude all nations but England from trading with the English colonies.

Smarting under a system that fixed low prices for their exports and artificially high prices for imports, and levied excessive taxes and duties, the northern colonies depended on trade for their prosperity and thus were ripe for traffic with the Roundsmen. They wooed the pirates, welcoming their infusion of cash and contraband estimated to be worth £1,000,000 a year; £100,000 poured annually into the economy of New York alone, and Arab and Mogul gold coins were common currency.

Piracy, Inc.

Colonial officials and merchants were happy to finance voyages of the "plate ships" (as they were called) for the gold and silver they brought back. The Roundsmen, or Red Sea Men, were happy too because even after settling with their backers, the returns were higher than at any time since Drake or the heyday of the Brethren of the Coast.

Pirates on the Round fitted out at Boston, New York, Philadelphia, and (to a lesser degree) in ports of the middle colonies of New Jersey, Delaware, and Maryland. The "chief refuge for pyrates" for half a century was Rhode Island, which served as a clearing-house for Eastern treasure. England seemed unable to curb them. A Royal Customs agent in Pennsylvania complained, "All the persons I have employed in searching for and apprehending these pirates, are abused and affronted, and called enemies of the country, for disturbing and hindering honest men, as they were pleased to call the pirates, from bringing their money and settling among them."[5] Pirates were routinely acquitted if brought to trial. In fact, one man who ingenuously pleaded guilty to piracy was acquitted by a jury that couldn't imagine anyone doing such a thing.

Above: *A view of Surat from the sea with shipping at anchor in the roadstead. Conquered by the Moguls in 1573, Surat became an important commercial center for the export of cloth and gold and in 1612 was chosen by the British for their first trading post in India.*

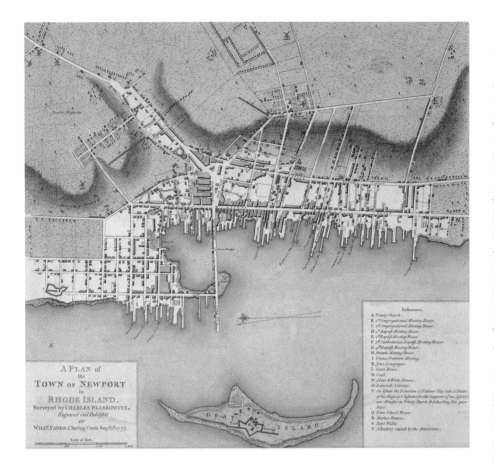

Above: *A plan of the town of Newport, Rhode Island. The fine harbor was used as a base by several pirates, notably Thomas Tew, and many more privateers. Many of the town's merchants were prepared to invest in pirate activities in the Indian Ocean, and several families became rich on the proceeds. In 1696 New England's surveyor-general of customs described Rhode Island as "the chief refuge for pirates."*

Partners in Piracy

Prominent colonists openly bankrolled pirate ventures. They found agents and brokers too in places like St. Croix island (then Santa Cruz, in the Danish West Indies) and the Bahamas, where Governor Trott was an intimate friend of pirates. Indeed, very few people in the colonies were unsympathetic to the pirates. Colonial officials consorted with known pirates, inviting them to dine and accepting lavish gifts in exchange for their protection. Men who had made fortunes pirating moved in the best circles, and Governor Markham of Pennsylvania wed his daughter to a pirate and helped him take a seat in the assembly.

Pirates were invited to Massachusetts by Governor Sir William Phips. Phips was a former adventurer, a sloop captain who had convinced King Charles II to fund his successful search for a Spanish treasure galleon that had wrecked on Silver Shoals off the north coast of Hispaniola in 1641. After the find in 1697, King James II got £20,000 as his royal share and Phips received a knighthood, £16,000, and eventually the governorship of the huge Massachusetts Bay Colony (that today forms the New England region), a position that allowed him to increase his wealth through pirate brokering.[6]

"A Parcel of Pyrates"

"We have a parcel of pyrates called the Red Sea Men in these parts," a New Yorker named Peter de la Noy wrote in 1695, "who get a great booty of Arabian gold. The Governor encourages them because they make due acknowledgements." Benjamin Fletcher (to whom de la Noy was referring) protected pirates, letting ships land for an "offering" of £700 collected by his agent. He openly accepted bribes and sold commissions through Mr. Nicoll, his secretary. The governor's wife and daughters wore dresses of India silk and gem-studded Mogul jewelry received from pirates such as the notorious Captain Tew, who was invited to dine often at the governor's table.

The city's civic leaders and businessmen financed voyages, furnished vessels, and supplied gunpowder, spirits, and other stores. Respectable merchants set up clearinghouses for pirated merchandise which sold, tax free, at bargain prices. Pirate brokering was the foundation of several great fortunes, including that of the New York Philipse family. Frederick Philipse, a colonel in the New York militia and a New York City councilor for twenty years, and his son Adolph, had a fleet that sailed regularly to Madagascar laden with manufactures, spirits, gunpowder, flour, and other stores that they sold at premium prices. Their ships brought back pirated booty and slaves. Robert Livingston, also a New York militiaman and a manor lord, was widely known for financing Red Sea ventures.

Captain Johnson's *History*

Just as the exploits of many of the "Brethren of the Coast" were immortalized by Esquemelin in his work *The Buccaneers of America*, the bloody and generally brief careers of many early eighteenth century pirates were chronicled by Captain Charles Johnson in *A General History of the Most Notorious Pirates*, first published in London in 1724, which became an international best-seller. Expanded in subsequent editions, the book remains a most valuable resource, furnishing a wealth of intimate details and information based on contemporary accounts, Admiralty trials, and gallows confessions, with a liberal sprinkling of the writer's own thoughts on the subject and lively passages of pirate speech as it might have been.

Tew: A Privateer Turns Roundsman

Thanks in large part to Johnson[7] we can see how the spectacular success of Rhode Island's Thomas Tew sparked the sea fever of the Round. Until "a shot carried away the rim of Tew's belly" and he died after holding "his Bowels with his Hands some small space," he was living proof of how a mariner of modest background could catapult to international fame and fortune.

In late 1692 Tew sailed aboard the *Amity* with a commission from the governor of Bermuda. The *Amity* was owned by a syndicate of Bermuda merchants and officials from whom Tew bought a share and the right to crew it with sixty seasoned privateers. Their mission was to assist the British Royal Africa Company to take a French trading post on the Guinea Coast. However, no sooner were they at sea than Tew called all men on deck and expressed an opinion that his fellow seamen shared:

> He thought it a very injudicious expedition which, did they succeed in, would be of no use to the public, and only advantage a private company of men, from whom they could expect no reward of their bravery; that he could see nothing but danger in the undertaking, without the least prospect of booty; that he could not suppose any man fond of fighting for fighting's sake, and few ventured their lives but with some view either of particular interest or public good, but here was not the least appearance of either. Wherefore, he was of opinion that they should turn their thoughts on what might better their circumstances. . . .[8]

Captain Johnson relates that "Tew proposed launching a course that should lead them to Ease and Plenty, in which they might pass the rest of their Days. That one bold Push would do their Business, and then might return home, not only without Danger, but even with Reputation." To a man the crew vowed: "A gold chain or a wooden leg, we'll stand by you."[9]

Tew Captures the Mogul's Flagship

With that the *Amity* headed around the Cape of Good Hope and into the Red Sea. In July 1693 after months of cruising they happened on the flagship of the Great Mogul's treasure fleet outward bound from Surat in India to Jedda in Arabia. Her three hundred man crew surrendered without a fight, "every one taking more care to run from the danger than to exert himself in the defense of the goods." They gave up £100,000 worth of gold and silver, coffers of gems, pearls, a king's ransom in "elephants teeth" (ivory), spices, bales of silk fabric, and a great quantity of gunpowder.

Tew proposed hunting down the other ships of the fleet, but at the urging of the quartermaster (a position of authority equal to that of the captain on most pirate voyages) he quit while he was ahead and made for

Below: *One family which founded a great fortune on the Pirate Round trade was the Philipses of New York. A respectable, established family, they had a family fleet which sailed regularly to Madagascar to trade goods at massive profit margins and return with pirate booty and slaves. This letter is from a ledger recording the family's transactions with pirates of St. Mary's, Madagascar, in the 1690s, and held today at the Public Record Office, London. The letter cautions the captain to be careful on his voyage.*

Left: *The nature of the Pirate Round was such that the profits to be had and the luxury goods to be obtained exercised a corruptive influence on officials and politicians. Governor Fletcher of New York (on the right in this illustration of him talking with Tew) openly entertained Thomas Tew in spite of the fact he had referred to him explicitly as a pirate, a man who had risen from modest means to fame and fortune as a result of the seizure of one of the Great Mogul's richly laden ships en route to India. As he had acquired his wealth, so Tew also lost his life attempting to repeat the feat.*

Madagascar, the Roundsmen's chief base. There he careened the *Amity* and shared out the plunder. Each pirate received one share worth £1,200 (some reports say £3,000). Tew received two shares and the quartermaster and surgeon a share and a half each. Twenty-six of the crew remained there, but the rest of the pirates accompanied Tew to Newport, Rhode Island, where all but a few pulpit-pounding clergymen hailed Tew as a triumphant hero. After all, the ship he had plundered belonged to "heathen Moors."

The merchants of Boston descended in droves to buy up the booty. Tew was fussed over by Newport society and invited to New York by Governor Fletcher. To complaints that he had received a known pirate and been seen riding in public and dining with him, the governor wrote to the Lords of Trade saying that he found him a most engaging man and that "at some times when the labours of my day were over it was some divertissement as well as information to me, to hear him talk."

Avery: the "Arch Pirate"
Tew enjoyed life in Newport for a while but in November 1694 he set out again. By that time scores of expeditions had sailed for the Red Sea in his wake. Within a year Tew was mortally wounded in an attack on one of the Great Mogul's treasure ships. On this last expedition he joined forces with Avery, the "Arch Pirate," who more than any other of the early Roundsmen excited the public's imagination.[10]

Avery, the son of a Plymouth innkeeper (or, as some sources state, of a prosperous ship-owning family with ties to the Jamaica trade), was the Arch Pirate. He was called "Long Ben" by his associates and widely known as John Avery, but he signed himself Henry Avery and that is his name as recorded in the Calendar of State Papers. Much of his life is sketchy. Following service in the navy and merchant marine, he seems to have been successively the captain of a logwood freighter plying the Bay of Campeche and an un-licensed slaver. An officer in the Royal Africa Company reported in 1693 that owing to the "kidnapping tricks of Long Ben, alias Every, and others of his kidney . . . who had seized them off without any payment," he had "never found the Negroes so shy and scarce." He also sailed with "Red Hand" Nicholls in the West Indies in the early 1690s.

Avery was under the protection of Cadwallader Jones, governor of the Bahamas, of whom it was said that "he highly caressed those Pirates that came" and "gave Commissions to pirates without and contrary to the advice of the Council." Jones had been over-thrown and imprisoned by the council at one point, but in February 1692 he was rescued from prison and restored to power by "some desperate Rogues, Pirates and others . . . a seditious rabble."

Long Ben's *Fancy*
All this led up to the exploits that were to make Long Ben the pirates' pirate, the best-known and most imitated of them all in his time, and the subject of spirited conversation from the drawing rooms of London to the brothels of every colony. In 1694 Avery was sailing master aboard the *Charles II*, a Bristol privateer hired by Spain to attack French smugglers based on Martinique who were trading with Spanish colonies. En route to the Caribbean the ship stopped at La Coruña for provisions, freight, and passengers. The crew hadn't been paid for eight months and soon after leaving port they mutinied and elected Avery captain. The ship, rechristened the *Fancy* (a name favored by pirates), then set a course for the Indian Ocean. At Johanna Island, off the Comoro Islands northwest of Madagascar, Avery seized a French pirate vessel jammed with plundered Moorish treasure and signed on most of her crew.

In early 1695, before leaving the island of Johanna, Avery or Every wrote a letter addressed to all English commanders, which eventually reached London. It read in part:

I was riding here in the *Fancy*, man-of-war, formerly the *Charles* of the Spanish Expedition . . . being then and now a ship of 46 guns, 150 men, and bound to seek our fortunes. I have never yet wronged any English or Dutch, nor ever intend whilst I am commander. . . . If you or any whom you may inform are desirous to know what we are at a distance, then make your ancient [ensign] up in a ball or bundle and hoist him at the mizen peak, the mizen being furled. I shall answer with the same, and never molest you, but my men are hungry, stout, and resolute, and should they exceed my desire I cannot help myself. . . . As yet an Englishman's friend. . . . Henry Every.[11]

Below: *Households in the ports of the eastern seaboard—Boston, Newport, Salem, and suchlike—were very often graced with fine objects brought back from the East by captains and crews, in addition to those furnished by the pirates' activities. Lacquerware, silk, fans, and ivory carvings were among the most favored items. This exquisite ivory chess figure was carved in China for export and has been dyed red.*

Above: *Alongside Tew, Henry Avery (or Every) was also a highly successful Roundsman, so much so that he was called the "Arch Pirate." His claim to fame, not to mention riches, was the capture of two of the Mogul's treasure ships (Tew actually apprehended the smaller of the two but was killed in the process). The incident had international repercussions because of the rage with which the Mogul greeted the news and the effect that had on legitimate trading by Western companies. This engraving shows Avery with the Mogul's ship,* Ganj-i-Sawai, *being seized in the background.*

"Exceeding Treasure"

Avery left Johanna with two Roundsmen he had encountered there, bound for the Red Sea entrance nearby the Arabian port of Mocha. While waiting to intercept the Mocha fleet the three vessels met up with Captain Tew, who joined them. Soon a former mate of Tew's, Captain Want, sailing a Spanish prize, and three other Rhode Island pirate vessels joined them to form a formidable fleet under Avery's command. Somehow in the night the pirates missed all but the last two vessels of the Mocha fleet as it passed by en route to Surat. They attacked these stragglers, Tew's *Amity* taking on the first *Fateh Mohamed*, the smaller of the two, which both belonged to the wealthiest merchant of Surat. During the short engagement Tew was felled by "a great shot."

The Roundsmen captured the *Fateh Mohamed* and discovered it was crammed with some £40,000 in gold and silver. Racing ahead, the *Fancy* caught up with and captured the *Ganj-i-Sawai*, a much larger vessel owned by the Great Mogul himself. Its name means "Exceeding Treasure" and the treasures it yielded truly surpassed anything yet seen. The ship, with eighty guns and four hundred soldiers all armed with matchlock rifles, was transporting a number of high-ranking Muslims, including many ladies,

home from the pilgrimage to Mecca. The pirates behaved abominably toward the passengers, particularly the women, many of whom killed themselves.

The Share-out

When they reached Réunion Island, a pirate base east of Madagascar, they had a breathtaking array of swag to divide; one of piracy's greatest hauls. It included more than five hundred thousand gold and silver coins, chests and chests of jewels, and a gold-trimmed saddle and bridle set with rubies, being sent as a present for the great Mogul. Each of the four hundred pirates who had participated got a share of £1,000 plus some gems. A number of youngsters under eighteen received £500 each (the amount a merchant seaman might make in his whole career), and a few boys under the age of fourteen were given £100 to be used "to apprentice themselves to an honest trade ashore." The four subordinate captains took a share and a half and Avery took the customary two shares for the commander, but it was felt he had cheated his associates and held back more from them.

The Mogul was enraged and did nothing to quell riots in Surat and Agra, during which one Englishman was stoned to death. Sixty-eight East India Company officials in Surat were imprisoned for almost a year until the company made good the loss. Meanwhile Avery's fleet split up, with ships heading for Madagascar, the Persian Gulf, and Ethiopia. Fifty of the *Fancy's* crew elected to settle on Réunion.

Across the Atlantic

Crossing the Atlantic, Avery made landfall at St. Thomas in the Virgin Islands, oblivious of the price on his head: £500 from the British government matched by £500 from the East India Company. Many merchants in St. Thomas filled their stores with the sumptuous Indian fabrics, jewels, and other pirated luxuries. The Caribbean was becoming an international emporium.

Governor Jones was no longer in the Bahamas; however, his replacement, Governor Trott, was equally a protector of pirates and welcomed Avery, who offered homage in the form of £7,000 worth of goods, some ivory, and two thousand pieces of eight. Trott expressed regret at being unable to issue the pardon Avery expected. Avery then sent a letter to the governor of Jamaica offering him a substantial bribe of £20,000, for a pardon. The Arch Pirate was refused again, most likely because the eyes of the world were upon him. The *Fancy's* crew trickled into the colonies, where pardons were obtained from several sources, Governors Fletcher and Markham, and John Greene, deputy governor of Rhode Island, being most helpful; and before long many of the pirates were back on the Round.

Governor Markham of Pennsylvania, a Quaker, was a notorious "Steddy friend" of pirates. "These Quaker have a neat way of getting money by encouraging the pyrates when they bring in a good store of gold," wrote an observer in 1703, when William Penn had replaced Markham. Penn had heard in London that the people of Pennsylvania "not onlie wink att but imbrace pirats, Shipps and men."

A hundred pounds sterling bought Markham's protection. For a somewhat larger amount an ex-pirate named Captain Robert Sneed was named a justice of the peace. Sneed surprised Markham by turning on him, prosecuting pirates, and accusing Markham of collusion. Sneed was reviled in the streets as an informer and lived in fear of his life while trying every avenue to bring the pirates to a "speedy tryall." He had several other encounters with the governor, who ordered him to stop sending "warrants up and down, whistling to scare People (meaning the Pyrates)."

Below: *The "pirate island" of Madagascar in a wonderfully decorative map from Joan Blaeu's* Atlas Major, *an eleven-volume work printed in Amsterdam between 1662 and 1665. The island was an ideal base because it commanded the main trade routes from India via the Cape of Good Hope to Europe, and it had fine harbors and was out of reach of the authorities. St. Mary's is visible here (as Isle Ste. Marie) with Ranter Bay immediately above it. Réunion is marked Isle Bourbon.*

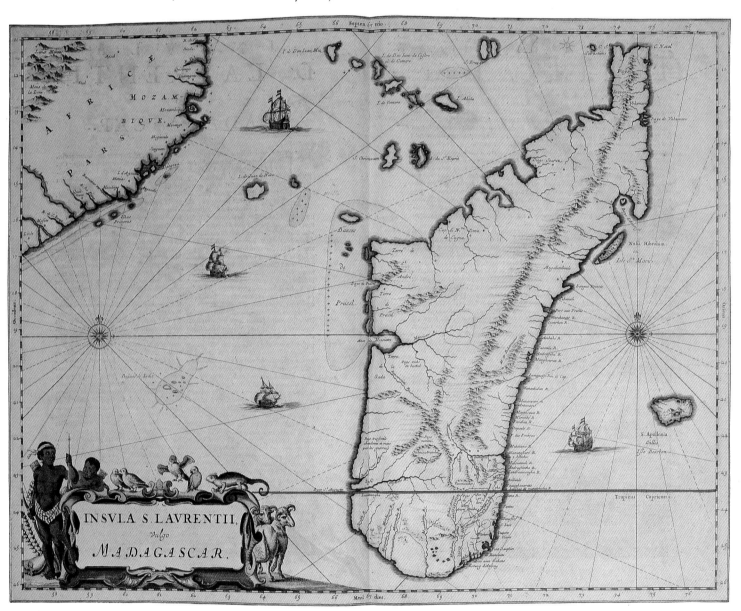

On the Run

Some of Avery's men landed a little sloop at Westport in County Mayo, Ireland, in June 1696. When the mariners offered to buy horses worth ten shillings for as much as £10 the local sheriff became suspicious and detained them. One who escaped, Robert Dunn, was soon arrested in an inn at Rochester where a curious chambermaid discovered £1,045 in gold coins concealed in his quilted jacket. Goldsmiths in the large towns were alerted and eventually twenty-four of Avery's men were arrested in England.

Avery himself was never caught. He had started calling himself Bridgeman and sailed for Ireland, where he vanished. Whatever his end, the legend of the Arch Pirate lived on, inspiring countless others to head for the Eastern seas.

"Steer For Madagascar!"

The long-distance nature of the Round necessitated secure bases to which the pirates could repair for water, provisions, and refreshment. Since pirates were almost always on the move, they needed a place to rendezvous, and a base close to the action but as far as possible from the reach of the law. Their first Eastern base was the scorched island of Perim, known to the pirates as Bab's Cay, at the mouth of the Red Sea. It was soon eclipsed by the island of Madagascar, 250 miles (400km) off the east coast of Africa, where English and French pirates clustered.

Lying within striking distance of the Indian Ocean and the Red Sea, the wildly beautiful tropical island became the pivot point for the Pirate Round. It boasted good harbors, innumerable coves with pristine beaches for careening, ample fresh water and provisions, including citrus fruits that were critical for preventing scurvy on the long voyages. Good food and copious drink were as important as fair maidens to sea-weary men, sick of maggoty victuals. They appreciated the island's "vast numbers of good, fat beef," chickens, eggs, and fresh fruit. The message "Gone to Madagascar for lymes" was often left at pirate meeting places.

Thickly forested mountains divided the island's primitively armed tribes, which seemed to be incessantly at war with one another, making it easy for the pirates to carve out a place for themselves, helping chieftains in battle and receiving slave prisoners.

Adam Baldridge

Self-styled "King of the Pirates" Adam Baldridge was a Jamaican and veteran buccaneer. He was the well-educated son of a planter who had fled after killing a man. He held sway over the tiny island of St. Mary's just off the Madagascar coast, where Tew had careened the *Amity*. He built a great stone castle and fort overlooking the superb harbor. Baldridge had dozens of warehouses filled with private plunder and acted as agent for Frederick Philipse, the New York entrepreneur, slave dealer, and pirate broker.[12]

Baldridge kept a journal that provides a fascinating glimpse into the Pirate Round. He notes the arrival of a Jamaican ship, the *Batchelor's Delight*, which had taken a Muslim ship. "They took so much money," he wrote, that each of the eighty men received "about £1,100" at the share-out. He provided them with cattle for which they bartered "a quantity of beads, five great guns [cannons] for a fortification, some powder and shot, six barrels of flour, and about 70 bars of iron." The ship went on to Port Dauphin, Madagascar's main port, and then set sail for Carolina, where pirates were generally well received.

As recognized ruler of local tribes, Baldridge received tribute in the form of produce, livestock, and sometimes even slaves, which he traded with the pirates for booty. In addition, he sold them ammunition, naval stores, and other supplies, which had been brought across the Atlantic, around the tip of Africa to St. Mary's on the ships of the New England syndicate he was agent for in the 1690s. Wine sold in St. Mary's for fifteen times its New York price. American merchants shipped rum worth two shillings a gallon in New York to Baldridge, who retailed it for three pounds sterling a gallon. Back in the colonies the common man was delighted to get his hand on calicoes, muslins, and other pirated luxuries that, free of taxes, sold at bargain rates. Profiteering merchants bought stolen cargoes wholesale.

Captain Kidd: "Milk and Water Pirate"

Of the host of adventurers who followed Avery to the Eastern seas the best remembered is Captain Kidd. A single exploit made Kidd the best-known pirate in history—and one of the unluckiest. If only he had been content to remain William Kidd, prominent New Yorker and family man, his name would now

Right: *Captain Kidd on the deck of the* Adventure Galley, *an image by Howard Pyle that was later engraved and used as an illustration for his* Howard Pyle's Book of Pirates. *Kidd is depicted as an unpleasant character brooding about his evil deeds in the Indian Ocean. In fact, Kidd became a pirate more by accident than design and it was his misfortune to become a pawn in a political game involving players in London, New York, and India. He was the chosen mariner for a more upmarket Pirate Round involving Governor Fletcher's replacement, the Irish peer the Earl of Bellamont, a backing syndicate of high ranking Whig politicians connected to the king, and New York financiers. Kidd had a dual task: a public one as privateer to seize French vessels, and a private, secret one as sponsored entrepreneur to seize pirate ships and their plunder.*

Below: *A portrait of Admiral Edward Russell, Earl of Orford, by Sir Godfrey Kneller. He was one of the secretive Whig peers backing Kidd's expedition and when news came through of the turn of events, Orford and his fellow aristocrats were quick to distance themselves from the venture.*

be forgotten, but he would surely have escaped the hangman's noose. Scrutiny of his ill-fated piratical career reveals that he was a mediocre pirate who was done in by indecision, bad judgment, and politics.[13]

Kidd, the son of a Presbyterian minister, was born in Scotland in about 1655. In 1689 he was in the West Indies in command of the *Blessed William*, a brigantine that made several successful privateering cruises. In 1691 his crew, led by Robert Culliford, mutinied. Most of the men were ex-pirates and they took off for the Red Sea on their own account, leaving Kidd stranded on Antigua. After this humiliation, he came to New York City and married Sarah Oort, a widow who fortunately happened to be very rich, a beauty, and the owner of an elegant mansion on the city's Wall Street. Kidd quickly became a highly regarded merchant with a pew in New York's fashionable Trinity Church.

Kidd's Commission

Despite his pleasant life, Kidd missed the sea. In 1695 he went to London to lobby for command of a privateer ship. King William III was at the time responding to increasing pressure from the East India Company to do something about the Roundsmen, who were not only preying on company vessels but endangering the company's tenuous trading relationships in the East with their assaults on Mogul and Arab ships. The king ordered strengthened naval patrols in the Red Sea area and began to tackle the problem of corrupt colonial officials. He replaced the infamous Fletcher with Richard Coote, earl of Bellamont, as governor of New England and charged him with putting an end to the North American pirates.

Kidd had testified against Fletcher to Bellamont's benefit and now enlisted the latter's aid in getting a command. He received a royal privateering commission empowering "our trusty and well beloved Captain Kid, Commander of the *Adventure Galley* to capture Tew, Wake, John Ireland and other pirates based in the colonies who commit many and great Piracies, robberies and depredations on the seas . . . to the great hindrance and discouragement of trade and navigation."

The idea behind the venture had rather less to do with suppressing the Red Sea Men than it did with making a fat profit for the joint stockholders who financed it, most of whom were also kingpins in the ruling Whig party. The two secretaries of state, the first lord of the Admiralty and the lord chancellor, the earl of Orford, were not, however, even mentioned in the grant, nor was King William, who had a one-tenth share of profits from any plunder. Kidd himself put up £600

Right: *William Kidd's privateering commission, dated December 11, 1695. This letter of marque, issued under the authority of King William III and bearing his portrait, licensed Kidd as captain of the* Adventure Galley *to seize any French ships encountered during his search for pirates in the Indian Ocean. It no doubt encouraged Kidd to believe that his piracies were legitimate privateering and helps to explain why he protested his innocence to the end. Instead, papers which would have served his defense were denied to him and all erstwhile friends became either inactively obstructive or outrightly hostile. Tried on separate counts of murder and piracy, Kidd appealed to the judge at the end, "It is a very hard sentence. I am the innocentest person of them all, only I have been sworn against by perjured persons." His plea was in vain.*

of the £6,000 required to outfit the *Adventure Galley*, a newly built 287-tonner with thirty-four cannons. It looked like a foolproof opportunity to make a quasi-legitimate fortune from French shipping and pirate plunder of all nations. In the flush of anticipation it seemed insignificant that none of the backers' names appeared publicly in connection with the venture, save that of Kidd's patron, Bellamont.

No Prey, No Pay

Kidd sailed for New York with high hopes, a hand-picked crew, and his royal commission, as well as a document granting him license to capture French ships. He knew that there would be no profit for him save for his share of captured prizes. Leaving the Nore, the anchorage off Chatham dockyard, Kidd failed to dip his flag in deference to a Royal Navy sloop. Perhaps in retaliation for his perceived arrogance, a press gang boarded and hustled off many of his best sailors. He was forced to replace them with assorted scum, many of scarcely veiled piratical leanings. It

was not an auspicious beginning. In New York he took on additional seamen, trying to make sure none of them were "Madagascar men" because, at that point, piracy was not on his agenda.

In September 1696 the *Adventure Galley* sailed for the Indian Ocean, aiming for the pirate nest of Madagascar. Things did not go well. The ship began to take on water. In the space of a week one-third of the crew perished from cholera. Weakened by scurvy during the nine thousand-mile (14,500km) voyage, the remainder of the crew began to mutter about going "on the account." At Johanna Island in the Comoro Gulf he took on fifty replacements, obviously veteran rovers. Kidd appears to have been tortured by indecision as he cruised the tropical waters. Months passed and no significant prey appeared. Should he adhere to the terms of his privateering commission or turn pirate? The crew became more mutinous and he allowed them to attempt culling a Moorish merchantman from its escort of Dutch and French ships. The effort failed and time

ADVENTURE GALLEY, 1695

IN APRIL 1696 Captain Kidd set off from London on a privateering voyage to the Indian Ocean. Five years later he was hanged for murder and piracy. His vessel was an armed merchant ship of 287 tons called the *Adventure Galley*. She had been built at Deptford on the banks of the Thames in 1695, and in common with a number of other ships of the period she had oarports and sweeps (the long oars that could be used in calms), which was why she was called a galley. She had thirty-four guns, carried a crew of 152 men, and was as fast and as powerful as one of the Royal Navy's smaller warships. In these circumstances it is surprising that when Kidd turned pirate he did not take more prizes, and he only captured the *Quedah Merchant* and her rich cargo by flying French flags and tricking her captain into surrender.

While most pirates had much smaller vessels than Captain Kidd's, there were a few who had similar, or even larger vessels. Blackbeard's famous ship the *Queen Anne's Revenge* was a captured French guineaman of thirty-six or forty guns. Black Sam Bellamy's ship the *Whydah* was a former slave ship of 300 tons that he armed with twenty-eight guns. And the Welsh pirate Bartholomew Roberts commanded several large ships of which the most formidable was the *Royal Fortune*, a French man-o'-war of forty-two guns that he captured off Martinique.

Key

1 Quarter gallery leading off the great cabin used by the captain.
2 Sweeps for propelling the vessel in flat calms.
3 Stern lanterns.
4 Quarter deck from which the captain and his officers controlled the ship.
5 Mizzen mast.
6 Windlass for hauling up the massive anchor and cable, a task that might take an hour's work.
7 Main mast.
8 Main hatch to provide light and ventilation to the deck below.
9 Water barrels.
10 Spare sails.
11 Ropes and cables.
12 The ship's bell, rung to mark the changing of the men on watch.
13 Foremast.
14 Fighting top.
15 Spare blocks and gear.
16 Head rails.
17 Anchor weighing about three thousand pounds (1,361kg).
18 Bowsprit.

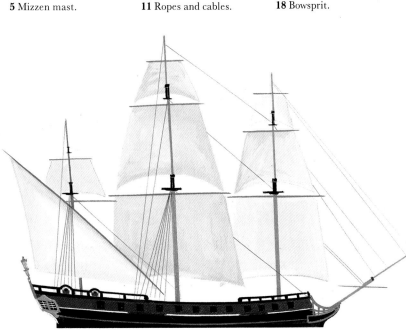

wore on. An Arab vessel that they plundered for provisions notified East India Company officials that English pirates were about. Near Goa two Portuguese naval vessels battled the *Adventure Galley*, tearing her rigging and splintering the hull.

Kidd Kills William Moore

The ship moved sluggishly over a vacant sea, through stifling air. No prizes appeared. The rotting food crawled with maggots. The water was foul. Days became weeks. Finally, just off the tip of India, a lone merchant ship was sighted. She turned out to be the *Loyal Captain*, another English ship, and when Kidd refused to plunder her, the gunner, a feisty man named William Moore, taunted Kidd and in the fight that ensued Kidd hit Moore in the head with a bucket. The gunner crumpled to the deck and next day he was dead. Kidd assured the surgeon that he had friends in England who would take care of "that matter" should it ever be necessary.

The *Adventure Galley* was leaking so badly that hourly shifts of eight men had to work the pumps around the clock. Cables were cinched around the hull to keep her from falling apart. More than a year had passed and the mirage of a treasure-laden prize con-

tinued to elude them. They took three small trading ships, one Portuguese, one Arab, and a Dutch one with a French East India Company pass. The assortment of cotton, candy, wax, opium, iron, butter, and coffee they found aboard didn't improve the mood of the mutinous crew.

The *Quedah Merchant*

Then in February 1698, as the *Adventure Galley* cruised along the Malabar coast, their dream ship sailed into view riding low in the water. The *Quedah Merchant* was owned by Indian merchants from Surat and carried a cargo valued at £710,000 belonging to Persian Armenians. The pirates took her easily. The ship had an English captain, Dutch officers, and a Muslim crew. But her pass was French, issued by the French East India Company, so Kidd with some qualms claimed her as a lawful prize. His men swarmed aboard, ripping into the hold crammed with gold, silks, jewels, muslins, sugar, guns, iron, and other goods. They had finally hit the jackpot. The memory of the past months' privations vanished before such an array of treasure.

Kidd took his ship and the *Quedah Merchant* into St. Mary's. In a strange twist of fate the

Below: *Kidd arraigned before Parliament in March 1701. Taken from his damp confinement in Newgate Prison to explain his actions before the assembled members of the House, Kidd remains the only pirate in British history to have had this opportunity. Inexplicably, he did not turn on his Whig sponsors and implicate them—something which the Tory members desperately wanted to hear so that they could exploit it politically. Instead he insisted on his honesty and that of the others involved. Either this was misplaced loyalty and deference, or perhaps he was ill and suffering the effects of his two-year imprisonment. The result was that, deprived of key documents for his defense and having to conduct his own cross-examinations in court, it is little wonder he was subsequently found guilty.*

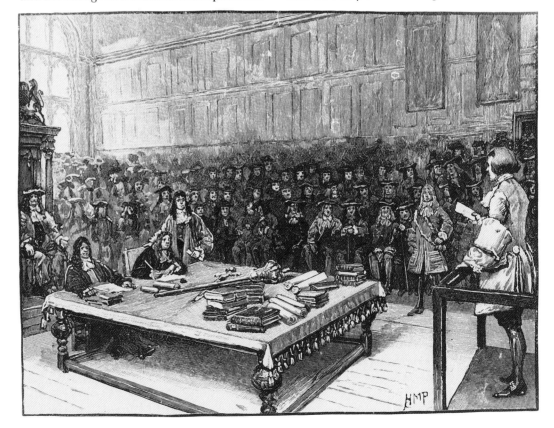

only other ship anchored there was an East India Company frigate, the *Mocha*, which had been captured by Robert Culliford, the pirate who had snatched Kidd's brigantine in the Caribbean. Culliford had a crew of forty and Kidd proposed to his larger contingent that they seize the *Mocha*. After all, Culliford was a pirate and Kidd's commission called for the capture of such rovers and their vessels.

Kidd's crew would have none of it. They turned on him, jeering at his leadership, and said they would rather fire guns at him than at the pirate. Under pressure Kidd made a mistake that would cost him dearly during his trials. He broke bulk, unloading and selling £10,000 worth of cargo and sharing it out among his crew. As soon as they had their share of the *Quedah* plunder, ninety-seven of Kidd's crew defected to Culliford. Kidd, thoroughly demoralized, was left with a skeleton crew of eighteen, a sinking ship, and a long trip home. He wasn't even sure Culliford, who now had the upper hand, would let him sail.

"The Scourge of the Indies"

After a tedious five-month wait for the northeast monsoon to drive him around the Cape of Good Hope, Kidd abandoned the derelict *Adventure Galley* and, picking up a raggle-taggle crew, sailed for the Caribbean in the *Quedah*. In London, meanwhile, the political crisis that was to spell Kidd's doom was taking shape. The Tories made much of the fact that Kidd, whose exploits had appeared in exaggerated form in a report on piracies in the Indian Ocean, was backed by leading Whigs. The Whig government, attacked as "a Corporation of Pirates," defended itself by labeling Kidd an "obnoxious pirate." In a final insult they excluded his name from a royal offer of pardon to all surrendering Indian Ocean pirates. Colonial authorities from the West Indies to Massachusetts were ordered to arrest him on sight.

Kidd was unaware he was the "Scourge of the Indies" until he anchored at the little island of Anguilla. When he heard he was a vicious pirate with a price on his head he remained confident that with the aid of his patron, Governor Bellamont, and upon producing the French passes from the ships he had plundered, he would be cleared of any charges. But not even the neutral Danes were willing to play host to such a wanted man, refusing his offer of forty-five thousand pieces

of eight to remain at St. Thomas until he could make contact with his powerful friends.

The fugitive Kidd had to reach Bellamont in New York. The bulky *Quedah* could never outrun one of the men-o'-war that were on the lookout for him, so he ran her up a river on the isolated southeast coast of Hispaniola. A portion of the cargo, including his share of gold bars, gold dust, silver plate, jewels, and silks, was transferred to his sloop. The remainder of the cargo was left under guard until he could clear himself.

The Noose Tightens

In his anonymous sloop Kidd and twenty-one men made it safely to Long Island. Bellamont, who was in Boston, lured him there with a deceptively welcoming letter. Before he left for Boston, Kidd sent the governor's young wife an enameled jewel box with some gems. He also sold off some of the *Quedah* cargo, which by Admiralty law should have been brought before a court before being disposed of, even under the new law that gave 100 percent of a prize to a commissioned privateer. He acted as if he were dealing with his own property, putting gold bars in keeping with a pirate friend from Rhode Island, and burying

Above: *Another evocative illustration by Pyle depicting Kidd burying his treasure. It is known that Kidd buried part of his treasure on Gardiners Island near New York, but it was all accounted for despite persistent rumors to the contrary. John Gardiner handed over eleven bags of gold and silver to Lord Bellamont. This treasure was claimed by the consortium which owned the* Quedah Merchant, *but they failed to supply the Admiralty Court with documents within the three-year period allowed. After their case had lapsed the sum of £6,472 which the treasure had realized at auction was used to fund the Greenwich Hospital.*

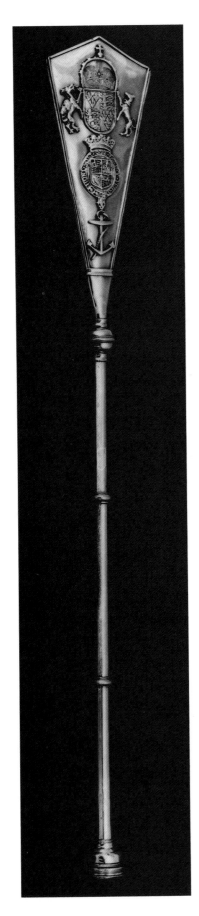

chests of gold and gems on Gardiner's Island, owned by his friend John Gardiner, who gave him a receipt for the treasure.

In Boston, Kidd tried to negotiate with Bellamont. He gave his wife a further bribe of gold bars worth about £1,000 presented in a green silk pouch. Her husband, betraying Kidd with no evident remorse, made her send them back and refused to meet with Kidd privately. Kidd was arrested and imprisoned. His parceled-out treasure was recovered for evidence. Governor Bellamont even sent a sloop to Antigua, St. Thomas, Curaçao, and Jamaica to search for booty Kidd might have sold. Despite the persistent belief that Kidd's treasure is buried on the island that the Gardiner family still owns, the cache there was recovered by Bellamont's men. Later, Bellamont was to write to London asking for the one-third share due him as vice-admiral of the American seas. Kidd's former friend, eager to dissociate himself from a project gone sour, wrote Lord Somers calling the prisoner "a monster . . . there was never a greater liar or thief in the world than Kidd." Throughout the freezing winter of 1699, Kidd was shackled in irons in a damp Boston prison. By the time he arrived in England the following April, the passions of Parliament and the public were inflamed by the "Kidd Affair."

"Jerked Into the Devil's Arms"

William Kidd, the reluctant pirate, never had a chance to acquit himself. Too many politicians were set on seeing him "jerked into the Devil's arms." Kidd was the scapegoat for both Whigs and Tories. During his four trials he could not prove his innocence because his log had been burned and his passes turned over to Bellamont, who denied having seen them. All his papers had disappeared, and prosecution and defense conspired against him. He was found guilty of murder and five counts of piracy and condemned to death.

William Kidd, honored New Yorker, pew holder in Trinity Church, was to hang like the vilest outlaw. On May 23, 1701, he left Newgate Prison in a procession led by a deputy marshal who carried on his shoulder the silver oar, symbol of the Admiralty Court. Kidd was in an open cart draped in black, a noose already around his neck.

A sympathetic warden had furnished him with a numbing amount of liquor so that he

was reeling drunk and scarcely aware of the macabre parade that wound its way through the squalid slums to the muddy shore at Wapping. Bad luck dogged him to the very end, for when he was "turned off" the makeshift gibbet at the river's edge, the rope broke and he fell to the ground. The second time the noose held. His corpse was chained to a post at the water's edge until the tide had washed over it three times in fulfillment of Admiralty law. Then Kidd's body was coated with tar, bound with iron bands, and encased in a metal case to hold it in place as the flesh rotted. The grisly corpse was displayed on a gibbet in the Thames Estuary, remaining for several years in order to serve as "a greater Terrour to all Persons from committing ye like Crimes for the time to come."

Of the six men convicted with Kidd, only one was executed. The others were reprieved. Two bribed their Newgate jailers and then embarked for America, sailing past Kidd's gruesome corpse. Kidd's share of the *Quedah Merchant* plunder was forfeited to the Crown. The gold, silver, gems, and rich fabrics were auctioned off for £6,472. Queen Anne agreed to turn the money over to the directors of Greenwich Hospital. The National Maritime Museum, which now occupies some of that hospital land and its buildings, is therefore a beneficiary of pirate treasure.

The Round Revived

Kidd's foray came at the end of the Pirate Round, which was done in by concerted government efforts on both sides of the Atlantic to suppress the Roundsmen, coupled with the waning of the Mogul empire. The pirates, deserters, and beach bums who had settled on Madagascar were reduced to poverty and despised by the natives whom they had so long abused.

Piracy didn't die out completely. After a lull of twenty years the Round had a brief revival during which Madagascar once again bloomed as a pirate entrepôt and the Eastern seas boasted the boldest and best of the sea rovers. Men like Christopher Condent, Edward England, Howell Davis, and John Taylor led the way from the New World after 1718, when the pirate stronghold on New Providence in the Bahamas had been wiped out by Woodes Rogers, and North American waters had become too dangerous.

Condent, a Plymouth man like so many of the earlier Roundsmen, was one of the first to sail east on the old Round route. Off Bombay he took an Arab ship carrying £150,000 in gold and silver, the richest prize since the end of the Round. At the share-out held on the beach at St. Mary's each man received close to £3,000.

There was such a glut of goods that packets of spices, bolts of silks, and gold-embellished muslins were left strewn on the sand. Condent and forty of his crew showed uncommon good sense by retiring on the strength of their phenomenal haul. They were granted French pardons by the governor of Réunion (formerly the Isle de Bourbon) Island, where about twenty of them settled. Condent married the governor's sister-in-law and became a wealthy shipowner in St. Malo, the port and former corsair base on the northern coast of France.

England the Irishman

Edward England and John Taylor were two veterans of New Providence who sailed on the final Round. The two pirates couldn't have been more different in personality. Taylor,

Right: Frank Schoonover's painting of privateers onboard the ship Pickering *attacking an unidentified East Indiaman.*

Left and far left: *Kidd was taken, drunk, to his place of execution in the traditional procession headed by the deputy marshal carrying the Admiralty Court's symbolic silver oar (far left). The marshal and his men had enough left from court funds to finance a drink to Kidd's health after the event. Big crowds had followed the procession and a mixed mob watched, from the urchins and tenement-dwellers to the comfortable classes in their carriages and members of the establishment. After the somewhat squalid hanging, Kidd's body was cut down and chained to a post until the Thames tide had ebbed and flowed over it thrice. The bloated body was then taken to Tilbury Point, tarred, and placed in a gibbet (left) in sight of every passing vessel. The birds were then free to strip it to the bone.*

captain of the *Victory*, had a reputation for ruthlessness. In contrast, England, captain of the *Fancy*, was a genial Irishman whom Captain Johnson characterized as "having a great deal of good nature . . . courageous, not over-avaricious, humane, but too often over-ruled." They joined forces in the Indian Ocean and in August 1720, having seized a number of prizes, they repaired to Johanna Island in the Comoro Gulf, the watering place frequented by both pirates and merchantmen.

They found two East Indiamen there. One of the great British merchant ships slipped out of the bay, but the *Cassandra* under James Macrae, son of a poor English cottager who had made the rare climb to a naval command, fought the pirate ships valiantly for several hours. The other East Indiaman, whose captain had deserted Macrae despite a vow to face any pirate attack together, watched from a safe distance. Thirteen crewmen were killed and twenty-four wounded on the *Cassandra*. Casualties were even greater on the pirate ships. Macrae had little hope in the face of such great odds. The pirates with their black and bloody flags flying forced

Macrae to run his ship aground. Most of the seamen who didn't escape in time were slaughtered when the pirates then swarmed aboard.

Despite Taylor's violent objections, Captain England insisted that Macrae, who was suffering from a severe head wound, be given safe passage in the all-but-sinking *Fancy*, with half his original cargo and a skeleton crew. During the seven weeks it took Macrae and his men to reach Bombay, most of them died of thirst. Macrae was greeted triumphantly as a hero by the British East India Company and was soon after appointed governor of Madras.

England, the humane pirate, fared less well. His own company deposed him and a few others for "softness" toward Macrae. They made a grueling passage to Madagascar in a small open boat, where England was reduced to begging and died soon afterward. (One of England's companions, who was described in Johnson's *General History* as "a man with a terrible pair of whiskers and a wooden leg, being stuck round with pistols," became Robert Louis Stevenson's inspiration for Long John Silver in *Treasure Island*.)

According to Captain Johnson, no part of the *Cassandra* booty was so highly valued as the surgeon's chest, "for they were all poxed to a great degree." After they had treated their venereal sores with mercury compound, the pirates set off under Taylor on a rampage that scored the single greatest haul of the Pirate Round's last season. Sailing in the *Cassandra* and the *Victory*, they took prize after prize, from Arab dhows to an East Indiaman, torturing and murdering the crews encountered.

Taylor Strikes it Rich

In April 1721 Taylor, on the *Cassandra*, joined with Oliver La Bouche (yet another refugee from the Bahamas), commander of the *Victory*. The two ships with two hundred ferocious cutthroats aboard sailed into the harbor at St.

Below: *The Kidd trial served as a good deterrent lesson as far as the East India Company was concerned and helped to soothe the anger of the Mogul. This painting shows the East India Company's yard at Deptford, near Greenwich, in about 1660 with ships being built and repaired.*

Right: *Edward England, another notorious enemy of the East Indian Company and other trading vessels in the Indian Ocean. Ironically, he was deposed by his crew for being too compassionate and ended his life in poverty on the island of Madagascar.*

Denis on the Isle de Bourbon. What they found there exceeded all expectations. Anchored in the harbor was the *Nossa Senhora do Cabo*, a Portuguese carrack that had been dismasted in a heavy storm while en route from Goa, the Portuguese enclave on the southwest coast of India. In addition to the usual eastern luxuries, the *Cabo* was laden with a stunning shipment of diamonds. A large share of the consignment belonged to the retiring viceroy of Goa, Luis de Meneses, count of Ericeira and marquis of Louriçal. Some of the diamonds were being sent to the king of Portugal, who was so put out at the loss that he banished Ericeira from court for ten years; most, however, were the result of his own private dealings and the personal financial loss must have been great.

The count gallantly defended his poorly armed vessel, surrendering only when his sword snapped in hand-to-hand combat on the quarterdeck. Taylor returned his diamond-studded gold sword hilt in recognition of his courage. He tried to return his personal belongings to him as well but the count spurned the offer, stating he wished no distinction to be made between himself and the other captives. As a consequence, the boorish pirates, who were ignorant of their value, shredded his collection of unique Oriental manuscripts to make wadding for their guns.

The island's governor paid a ransom for the viceroy, who was set free. The pirates transferred armaments and cargo from their weatherbeaten vessels to the prize and sailed off to St. Mary's for their share-out of the £1,000,000 worth of plunder. The *Cabo* cargo, exclusive of the diamonds, was worth some £375,000. The gems alone were worth more than £500,000. Each of the pirates received more than £4,000 and a handful of gems. Captain Johnson wrote that each man got forty-two small diamonds, or less if the gems were larger. "An ignorant or merry fellow, who had only one in this division, as being adjudged equal to forty-two small, muttered very much at the lot and went and broke it in a mortar, swearing afterwards he had a better share than any of them, for he had beat it, he said, into forty-three sparks."[14]

The End of the Pirate Round

Others followed them to prey on shipping in the Indian Ocean, the Red Sea, the Persian Gulf, and along the African coasts. But their fling was short-lived. The nations that had for

so long used piracy as a weapon against Spain and one another now had their place in the sun, and the unruly pirates had become a universal menace and an embarrassment. The British dealt with the pirate menace by establishing colonial Admiralty courts and passing the Piracy Act of 1721. The same year, a squadron of Admiralty warships destroyed Indian Ocean pirate strongholds on Mauritius and Réunion. The French navy concentrated on pirates in the Persian Gulf, and the Dutch supplied three ships to protect the Mocha fleet in the Red Sea.

Their long-overdue cooperation eradicated all but native pirates from the Eastern seas. By the end of 1721 most of the new surge of English and American pirates had vanished into retirement, sailed back to the West Indies, or drifted around the Cape of Good Hope to the three thousand-mile (4,830km) Guinea Coast. There, in the estuary overlooked by Cape Sierra Leone on Africa's western coast, where the deep-water pirates had traditionally stopped off for "whoring and drinking," the long-distance rovers of the revived Pirate Round had their final fling, preying on trading ships laden with gold, slaves, and ivory.

CHAPTER EIGHT

FRENCH AND
AMERICAN PRIVATEERS

~

***P**rivateer: a vessel of war, armed and equipped by particular merchants, and furnished with a military commission by the admiralty. . . . to cruise against the enemy, and take, sink, or burn their shipping, or otherwise annoy them as opportunity offers.*

AN UNIVERSAL DICTIONARY OF THE MARINE, 1780[1]

THE LINE between pirate and privateer was a fine one throughout history but never more so than between 1690 and 1865, when commerce warfare played such an imposing role in maritime warfare. A letter of marque—an official commission issued by a sovereign state authorizing attacks on enemy vessels—formed the thin line between legal and illegal activity. But on which side a vessel or individual rested often lay in the eye of the beholder.

From medieval times, monarchs added privateers to their naval vessels when pursuing commerce warfare (attacks on merchant ships). Letters of reprisal, similar to letters of marque but more limited in scope, allowed shipowners and captains to seize enemy vessels and property to obtain reparation for losses sustained by enemy action. Letters of marque placed no limits on the amount of property their holders could seize, but individuals operating under letters of reprisal were authorized to seize property only to the true value of losses they had sustained and the full cost of recovering that amount. Ships licensed by either letters of marque or letters of reprisal were commonly referred to as privateers in English-speaking areas, and as corsairs in France.[2]

Such commissions had the dual purpose of harnessing private enterprise to the public's service, while providing a legal outlet for activities that would be difficult to stop in time of war, as aggrieved parties sought to recover losses suffered from enemy action. Ships and cargoes captured by privateers increased the wealth of the captor, while the licensing fees and taxes (usually a portion of the value of ships and goods captured) contributed to the government's treasury and hurt the enemy. Had privateers always operated according to the law, the system might well have functioned in everyone's interest. In practice privateers proved difficult to control, and once away from official scrutiny their plundering often became indiscriminate. They sometimes preyed upon the vessels of neutral or friendly nations, not just those of the enemy.

The New World

Both piracy and privateering spread to the New World in the sixteenth century. When England, France, Spain, Portugal, and the Netherlands went to war, the West Indies became the favorite haunt of seaborne commerce raiders. Governments in Europe regularly signed peace treaties that ended wars without considering the grievances or goals of all their colonists in America. When this happened, privateers who would continue their attacks became pirates and were outlawed.

Francis Drake's raids on Spanish shipping in the Caribbean epitomize the great age of English privateering in the reign of Elizabeth I (1558-1603). A century later, French privateering reached its peak during wars with the Dutch and English. The tenuousness of imperial control in the Americas was recognized by the Treaty of Whitehall of 1686 whereby England and France agreed that hostilities in the New World should not be considered cause for war in Europe.

Bart and DuGuay-Trouin

Diplomats may have succeeded in separating European warfare from that in the western hemisphere, but wars continued in both regions and both sides resorted to privateering, though France more than England because it was usually the weaker naval power that used privateers for commerce raiding.[3] Two of France's greatest naval heroes, Jean

Left: *Bold-looking privateers hunting their prey. This painting by John Schoonover was commissioned to illustrate "Privateers of '76—a Story of the Revolution," by Ralph D. Paine. It was published in* American Boy *magazine in July 1923.*

Below: *A naval dirk and scabbard. The dirk has an ivory grip and diamond-section blade. The standard weapons in regular use in the Royal Navy during the eighteenth and nineteenth centuries were swords, dirks, and cutlasses. These were augmented by pistols and muskets issued prior to going into battle.*

Below: *An engraved portrait of Jean Bart, leader of the privateers at Dunkirk, a notorious center for piracy and smuggling in the sixteenth and seventeenth centuries. Bart rose from humble origins to become commodore in the French navy and was ennobled by King Louis XIV. During his privateering days he was the scourge of the Dutch herring fleets and his North Sea squadron raided the northeast coast of England. He was caught by the English once but escaped from Plymouth and rowed back to France.*

Bart and Réné DuGuay-Trouin, commanded privateers before entering the navy. Bart was born at Dunkirk, long a center of smuggling and privateering, in 1650. He went to sea at the age of twelve and soon entered the Dutch navy, in which he served under the great Michel de Ruyter before returning home at the outbreak of the war that pitted France and England against the Netherlands in 1672. The naval officer corps of France was largely limited at the time to members of the gentry and aristocracy, so Bart, unable to obtain an officer's commission, went to sea in command of a privateer. In his first cruise he

captured five ships. Shortly thereafter he became leader of the privateers based at Dunkirk, and before peace was signed in 1678 ships under his command took eighty-one prizes. His fame led finally to a lieutenancy in the French navy.

In 1688 France was again at war with the Netherlands, which was now allied with England. Commanding a mixed force of French naval ships and privateers, Bart soon put to sea. In 1691 his squadron captured two English warships and the merchantmen under their protection. In November 1692, Bart commanded the three frigates that cut twenty ships out of a convoy bound for Holland from the Baltic and also captured one of the convoy escorts. Louis XIV recognized Bart's achievements by ennobling him in 1694, though his manner remained that of the rough, unsophisticated companions of his youth. England and Holland countered the commerce raiding from ports such as Dunkirk and St. Malo by blockading them, but Bart slipped by the blockaders one foggy night in 1696 and led five naval vessels and two privateers to the coast of Holland, where they fought a three-hour battle against five warships, capturing every one of the escorts and twenty-five of the merchantmen. This victory led to his promotion to *chef d'escadre,* the equivalent of commodore in other navies. A year later the Treaty of Ryswick brought the war to an end. First the peace, 1697–1702, and then his death from pleurisy in 1702 robbed Bart of the opportunity to test his abilities as a fleet commander. He was a great loss to France because no one had surpassed Bart as a commerce raider.

During the War of the Spanish Succession *guerre de course* (commerce raiding) was the official French naval strategy (replacing *guerre d'escarde,* or "purely naval warfare") and there rose a second great practitioner, Réné DuGuay-Trouin. Like Jean Bart, he came from common stock. The son of a St. Malo shipping family, DuGuay-Trouin was born in 1673, went to sea at sixteen, and commanded a privateer owned by his family only two years later. King Louis XIV rented some of his warships to private investors who sent them to sea in search of prizes. As the commander of one such ship, DuGuay-Trouin was sent with a squadron to help defend Cadiz from an expected attack. En route the French force was attacked by one superior in number and guns. DuGuay-Trouin played a leading role in fighting off the attack and as a reward the king granted him a commission as *capitaine de frégate* in the French navy. As a naval officer DuGuay-Trouin took command of fourteen of the king's warships, all sailing as privateers, and in 1706 intercepted a convoy carrying troops to Portugal. DuGuay-Trouin's force captured three ships of the line and sixty of the convoy's eighty ships, and sank another ship of the line. Five years later DuGuay-Trouin achieved a remarkable triumph when he led a fleet, again consisting of warships acting as privateers, across the Atlantic to capture Rio de Janeiro and force its governor to pay a ransom to prevent its destruction. Investors in this enterprise almost doubled their money and DuGuay-Trouin was promoted to admiral.[4] In 1713 the Treaty of Utrecht brought peace between England and France for a quarter of a century. DuGuay-Trouin continued in the navy, rising to the rank of vice-admiral in 1728. His later years were spent in the eastern Mediterranean protecting French commerce, and by his death in 1736 he was revered as one of his nation's greatest naval leaders, to be rivaled only by the Bailli de Suffren a half century later.

The Great Age of Privateering

The years of peace after 1713 brought changes that altered private warfare at sea. Nation-states, including Britain and France, developed bureaucracies to control their empires more tightly. Moreover, technological advances and maritime experience rendered the Atlantic Ocean less of a barrier, and the growth of the North American economy spurred regular communication between mother countries and their colonies. Finally, nations had constructed a significant number of purpose-built warships to protect commerce. Thus by the mid-1700s the great age of piracy in the western world had passed into history.

But not that of privateering—the resumption of warfare in 1739 marked the start of the great age of privateering in North America. Indeed, commerce raiding by privately owned and manned vessels became so widespread during the colonial wars of the mid-century, the American Revolution, the Quasi-War between the United States and France, and the War of 1812, that it played a

major role in the economy of the region. As a weak naval power, the United States adopted *guerre de course* out of necessity, wedding private enterprise and state policy in a marriage of convenience.

When Britain's thirteen colonies rebelled against the mother country in 1775 they

Above: *A document issued by the Prize Office in London on May 4, 1703, referring to the capture of prizes by the captain of the* Eagle. *All privateers were expected to report details of prizes to the office, which would determine their value.*

adopted laws based on colonial precedents, including the rules and regulations governing privateering. When Britain went to war during the eighteenth century, the monarch ordered the lords of the Admiralty to authorize issuance of letters of marque by colonial governors. New instructions required the captor to take or send the prize and its cargo to a port and appear before a Court of Admiralty, which was empowered to determine whether the vessel belonged to an enemy nation and was thus a legal prize. The court would also supervise the sale of the prize and the distribution of funds to the sailors, officers, and owners of the privateer. In England the High Court of Admiralty conducted such proceedings, but after 1689 that court usually assigned its powers in the colonies to the governor, who frequently received a commission as a vice-admiral so that he could preside over Admiralty courts. France followed a similar system and both individual American states and the Continental Congress continued British practices post independence.

King George's War

Thus American practice was based on experience of Britain's wars with Spain and France between 1739 and 1763. The first of those wars, known in continental Europe as the War of the Austrian Succession, in Britain as the War of Jenkins' Ear, and in America as King George's War, began when Robert Jenkins, a merchant captain, spoke in Parliament and related tales of Spanish cruelty (including the cutting off of his own ear) to foreigners accused of trading illegally in Spanish colonies. Protests by Britain led to Spanish promises of reparations to British shipowners and mariners by May 25, 1739. When Spain defaulted on the payments, King George II sent warrants to his governors in America that stated:

> We have thought fit ... for Procuring Reparations, and Satisfaction for Our injured Subjects, to order Reprisals to be made upon the Crown and Subjects of Spain. And We do therefore ... empower you to issue forth, and grant Commissions of Marque and Reprisal ... for Arming and Fitting out private Ships of War, for the Apprehending, Seizing, and Taking of Ships, Vessels, and Goods belonging to the King of Spain, his Vassels, and Subjects.[5]

During 1740 the war between Britain and Spain merged with another pitting Britain against France. Thus French vessels, and those of her colonies in Canada and the West Indies, also became targets for British and American privateers after 1744. In 1740 and 1744 Parliament passed Prize Acts to regulate them. In British North America more than three hundred groups and individuals obtained letters of marque and fitted out vessels, mostly sloops and brigantines. Service in privateersmen proved attractive to mariners, who generally received higher wages than in merchantmen. Furthermore, they had the possibility of earning prize money, a portion of the proceeds from the sale of captured vessels and their cargoes. New York City and Newport, Rhode Island, fitted out the largest number of privateersmen even though both ports were relatively remote from the Caribbean, from where large numbers of French and Spanish ships exported valuable cargoes of sugar, cocoa, and tobacco.

The kings of France and Spain issued letters of marque authorizing the seizure of British vessels, including those of her American colonies. Privateers from the Bourbon nations and their colonies divided their operations between Britain's North American and Caribbean colonies because numerous vessels participated in the northern fish, timber, tobacco, grain, rice, and other trades that linked the dominions of George II. French Louisbourg on Cape Breton Island became a nest for privateers, many of whom preyed on New England fishing fleets. Putting a stop to privateering was a major motive for the joint Royal Navy–colonial militia attack on Louisbourg in 1745. In the war, over thirty-six thousand American colonists served in privateers, double the number of men who participated in expeditions against Cartagena, Louisbourg, and Quebec.[6] The Treaty of Aix-la-Chapelle in 1748 brought peace and ended privateering for eight years.

The Seven Years' War

Anglo-French hostilities in India and North America from 1754 led to renewed privateering, especially once war was officially declared in 1756. The capture of Louisbourg in 1758, Martinique and Guadeloupe in 1759, and Dominica in 1760 denied French privateers their best American bases, but did nothing to limit their depredations on the

Below: *The British action at Louisburg in 1758. The French had established a great fortress there to defend the approaches to the St. Lawrence River, and during the early eighteenth century it became a base for privateers who harassed the New England fishing fleets. The British attacked in 1745 and again in 1758 when an expedition led by Admiral Boscawen besieged the fortress, took the town, and captured or burned all the ships in the harbor.*

other side of the Atlantic. Approximately 10 percent of British shipping fell victim to French privateers, most of which operated from ports on the English Channel and Bay of Biscay. The Royal Navy kept most French shipping blockaded in port.

The War of Independence

Triumphant over France in 1763, Britain instituted policies that led thirteen of her North American colonies to rebel and declare their independence only a decade later. The new nation was closely bound to the sea, and keeping open the nation's sea lines of communication would necessitate naval power. Thus the Continental Congress and eleven of the thirteen states formed navies. Few of the leaders who voted to establish those services believed they possessed adequate resources to defend American commerce or to engage the Royal Navy directly, but many thought that American losses at sea could be compensated for by British prizes, and that attacks would lead mercantile interests in the mother country to pressure the government into accepting American independence. Thus

the rebels turned to commerce raiding, the traditional strategy of the weaker naval power, for the maritime component of the war against Great Britain.

The Congress laid the basis for a Continental Navy in October 1775 when it voted to arm two vessels as warships and formed a Naval Committee. On November 1, the General Court of Massachusetts became the first American government to authorize privateering and established three Admiralty courts to adjudicate cases involving captured vessels. The Continental Congress was unwilling to go as far. Thus when Congress passed legislation on November 25, it allowed the capture only of warships, transports, and supply ships, exempting civilian-owned vessels. By spring, events threatened to overtake the Congress as other states either enacted privateering legislation or discussed it, so on March 23, 1776, Congress extended its list of legitimate prizes to include "all ships and other vessels, their tackle, apparel, and furniture, and all goods, wares, and merchandise, belonging to any inhabitant or inhabitants of Great Britain." Ten days later, Congress approved a form letter of marque that was subsequently adopted by eleven states.[7]

Privateering proved highly controversial in the former colonies. Critics argued that it siphoned off sailors, naval stores, and the time of artisans needed to fit out and man public vessels. The Continental Congress and state governments reserved to themselves two-thirds of the proceeds from the sale of prizes captured by public warships. Privately fitted-out vessels retained the entire proceeds for the captors, making service in privateers potentially much more profitable. Discipline was less regular than onboard men-o'-war, and less scrupulous privateer captains could turn a blind eye or even participate when the crew decided to appropriate part of the cargo for immediate use rather than wait to go through sometimes lengthy court proceedings. In addition, privateers were devoted full-time to commerce raiding and avoided carrying supplies, transporting diplomats, and other less profitable endeavors. Many seamen also believed it less dangerous to serve in privateers (which usually fled from warships) than in ships of the Continental Navy, which might engage vessels of the Royal Navy. To counter such occurrences the government often laid embargoes on privateers, refusing to let them sail until public ships were manned.[8]

The government rejected an outright ban on privateering because it harnessed resources that the state and national govern-

Below: *An English privateer engaging a French privateer, in a painting by Samuel Scott, in about 1750. This fine painting gives a good idea of the size and appearance of the small, armed ships that were much used for privateering during this period. Some decades later, in a burst of patriotic fervor and strong feelings of a divine revolutionary mission, the French Convention proclaimed in January 1793, after declaring war on England, that, "you corsairs must board the enemy axe in hand and cut down those proud islanders, the despots of the ocean."*

ments, unable to support the ships they already had, could not have employed. It also gave shipowners whose normal trade was disrupted by war a way to use their ships and perhaps to turn a profit. To safeguard against abuses, Congress required that the master of a privateer post a five or ten thousand dollar bond, depending on the size of his ship, for good behavior, and with each commission issued a warning:

> If you, or any of your officers or crew, shall, in cold blood, kill or maim, or by torture or otherwise, cruelly, inhumanly, and contrary to common usage, and the practice of civilized nations in war, treat any person or persons surprized in the ship or vessel you shall take, the offender shall be severely punished.[9]

Commerce raiding by privateers contributed to the common cause, not simply by capturing cargoes needed by Americans but also by forcing Britain to disperse its forces, and thus preventing it from attacking American shipping or the long and largely defenseless American coast.

American shipowners and sailors did not think in such strategic terms. Although many cited patriotic motives, profits were at least as strong an incentive. During the first year of the war 136 American privateers put to sea. Vice-Admiral Richard Howe's secretary recorded that "the Rebels are fitting out every Vessel that can sail" as a privateer—a situation confirmed for Boston by David Cobb, who wrote that "the Spirit of Privateering is got to the highest pitch of enthusiasm, almost every Vessell from 20 Tons to 400 is fitting out here [as a privateer]."[10]

The Admiral and the Infestation
Most privateers from New England ports cruised the Grand Banks, where they preyed upon fishing vessels and merchantmen trading between Great Britain and her remaining loyal colonies. Privateers with larger vessels and those based in southern ports preferred the Caribbean, which required longer voyages but promised greater profits. British officials were quick to respond to the swarm of predators. In February 1776 Admiral Molyneux Shuldman, the British naval commander in America, wrote the Admiralty to advise "that all supplies to this country . . . be

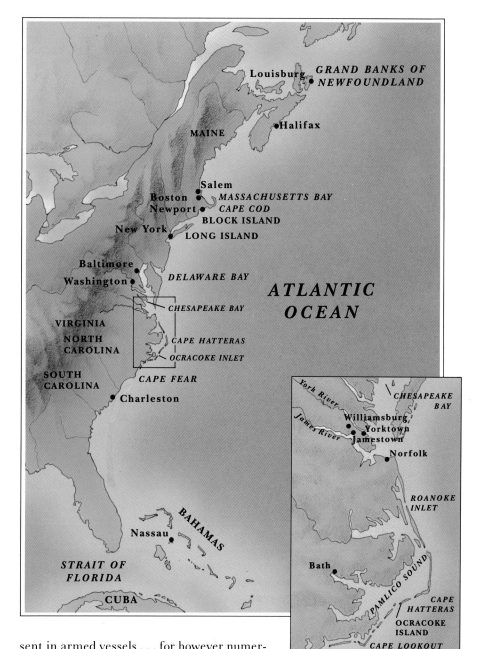

sent in armed vessels . . . for however numerous our cruisers may be or however attentive our officers to their duty, it has been found impossible to prevent some of our . . . small vessels falling into the hands of the rebels." Conditions had not improved three months later when the captain of the *Phoenix*, stationed at New York, reported he was "apprehensive [that privateers] will in a very short time Infest this Coast so, that no Vessel unless well Armed will be able to approach this Port."[11]

Shortly thereafter the Admiralty organized a convoy system. Ships, sometimes as many as 100, gathered at Portsmouth on England's south coast, or at Dublin in

Above: *A map of the east coast of North America showing the principal privateer ports and harbors (with the main region highlighted) situated along a very lengthy coast that was difficult to defend. To the north, the Grand Banks of Newfoundland were busy fishing grounds as well as a route for British ships trading with her colonies; to the south, the Caribbean remained a place of rich pickings for both privateers and pirates.*

Ireland, and crossed the Atlantic under the protection of warships. But some ships always fell behind and privateers picked off the stragglers. By the end of 1778 only one of the fourteen merchantmen purchased by Congress in 1775 remained in service, nine of the thirteen frigates it ordered built in 1776 were lost, and only one of the three cutters commissioned in Europe still sailed.[12] But there were still plenty of privateers, and they, more than the Continental Navy, represented American hopes at sea.

More and More Commissions

The number of investors sending out privateers rose continually as the war progressed. Congress issued thirty-four commissions in 1776, but the number rose year after year and the total for the war was around 1,697 letters of marque involving more than 1,300 oceangoing vessels.[13] The vast majority of these went to Americans but a few were issued to foreign nationals such as French privateers sailing out of Guadeloupe and Martinique.

States also issued letters of marque during the war. Massachusetts accounted for 998 commissions (to seven hundred vessels), one-third of those issued by states, and her ships took almost 1,200 prizes.[14] Indeed, so eager were citizens of the Bay State, that a group from New Bedford and Dartmouth fitted out a vessel and captured the British sloop of war *Falcon* off Martha's Vineyard six months before the state assembly authorized privateering on November 1, 1775.

Pennsylvania issued the second-largest number of commissions, 448 (100 in 1779 alone). Maryland issued 248, Connecticut 202, and Rhode Island 193. Records for other states are incomplete but newspaper notices of prize hearings in New England states and New Jersey indicate that privateers sent 2,106 captured ships into those states for adjudication by Admiralty courts.[15]

Americans in Europe

American privateers also took the war to Britain's home islands. The *Hawke*, a schooner

Above: *A view of Boston's waterfront in the eighteenth century. Boston and Newport, Rhode Island, were two of the major centers for privateers who cruised the coast of New England and the Grand Banks of Newfoundland preying on fishermen and merchant ships. An important port and city in its own right, Boston was also a center of revolutionary activity and an important commercial hub for the merchants and pirates involved in the Pirate Round.*

Below: *A nineteenth-century French engraving showing French privateers attacking a Dutch ship off the coast. Furious hand-to-hand fighting is taking place as the attackers come alongside the victim and swarm aboard. The French corsairs operating "la course" out of St. Malo, Dunkirk, La Rochelle, and Nantes, had a long pedigree, and with their long enmity with England they were natural allies, directly or indirectly, for the Americans —both countries proclaimed the newly discovered Rights of Man, the greatest transgressor of which they believed to be England.*

out of Newburyport, Massachusetts, was one of the first privateers to cross the Atlantic. It took five British prizes before entering the harbor at Bilbao, Spain, in early October 1776. Others followed, and by the summer of 1777 the Admiralty felt forced to station four warships in the Irish Sea to protect British commerce.[16] Lord George Germain, secretary of state for the American Colonies, was driven to exclaim:

> We have lately had so many privateers upon our coasts and such encouragement given them by the French, that I was apprehensive a few weeks ago that we should have been obliged to have declared war.[17]

The formal outbreak of war between France and England in 1778 did nothing to improve conditions for British shippers. In early 1779, for example, the *Hampden* and *General Sullivan* of New Hampshire and the *Black Prince, Pilgrim,* and *Franklin* of Massachusetts operated in European waters.[18] That May a Boston observer wrote that "privateering was never more in vogue."[19] They were joined by other ships that never entered an American port. Prior to France's joining the war, its merchants, perhaps remembering the profits made raiding British commerce in previous wars, quickly sought letters of marque from American diplomats in France. Dunkirk, the home of Jean Bart, had been a center of privateering for centuries, and merchants there fitted out seventy-eight privateering vessels during the American Revolution, including six that sailed under the U.S. flag.[20]

Three of the six sailed under commissions issued by Benjamin Franklin, who hoped the privateers could capture British sailors who could be exchanged for American seamen held prisoner by the British. His efforts to

Above: *An engraved portrait of John Paul Jones with drawn sword on the deck of his ship. He was born in Scotland, but when Britain declared war on the American colonists in 1776 he joined the rebels. He led several devastating attacks on British warships and made a number of daring raids on the British mainland.*

obtain their release met little success. In 1778 Continental Navy Captain John Paul Jones and his ship the *Ranger* captured the *Drake*, a similar-sized vessel of the Royal Navy. Jones took the *Drake*, with its officers and crew, to France, where he and Franklin hoped to exchange the prisoners for Americans held in English prisons. That plan came to naught when French authorities forced them to transfer control of the prisoners to port officials and then exchanged them for their own countrymen.

By early 1779 almost five hundred American seamen languished in British prisons, and it became clear that their only hope lay in an exchange for a like number of British mariners. Thus when John and Charles Torris, merchants of Dunkirk, and Stephen Marchant, a shipmaster from Boston, sought a U.S. letter of marque in May 1779 for their

ship, the ex-smuggling cutter *Friendship*, recently renamed *Black Prince*, Franklin issued it. Between June 12 and September 24, the *Black Prince* made four cruises in the English Channel and Irish Sea taking thirty-four prizes, of which it burned three, ransomed twenty-one, had eight recaptured by the British, and brought into port only two. In all it took eighty-six prisoners, thirty-four of whom it paroled and the rest it brought into French ports for Franklin to exchange for Americans.

Franklin subsequently granted letters of marque for two other ships, the *Black Princess* and the *Fearnot*, operated by the same group of men out of Dunkirk.[21] Franklin never recorded whether he thought the results worth the effort, but there is no doubt that his privateers annoyed the British, in whose minds they were linked to John Paul Jones's audacious Irish Sea cruise of 1778, and the cruise he made around the British Isles in 1779 in command of a squadron consisting of the *Bonhomme Richard* and *Alliance* of the Continental Navy, and four French privateers. Jones and his ship took several prizes and captured two Royal Navy ships, the *Serapis* and *Countess of Scarborough*. Jones drew particular ire from the British both because of his Scottish birth and because his operations included landings on the coasts of England and Scotland. Thus Jones was often referred to as a "pirate," which he never was, or more charitably as a "privateer," something he also was not, but a term often used by the British for Continental and state navy vessels and officers. Only sovereign nations could, under international law, establish navies or issue letters of marque, so that the reference to Americans as privateers instead of naval officers did not reflect a refusal to recognize the former colonies as independent; rather, it signified a reluctance to accord their ships and men the respect due a regularly constituted navy.

America's Backpond

American commerce raiders were even busier in the Caribbean than around the British Isles, and it was there that American privateers came closest to totally disrupting British commerce. Yankee mariners were well acquainted with the waters of the West Indies, which were closer to the rebelling colonies than to the mother country, and foreign governments gave more support to privateering in the islands.

In July 1776 the Continental Congress sent William Bingham to Martinique with blank letters of marque. With French connivance he operated a Court of Admiralty to adjudicate prizes brought to the island by privateers sailing under the U.S. flag.[22] In April 1777 Lord Macartney, governor of Grenada, Tobago, and the Grenadines, sent officials in London a list of thirty-one American privateers operating out of Martinique, and thirty prizes recently captured by them.[23] In December a British informant counted eighteen American privateersmen in the harbor at St. Pierre at one time.[24] Between October 1776 and May 1778 the Royal Navy captured ten American privateers, but this was not enough to protect British ships in the area.[25]

Britain retaliated against American and French privateers by issuing letters of marque of her own, and came close to matching the score of property captured. The vice-admiralty court in Halifax, Nova Scotia, for example, heard cases involving captures made by fifty-three privateers.[26] On balance it is difficult to calculate the impact of privateering on the outcome of the American Revolution. During the war the Continental Congress issued letters of marque to 1,697 vessels, and these, combined with privateers commissioned by state governments, captured approximately six hundred British prizes worth a total of $18,000,000—figures three times those for the Continental Navy. Yet, Royal Navy vessels and British privateers captured as many American ships. Privateering certainly did not win the war, but it made British merchants and mariners feel its effects; it forced the Admiralty to assign ships to convoy duty and to dispatch others all around the North Atlantic and the Caribbean to hunt down privateers; and it provided employment for American ships and sailors. The cargoes they sent in to port provided Americans with goods the mother country would have denied them, and served as proof that Britons were suffering in the war, thereby bolstering American morale.

The Anglo-French Wars

The peace that followed the War for American Independence ended in 1793 when Great Britain and France returned to war. Britain renewed her campaign to limit rights of neutral shippers to use of the seas; to the Rule of 1756 (unilaterally proclaimed) the English added an expanded list of contraband goods that included foodstuffs for the first time in history. Cognizant that French harvests had been very poor in 1792, Britain acted to cut her enemy off from outside sources of grain. On March 25, 1793, Britain and Russia signed a treaty agreeing to pre-

Below: *A bust of Captain John Paul Jones by the French sculptor Houdon. His actions against the British led to his becoming an American naval hero and he was awarded a gold medal by Congress. It also, naturally, endeared him to the French, and the king of France made him a chevalier.*

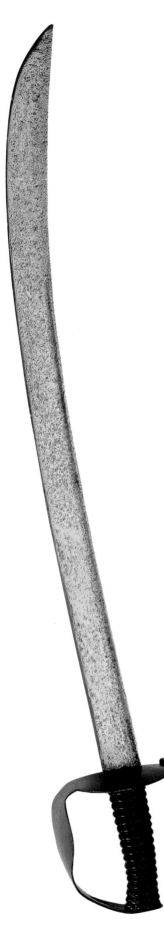

vent French import of grain from any nation.

France, her allies, and most of the neutral nations wished to expand neutral rights and so denounced the Anglo-Russian treaty. French leaders proposed adding noninterference with fishermen and the abolition of privateering to expanded protections for trade. Britain would never accept such views in the eighteenth or nineteenth centuries.

America Tries to be Neutral

The bounds of protection to be accorded neutral shipping were first tested by Americans. At the start of her war with Britain in February 1793, France did not invoke the terms of the Franco-American Alliance of 1778, which allowed France to call on the United States for assistance in protecting her possessions in the western hemisphere. Instead France simply threw her Caribbean Islands open to American traders in the hope that trade in American-flagged vessels would keep supplied the islands that were soon to be cut off from France by a British blockade.

Britain responded with Orders in Council instructing the Royal Navy to enforce the doctrine that "trade illegal in time of peace is illegal in time of war" from the Rule of 1756. When British warships began seizing U.S. ships caught trading with French possessions or carrying French colonial goods, the French began issuing letters of marque. On April 8, 1793, Edmund Charles Genêt, France's new minister to the United States, landed in Charleston with plans to use the United States as a base for privateering against the British. With him he brought 250 blank letters of marque, four of which he immediately issued to ships fitting out as privateers. When those privateers took British prizes into Philadelphia and New York for adjudication by French consuls who also served as admiralty judges, U.S. officials protested that such activity violated President George Washington's April 22, 1793, proclamation of neutrality, and they banned privateers from American ports.[27]

This action angered French officials, who were further alarmed when the United States and Britain settled their outstanding disputes by signing the Jay Treaty. When it became clear that Americans would follow British commercial regulations, the French reacted by issuing a decree (July 2, 1796) saying that France would treat neutral ships in the manner their government allowed Britain to treat them. During the next six months French forces seized over three hundred American ships in the Caribbean alone.

The Quasi-War

French privateers soon began operations off the coast of the United States, leading the government of John Adams both to send diplomats to Paris and to reestablish an American navy. In 1785 Congress had sold the *Alliance*, the last ship of the Continental Navy, and with the ratification of the Constitution in 1788 all states gave up their right to form navies. Thus for a decade the United States had been without a naval force. The first duty of the new U.S. Navy, authorized July 1, 1798, was to clear U.S. waters of French privateers, and the first vessel captured by the infant navy, during what would later be called the Quasi-War, was *la Croyable*, a French privateer that had plundered the cargo of an American ship off New Jersey.[28]

After most French privateers were swept from U.S. waters by mid-1798, the Caribbean became the chief theater of U.S. Navy operations for the rest of the war. This deployment resulted from the continued success of French privateers, which took 489 American prizes in 1797 and 1798.[29]

By 1799 French privateers no longer posed a major threat to U.S. shipping. One factor in this was the recall to France of Guadeloupe governor Victor Hugues when officials in Paris concluded he was not only failing to enforce French laws governing privateering, but that he had actually encouraged and personally invested in activities that crossed legal limits and amounted to piracy. His removal contributed to a decline in American losses around the island, from 89 vessels in 1798 to 38 the next year. French privateers shifted their operations to the north coast of South America, using Cayenne as a base, but there was less American commerce in that area. The U.S. Navy and Britain's Royal Navy contained French activity in that region fairly well until 1800, when Victor Hugues, cleared of charges in Paris, became governor of Cayenne and U.S. losses tripled in the area,[30] before the conclusion of the war brought French attacks to an end.

Robert Surcouf's Private War

Few U.S. ships sailed the Indian Ocean

during the decades either side of 1800, but plenty of British merchantmen did. With most of France's ports closely blockaded by Britain, a number of French privateers set sail for the Indian Ocean. Foremost among these ranked Robert Surcouf of St. Malo, who had gone to sea at age thirteen and engaged in the slave trade between Africa and Mauritius, rising to command a slave ship in 1794. Shortly after France outlawed the slave trade, Surcouf abandoned it for privateering. Taking command of the *Emille*, a defensively armed vessel that had been denied a letter of marque, Surcouf captured a number of British vessels in the Bay of Bengal, including the East Indiaman *Triton*. When the governor of the Île de France (Mauritius) deprived him of the prizes because he lacked a letter of marque, Surcouf went to France and got the decision reversed. On his return, he cruised for two years in the *Clarisse* and *Confiance*, taking dozens of British ships, including the *Kent*, another rich East Indiaman. Surcouf returned to France a rich man during the

brief peace brought by the Treaty of Amiens in 1802. When the war resumed in 1803 Napoleon offered him a commission in the French Navy, but Surcouf preferred to invest in privateers sailing from St. Malo. In 1807 he had the *Revenant* constructed for his own command and sailed it to Mauritius. In it he made two successful cruises, then returned to St. Malo and remained ashore, financing privateering expeditions led by his former lieutenants. With the French Navy almost non-existent following its defeat at Trafalgar in 1805, Surcouf enjoyed great popularity for his attacks on British shipping; Napoleon made him a baron of the French Empire.

The War of 1812

Peace between the United States and France brought an end to American privateering for a decade, though it did not stop American losses. Britain and France continued at war and both did all in their power to deprive the other of overseas trade. After the Battle of Trafalgar had brought to an end Napoleon's

Far Left: *A naval cutlass from 1800 or thereabouts. This was the standard weapon for close fighting on deck. Cutlass drill continued in the Royal Navy until 1901 even though boarding enemy ships was no longer a usual tactic and firearms were more effective for general use. By the mid-nineteenth century Wilkinson of London were making cutlass blades that could cut through lead and breastplates.*

Below: *The destruction of the American fleet at Penobscot Bay, by Dominic Serres. On August 14, 1779, a British fleet attacked the American ships in this bay on the coast of Maine, some 200 miles (320km) north of Boston. It was one of the few British naval and military successes during the course of the Revolutionary War.*

plans for invading the British Isles, the French emperor devised the Continental System to exclude Britain economically from the rest of Europe. Britain responded with a blockade to prevent neutral trade with Europe. As the largest neutral trader, the United States was the most affected, and American trading vessels again fell victim to British and French warships and privateers. Such losses, or at least public complaints concerning them, stopped in 1807 when the U.S. government imposed an embargo on trade from American ports in an effort to force European recognition of neutral maritime rights. The embargo and the subsequent Non-Intercourse Act failed to achieve the desired results, and after much diplomatic maneuvering on all sides, the United States government declared war on Great Britain on June 18, 1812, to protect those rights.

The War of 1812 was far more popular than the Quasi-War with France, in part because it was directed against an enemy with literally thousands of ships that could be seized. There was little of the debate that had accompanied privateering during the Revolution. Eight days after voting for war, Congress enacted legislation encouraging and regulating privateering.[31] Shipowners and merchants had anticipated such action and on July 1, 1812, less than a week after passage of the legislation, a New England newspaper reported:

> The people of the Eastern States are laboring almost night and day to fit out privateers. Two have already sailed from Salem and ten others are getting ready for sea.

This was in New England, where congressmen had voted against declaring war. Three days later a Baltimore newspaper reported similar activity, and on July 15 *Niles' Weekly Register*, also in Baltimore, predicted:

Below: *A schooner commanded by Robert Surcouf attacking the merchant ship* Hope. *Surcouf was from St. Malo but spent a profitable ten years operating as a privateer in the Indian Ocean. Using the French island of Mauritius as a base, he made numerous attacks on British ships and secured his richest prize with the* Kent, *a thirty-eight gun East Indiaman. His success prompted the East India Company to offer a reward of 2,500,000 francs for his capture. Accused by an English prisoner that the French fought for profit but the English for honor, Surcouf is supposed to have replied: "That proves that each of us fights to acquire something he does not possess."*

In sixty days, counting the day on which war was declared, there will be afloat from the United States not less than one hundred and fifty privateers. . . . Sixty-five were [already] at sea on the 15th inst[ant].[32]

During the opening months of the war virtually any vessel large enough to carry a single large gun and a crew of fifty or sixty armed men could hope to capture British merchantmen, which sailed unguarded and often unarmed because the Royal Navy had swept the French from the sea. The small American privateers generally made for the West Indies or waters off Nova Scotia, Newfoundland, and the mouth of the St. Lawrence River. By mid-October New York alone boasted twenty-six privateers, half of which mounted only one to four guns.

The *Yankee* Makes a Good Return
Several of these small vessels enjoyed noteworthy success. *Jack's Favorite* from New York, carrying five guns and eighty men, took five prizes during its first cruise. Two were sent into port and sold, with the handsome profit distributed, half to the owners of the privateer, half divided among the officers and crew. The *Jefferson*, a small schooner with two guns and forty men operating out of the port of Salem, Massachusetts, captured a brig, four schooners, as well as a shallop, all carrying dry goods. Of these early privateers, the schooner *Fair Trader* made the most captures, a ship, a brig, and five schooners, before herself falling prey to a Royal Navy brig on July 16,[33] just shy of a month after the start of the war. Such cruises are evidence that while privateering could bring great profits, it could also result in significant losses, especially for an individual who risked all his money in a single vessel instead of purchasing shares in a number of privateers.

The British navy quickly responded to the American onslaught. Between the outbreak of war in June and the end of August, the Royal Navy squadron at Halifax captured or destroyed more than twenty American privateers, several of which were attacked in the creeks around the Bay of Fundy.[34]

Larger vessels took longer to arm, provision, and man, so few were ready for action until the fall of 1812. On September 7, 1812, the *America*, one of the most successful privateers, set sail from Salem, Massachusetts.

Armed with twenty guns and carrying 120 men, the 350-ton vessel took its first prize, the brig *James and Charlotte*, on September 23. Before returning to Salem on January 7, 1813, the *America* took another five British prizes, bringing the value of its captures to $58,000. Three additional cruises brought a further thirty-four prizes by April 1815. The four cruises netted for her owners, George Crowninshield & Sons, the considerable sum of $600,000, making the *America* one of the most successful privateers of the war.[35]

The *Yankee*, a 168-ton brig armed with a "long tom" (a long-range twelve-pound cannon), and fourteen nine- and six-pounders, had an equally spectacular career. Putting to sea from Bristol, Rhode Island, in mid-July 1812, the *Yankee* headed for the coast of Nova Scotia where it encountered the much larger,

Above: *A painting by Frank Schoonover entitled* They Rushed into the Moonlight. *It is an illustration from "Privateers of '76—a Story of the Revolution," by Ralph D. Paine.*

Above: *A painting of Crowninshield Wharf at Salem, 1806, by George Ropes, Jr. This busy harbor in Massachusetts was an operational base for many privateers, contributing more sailors and ships than any other during the Revolutionary War. It was active again during the War of 1812 and was also much used for the Eastern trade. Moored alongside the quay in this picture are the famous privateer* America, *as well as* Fame, Prudent, *and* Belisaurus. America *was one of the most successful privateers of all.*

Right: *A brass-mounted sea service pistol and ramrod. This flintlock is typical of the type issued to British naval officers between 1760 and 1820. Normally such pistols had a belt hook or lanyard ring because seamen needed both hands free when boarding an enemy ship.*

but more lightly armed and manned, British privateer *Royal Bounty*. After several exchanges of fire, the sails and rigging on the British vessel were cut to shreds and her helmsman killed by small-arms fire. This allowed the *Yankee* to cross the bow of the *Royal Bounty* and rake her fore and aft, forcing the larger ship to surrender. After taking several other prizes the *Yankee* returned to port. In October the *Yankee* sailed to the African coast, where she captured a succession of merchant ships loaded with rich cargoes of gold dust, ivory, camwood, and dry goods, before returning to Rhode Island. The *Yankee* then conducted five more predatory cruises, mostly along North America or off Ireland. All were successful, but none as spectacular as the first. In total the *Yankee* captured nine ships, twenty-five brigs, five schooners, and one sloop, seizing or destroying property worth $5,000,000.[36]

Britain Fights Back

Few ships had as spectacular successes as the aptly named *America* and *Yankee*, perhaps because, although British ships carried particularly valuable cargoes in the Caribbean, their owners were more used to having their ships attacked, and thus protected them better. Indeed, so many American privateers cruised the Caribbean within weeks of the

outbreak of war that by October 1812 British vessels around Jamaica sailed "in small squads of 4 or 6 ships" for protection against the American raiders.[37]

On January 13, 1813, Rear-Admiral Sir George Cockburn arrived in America to enforce the blockade of the Chesapeake and Delaware bays, proclaimed the previous month. Shortly thereafter, Admiral Warren, Cockburn's senior, extended the British blockade to all U.S. ports between New York and the Carolinas, then extended it again to include the eastern entrance to Long Island Sound. This made it difficult for privateering vessels outside New England to get to sea. America countered by ordering its warships to create "a powerful diversion" by attacking British merchantmen rather than warships, but few ships eluded the blockade to execute the strategy.[38]

Cockburn's squadron was particularly successful in closing the Chesapeake to commerce and in preventing commerce raiders at Baltimore from getting to sea. During the War of 1812 Baltimore sent 122 privateers to sea, more than any other American port. In addition, schooners sailing from Baltimore ranked among the best in design, and their officers and crew as capable as any others. Baltimore's privateers took over five hundred

prizes, almost 40 percent of the total captured by American privateersmen in 1813 and 1814. Baltimore's privateers "constituted," in the words of Jerome Garitee, "virtually the only challenge and the only obstacle to Britain's efforts to strangle America's seaborne commerce,"[39] though at a very heavy cost. During 1813, twenty Baltimore privateering vessels were lost to the British or to bad weather, and the following year another twelve were put out of action. Still, their continued success made Baltimore a target equal to Washington in enemy operations in the closing year of the war. By the summer of 1814, Europe was at peace, Napoleon having abdicated in April, and American privateers, with those from Baltimore in the forefront, formed the only threat to Britain at sea.

The most important incident involving a privateer in 1814 took place three thousand miles (4,828km) from the Chesapeake. Late in the summer, the *General Armstrong,* commanded by Captain Reid, put to sea from New York and crossed the Atlantic to Fayal in the Azores. The Royal Navy brig *Carnation* (eighteen guns), frigate *Rota* (thirty-eight), and the ship of the line *Plantagenet* (seventy-four) arrived later that same day and launched a massive attack. Reid defended his ship so stoutly that the British lost sixty-three killed and eighty-five wounded. In the end Reid accepted the inevitable. He ordered his ship to be scuttled and led his men ashore. Rarely in history has a single vessel inflicted such disproportionately heavy casualties on so superior an opponent.[40]

The loss was even greater to the British in strategic terms. The ships that engaged the *General Armstrong* were part of the fleet en route to attack New Orleans. As other ships reached Fayal, they paused for over a week to help bury the dead and care for the wounded. Their delay proved crucial to the outcome of the battle because it allowed additional reinforcements to reach New Orleans and gave Major General Andrew Jackson precious time to construct additional defenses around the city.

Jean Lafitte

A section of those defensive works was manned by a controversial band of privateers —or pirates, depending on one's perspective—led by Jean Lafitte, one of the most colorful and controversial figures of the era.

Born in Port-au-Prince, Haiti, in 1782, Lafitte and his elder brother Pierre moved to New Orleans when Haitian blacks rebelled and expelled the French. After briefly operating a blacksmith shop in 1805, the Lafitte brothers turned to trading in smuggled goods and slaves. By 1811 Jean Lafitte had become the leader of a large band of disreputable characters operating from islands in Barataria Bay, south of New Orleans. Between 1803 and 1810 Britain had occupied France's island possessions, from which a number of privateers moved to Barataria with French letters of marque authorizing them to attack British shipping. Other Baratarians held letters of marque from the Republic of Cartagena (established in 1811 in what is now Colombia) authorizing them to prey upon Spanish commerce. As many as three thousand men sailed in thirty ships, mostly small brigs and schooners, returning to Barataria with their booty. Jean Lafitte does not appear to have commanded ships himself, but instead built and managed warehouses, transferred illegal goods through a maze of waterways, and conducted auctions of captured slaves and merchandise without paying American customs duties. As the leader of men who were, in the eyes of the law, pirates, Lafitte was a pirate.[41]

When the United States declared war on Great Britain in June 1812, six New Orleans residents received letters of marque and reprisal to prey upon British commerce, but only one vessel, the *Spy,* enjoyed any success.[42] With British warships hovering off the coast, Baratarians preferred to target Spanish shipping and continue selling captured goods. In November 1812 Jean Lafitte was caught smuggling but jumped bail the following spring. On November 23, 1813, the governor of Louisiana posted a $500 reward for the capture of Jean Lafitte, who countered with a $5,000 reward for the delivery of the governor to Barataria.[43]

Meanwhile the War of 1812 approached a climax as Britain prepared invasions of northern New York state, the Chesapeake, and the Gulf Coast. On September 3, 1814, emissaries of the British force preparing to attack New Orleans offered Lafitte $30,000, a commission in the British military, and immunity from punishment for past transgressions if he and his men would assist them against the Americans. When Lafitte passed information about British plans to

THE LIFE OF

LAFITTE,

THE FAMOUS PIRATE OF THE GULF OF MEXICO.

Lafitte boarding the Queen East Indiaman.

With a History of the Pirates of Barrataria—and an account of their volunteering for the defence of New Orleans; and their daring intrepidity under General Jackson, during the battle of the 8th of January, 1815. For which important service they were pardoned by President Madison.

U.S. officials, most thought it a ruse aimed at getting them to cancel an expedition being formed to attack the outlaws' settlement. In September a joint navy-army force of two schooners and six gunboats with seventy soldiers burned Lafitte's headquarters at Barataria, imprisoned eighty men, and captured sixteen of their vessels. Lafitte was away at the time so he escaped, but the prisoners were taken to New Orleans and charged with piracy.[44]

Shortly, intelligence confirming Lafitte's information arrived in New Orleans. In a mad scramble to prepare defenses, Louisiana governor William Claiborne accepted Lafitte's offer to help, though Major General Jackson, the U.S. commander, had earlier denounced the Baratarians as "hellish banditti."[45] Some of Lafitte's men fought with the army on the river below New Orleans, but most served on the outskirts of the city in three companies of artillery that on December 28 turned back a British reconnaissance force. Lafitte and the Baratarians supplied maps and expert knowledge of the

area; cannons and cannonballs; and flints, powder, and musketballs, all of which Jackson needed because he had seriously depleted his own supplies during the campaign against the Creek Indians. The assistance of the Baratarians in defeating the British on January 8, 1815, earned them a presidential pardon for their illegal activities prior to that time.[46]

Though accepting the pardon, Lafitte soon returned to his previous activities, established a base on Galveston Island, Texas, and, flying the flags of various "countries" in revolt against Spain, preyed upon Spanish commerce. When such "legal" pickings were scarce, men from Galveston attacked any vessel that appeared. At no time did they follow international laws, which required submitting their captures to prize courts, nor did they pay any fees or taxes to the "governments" whose flags they flew. Lafitte did punish the leader of a band that raided the coast of Louisiana in 1819, but another group captured an American merchantman in 1820 and the U.S. government sent an expedition to destroy the pirate settlement. Lafitte then dropped from sight for a decade before re-appearing in Charleston under the name John Lafflin. From then until his death in 1854 he tried a number of jobs, including manufacturing gunpowder in St. Louis.[47] For two decades Jean Lafitte had lived a most colorful life, mixing privateering and traffic in pirate spoils. New Orleans society welcomed him and he was hailed a patriot in 1815. He was a romantic figure who lived on into a less tolerant era. The great age of privateering was nearly over.

The Last Years

Pirates claiming to be privateers continued to operate in the West Indies for another decade. The extent of the region, its thin population, weak governmental institutions, and great wealth had attracted commerce raiders, some of whom operated legally, since the days of Sir Francis Drake. Between 1810 and 1825 the Latin American wars of independence formed an excellent incubator for buccaneers, especially post-1815. A half dozen revolutionary governments distributed letters of marque; some issued commissions to individuals of any nationality and for ships that never made port in territory controlled by the government. In 1823 a Baltimore

Left: *Lafitte boarding the East Indiaman* Queen *in the Indian Ocean in 1807, as depicted in* The Pirates' Own Book *published in Boston in 1837. Haitian-born Lafitte was a colorful character who at various times was a privateer, smuggler, slaver, and pirate. It is doubtful if this incident ever actually occurred because his operations seem to have been confined to New Orleans and the Gulf of Mexico.*

newspaper estimated that there had been almost three thousand attacks against merchant vessels in the Caribbean since the end of the War of 1812.[48]

Many of the privateer-pirates operated without even a ship. Bands of men in open boats would wait for a merchantman to get becalmed, then row out and board the vessel. Small coves and inlets on Cuba, Hispaniola, and Puerto Rico provided excellent cover, and merchants in Havana and other ports proved ready buyers of the loot. Buccaneers

turned to torture to find gold and silver hidden aboard a captured vessel. When the United States established the West India Squadron to protect a burgeoning trade between its east coast and Gulf ports, the pirates turned to murder to cover their crimes. Charles Gibbs, the leader of a gang of cutthroats that operated off Cuba, claimed that his men murdered the crews of twenty vessels, half the number they captured between 1818 and 1824.[49] By the late 1820s British and American naval action,

Below: *Frank Schoonover's beautifully evocative painting of Jean Lafitte that was commissioned as an illustration for the story "The Haunts of Jean Lafitte" in* Harper's Monthly Magazine *in December 1911. Operating mostly among the islands in Barataria Bay, south of New Orleans, Schoonover has captured the atmosphere of the country where Lafitte had his pirate lair within a labyrinth of lakes and bayous.*

and the end of the Latin American wars of independence, ultimately brought all the Caribbean pirates under control.[50]

American Policy

Revulsion at the crimes committed in the Caribbean under the guise of conducting privateering against Spain helped to turn public opinion against privately armed ships. During the long peace of the nineteenth century, safe passage of Western waters, including the Atlantic Ocean, Mediterranean, and Caribbean, came to be taken as a right by ships of all nations. The industrial revolution, free trade, steam navigation, and transatlantic cables promised progress that sea warfare could not be allowed to hinder. In 1856 diplomats signed the Declaration of Paris, outlawing privateering, tightening conditions under which blockades would be considered legal, and accepting the doctrine that "free ships make free goods," thus providing that cargoes took on the nationality of the vessels carrying them, while at the same time agreeing that cargoes belonging to neutrals could not be seized from belligerent ships. Seven European nations signed the Declaration of Paris and forty-four other states acceded to its terms, but the United States, Spain, Mexico, and Venezuela, all nations with weak navies, refused to sign.[51]

American rejection was based on its experience in the War of 1812, during most of which privateers represented its only effective force at sea. Accurate figures for captures by American privateers during the war are elusive. America issued 1,100 letters of marque, but how many achieved any level of success and just how much success is more difficult to calculate. One historian estimates that only 517 privateers, slightly less than half of those holding commissions, made any captures at all, and that between them the successful ships captured 1,300 British prizes. *Niles' Weekly Register* put the number of captures closer to 2,500 of which 750 were recaptured by the British. A modern analyst calculates that if Newfoundland fishing vessels and small West Indian craft are included the total "was probably from 1,300 to 2,500."[52]

United States policymakers were impressed enough by their success to give privately financed commerce raiders an important role in American naval strategy, a decision it would come to regret, along with its refusal to sign the Declaration of Paris, at the start of its Civil War in 1861, when one of the first actions of the rebelling Southern states was to issue letters of marque.

Confederate Privateers, 1861

Six days after the surrender of Fort Sumter, Confederate President Jefferson Davis responded to President Abraham Lincoln's call for volunteers to force the Southern states to return to the Union by issuing a proclamation of his own. It invited:

> all those who may desire, by service in private-armed vessels on the high seas, to aid this Government in resisting [Northern] aggression, to make application for commissions or letters of marque and reprisal to be issued under the seal of these Confederate States.[53]

Davis also called the Confederate Congress into special session, and on May 6 it adopted regulations to govern privateers. The Union government countered by denying the legal existence of the Confederate government, thus making anyone seizing U.S. property under its auspices a pirate. It also sent a message to Great Britain offering to adhere to the Declaration of London, but Britain rejected the offer.[54]

Several groups responded to the Confederacy's call for privateers. First to receive a letter of marque was the *Triton*, a 30-ton schooner out of Brunswick, Georgia. There is no indication that its three investors ever received a return on their money, but applications poured in, with the greatest number coming from New Orleans, the Confederacy's largest city, where the *Calhoun* became the first Confederate privateer to put to sea and the first to send in a prize, the *Ocean Eagle*, a 290-ton bark carrying lime.[55]

Later that same summer investors transformed the 128-foot-long (39m) icebreaker *Enoch Train* into the privateer ram *Manassas*, the world's first steam-driven, ironclad commerce raider; other citizens of New Orleans constructed the *Pioneer*, a submarine, but both vessels were pressed into government service before making a privateering voyage, and the *Pioneer* was lost defending New Orleans.[56]

On the east coast more Yankee shipping fell victim to privateers off Cape Hatteras

Right: *Another interesting piece by Frank Schoonover, this one dating from 1921 and entitled* A Yankee Ship in Pirate Waters. *An American seaman appears to be under attack from native pirates in Caribbean or Far Eastern waters and is using the butt of his pistol as a club during the close fighting on the deck of his ship. In the early nineteenth century the Caribbean became particularly dangerous and anarchic with thousands of attacks being carried out on merchant ships without provocation as revolutions spread throughout the region.*

than anywhere else. Confederates used lighthouses on the Outer Banks to keep watch, and in the opening weeks of the war the half-dozen vessels of the North Carolina Navy waited inside the barrier islands until a victim was spotted, then sallied forth to attack. Activity was limited, however, for on August 28-29, 1861, a Union force occupied Forts Hatteras and Clark on either side of Hatteras Inlet. This deprived Confederates of one of their best commerce raiding bases and gave the Union navy a sheltered harbor from which to blockade the area known as the "Crossroads of the Atlantic."[57]

Though hailed as patriots in the South, the privateers were reviled in the North. To discourage men from serving in privateers, Union officials treated any they captured as pirates. When the U.S. Navy brig *Perry* captured the *Savannah*, a privateer out of Charleston, the officers and men were imprisoned in New York City and charged with piracy.

By 1862 most Southerners preferred blockade-running to privateering. Eluding Union cruisers was safer than engaging other ships, and the profits could be just as great. In 1862 investors on the Gulf Coast obtained letters of marque for four steamers and a schooner, but only the latter ever got to sea. Within less than a year only one Confederate privateer, the *Retribution*, a converted tug, remained in service. Armed with cannons purchased with proceeds from the sale of cotton it ran

through the embargo, the *Retribution* began a short-lived career as a privateer. Sailing to the Bahamas, it first captured the schooner *Hannah* on January 31 and then the brig *Emily Fisher* on February 19. Finding the *Retribution* in serious need of repair, its captain, John Parker, took it into Nassau and sold it. With this action Confederate privateering came to an end.[58]

Epilogue

The capture of their ports and the Union blockade made returning prizes to the South more and more difficult as the war progressed. The South had other, more famous commerce raiders, but they were regularly commissioned vessels of the Confederate States Navy, not privateers. Together the *Alabama*, *Florida*, and *Shenandoah* took a heavy toll on the U.S. merchant marine and whaling fleet, driving hundreds of owners to transfer registry of their vessels to foreign flags. The Union economy was badly hurt by Confederate commerce raiding, whether executed by privateers or by government cruisers, but it did not influence the outcome of the Civil War.

With the end of that war came an end to the centuries-old practice of nations licensing private ships of war. In 1871 Prussia attempted to adopt a revised form of privateering, but its war with France ended before a system could be devised. Finally, in 1907 diplomats at the Second Hague International Peace Conference agreed that all vessels of war, regardless of type, must be under the total control of an independent national government and commanded by an officer commissioned in the service of the state.[59]

During the twentieth century weaker naval powers have resorted to commerce warfare—as did the United States in the Pacific—but they have employed naval surface ships, submarines, and airplanes. Privateering, which buttressed weak naval powers for centuries and provided opportunities for investors and sailors, is simply outdated. In the age of total war, modern states harness resources through taxation and conscription rather than appeals to financial gain. Privateering is neither necessary nor appropriate. Its near-cousin, piracy, continues in a few places, most notably in the East Indies and South China Sea, and modern liberation movements employ terrorism, not privateers, to strike at those they oppose.

Left: *An aquatint engraving of Charleston, South Carolina, in the mid-nineteenth century. It is a city with a rich maritime history, including pirate and privateering activity: Blackbeard attacked it, it was host to a number of famous pirate trials and executions (including Stede Bonnet), privateers operated from it, and the Civil War began there with the attack on Fort Sumter in its harbor. The Confederacy retained Charleston until 1865, operating blockade runners and privateers for the war effort.*

CHAPTER NINE

THE
EASTERN SEAS

~

That piracy does exist to a very great extent even in the neighbourhood of our settlements is notorious. . . . The most casual view of a chart of these seas is sufficient to convince anyone that no corner of the globe is more favourably adapted for the secure and successful practice of piracy.

EDWARD PRESGRAVE, 1828[1]

THE EPIGRAPH to this chapter comes from a report written in 1828 by Edward Presgrave, registrar of Imports and Exports at Singapore. Compiled when the British settlement on the island was little more than nine years old, it reiterates a persistent fear that the menace of piracy was in danger of undermining the promising but still fragile economy of the newly founded entrepôt. Such worries had preoccupied the European settlers since their initial occupation. In 1823, Stamford Raffles considered the threat of piracy among the most important problems with which his successor would have to deal.[2] While he noted that attacks on European vessels were comparatively rare, he pointed out the growing danger that fear of piracy would deter the "country" or local trade from attempting the passage through the Strait of Malacca. Vital commerce would then be diverted to the rival British settlement of Penang or to the independent state of Aceh in northern Sumatra. His principal suggestion—never fully realized in the years that followed—was for an anti-piracy campaign that coordinated the efforts of the British, the Dutch, and "the principal native states."

Presgrave's report was perhaps the first attempt to set down a detailed factual account of pirate activity in the seas around Singapore. He considered piracy an inevitable result of the collapse of the old Malay empire of Malacca, which had flourished since the fourteenth century, but was destroyed by the Portuguese in the early years of the sixteenth. Ousted from Malacca, Sultan Mahmud had settled with his adherents at Johor on the southern tip of the Malayan peninsula and established the Johor–Riau Empire. This loose-knit federation of petty states and kingdoms stretched from the islands of the Riau Archipelago to the east

coast of Sumatra. But this empire in turn decayed, and its central authority rapidly declined as former adherents were dispersed among the surrounding islands. By the early nineteenth century Johor and the congeries of islands of the Riau Archipelago that controlled the southern end of the Strait of Malacca—Bintan, Galang, Karimun, and a host of smaller islands—were renowned as the haunt of pirates pledging allegiance to local chiefs and rulers. Nominally under the authority of the sultan of Johor, in practice they functioned as largely independent fiefdoms. Many of the inhabitants operated as pirates for part of the year, while for the remaining months "these savage islanders" harvested exotic algae produce that serviced a flourishing export trade with China.

But much of the revenue from this trade was diverted into the pockets of the sultan's greedy functionaries, and Presgrave considered the "oppressive nature of the government . . . among the chief causes which drive these people to seek a livelihood rather by piracy than by honest and patient labour." Somewhat inconsistently, Presgrave also stated—as did almost all European writers on the subject—that piracy was an ingrained racial characteristic of the Malay. Thus, while economic necessity played its part, piracy was also a matter of aristocratic pride, as Raffles himself had discovered in his dealings with the sultan of Johor. Responding to the latter's complaints about the inadequacy of his allowance from the British after the cession of Singapore, Raffles had suggested a scheme that would allow the sultan to engage profitably in commerce. In the face of amused incredulity that a Malay ruler should demean himself with trade, Raffles was barely able to conceal his fury, and inquired why commerce

Left: *The capture of war chief Haji Samman's fort by the boats of the* Iris *and* Phlegethon *in August 1846, one of the many expeditions against Dyak strongholds during that decade. The action shown here involved a large Dyak contingent allied to Raja Brooke. The* Phlegethon *was a steamer belonging to the East India Company.*

Below: *A naval boarding ax from 1870 with its typically curved blade and spike at the back. This was a practical tool for cutting through rigging and wreckage during an action, but it was also a highly effective, if brutal, weapon for hand-to-hand fighting.*

should be shameful while piracy was in no way frowned upon. To which the sultan replied, "Piracy is our birthright and so brings no disgrace."[3]

Piracy took the form of an annual cycle whose very regularity indicates how far such activities were an integral part of the social and economic structure of the archipelago. For the inhabitants of these islands, the months of February to April were taken up with the collection of agar-agar (an edible marine algae). In May the rocks were clear of the algae, and in June, when the southeast monsoon had set in and fine sailing weather was prevalent, the fleets set out in search of plunder. These annual voyages took the proas up through the Strait of Malacca as far north as Kedah. By the end of October almost all the fleets had returned and disposed of their booty, after which they "pass listless lives till the weather again permits them to collect their marine productions, and the season recall them on their predatory expeditions."

Malay Proas Attack

The mode of attack of these marauders had been described in the *Singapore Chronicle* in 1826. While vessels under way were rarely attacked, the favored tactic of the pirates was to lie up concealed and wait to attack grounded vessels (not uncommon in the coastal reaches of these shallow seas), or those "becalmed in the interval between land and sea breezes." Several of the proas would then fall on the vessel "and station themselves under the bows and quarters of a ship when she no longer has steerage way, and [is] incapable of pointing her guns. The action continues often for several hours, doing very little mischief, but when the crew are exhausted with the defence or have expended their ammunition, the pirates take this opportunity of boarding in a mass." The pirates' own tactics also suggested a possible means of defense, that was to stand patiently upon the defensive, and not attempt any actions that would tire the defenders, but rather to wait for an attempted boarding and then take the offensive:

Boarding nettings, pikes and pistols appear to us to afford the most effectual security, and indeed we conceive that a vessel thus defended by a resolute crew of Europeans,

stands but little danger from any open attack of pirates whatsoever, for their guns are so ill-served, that neither the hull nor rigging of a vessel can receive much damage from them, however protracted the contest.[4]

Presgrave considered that there was ample evidence that the pirate fleets were fully supported by local rulers, generally impoverished figures for whom piracy was a more lucrative undertaking than the "more tedious and uncertain profits of commerce." A well-regulated system for the disposal of booty was also in operation. In Singapore before the coming of the British, the Temenggong would supply the pirates with arms and ammunition, as well as money advances, in return for a share of the plunder: the hulls of captured proas, all guns above a certain size, various types of weapons, and some of the female captives all became due to him in direct proportion to the success of the cruise. A similarly organized system was also found aboard the boats themselves, which generally carried from forty to eighty men. During a cruise, the crews came under the authority of the *panglima*, or captain, whose word was law and who held power of life and death, and the *juramudi*, or helmsman. When a prize was taken, the crew were allowed to board and plunder, each taking all he could for himself, with the exception of female captives who became the property of the *panglima*. Each crew member was permitted one male captive, any further prisoners being handed over to the *panglima*. Gold and silver could be taken up to a value of $100, anything in excess also being shared with the *panglima*. This booty was considered distinct from the main cargo, which was divided into two halves, one half going to the *panglima*, the other to the crew.

In emphasizing geography as a major factor in the marauders' favor, and the political and social structures of kingdoms for whom sea-raiding was a legitimate and time-honored activity, Presgrave highlighted the two major disadvantages faced by the Euro-

Right: *A chart of the East Indies made by Pieter Goos of Amsterdam for the Dutch East India Company in about 1660. Made of vellum, its illustrations portray the diversity of riches and wealth of the exotic and alluring East which was to lure pirates to the Indian Ocean from as far away as the Caribbean.*

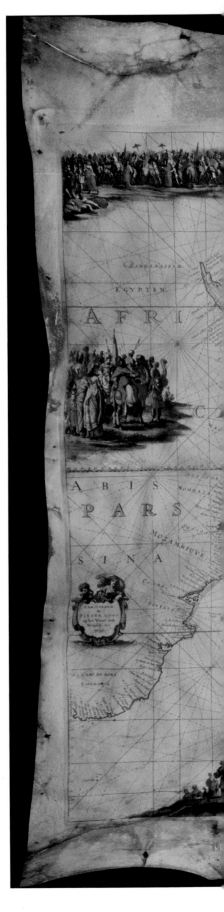

pean colonial administrations in the fight against piracy. The problems of geography would in time be overcome by the use of superior technology and the adoption of anti-piracy measures adapted to the specific physical environment. But the political problem was to prove more complex and less easily solved, for it involved not only the changing structures of the local kingdoms and rulers during a period of transition and upheaval, but was also to encompass the larger international rivalries of the European colonial powers—principally the British and the Dutch—who were attempting to establish political and commercial hegemony in the archipelago. And perhaps the most taxing aspect of this problem lay in the very definition of piracy.

Colonial Complications

Despite a seemingly clear-cut legal description, piracy throughout the ages has always been subject to difficulties of definition: partisan interpretations and political considerations have always played their part, and nowhere was this more true than in Southeast Asia, where the suppression of piracy was often subsumed within the larger political maneuverings of the great European powers. Although those involved in piracy suppression often showed little concern for the niceties of international law when confronted with suspicious or hostile craft, the question of proving piracy became a major headache for the colonial authorities. For if the raiders' actions were sanctioned by their own rulers, and the legitimacy of those rulers was recognized by the British, then legally they could not be considered pirates. In several cases pirates caught red-handed were subjected to the full process of the law, taken at great expense to be tried at Calcutta, only to be released on technicalities and returned as free men to the Straits Settlements (hereafter called the Straits, as distinct from the Malacca Strait).

On the European side, three distinct and sometimes opposed groups were concerned with the suppression of piracy in the Straits, each with its own priorities: those whose commercial interests were directly involved, the local authorities charged with the task of eradicating piracy, and lastly the Supreme Government in Calcutta. To the merchant community of Singapore, the matter was simple. The menace that threatened their present prosperity must be destroyed, preferably at no cost to themselves. If this involved a more active role in the political affairs of the mainland, so much the better, since colonial expansion would bring further commercial benefits in its wake.[5]

The Treaty of London, signed by the British and Dutch in 1824, signaled the end of the Johor–Riau empire. Under its terms

Below: *A view taken on the esplanade at Calcutta, from an aquatint engraving by Thomas Daniell and his nephew William in 1797. It captures the maritime and trading atmosphere of the seat of British colonial power and authority in the East.*

the Dutch withdrew from Malacca and surrendered all political and commercial rights in the Malayan peninsula; British rights to Singapore were recognized, and in exchange the British abandoned their interests in Sumatra and agreed not to form any settlements to the south of the Straits. Thus the treaty not only created two distinct spheres of influence, it also effectively dismembered

the remnants of the Johor–Riau empire, dividing its territories between the two European powers. In addition, the treaty enjoined the two signatories: "to concur effectually in repressing piracy in those seas: they will not grant either asylum or protection to vessels engaged in piracy, and they will, in no case, permit the ships or merchandise captured by such vessels to be introduced, deposited, or sold, in any of their possessions."

Although the treaty contained provisions for mutual cooperation for the suppression of piracy, in reality commercial jealousy and mutual suspicion more often than not hindered effective joint action, leading instead to mutual recrimination and accusations of bad faith.

Admiral Owen in the Strait

At the time of the signing of the 1824 treaty, the forces at the disposal of the authorities in the Straits consisted of a brig of six guns and a cruiser of twelve guns. The schooner *Zephyr*, destined to feature for many years to come in antipiracy work under the command of James Congalton, arrived shortly afterward, but her shortcomings were highlighted in 1827 when she was becalmed during an encounter with pirates off the Dindings and watched helplessly as they rowed away. Such humiliations led to an increasing demand for the use of steamers in the fight against the pirates, a weapon that had been successfully employed by the Dutch, and whose advantages were cogently argued in an article that appeared in the *Singapore Chronicle* in 1826: the generally calm seas of the archipelago, combined with abundant sources of fuel, made steaming conditions ideal and pirates who relied on "calms and shoal water," would "be pursued to certain destruction"; "in short, from the steadiness, rapidity and certainty of such attacks, they would find themselves reduced to a condition of the utmost precarious[ness] and insecurity."[6]

The arguments for supplying steamers would eventually prove conclusive, but for several years government parsimony won the day, and the pirates had to be fought by cheaper means. Throughout the decade of the 1820s a motley collection of craft came and went in the Straits for the purpose of suppressing piracy: flat-bottomed boats that had seen service in the Burmese war of 1823–24, government schooners and yachts,

Below: *The sacking of Ras-ul-Khymah from the southwest, at 2:30pm on November 13, 1809, by a British force under the command of Colonel Smith and Captain Wainwright. Until this action the Wahabi pirates had ruled unopposed throughout the Persian Gulf and ranged as far as Bombay, attacking East Indiamen and British warships. In 1804 British servicemen had been taken as captives and paraded in Ras-ul-Khymah. The punitive expedition mounted in 1809 cleared the Gulf pirates and enabled British maritime commerce in the area to resume—at least until 1816 when a new Red Sea piracy campaign began.*

and light craft built after the fashion of Malay boats, designed for speed and with a shallow draft in order to pursue pirates into shoal water. The difficulty in persuading the Indian government of the urgency of more forceful protection for her settlements to the east is illustrated in the response to the suggestion of Charles Malcolm, the marine superintendent at Bombay, who in 1829 suggested that since piracy in the Persian Gulf had been successfully dealt with, a steamer of the company's marine might be spared for the Straits. Arguing that the Dutch were doing far more to suppress piracy, he suggested that the British should maintain a similar force in their own territories. Such pleas cut little ice with the government, which stated that it could not spare the vessel, the Straits Settlements could not afford to maintain it, and anyway it was not suitable for the suppression of what it dismissively termed "boat piracy." The necessary protection would be supplied by the occasional visits of naval warships.[7]

In 1830, however, a more forceful sweep against the pirates came with the arrival of Rear-Admiral Edward Owen in his flagship HMS *Southampton*. Owen, who had seen action against French privateers in the early 1800s and had served as commander-in-chief in the West Indies in 1822–25, was no stranger to the ways of pirates. He investigated the situation, making several voyages in search of marauders. Officials in the Straits, he concluded, had become demoralized over the years and had lapsed into apathy because of their lack of success.

In the absence of any likelihood of securing convictions against captured pirates, Owen argued for a more pragmatic approach to ridding the seas of pirates, one that would avoid the unsatisfactory judicial procedures then current. Commanders who encountered suspicious vessels should hold off from making arrests and allow the crews the opportunity to escape, so that their boats could then be destroyed.[8] Owen also argued in favor of shore posts that could control the river mouths of troublesome areas, as well as back up a force that he envisaged as consisting of a contingent of light boats each carrying twenty to twenty-five men, acting in concert and protected by a larger warship.

Official sanction for the construction of

Above: *Singapore in the 1840s. Founded in 1819, this colony's rapidly growing seaborne trade attracted local pirates during the nineteenth century, and protests from local Chinese merchants in 1833 resulted in the Royal Navy's sending warships to hunt down the perpetrators.*

such vessels was granted, and in 1831 Governor Robert Ibbetson was able to report that two were under construction at Malacca: they would be fitted with masts and sails in the Malay fashion, would each carry one large gun, and would be some forty to forty-five feet (12-14m) in length.[9] These, he suggested, might be used in conjunction with decoy ships disguised as merchant vessels, but with a strong force of men onboard. A loss inflicted on the pirates in this way would not only be an immediate setback to them, but would make them more cautious in the future about attacking seemingly defenseless vessels. This idea was used effectively several times. Owen's stay in the Straits, however, was brief, and after his departure toward the end of 1830, the impetus again waned.

"A heavy burden for a young colony."[10]

By the mid-1830s any benefits of Owen's piracy suppression work of 1830 had been lost and the number of reported cases of piracy was again rising. Such was the concern in Singapore that in May 1833 a petition, organized and signed by the Chinese merchants of the settlement, was delivered to Governor Ibbetson. These businessmen estimated the annual value of Singapore's trade "at about two millions of Spanish dollars per annum," but pointed out that it was in fact worth far more since the settlement acted as a central point for the diffusion of goods throughout the Malay archipelago in both directions. Losses of cargo to pirates both pushed up prices and depressed trade, and far from eliminating

the scourge, the growth of European commerce had acted like a magnet to the fleets of proas cruising the Straits. The police magistrate in Singapore, Mr. Wingrove, estimated that there were at this time between forty and fifty "piratical prows" cruising the seaways of the east coast.[11]

The merchants demanded effective action, not the piecemeal punitive raids followed by inactivity that had characterized so much antipiracy work in the past. First among their demands was a "permanent and constant" naval presence in the Strait of Malacca which would act as a deterrent. The suggestion of the Indian government in 1835 that taxes might be levied to pay for piracy suppression met with a predictable and immediate outcry from the merchants of Singapore, who quickly succeeded in having the measure quashed. But piracy continued to increase in frequency and ferocity.

Captain Chads of the "Andrew Mac"

The result of this upsurge of piratical activity was that in 1836 an antipiracy commission was authorized with the intention of striking a fatal blow against known strongholds and formulating long-term measures for the protection of trade in the archipelago. The commission was placed in the charge of two officers. The first was Captain Henry Ducie Chads, the commanding officer of the twenty-eight-gun frigate HMS *Andromache*, a man of long experience who had entered the Royal Navy in 1803 and had seen service in the Caribbean and Burma before his present command. Renowned as a most religious man who spent "a part of each morning and every evening in the study of his Bible and prayer,"[12] his ship was known for the quality of its gunnery.[13] Samuel Bonham, who accompanied the commission as representative of the government of the Straits Settlements, was an able and popular administrator who was shortly to become governor.

As far as Bonham and Chads were concerned, the first priority was decisive action against the known pirate haunts at Galang in the Riau Archipelago south of Singapore, where, under the influence of the sultan of Lingga, a thriving pirate community had been settled.

The *Andromache* set off from Penang and cruised down the strait toward Singapore. No pirates were discovered until May 30, 1836, as the *Andromache* approached the Aroa Islands, midway between Penang and Singapore. Disguised as a merchant vessel, *Andromache* stood off the islands while boats were lowered to search closer inshore. The fighting methods of the pirates were well known, and Chads had issued instructions to board any proas with extreme caution, giving strict orders to return to their boats the instant the pirates retreated below. The search party consisted of the ship's pinnace, two cutters, a jolly boat, and a gig, under the overall command of Lieutenant Reed. Dividing themselves into two parties, the boats set off to search the shoreline of the main island,

arranging to meet up at the south side, which it was known was used by pirates for replenishing their water supplies and repairing their boats.

The Galang Pirates

As the gig had been dispatched out to sea to investigate a suspicious sighting, Reed's pinnace, crewed by thirteen seamen and with five marines and armed with a twelve-pounder carronade (a ship's short, large-caliber gun), arrived alone at the rendezvous, where three recently launched proas were discovered. Banging gongs and shouting, the proas (carrying about 130 men) advanced on the lone pinnace, and a lengthy battle began. The timely arrival of *Andromache*'s cutter tipped the balance and led to a general rout as the pirates gave up the battle and attempted to escape. The smaller proa was abandoned as her crew made for the shore, and while a gig set off in pursuit of the fleeing proa, the remainder of the force set to work destroying the other large vessel.

Leaving the cutter and the jolly boat to kill as many of the fleeing pirates as possible, Reed's pinnace followed the gig in pursuit of the last proa. The final act of the drama took place under a tropical moon, as the enemy,

> having at length, like a hunted wolf, turned to bay, giving shot for shot as long as she was able. The whole crew having jumped into the sea, the work of slaughter began,

Below: *A night attack on the* panglima's *proa that took place in September 1843. The* panglima raja, *one of Brooke's Malay allies, was severely wounded and only saved from death by Brooke's intervention.*

with muskets, pikes, pistols, and cutlasses. I sickened at the sight, but it was dire necessity. They asked no quarter, and received none; but the expression of despair on some of their faces as, exhausted with diving and swimming, they turned them up towards us merely to receive the death-shot or thrust, froze my blood. My pistol and cutlass lay idle.... I saw one man, a most muscular-looking savage, receive four shots and three thrusts from a pike, and still he swam and dived. A blow from a cutlass then laid open his head, and he was finished with a pistol. Such tenacity of life is almost incredible.[14]

The following morning the islands were searched and nine prisoners taken. Some 113 Malays had been killed in the fight, without a single casualty in the British boats, a graphic illustration of Montagu Burrows's assertion that "no innate courage, or even rudimentary discipline, could make spears, krisses and jingalls a match for six-pounders, muskets and cutlasses in the hands of British sailors."[15]

Chads then proceeded to Singapore to pick up Bonham, disguising the *Andromache* as an Arab trader in order not to alert the numerous informers who infested the port. After discussion with Bonham, it was decided that now that it was known that all the inhabitants of Galang were connected with piracy in one way or another, and in addition that "an English brig had been carried in there a short time since . . . it was resolved . . . for the welfare of the commercial community and for the cause of humanity, that this place, with every boat found there should be utterly destroyed."[16]

The raid on Galang itself proved something of an anticlimax. The Dutch Resident voiced his disapproval of the mission, arguing that it would upset negotiations that were then ongoing with the sultan of Lingga, but in Chads's opinion these reasons were not considered of sufficient weight to defer the punishment called for by the aggression on the British flag.[17] Galang, a cluster of islands pierced with numerous shallow creeks, was quickly disposed of. Three villages were found and destroyed, while dozens of proas, many armed and ready for sea, were burned. A captured Chinese junk was also discovered, but the unnamed British brig had been burned to the water line as soon as her cargo had been landed some time before. Only a

Left: *The ship's figurehead of HMS Harlequin, a naval brig armed with sixteen guns. She was sent to the East Indies Station and took part in several punitive actions against pirates on the Sumatran coast in the 1840s. The pirates, however, often proved elusive and the attacks on coastal villages were very often hard fought battles.*

Above: *An engraving of James Brooke after the portrait by Francis Grant. Brooke came to the region as a private trader in 1838. He became raja of Sarawak and embarked on a vigorous campaign to exterminate piracy in the region. The portrait helped to establish his image as a romantic hero in the eyes of the British public.*

few pirates were killed, and a few British sailors were wounded (including Lieutenant Reed, who had served so conspicuously in former actions) when some gunpowder exploded during the destruction of a proa.

In 1837 an act finally granted the Admiralty jurisdiction to Singapore, for which both merchants and naval officers had been calling for the best part of a decade. But as the *Singapore Free Press* of September 28, 1837, acidly noted, the settlement's right to try pirates had been granted at the very moment when the means of catching them—naval warships—had been transferred elsewhere to a sideshow in the kingdom of Aceh on the western side of the strait.

James Brooke and the Dyaks of Borneo

In neatly carving out exclusive spheres of influence for the two signatories, the London Treaty of 1824 contained a significant omission that was to have huge repercussions for the history of the archipelago in the following decades. In concentrating on those points where Dutch and British interests were either contiguous or in conflict, it entirely passed over any mention of the island of Borneo. At the time the treaty was signed, Borneo was of little interest or apparent commercial potential, but a decade later, as the European commercial network expanded within the archipelago, and Singapore merchants cast around both for new markets and sources of raw materials, the island, over which the Dutch had no formal claim, became an obvious and tempting target.

The man destined to seize this opportunity was a figure in the heroic mold of Raffles—a man excited by the commercial opportunities of the islands, fired by the spirit of adventure, and driven by a sense of Britain's imperial destiny. Like Raffles, James Brooke was driven by a contempt for the Dutch and for British policy that, disgracefully, seemed to be ceding control of the archipelago to the great national rival. Brooke came from a family of East India Company employees and had himself served briefly in the company's army before arriving in the East in 1839 in his schooner, the *Royalist*, purchased with money inherited on the death of his father in 1835. Here chance and opportunity coincided to direct the future course of the young man's life. While at Singapore he learned of the rebellion in progress against the governor of Sarawak, at this time a province under the nominal control of the Sultanate of Brunei.

Brooke visited Sarawak briefly, but on his return a year later found the same state of affairs as before. In return for his critical role in suppressing the rebellion, Brooke was promised the governorship of the province and in September 1841, after forcing the issue, became governor. In the years that followed, Brooke and his successors extended the boundaries of his domain and established

the dynasty of the White Rajas that ruled Sarawak until World War II. But in the 1840s Brooke's position was still insecure. And one of the most pressing problems with which he had to deal was the endemic piracy of the northern coast of Borneo. While the Ilanuns and Balaninis from the east caused their fair share of trouble along his coastline, Brooke's more immediate problems were nearer home in the Dyak pirate groups based in riverine villages and stockades along the northern coast of Borneo. The campaigns mounted by Brooke against these strongholds were to prove a ferocious and effective demonstration of the superiority of European military technology and organization over local methods of warfare, and it was their very efficiency that was nearly to bring about Brooke's own downfall.

Brooke's rule in Sarawak was not backed by any imperial force, and while he had the support of most of those concerned with the development of the area, he had no European army or navy to act on his behalf. Thus his meeting with Henry Keppel in Singapore in 1843 was to supply Brooke with a vital ally. Keppel had come to the Straits Settlements after service in China, and as an impecunious and ambitious young naval officer was on the lookout for adventures that might further his career. His original commission had been to investigate Ilanun and Balanini piracy, but Brooke and Bonham were soon able to convince the fiery young commander that the Dyaks of the Saribas and Batang Lupor rivers demanded more urgent attention, and equally important, offered certain scope for adventure. Henry Keppel fell under the spell of Brooke's personality and sense of imperial destiny, and in later years, when the raja's actions came under critical scrutiny in England, was to act as his staunchest apologist and spokesman.[18]

The Ibans

The pirates who had most actively menaced Brooke's control of Sarawak and the trade of the region were the Ibans of the Saribas, who lived along the river of that name to the east of Brooke's capital of Kuching. The Saribas pirates were made up of Malay groups who had migrated from the Johor Empire around the end of the seventeenth century, and the much more numerous indigenous Sea Dyaks, renowned for their love of warfare and their

Right: *A Dyak warrior of Borneo. These warlike people made formidable pirates when they took to the sea. They had fleets of long native canoes or* bangkongs *that were armed with swivel guns. Rowed by sixty men, these shallow-draft vessels could hide in narrow creeks and rivers, and make hit-and-run raids on merchant shipping.*

Below: *A panoramic view of Kuching taken from Captain Drinkwater Bethune's work,* Views in the Eastern Archipelago, *published in 1848. It was in the settlement at Kuching in Sarawak that Brooke had his headquarters. Lieutenant Cree visited in 1843 and described it as "merely a collection of Malay houses built on piles at the edge of the river which is here about 100 yards wide."*

head-hunting practices. Keppel estimated that the Malay community of Saribas was never more than 1,500 men, and that in the early days their plundering was limited to those vessels that such a force could overcome at sea, the captured crews being always taken into slavery. The Dyaks, on the other hand, comprised numerous communities totaling several thousand warriors; their warfare was normally restricted to intertribal feuds, their only weapons the spear and the sword. However, with the coming of the Malays,

> in course of time these Dyaks became expert seamen; they built a description of prahu, or bangkong, peculiarly suited to their stealthy and rapid movements; and, together with the Malays, formed the fleets composed of one hundred or more prahus, which swept the seas, and devastated the seas of Borneo over a distance of 800 miles [1,300 km].[19]

As the Dyaks became far more aware of their power, their chiefs attained a more equal relationship with the Malays, and plunder was divided more equitably. According to Keppel, the Dyak thirst for heads, rather than slaves, introduced a more bloodthirsty element

Above: *A brass-barrelled musketoon from 1758. These short firearms were well suited to shipboard use with their wood and brass fittings. They were designed as scatter guns to fire a spray of pistol balls or big lead pellets. When out of ammunition the wooden stock could make do as a club.*

into their activities. The Dyak boat, the *bangkong*, was both lighter and smaller than the Malay craft, drawing very little water and with a long overhanging stem and stern. The biggest of the *bangkongs* measured one hundred feet (30m) in length by nine to ten feet (3m) in the beam, and were rowed by sixty to eighty paddles, so nimbly that they could be turned in their own length while going at full speed. Beside the Dyaks, each *bangkong* also had a few Malays armed with muskets onboard, and sometimes with small swivel guns. These boats had the added advantage that, being strung together with rattan rather than nailed, they could, under pursuit, be beached, dismantled, and the parts spirited away into the jungle, to be reassembled when the coast was clear.

The Saribas Expedition

Keppel and Brooke arrived in Kuching in May 1843 and, in response to news that the Saribas were on the move with more than three hundred war boats, they decided upon an immediate attack on their strongholds. On the morning of July 8, 1843, a force consisting of the *Dido's* pinnace, gig, and two cutters, the *Jolly Bachelor* (a gunboat built by Raja Brooke with a brass six-pounder), and a thirty-five-ton tope carrying the ammunition, entered the Saribas River. Manning the boats were eighty officers and men from *Dido*. In addition, a contingent of four hundred Dyaks raised by Brooke, and 180 men under local chiefs, accompanied the force. By the following day the expedition had advanced as far as Boling, about forty miles (60km) up-

stream. Here the river became shallower and the tope, drawing more water, was left behind under guard. On July 11 the main party reached Padeh. All through the previous night, as they approached their objective, the continuous booming of gongs and sporadic cannon fire had told them of the pirates' awareness of their presence. Just before Padeh the river was blocked by a boom made of some tree trunks lashed together. Spotting a gap, Keppel took his gig (in which James Brooke was also traveling) through, but then found himself drifting toward the waiting enemy, who rushed down the bank toward the boat while those in the three forts on the farther side laid down a heavy fire. For some moments it looked as if the gig might be captured, but in the nick of time they succeeded in turning her and by then the rest of the force was breaking through the boom. Soon a force was landed and a bayonet charge took the first of the pirate forts, throwing the defenders into confusion and precipitating a panic-stricken retreat.

The next day Brooke took a small force farther upriver while Keppel stayed at Padeh with the wounded. That night Brooke was ambushed, but a relieving force sent by Keppel saved the day and led to the Dyaks' complete surrender. After lecturing the chiefs on the benefits of peaceful trading, Brooke invited them to a meeting at Kuching, and the force then turned its attention to the strongholds at Paku and Rembas. Paku was taken with little resistance on July 14 and the stockades were burned to the ground. On the morning of July 17 the force advanced on the much stronger position at Rembas. First a number of booms across the river had to be

cut, and a mile below the town seven hundred of the Dyak levies were landed with orders to creep through the jungle and attack the fort from the rear. Although the strongest of the pirate forts, news of the other actions had sufficiently demoralized its defenders to the extent that they abandoned the fort almost without a shot when attacked from both front and rear.

Return of the *Dido*

The *Dido* sailed for Hong Kong at the conclusion of this short and devastating campaign, but she returned in 1844 to continue the work. In a strongly fortified position at Patusan, fifty miles (80km) up the Batang Lupar, five thousand followers of Serip Sahap and Serip Mular were gathered, emerging in small parties to cruise along the coast in search of heads and booty. The *Dido* returned with the East India Company's steamer *Phlegethon*, and in early August a fresh attack was under way. The four fortresses at Patusan, which protected further native strongholds upriver, were taken with little difficulty, although the force sustained one fatal casualty, John Ellis of the *Dido*, "cut in two by a cannon shot while in the act of

Left: A war dance of the Dyaks, reproduced from Captain Marryat's Borneo and the Indian Archipelago, *published in 1848. Marryat served on HMS* Samarang *from 1843 to 1847 during her cruise to the Far East. On that trip there were many encounters with pirates. This dance was really held as a friendly demonstration, although the dancers were carrying severed human heads in the baskets that hang from their shoulders.*

Right: *A large knife or* wedung *from the Malay Archipelago. The grip is made of dark horn mounted with silver and the blade is heavy, back-edged, and made of etched pattern-welded steel. Although the indigenous pirates greatly outnumbered the forces sent against them, their swords, daggers, and spears were no match for the British who were armed with warships and gunboats. In the many battles that took place in the waters around Borneo and the Malay peninsula, the British sailors' firearms and their ships' broadsides overwhelmed the pirates.*

ramming home a cartridge in the bow gun of the *Jolly Bachelor*."[20]

Beyond Patusan two tributaries branched off from the Batang Lupar, the Undop, on which the fort of the Malay Serip Mular was situated, and the Sekrang, on whose upper reaches were several Dyak forts. The Undop was selected as the first target, and after slow progress up a river blocked by obstacles, the first fort, the headquarters of Serip Mular, was found to be abandoned. Undop was only fifteen miles (24km) farther, but took two days to reach and a short battle to secure. Keppel then turned his attention to the Dyak strongholds on the Sekrang. Progress was slow, but for two days all went well apart from intermittent skirmishing. An ambush on the advancing party of Sarawak levies under Patinggi Ali, however, soon turned into a major incident. While a raft was launched across the river to cut off their retreat, six war proas bore down on the levies. Keppel heard the sounds of the clash, and on moving upstream came upon the fight, an inextricable mass of boats slowly drifting en masse downstream:

> About twenty boats were jammed together, forming one confused mass; some bottom up; the bows and sterns of others only visible; mixed up, pell-mell, with huge rafts; and amongst which were nearly all our advanced little division. Headless trunks as well as heads without bodies were lying about in all directions; parties were engaged hand to hand, spearing and krissing each other. Others were striving to swim for their lives.[21]

Keppel and Brooke succeeded in breaking up this congealed body of men and boats by taking the gig through and diverting the pirates. This plan succeeded, and once the initiative had been regained the stronghold was taken, though after very fierce fighting. Casualties among Keppel's men amounted to thirty killed and fifty-six wounded. No accurate figures were possible for the enemy. The main fort at Jarangan, a few miles farther upriver, was then taken without difficulty.

The two expeditions had inflicted massive destruction both on the pirates themselves and on their strongholds and supplies. Casualties were never accurately computed but must have been immense, and for a period

certainly crippled the pirate stranglehold on the coast. Perhaps more important, these antipiracy activities served to support and consolidate Brooke's control of his new kingdom at a critical moment in its history. To a martial race like the Dyaks, the slaughter of this campaign was perhaps the only way of finally demonstrating the white man's right to rule.

The Battle of Bantung Maru

But within four years the Dyaks were again marauding, and in 1848 Keppel was once more sent to Borneo, this time as commander of HMS *Maeander*. He had achieved little, however, before he was recalled to China, whereupon, on March 1, 1849, between sixty and 100 Saribas war proas swept up the Sadong River, raiding farmhouses and taking over 100 heads. Brooke immediately put a large force of over three thousand men to sea, and although he defeated a Sekrang force of 150 proas and prevented them joining up with the Saribas, he did not manage to corner the main fleet.

Help was soon at hand, however, with the arrival in May 1849 of HMS *Albatross* under Commander Farquhar, and toward the end of July Brooke left Kuching at the head of a powerful flotilla. In addition to HM brig *Royalist* and the company's steamer *Nemesis*, there were three boats from the *Albatross*, three from the *Nemesis*, the *Royalist*'s cutter, and the *Maeander*'s steam tender *Ranee*. Brooke himself traveled in his own locally built *Singh Rajah* (Lion King), escorted by seventeen proas manned by Sarawak Malays. With the various other detachments of Dyaks, the total native force consisted of seventy fighting proas and 3,500 men. This force proceeded to the mouth of the Batang Lupar River, where they learned that a large Saribas fleet had left the river just before their arrival. Brooke and Farquhar then evolved a plan to trap the pirates as they returned, denying them refuge in the jungle, thereby forcing them to fight in deep water, where the proas were at their most vulnerable against steam vessels.

As well as blocking the entrance to the Batang Lupar, the force also closed off the mouth of the neighboring Kaluka, which gave inland access to the Saribas country, and placed men on the flat sandy promontory

Above: *The attack on Paddi by the boats of HMS* Dido. *In May 1843 Brooke and Henry Keppel assembled a force of eighty men from the* Dido, *plus nearly six hundred friendly Dyaks, and set off up the Saribas River in boats. On July 11 they reached Padeh where the river was blocked by a boom of felled tree trunks. Undaunted by fire from the pirates' forts, they broke through and forced the pirates to flee or surrender.*

THE
Jane Ann & the Pirate.

TO A GENEROUS PUBLIC.

I am a poor young man who have had the misfortune of having my Tongue cut out of my mouth on my passage home from the Coast of China, to Liverpool, in 1845, by the Malay Pirates, on the Coast of Malacca. There were Fourteen of our Crew taken prisoners and kept on shore four months; some of whom had their eyes put out, some their legs cut off, for myself I had my Tongue cut out.

We were taken about 120 miles to sea; we were then given a raft and let go, and were three days and three nights on the raft, and ten out of fourteen were lost. We were picked up by the ship James, bound to Boston, in America, and after our arrival we were sent home to Liverpool, in the ship Sarah James.

Two of my companions had trades before they went to sea, but unfortunately for me having no Father or Mother living, I went to sea quite young. I am now obliged to appeal to a Generous Public for support, and any small donation you please to give will be thankfully received by

Your obedient servant,
WILLIAM EDWARDS.

P.S.—I sailed from Liverpool on the 28th day of May, 1844, on board the Jane Ann, belonging to Mr. Spade, William Jones, Captain. Signed by Mr. Rushton, Magistrate, Liverpool, Mr. Smith, and Mr. Williams, after I landed in Liverpool on the 10th December, 1845.

J. Southward, Printer, 9, Upper Pitt Street, Liverpool.

Above: *A handbill printed by a Liverpudlian victim of Malay pirates in 1845 appealing for donations. The text offers a vivid description of the type of fate befalling Westerners who fell into the hands of pirates in the region.*

that ran between the two rivers. On the evening of July 31, Malay scout boats signaled that the pirate fleet was approaching the mouth of the Kaluka, across which Raja Brooke's division was spread. On seeing the river closed to them, the fleet veered off toward the Batang Lupar, only to find access similarly denied to them. A brief stillness descended over the scene as the pirates took stock of the situation, and then over the darkness came the booming of a great gong, that could be heard for several miles. This was a call to a council of war among the Saribas, and after a brief pause its decision became

known, as the fleet headed en masse for the entrance to the Batang Lupar.

Brooke and Farquhar's forces were perfectly positioned to inflict the maximum damage: with the river mouths blocked and the open sea guarded by the steamer *Nemesis*, the pirates quickly became prey to confusion and panic. Seventeen of the larger proas, attempting to head out to sea, were destroyed, while on the shore side the line of battle spread out along a front nearly ten miles (16km) long. The fight lasted much of the night and only as dawn broke did the full extent of the devastation become apparent:

> The results of the night's action became visible with the morning light. On the eastern point, or Buting Marrow, lay upwards of sixty prahus; and on the beach, for a long distance, were strewed the débris of the large pirate fleet. Boats which had been swamped were carried backwards and forwards by the tide. About 2,500 of the enemy sought refuge in the jungle.[22]

No one will ever know precisely how many Saribas died during the Battle of Bantung Maru, but the figure was probably in the region of eight hundred men. The Court of Admiralty, in awarding head money totaling £21,700 for the action, accepted a figure of

five hundred men, and this was no doubt a conservative estimate. The expedition reached Kuching again on August 24 and a few weeks later a great peace conference, at which the Dyak chiefs came in and swore allegiance, was held. While the Battle of Bantung Maru cannot be said to have wiped out the Dyak pirates at a stroke, it had dealt them a devastating blow from which they never fully recovered.

For Brooke and Farquhar the results were less happy. Liberal sentiment had turned against Brooke and he became the subject of very bitter attacks in the British Parliament, accused of the ruthless massacre of natives involved in legitimate intertribal warfare rather than piracy. In addition, the huge sums being paid out in head money, both in Southeast Asia and in the China Seas, were becoming regarded as scandalous. The motions of censure against Brooke were defeated, and he was exonerated in a subsequent Commission of Inquiry that was held in Singapore, but that experience left him embittered against the country in whose service he believed himself to be acting. But more importantly perhaps, such criticism signaled the end of an age when romantic freebooters—pirate and colonist alike—could carve out kingdoms with little heed to the world outside.

Pirates of the Sulu Sea

These pirates had a saying that "it is difficult to catch fish, but easy to catch a Bornean," and, on the other hand, the Borneans, due to being harassed by the pirates, called the easterly wind during the southwest monsoon "the pirate's wind."[23]

The slave-raiding marauders from the islands of Mindanao and the Sulu Archipelago—the Ilanun and Balanini people, respectively—were organized, ruthless, and numerous, and by the 1830s had become the most feared marauders in the archipelago. Although many observers, including James Brooke, referred to the Ilanuns as hereditary pirates, the "calling" of piracy was not of great antiquity among them, and had developed only since the late seventeenth century. William Dampier, who lived for some months among the Ilanun people on the island of Mindanao during 1686–87, gave a detailed account of their society. He found them to be a prosperous and stable people with a developed commercial life, who built "good and serviceable ships and barks for the sea," trading in beeswax and gold with Manila, and buying in return "their callicoes, muslins, and China silk."[24] And while they were a martial race who also built some "ships of war," he makes no mention of any piratical propensities. From such an omission by so

Below: *A view of native houses in Borneo made of reed and bamboo and thatched with palm leaves and matting. The local style was often to build houses on piles along the edges of the rivers.*

Above: *A Dyak attack with poisoned arrows on the boats of* Iris *and* Phlegethon *during their expedition against Haji Samman's fort in 1846.*

Far right: *The pirates of southeast Asia used a variety of weapons, including short swords, knives, daggers, spears, and blowpipes. This is a* dao *from Sulu archipelago, decorated with tufts of human hair. It was captured during an action on September 2, 1879, when HMS* Kestrel *bombarded the pirate village of Taribas on the northeast coast of Borneo.*

observant a recorder as Dampier, it seems safe to assume that at this period large-scale marauding was not a major factor in their lives. Yet by the middle of the nineteenth century, their economic decline in the face of increasing European monopolization of trade had turned them to slave raiding, to such an extent that the months when the monsoon winds brought them west to the waters of the Strait, had become known as the "Lanun Season."

Edward Presgrave's report of 1828 had drawn attention to these Ilanun fleets, whose proas regularly appeared in Malayan waters. Like other pirates of the archipelago, their movements were determined by the monsoon winds. They appeared between the months of August and October; by the middle of October the monsoon winds were too strong for successful piracy, but favorable for the return voyage to the eastern islands. The authorities were not the Ilanun's only enemies in these parts, for in venturing this far afield they also encountered the hostility of locally based pirates, "so much so that if a Lanun prow appear in sight at the moment the former are in the act of taking a prize, their enmity must be gratified before the appetite for plunder is indulged."[25]

Ilanuns of the Lagoon

The southwestern shores of the island of Mindanao are formed in a great curving bay, on the shore of which the sultan's capital of Magindanao was situated, and here the sultan received European traders mingled with the sea rovers who visited his capital. However, the main base of the pirates, and the reason they were known to the Spanish as *Los Illanos de la Laguna*, was on the waters of an almost impregnable lagoon, separated from the bay by a dense web of swamp and mangrove forest, whose stiltlike roots stretching out into the sea formed an impenetrable wall through which Europeans ventured at their peril.

The Ilanuns had taken advantage of these natural features to create an intricate defensive base into which their boats seemed to melt, even when hotly chased: the proas simply disappeared into the depths of the mangrove swamp, and any pursuers foolhardy enough to approach their escape route "were saluted by a discharge of round and grape, from heavy brass guns placed in battery, and so far within this dangerous jungle, that attack was impossible."[26] Escaped slaves reported that within the enclosed waters of the lagoon the Ilanuns maintained extensive shipyards, using the old proas as floating homes for their families and as storehouses for booty, which could be moved to any part of the lagoon in an emergency.

The Ilanun boats themselves were frighteningly efficient fighting machines, bigger than most Malay craft and built for speed in the shallow seas of the archipelago. Several points in their construction, crewing, and fighting methods were strongly reminiscent of the corsair galleys of the Mediterranean, a resemblance that was mirrored in the extent to which slavery formed a crucial mainstay in both the economic and political structures of Ilanun society. (Such similarities had not escaped John Hunt, who visited Sulu on a diplomatic mission in 1814, and dubbed it the "Algiers of the East.")

In terms of construction, the proas were sharp-bowed and wide-beamed, generally exceeding ninety feet (27.5m) in length and with double tiers of oars. The rowers (who might number up to 100 in the largest vessels) were slaves and were not expected (or trusted) to fight except in the direst emergency. The cabin space, which was solidly built with heavy timber, took up a large portion of the upper works of the boat, and was home to a heavy brass gun pointing directly forward. Above the cabin stood the fighting platform, and on this some thirty or forty warriors stood, dressed in scarlet, with various pieces of armor and chain mail. Armed with kris and spear and the great two-handed Lanun sword, their frightful yells struck fear into their enemies and victims.

Unless caught unawares or by trickery, a well-disciplined and well-armed European vessel threatened by Ilanun proas generally had the advantage as long as they could be held off, for the Ilanuns relied on boarding a vessel and taking her by overwhelming force

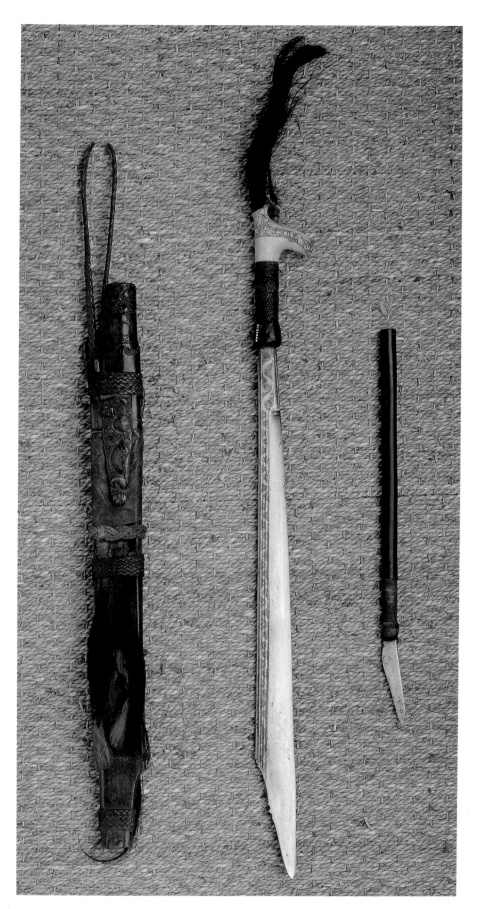

of numbers. If a merchant ship's gunnery was poor and failed to prevent the proa from getting within boarding range, then her outlook was poor, but with accurate fire and:

> with grape and canister fairly directed, the slaughter would be so great that they would be glad to sheer off before they neared a vessel. This is, of course, supposing a calm; for in a breeze, they would never have the hardihood to venture far from land with a

ship in sight, and would be sorry to be caught at a distance . . .[27]

The Ilanuns took to the seas in a number of well-defined divisions that, when occasion demanded, were capable of operating together in a single fleet of up to four hundred sail. But this was exceptional, and generally the fleet was divided into smaller divisions. From their home base on Mindanao, the fleet rendezvoused at their outpost at Tempasuk on the northern coast of Borneo, and here they split into fleets that quartered the whole of the archipelago and beyond. James Brooke of Sarawak, who had a peaceful, if cautious, meeting with a mixed fleet of Ilanun and Maluku pirates at Kuching, learned that their cruise had lasted upward of three years since leaving Magindanao, during which time they had cruised among the Moluccas and the islands to the east, around Celebes and up the Macassar Strait.[28]

And while they were feared in waters under British control, it was the Spanish possessions in the Philippines that suffered most severely from their depredations, as their boats raided for slaves throughout the islands. At Cavite in the Bay of Manila, they even took on and crippled the Spanish gunboat establishment. Even though the Spanish maintained a station at Zamboanga, garrisoned by some of their most experienced officers, they themselves admitted that they rarely bested the Ilanun boats. Not only their seamanship but their cunning and stealth were legendary. If the Spanish were keeping a particularly close watch for them, they would move their proas a small distance each night, hiding up in the mangrove by day, until they had slowly crept past the enemy.[29]

While European accounts have emphasized attacks on European vessels, it should be remembered that the overwhelming proportion of victims consisted of the anonymous and uncounted inhabitants of coastal villages and trading communities. In fact, direct confrontations with Spanish or European warships were the exception, and the Ilanuns had long learned to distinguish between well-armed warships and merchantmen by the color of their canvas, and to give the former a wide berth.

The Balanini Pirates

Almost as notorious as the Ilanuns were their

Below: *An Ilanun pirate from Tempasuk, Borneo. The typical Ilanun garments consisted of a sarong, headcloth, sleeping cloth, and embroidered belt. By the middle of the nineteenth century these pirates were the most feared marauders roaming the seas of southeast Asia.*

allies the Balanini, who based themselves on the string of islands forming the Sulu Archipelago between Mindanao and Borneo. Their way of life was similar, and indeed their fleets sometimes joined up with the Ilanuns for the purpose of slave raiding. Like the Ilanuns, they were similarly wide-ranging in their cruises:

> They have been traced along the whole coast of Borneo, into the Archipelago off the Malay Peninsula, and I am credibly informed (indeed I had it from a Chief, whom I believe to be a Pirate leader) that they trade to Singapore, leaving their warboats at the Natunas, or Anambas. . . .[30]

While their boats also were of similar build they did, according to Rodney Mundy, have one peculiarity among their weaponry that must have terrorized their victims. The Balanini, he wrote,

> seldom carry large guns like the Ilanuns, but, in addition to the usual arms, viz., lelahs (small brass guns), swords, spears, stones, &c., they use a long pole with a barbed iron at the end, with which, during an engagement or fight, they hook their enemies.[31]

The sultan of Sulu also had a power base too weak to oppose his subordinate chiefs or *datus*, and it was they who "participated in the profits, are receivers of, and traffic in the plunder. . . ."[32] Lieutenant William Spiers, a naval officer who visited Sulu in command of a trading vessel in 1821, reported that Sulu "may rather be said to be an aristocracy than a monarchy." The sultan and his sixty thousand or so subjects lived in uneasy proximity to the Spanish Empire of the Philippines, which several times had attempted to destroy them. They, in turn, carried on a constant series of marauding attacks along the coast of the Philippines. Sulu in the nineteenth century was an empire in decay, a polity that at its height had exerted control over Brunei and northeast Borneo, but that now was crumbling into its constituent parts, impoverished and ground down by internal instabilities and the strong external pressures of European colonial expansion and commerce.

It should be remembered that the slave-raiding activities of these states, so promptly condemned under the blanket term of "piracy" by the European powers, were just as much a means of enlarging and consolidating the power bases of conflicting chiefs, and in fact functioned as part of the existing political structures of the archipelago. Thus, viewed from within, the term "piracy" is difficult to sustain. In its practical effects, however, particularly when these were directed against European shipping, the English, Dutch, and Spanish authorities could hardly be blamed for reacting to it in these terms (even if the word itself was inextricably bound up with larger strategic implications and resonances).

The *Seaflower* Incident

Lieutenant Spiers, whose report had provided the Bengal authorities with its first useful account of the situation in Sulu for many years, served to reinforce deeply ingrained suspicions about the tribes who had also been responsible for the still unavenged massacre of the East India Company settlement on the island of Balambangam in 1775. For Spiers's narrative was written in the light of the attempted piracy upon his own vessel.[33]

The *Seaflower* had sailed from Calcutta in April 1821 and arrived at Sulu in July. Here she was received with the "greatest apparent friendliness" and Spiers stayed for ten days, making arrangements to pick up a cargo of "tortoiseshell, pearl shell, wax, brass guns, etc." stored at another island in the group. On August 2 Spiers set sail, taking with him the *datu* with whom he was dealing, as well as a letter from the sultan enjoining all his subjects to treat the English traders well. Arriving at their destination after a voyage of about ten days, during which time the guests had won the trust of their hosts, the crew was suddenly set upon by a large party of Sulus who had boarded the ship at a signal from the *datu* and "began to put their diabolical design into execution of taking the ship and murdering her unsuspecting crew." The attempted piracy was put down with great loss of life, with up to fifty of the attackers killed. Spiers was wounded, and the ship was only saved by the chief officer Mr. Colicut who, though "wounded in three places and bleeding most profusely . . . only remembering that the charge devolved on him he went to the mast head and from it piloted the ship through the narrow channel into the open sea in safety."

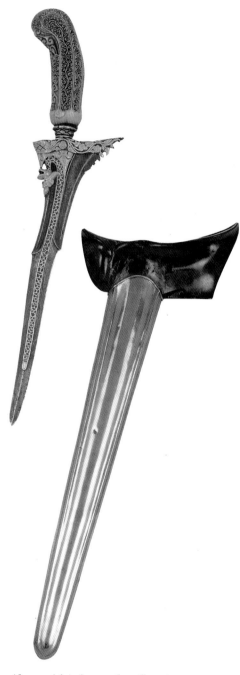

Above: *A kris from southern Sumatra in the late seventeenth or early eighteenth century. The hilt is of finely carved ivory and the blade is of pattern-welded steel that is chiseled and gilt near the hilt. The wooden scabbard is overlaid with "red" gold that was probably added later. The kris is replete with symbolic design elements: a straight blade is a sleeping snake, a wavy blade is a running snake; the hilt —no matter how stylized—represents the eagle demon,* Garuda, *as a helper in battle.*

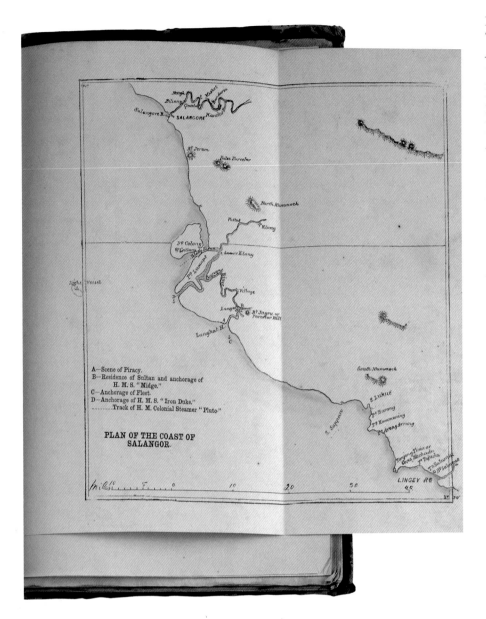

PLAN OF THE COAST OF SALANGOR.

A—Scene of Piracy.
B—Residence of Sultan and anchorage of H. M. S. "Midge."
C—Anchorage of Fleet.
D—Anchorage of H. M. S. "Iron Duke."
........Track of H. M. Colonial Steamer "Pluto."

Above: *This map is from the* British China Station Records: Piracy in the Straits of Malacca 1873-74. *It shows the coast of Salangore, which lies between Perak and Malacca in the Malayan peninsula (near modern-day Kuala Lumpur). "Pirates here were the most daring and bloodthirsty of all Malayan pirates and were supported by nobles, even royals of Bugghese descent who were more warriorlike than ordinary Malayan chiefs. The pirates have stockaded defences up the creeks. Piracy at Salangore is continuous, well organized and daring," is how one British official described the place.*

In their early dealings with the Sulus, mistrust was compounded by ignorance and commercial cupidity. Responding to Spiers's tale, the Bengal authorities confessed themselves ignorant even as to whether the "Island of Saloo be an independent state, or whether it was subordinate to the Netherlands Government," and the desire for punishment conflicted with the need to maintain friendly relations with islands so advantageously placed for the "quick intercourse with Cochin China and other places on the west coast of the China Seas." A punitive expedition was considered but abandoned since it would "leave but a transient effect on the minds of this numerous race of pirates," and Spiers's treatment was quietly forgotten.

Last Years of the Sulu Pirates

The fate of the Dutch schooner *Maria Frederika*, which was attacked by Ilanuns in the 1830s, shows their ferocious methods of intimidation. While she was becalmed off Lombok, the vessel was approached by two Lanun proas and asked for supplies. While the captain was belowdecks, one of his men, who apparently bore him a grudge, invited the Ilanuns onboard. Immediately, forty warriors swarmed over the bulwarks and quickly overran the ship. The Europeans were then landed at Tungku, buried up to their waists in sand, and hacked to pieces by Ilanun swords. The captain, Andrew Gregory, was killed by an elderly Lanun chief, Raja Muda, who "walked up to him, and with one blow cleft him from the shoulder to the side with his kempilan or heavy Lanun sword."[34]

The years that followed were to see a number of piecemeal and uncoordinated attempts to destroy the Ilanun and Balanini pirates by all the colonial powers in the region. In 1844 the French attempted to take the island of Basilan, while two years later in August 1846 British forces destroyed the Ilanun colonies at Tempasuk and Pandassan on the northern coast of Borneo. In 1848, the Spanish, followed by the Dutch, bombarded islands in the Sulu Archipelago on separate expeditions. But Ilanun and Balanini proas still appeared in Singapore waters in the late 1840s. With the changing political situation and the appointment of James Brooke as commissioner in Borneo, a treaty was signed with Sulu in 1849 that contained provisions for the suppression of piracy. However, this was effectively nullified by a Spanish attack on Sulu in 1851 that destroyed the sultan's stockade and forced him to flee his capital. The Spanish later signed their own treaty with Sulu, thus, temporarily at least, establishing their own political supremacy in the area.

Pressure from the Singapore Chamber of Commerce in 1861 again led to the planning of a joint Anglo-Dutch expedition against the Ilanuns and Balanini. Cruising in search of the marauders was, it was argued, only a temporary solution, but one massive blow, followed by regular policing of the seas around Borneo, could finally smash the power of the Sulu pirates. This scheme too fell foul of a Spanish refusal to allow the ships of other nations into her territories, although it did prompt the Spanish themselves to launch an attack that inflicted some damage on the pirates. Meanwhile, in May 1862, the Sarawak steamer *Rainbow*, with her gunboat the *Jolly Bachelor*, on her way to install a resident and build a fort at Bintulu, fell in with part of the Balanini fleet and inflicted a stinging defeat on the pirates, killing a great number and managing to rescue the slaves held onboard.[35]

At any rate, the grand Anglo–Dutch scheme was scaled down to a large cruising operation, much to the fury of Brooke, who likened it to "searching for mosquitoes with elephants."[36] Brooke was proved right; the squadron achieved little, and when it departed, the pirates returned. Reports in the following years—as the European grip over both commerce and territory became established—indicate the lessening power of the pirates as their bolt-holes were sought out and destroyed. In 1876 Sulu was permanently occupied by the Spanish, and while the pirates from the islands continued to roam the seas of the archipelago, their days as a force capable of severely affecting trade were coming to an end.

Partly due to her own resources and partly to the geographical accident of her position at the meeting point of the ambitions of three European powers, Sulu had withstood the onslaught of European colonial expansion longer than any other sultanate in the Malay world. But inevitably her days were numbered, as was perceptively realized as early as the 1860s by the disconsolate Ilanun who came to sell his brass gun to William Wyndham, the British merchant at Sulu, saying that:

> since the English have been settled at Labuan, there are so many steamers about, it was no use pirating: so he sold his brass gun and returned home.[37]

Below: *The ceremony of hoisting the Union flag on the island of Labuan, northwest Borneo, by Captain Rodney Mundy of HMS* Iris *on December 24, 1846, as depicted in Captain Drinkwater Bethune's* Views in the Eastern Archipelago.

CHAPTER TEN

CHINESE
PIRATES
~

For I shall sing of battles, blood, and rage
Which princes and their people did engage, and haughty
souls that moved with mutual hate,
In fighting fields pursued and found their fate.

JOHN DRYDEN, AENIUS, VIII[1]

IN CHINA WE see at work the very same pressures that had given rise to piracy elsewhere, but we also see them playing themselves out in somewhat different ways owing to the geopolitical circumstances arising from the well-established patterns of continental bureaucracy.

By the time of the age of discovery and the first European raids upon the Spanish Main during the late-fifteenth and early-sixteenth centuries, the dynamics of state-building in China had largely worked themselves out in the form of a unified agrarian bureaucracy that rested on principles of Confucian Legalism that buttressed an authoritarian imperial power whose danger zones lay to the northwest. Traditionally, it was the nomads of the steppe rather than raiders from the sea who constituted China's greatest military threat in the form of periodic conquests of all or parts of the Middle Kingdom.

The geopolitical setting of the Chinese coast was characterized by a single system of sovereignty that extended from the Liaotung peninsula to Vietnam. This stood in marked contrast to the competitive, multicentered political situations that prevailed within the Mediterranean, the Caribbean, and the relatively shallow seas surrounding the Malay peninsula and the Indonesian archipelago where Europeans and Asians engaged one another in competitive processes of state-building and colonization.

Because much of this activity took place at a time prior to the advent of large, standing navies, sovereigns, as we have seen, often had recourse to private men of the sea whose energies were co-opted through letters of marque and reprisal and who, under the guise of "privateers," received encouragement to raid enemy shipping or neighboring shores. In these regions, maritime power

centers competed with one another in profiting from piracy, plunder, and raiding to force better conditions of trade and colonization.

Similar conditions, however, did not prevail in China, where throughout most of history, control of the seas was not a major preoccupation, and the government's jurisdiction seldom extended beyond what the eye could see. When it did, the goal was more to limit the impact of the coastal region and its ability to cause trouble than to co-opt its potential energies in outward expansion or a search for wealth and power. There was little attempt to spread Chinese influence into areas with no previous foothold, for the belief was that profits to be made from outside were potentially fewer than those to be generated from within. Most Chinese needs were satisfied by domestic trade, which was centralized under state supervision.[2]

The Mysterious Voyages of Cheng Ho

One exception occurred early in the fifteenth century with the long voyages of the eunuch Cheng Ho. But unlike in Europe, where maritime endeavors were often initiated by ambitious individuals who competed with one another in seeking state support, the Chinese voyages were a state-sponsored endeavor whose ultimate goal, though shrouded in mystery, seems to have been the establishment of a Chinese world order in Asia. Six maritime expeditions were organized to the "Western Oceans"; the first one took a group of 317 vessels and 27,870 men to Calicut on the southwest coast of India in 1405; the fourth voyage continued on to Hormuz on the Persian Gulf in 1413; while the fifth reached ports on the east African coast in 1417. The enterprise yielded a vast assort-

Left: *The capture of John Turner, chief mate of the ship* Tay, *by Ching Yih's pirates in 1806. Turner was held captive for five months until a ransom was paid for his release. He witnessed scenes of horrendous cruelty and later wrote an account of his ordeal that was published in the* Naval Chronicle.

Below: *A pennant captured from a Chinese junk during the Opium Wars. The naval surgeon Edward Cree noted in his journal on October 20, 1849: "We could now count fifty junks. . . . The big junk carried a red and blue ensign and all the junks were decorated with numerous flags."*

ment of exotic goods and spices, and opportunities for trade under China's tribute system.[3]

Despite the fact that Cheng Ho had carried out the greatest series of maritime explorations prior to the European voyages of discovery at the end of the fifteenth century, the opportunities were not followed through. The mission was suddenly called off; no one knows why, but perhaps it was due to ongoing or renewed Mongol threats from the northwest.[4]

Thereafter the Chinese posture toward the sea changed as the government focused on preventing or containing potential threats through the same kind of strategies as on the land. Since Chinese intercourse with states of comparable power was limited by both land and sea, their interaction with foreigners was geared more to preventing contact than profiting from it. Controlling foreigners was preferable to cooperating with them. "Defense" was to be obtained through alternating practices of battle and negotiation, "sea-war" and pacification.[5]

Although Cheng Ho's voyages had given employment to thousands of individual seafarers, they gave no sanction to individual missions of exploration, plunder, or profit. China afforded few opportunities for a maverick Columbus or Drake.

Petty Piracy

Within this setting, piracy, throughout most of history, was "petty piracy," an economic survival strategy on the part of individuals who could make it no other way in society. Petty pirates were, above all, fishermen, single and in the prime of life, who hailed from the maritime regions of the southeast coast.[6] Often unable to discharge their financial obligations, fishermen found themselves compelled to supplement their incomes through small-scale trade. Yet even then the livelihood was often so miserable that, for many, a successful pirate foray was the sole hope for a better life.[7] For fishermen pushed to the brink, piracy as a temporary survival strategy made sense. As practiced in China, petty piracy was also an enterprise that accorded well with fishing, a seasonal pursuit occupying only 120 to 150 days a year.[8]

During the summer when fishing was poor and dangerous, financially pressed fishermen took advantage of the southerly winds to sail

Below: *A watercolor sketch by Edward Cree entitled* A Boatload of Piratical Rascals. *Cree served as a surgeon with the Royal Navy and took part in the expeditions against the pirates in Bias Bay in the late 1840s; he witnessed the destruction of Shap-'ng-tsai's fleet in the Gulf of Tonkin. A talented amateur artist, he kept an illustrated journal throughout his naval career.*

north and plunder along the coast. Then, with the changing winds and the approach of fall, they would sail south, return home, and resume their fishing. With almost predictable regularity, piracy along the South China coast increased dramatically during the third and fourth lunar months.[9]

The leaders of petty pirate gangs were almost always fishermen who, aside from possessing the major tool of the trade, a vessel, were relatively undifferentiated from their peers. Their organizations consisted of informal ad hoc associations that took shape within hours or, at most, days of a given leader's decision to turn pirate. Would-be leaders, relying on networks of family, friends, and voluntary associations, seldom had trouble recruiting a dozen or so followers for a given mission.

Once at sea, such gangs often increased their manpower through the forced or voluntary labor of captives. Outstanding captives who found favor with gang leaders might even be catapulted into leadership positions. Such promotions sometimes grew out of homosexual relations initiated by a gang leader, who would then reward the captive by commissioning him as the boss or skipper of a newly taken craft. At maximum strength, petty pirate gangs consisted of no more than ten to thirty men and a junk or two.[10]

Ships and Weapons

Petty piracy was an operation with low overheads that could be conducted with implements at hand. In addition to the standard fishing vessels that often doubled as pirate craft, the knives, pointed bamboo pikes, and cutting blades that completed the pirates' arsenal would have been standard equipment on most South China junks. Outfitting an expedition thus amounted to little more than recruiting accomplices, readying weapons, and procuring provisions.

The object was the heist, a short, swift, lightning-fast attack leveled against a single craft at sea. Captives or junks were often ransomed for silver yuan. Such everyday items as bean bran, dried fish, clothing, wine, betel nuts, vegetables, oil, rice, firewood, porcelain, iron nails, tea leaves, and sugar could be sold for cash in home bases.

These petty pirate enterprises were brief. Their guerrilla-like tactics consisted of striking swift blows and then retreating before

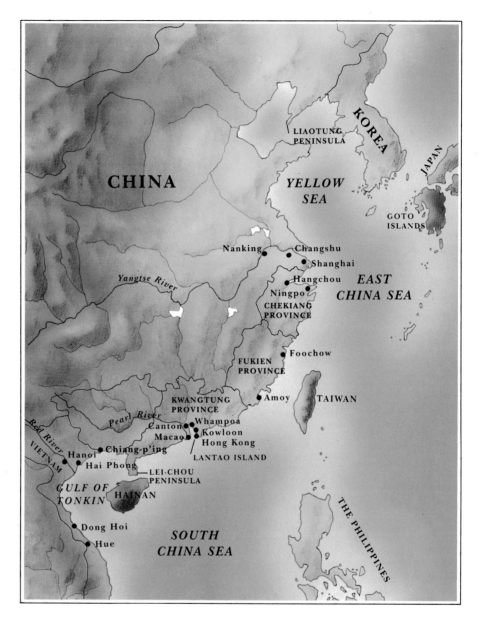

stunned victims could recover their senses or offer resistance. By the time constabulary forces reached the scene, the pirates had usually vanished. Petty pirates typically remained at sea only a few days before returning to their bases to dispose of booty and divide the proceeds.

Allocation of their prizes was also straightforward: single shares for each of the crew members and double shares for the head of the gang and the provider of the vessel if they were not the same individual. Beyond that, codes of conduct, articles of cooperation, and mechanisms of punishment seem to have been scarcely specified. After a rather successful mission, many gangs dispersed, never to come together again. Others carried out

Above: *A map of the coast of China showing the principal ports and trading centers. While pirates operated up and down the coast at different periods, the areas that became notorious for pirate attacks were the Gulf of Tonkin and the shores and coastal waters of the South China Sea, particularly around the Lei-chou peninsula and the island of Hainan.*

sporadic activities over a period of several months.[11] Although the remuneration from such ventures was usually modest, an average strike seems to have yielded to participants somewhere between ten and fifteen silver yuan, or a sum equivalent to about three-and-a-half months' earnings for an agricultural laborer.

During the eighteenth and nineteenth centuries, petty pirates made their headquarters on the periphery of the Chinese empire around the island of Hainan or across the border in such coastal cities as Chiang-p'ing, which was technically a part of Vietnam until 1885.[12]

As an individual survival strategy, practiced on a local level, there were limits to the potential of petty piracy to expand beyond a certain point. Periods of prolonged economic exigency, together with overpopulation and increased maritime trade, caused the phenomenon to intensify, but its methods of operation remained the same as leaders, scarcely distinguishable from their followers, seemingly lacked the means to transform the scale and longevity of their endeavor. Yet, these conditions notwithstanding, piracy in China did experience periods of dramatic growth. In nearly every instance, what was needed was a raison d'être, some economic or political circumstance to give it momentum and sustain it thereafter.

Economic Piracy

When the state's economic policy so contravened perceived social and economic needs that commerce in contraband provided a real reason for its existence, "economic piracy"

Below: *A view of Macao near the Canton River in 1784, painted by John Webber. Merchant shipping sailing to and from Canton, and the neighboring ports of Macao and Hong Kong, attracted numerous pirate attacks. By 1800 the pirate confederation was powerful and was openly running a protection/extortion racket based at Macao.*

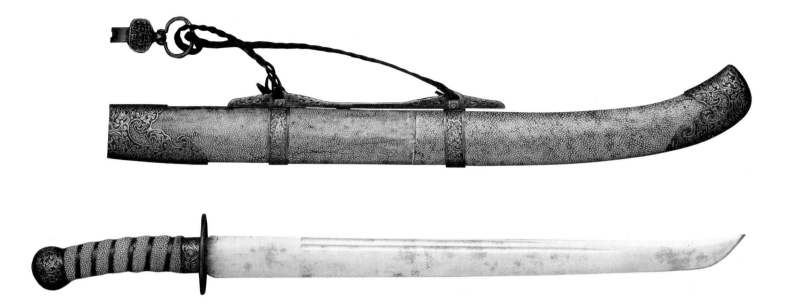

resulted in conjunction with smuggling and a host of other underworld maritime activities. One classic example, which in a sense foreshadowed the passage of the Navigation Acts[13] in the New World, occurred when interdicted trade between China and Japan gave rise to a brisk, clandestine exchange during the middle of the sixteenth century and to attacks by *wako* (*wo-k'ou* in Chinese).

Demand and Supply

During this time, the Chinese impetus to smuggle was driven, perhaps more than anything else, by the demand for silver, which focused increasingly on Japan, following the discovery early in the century of silver, copper, and gold on its western coast. Conversely there was a large demand in Japan for the silk and textiles of China. Yet there were few recognized means by which these commodities could be exchanged. In the aftermath of Cheng Ho's voyages, Chinese prohibitions forbidding coastal traders from voyaging overseas for private purposes and conducting trade with "outer barbarians" were reinstated.[14]

This meant that the only recognized opportunities for trade were under the tribute system, and by the mid-sixteenth century the tribute or "tally" trade between China and Japan had nearly petered out.[15]

Smuggling flourished as market demands were increasingly met through illicit maritime traffic instead of through the more cumbersome channels of tribute. In time, smuggling swelled to such proportions that it ultimately

displaced the function of the tribute trade itself. Along with it, new patterns of exchange and methods of finance emerged.[16]

Initially, the bases of these merchants were in the small islands just off the coast of China.[17] Most prominent was Shuang-hsü-kang (Shang-yü) in the Chushan Islands near Ningpo, which developed about 1540. It was dominated by the Hsü brothers, but most notably, Hsü Tung of She county, Anhwei, whose operations extended from Malacca to Japan.

Wako: the "Japanese" Pirates

What turned this operation from covert exchange into outright piracy was the destruction of the base at Shuang-hsü-kang in 1547, the killing of Hsü Tung in about 1548–49, and the disruption of the relatively stable networks of commerce that had grown up there. These actions pushed local resistance to even greater heights and provided the impetus for the rise of a new harbor, Yüeh-kang, as the preeminent smuggling center on the coast of Fukien.[18] At the same time, the collapse of Ouchi power in Japan in 1551 made the ports of many *daimyo*[19] in western Japan available to the *wako*. Although the term *wako* literally denotes "Japanese" pirates, in fact most of the *wako* raiding was actually carried on by Chinese.

Their leader, Wang Chih, was a Chinese who had made a fortune trading illicitly in Patanai, Thailand, and possessed secure bases in the Goto Islands west of Hirado,

Above: *An ornate Qing dynasty* dao *sword with a plain, straight, single-edged blade nineteen inches (47cm) long with double fuller, curving slightly at the hatchet point. It has a shagreen grip with brass guard and pommel. The scabbard is shagreen-covered with brass fittings and a leather hanging thong.*

Japan. The high tide of the *wako* era occurred between 1549 and 1561, with the cities of the lower Yangtze bearing the brunt of attacks.

The government responded with simultaneous campaigns of "sea-war" and "pacification." By the end of 1557 offensive measures against the pirates were beginning to take effect, and Wang Chih was induced to enter into negotiations with the state. Upon securing a promise for the partial legalization of maritime trade in Chekiang, Wang Chih surrendered to his fellow townsman Hu Tsung-hsien. But higher level court intrigue ultimately led the emperor to renege on those promises and even execute Wang Chih in 1559.

Thereafter, the imperial forces gradually began to regain control of coastal Fukien in 1564 and coastal Kwangtung in 1566. Even more than military measures, however, it was the legalization in 1567 of trade to all points, except Japan, that brought an end to the piracy. Goods, previously in scarce supply and high demand, now appeared in abundance. Restrictions on trade to Japan

were overcome by the Portuguese, who had come on the scene in the 1520s and who, after extended contacts with local Chinese authorities, were finally granted "official" recognition of their settlement at Macao, which was then used as a base to carry out trade between China and Japan. Through the agency of the Portuguese, Chinese silks reached Japan, and Japanese silver, along with that from the mines of Mexico and Peru, arrived in China. At the same time, Taiwan also became the site of a very brisk exchange between Chinese and Japanese, and ultimately Dutch, merchants.

Political Piracy in China

Despite the fact that Chinese rulers were not in the habit of sponsoring pirates for purposes of trading, raiding, or colonization, the Chinese political process occasionally afforded opportunities for the growth of piracy, especially during times of political dislocation and dynastic change. One clear instance occurred during the transition from the native Ming to the Manchu Ch'ing dynasty (1629–84), where

Left: *A model of an ocean-going Foochow pole junk of the type used to transport wood from Foochow to Shanghai. Junks such as this were frequently captured by the pirates, armed with guns, and used in their pirate fleets as war junks.*

Above: *Shipping and factories along the waterfront at Canton, the busy port that was at the heart of one of China's richest trading areas and thus attracted shipping from far and wide. The merchant ships sailing up and down the Pearl River and into the Bocca Tigris estuary were at the mercy of one of the largest and most formidable confederations of pirates the world has ever seen.*

members of a powerful, maritime mercantile family named Cheng ended up in different political camps, and in the process challenged all contenders for control of the coast.

The pirate patriarch of this prominent family was Cheng Chih-lung, the son of a petty official of Ch'üan-chou, who possessed something of a social pedigree, but not enough to preclude his going abroad to Macao to seek his fortune among the Europeans. After having linked up with merchants in Manila, Taiwan, and Hirado (Japan), Cheng Chih-lung in 1624 joined a band of pirates who preyed on Dutch and Chinese trade.[20]

The beleaguered Ming dealt with the situation in the time-honored fashion of trying to buy them off and win their "return to allegiance" as pirate-suppressors and defenders of the coast. After a three-year courtship, Cheng Chih-lung finally submitted and in 1628 won official promotions by capturing

other pirates. In 1629 he was charged with the defense of Amoy and was allowed to keep his forces intact. Cheng Chih-lung financed his operation through "water payments" and profits from trade, and, at the same time, remitted funds to the capital as payments to various officials.[21] The episode catapulted him into high official circles, where he was confirmed as a military commander who used the wealth from his maritime empire to garner prestige at court.

What changed this from a routine situation by which Chinese dynasts co-opted maverick energies from the coast was the politics of the Ming–Ch'ing transition, where Cheng Chih-lung ultimately found himself solicited by both camps. He was given the title "Earl of Nan-an" by one of the southern Ming rulers and ordered to supply troops for the city's defense. But, unable to afford separation from his maritime bases, Cheng Chih-lung refused to support the inland expeditions of his patrons and began to negotiate instead with the enemy Ch'ing, to whom he finally surrendered after their conquest of Foochow in 1646.

The Pirate Army of Cheng Ch'eng-kung

Meanwhile, Chih-lung's son Cheng Ch'eng-kung (who the Portuguese called Coxinga) refused to follow his father in surrendering to the Ch'ing. Instead, he raised an army and continued to serve as a general of the southern Ming. Between 1654 and 1656 he, too, was courted by both the Ming and the Ch'ing and in early 1655 perfected the organization of his forces in Fukien by establishing seventy-two military stations. He ultimately accepted the southern Ming title of "Yen-p'ing prince." In his ensuing battles with the Ch'ing, he was defeated at Nanking in 1659; this forced his retreat to Amoy.

Cheng Ch'eng-kung, however, was far from finished. His empire still retained strong coastal outposts and in 1660 his forces turned the tables and defeated the Ch'ing during a major campaign at Amoy. Thereafter, when negotiations failed and Cheng Ch'eng-kung still refused to be co-opted, he forced the Ch'ing to retaliate with a very long and costly campaign. In hopes of further dividing the Cheng forces, the Manchus executed the family patriarch, Cheng Chih-lung, in 1661 (who, after having been removed from his forces at the time of his surrender in 1646, had been held under house arrest in Beijing). Feeling the squeeze, his son, Cheng Ch'eng-kung, evacuated the bulk of his forces from the Chinese mainland to Taiwan, which he conquered from the Dutch in 1661.

Instead of trying to gain the cooperation of the Dutch, Portuguese, or other elements along the coast, the Ch'ing, seeking to minimize opportunities for contact between any potential allies and members of the Cheng family, imposed an evacuation that forced all coastal inhabitants to move inland approximately ten miles (16km). These measures were extended throughout Fukien in 1661 and to Kwangtung and Chekiang in 1662–63. By 1665, most of the coast had been devastated, with many of its towns and villages burned to the ground. Reprieve did not come until the final defeat of the Chengs and the ultimate pacification of Taiwan by the Ch'ing in 1683.

Above: *A Chinese lacquered tea caddy dating from the eighteenth century. Beautifully decorated and finely crafted items like this were much prized in Europe and North America. As the Chinese export trade expanded and flourished, so the number of ships voyaging to and from China with rich cargoes increased—making inviting targets for pirates.*

International Piracy and Privateering

While Chinese politics may have provided little encouragement to piracy and privateering in the familiar Western sense, this was not true across the border in Vietnam, where sovereigns engaged in a more classical use of privateering to further state-building ends, and in the process gave China's petty pirates a chance to expand the scale of their activity.

During the late eighteenth century, Vietnam was wracked by a rebellion that brought an end to the long-standing political arrangement in which, since the sixteenth century, the country had been under the nominal rule of the late Lê dynasty but was effectively governed by two rival families: the Trinh in the north (at Hanoi) and the Nguyen in the south (at Hue). The so-called Tay-son Rebellion took its name from the native village of the three brothers, Nguyen Van Lu, Nguyen Van Nhac, and Nguyen Van Hue, who led it.[22] As merchants engaged in commerce with the hill people of Binh Dinh province, the brothers gathered a band of followers and in 1773 succeeded in seizing the provincial capital of Qui Nhon. In 1775, they evicted the Nguyen from their capital at Hue and forced the Nguyen heir-apparent Phuc Anh to seek refuge in the Gulf of Siam. In 1785, with the south temporarily secured, the Tay-son drove the Trinh from Hanoi, which they entered in 1786. At this point the Lê emperor requested aid from China, and in 1788 three Chinese armies invaded Vietnam to restore his throne. At the same time Phuc Anh and his followers staged a counterattack in the south.

To meet this challenge, the Tay-son declared their most able leader, Nguyen Van Hue, emperor and totally routed the Chinese expedition; after which the Chinese emperor, Ch'ien-lung, recognizing Tay-son mastery of the country, officially invested Nguyen Van Hue as the king of Annam.[23]

Chinese Pirates Under the Tay-son

These state-building endeavors in Vietnam held out wonderful opportunities to pirates in China who were willing to join the cause. Prior to 1776, Chi T'ing and Li Ts'ai, two businessmen turned pirates, joined the Tay-son and recruited the Loyal and Harmonious armies, respectively. Their efforts enabled the Tay-son to take Quang Ngai.

The most intense phase of Tay-son recruit-

ment occurred in 1792 when, with his hold upon the throne growing more precarious each day, the Tay-son emperor sent his fleet of 100 junks and three divisions led by twelve brigadier generals across the border to enlist privateers from among the "scum" of the coast. During June and July alone, the Tay-son ruler commissioned forty Chinese pirate junks to conduct expeditions along the coasts of Kwangtung, Fukien, and Chekiang provinces. Thereafter, Chinese pirates participated in every major Tay-son naval encounter.[24]

The Chinese who answered the Tay-son call were the petty pirates of the South China coast: among whom the most well known was Cheng Ch'i, the scion of a family with a long history in piracy. By 1786 Cheng Ch'i was already well-launched on his career as a pirate and in 1788 he had joined the Tay-son.[25]

By 1795 Cheng Ch'i and his associates Huang Ta-hsing and Ch'en Ch'ang-fa had formed a gang that operated out of Chiang-p'ing on the China-Vietnam border. From there Cheng Ch'i reached out in several directions until, at his most powerful, he had at least nine different groups under his com-

mand. After his defeat at Qui Nhon in early 1801, Cheng Ch'i fled back to China and took up residence in Kwangtung.[26] There he remained, raiding forts and seizing salt junks, until January 1802.

Then just before the Tay-son denouement, Cheng Ch'i returned to Vietnam and presented his fleet of two hundred junks to the Tay-son for use in their attempt to retake Hue. In return he received the prestigous rank of "Master of the Horses." For this effort more than 100 pirates were deployed at Nhat Le, a port near Dong Hoi, where on February 3, 1802, the forces of Phuc Anh engaged the pirates in battle. A sudden northeast wind enabled Phuc Anh to capture twenty pirate vessels and forced the remainder to flee to Tien Coc, where they were attacked again.

By this time the Tay-son were nearly finished. Their final battle occurred at Hanoi, where forty of Cheng Ch'i's vessels were recruited to guard the port. Their effort was to little avail and was totally unable to stem the enemy advance. On July 20, a victorious Phuc Anh entered the city, captured the

Above: *Cochin villagers spearing survivors from Shap-'ng-tsai's junks following the Royal Navy attack in October 1849. Accompanying the journal drawing, Edward Cree wrote an entry: "The Cochins were chasing the poor wretches in their sampans and spearing them in the water."*

Tay-son emperor, and paraded him through the streets in a cage. One of the first acts of the new emperor was to send a tribute mission to China that included the three captured pirate leaders as a sign that Chinese piracy would no longer be countenanced in Vietnam. Six weeks later Phuc Anh's officials dealt the pirates yet another stunning blow by beheading their leader Cheng Ch'i and attacking their base at Chiang-p'ing.[27]

The pirates, however, had learned their lessons well. The result was a system of piracy so well entrenched that neither the defeat of the Tay-son, and the death of four of their most important leaders, nor the loss of their headquarters, could eliminate it. Pirates were now too well organized to melt inconspicuously back into the society from which they had come. Ironically, the high point of both the Cheng family's participation in piracy, and Chinese piracy itself, came after the defeat of the Tay-son, when, bereft of sponsors in Vietnam or anywhere else, Chinese pirates returned to their homes and organized a confederation. This confederation enabled them to survive, not in some remote corner of the world preying on an occasional ship, but rather under hostile circumstances as a state-within-a-state, amid one of the richest trading networks and most heavily populated regions of the world. It was also not the product of flamboyant mavericks who executed colorful raids or circumnavigations of the globe, but rather the work of those individuals who outmaneuvered their own government in mobilizing the resources at hand.

In most regions of the world, even pirates who operated in their home waters tended to prey on the shipping and goods of foreigners. Breaking this rule often spelled the beginning of their own demise. What finally emerged in China, by contrast, was Chinese pirates preying on Chinese (and other) shipping, in a big way.

Initially, upon returning to China from Vietnam, Chinese pirates found themselves involved in an internecine competition for resources. Within an atmosphere of strife, bands that had once been loosely allied now turned rapaciously against one another in a free-for-all that continued until 1805. At that time the leadership of the pirates had passed indisputably into the waiting hands of another member of the Cheng family,

Cheng Ch'i's distant cousin, Cheng I (Cheng the first).

Cheng I was the eldest son of temple-builder Cheng Lien-ch'ang and was five years younger than Cheng Ch'i. Most of Cheng I's early life is lost to history. We know only that he joined the Tay-son cause, returned to China in 1801, and joined with Cheng Ch'i for an attack on the salt fleets in September (see earlier discussion). We also know that he settled briefly in Tung-hai, a village on an island in Kuang-chou bay, and married the prostitute Shih Yang, who would later be known simply as Cheng I Sao (the wife of Cheng I).

The Confederation

The major accomplishment of Cheng I and his wife was the unification of the warring pirate gangs into a formidable confederation that, by 1804, included some four hundred junks and seventy thousand men.[28] In con-

Above: *In common with pirates elsewhere, Chinese pirates went into action with a varied arsenal of weapons. While fine swords like these long, heavy ones would have had their place, more typical were knives, short swords like billhooks, and bamboo spears and sharp-bladed pikes.*

Far right: *Chinese ransom or extortion notes from the nineteenth century. The Chinese pirates were highly organized and even bureaucratic, keeping records, drawing up contracts, and so on. They issued threats and then protection documents once the victim paid. Merchants were an obvious target, but so too were coastal villages that were often threatened with dire retribution if they failed to pay.*

trast to the ad hoc procedures that gave rise to petty pirate gangs, the confederation came into being as the result of a written agreement (*li-ho-yüeh*) signed by Kwangtung's seven major pirate leaders in 1805. Its goal was to regularize the internal operating procedures of the member units, to prescribe methods of conduct and inter-group communication when at sea, and to stipulate how business transactions with outsiders were to be conducted.[29]

In the name of order, each vessel was to be registered with one fleet and clearly identified. Anyone caught tampering with this registration process would be punished. Provisions prohibiting pirates from fighting one another for prizes already taken, and from undertaking unauthorized activities on their own, sought to prevent internal conflict. Since much of their income would derive from the sale of protection, members also agreed to honor each other's contracts of sale. Implicit in the document was also the pirates' view of their confederation as an ongoing organization with a future as well as a present. This view is evidenced by provisions allowing for deferred payments by confederation members lacking in cash for indemnities or other internal obligations. In reserving, for the confederation as a whole, the right to distribute confiscated property and punish offenders, the founders created an organization that functioned as a final unit of accounting and an ultimate "court" of arbitration.

In contrast to the loose gangs of petty pirates, the confederation was predicated on concepts of hierarchy and intergang affiliation. It was initially composed of seven great fleets, later six. Consisting of between seventy and three hundred vessels each, they were commonly referred to as the Red, Black, White, Green, Blue, and Yellow Flag fleets. The largest and most important, the Red Flag Fleet, was composed of more than three hundred junks and between twenty thousand and forty thousand pirates.

The "admirals" of the fleets were drawn largely from the ranks of those who had fought in Vietnam. Wu-shih Er, leader of the Blue Flag Fleet, became a pirate after having been captured. Early in his career, he had made a living by extorting blackmail from the ports in Kwangtung. After joining the Tay-son, he was eventually given the title

"Great Admiral Who Pacifies the Seas." After the Tay-son defeat at Hue (in June 1801), Wu struck up an alliance with Cheng Ch'i to attack the salt fleets at Tien-pai and later joined Cheng I in a series of raids. With a fleet of 160 junks, he ultimately became the master of the Lei-chou peninsula.[30]

Kuo P'o-tai, leader of the Black Flag Fleet, was the son of a fisherman from Pan-yü county, Kwangtung. At age fourteen he was captured at sea by Cheng I, whom he then joined in serving the Tay-son. There he reached the position of being allowed to dispense newly acquired cannons to his subordinates. Back in China, he ultimately commanded a fleet of more than 100 vessels and ten thousand men.[31] Similarly the leaders of the Yellow and White Flag fleets had also made the acquaintance of Cheng I in Vietnam while serving under the Tay-son. The leader of the Green Flag Fleet was an acquaintance of Cheng I's, but whether he ever served the Tay-son is not known.

Each large fleet, in turn, was composed of a number of squadrons of between ten and forty vessels each. These units were formed from the independent gangs that had once flourished at Chiang-p'ing and had later constituted the basis for the privateer fleets of the Tay-son. As intermediary units between the fleet and the individual junks, the squadrons were the major "building blocks" of the confederation. Although it is impossible to know how many there were at any given time, one of the largest, with thirty-six junks, boasted 1,422 men and thirty-four women.[32]

Commanders and Crews

Below the squadrons were the individual junks, under bosses or skippers known as *lao-pan*, who at one time may have functioned as the commanders of petty pirate gangs. *Lao-pan* were often responsible for several ships and were frequently assigned to newly captured craft. Each vessel also had a headman who shared responsibility for its management with the *lao-pan*. The headmen were readily distinguishable from the rank and file by their better dress and fare, and it was they who took command of the ships during combat. Those appointed as headmen were individuals who had caught their superiors' eyes as men capable of handling responsibility. Headmen possessed certain powers of

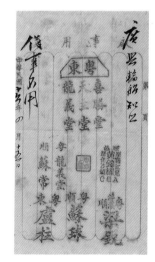

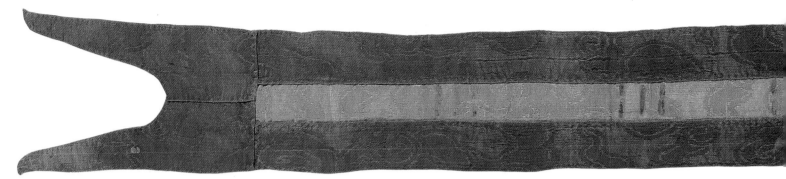

Above: *A Chinese junk pennant. Just as in the West, a variety of flags and pennants were used to identify vessels and their owners. The imperial flag was flown by naval vessels and institutions with the authority of the emperor, and government vessels always had identifying characters on their sails. Pirate fleets used different colored flags to identify the various squadrons, and the commander often flew a large flag decorated with elaborate, often symbolic, designs.*

Left: *A Chinese pirate beheading his victims and hanging the heads on a string around his neck. Decapitation was common in the East and the pirates collected heads almost as trophies. These are being worn in an intimidatory fashion probably during a raid on a village that has ignored a demand for protection money.*

appointment and frequently assigned tasks and rank to other crewmen.[33]

Helmsmen were in charge of the general management of the sails and steering; there were usually two per vessel. Given the need for experience at the helm, they were often hired from the outside. So widespread was the practice that in 1804 the governor-general complained that all the good helmsmen were leaving the naval forces because the pirates were paying them higher wages.[34] Under the helmsmen were three or four people charged with deck duties and two or three who manned the cannons, threw anchors, and burned incense.

Pursers kept track of protection contracts and booty. All prizes taken were to be surrendered to the common fund for redistribution. Such goods were to be registered by the pirates' purser and distributed by the fleet leader. Customarily, 20 percent of the booty would be returned to the original captor, and the remainder, referred to as the "public fund," would be placed in a joint treasury or storehouse. Currency, too, was to be turned over to the squadron leaders, who would

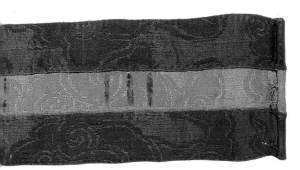

remit a certain portion to the fleet leader and a small amount to the captor. The remainder was to be reserved for purchasing supplies and provisioning vessels that were unsuccessful in their own pursuits.[35]

Pirate Bases

Since much water-based activity ultimately depended on the land for supply and shelter, continental headquarters were necessary to the success of both petty and professional pirates. While most of the eighteenth and early nineteenth century petty pirates made their headquarters on the periphery of the Chinese empire, around the island of Hainan or in Vietnamese coastal waters, the pirates of the confederation dominated the seas and set up their headquarters much nearer the busiest shipping lanes, those centered on Canton. At that same time, they allocated specific operating territory to each fleet.

Upon returning to China from Vietnam, the pirates set up their first base of operation in the Lei-chou peninsula, whose relative isolation rendered it, like Chiang-p'ing, far from strong as an administrative center. They next took possession of Nao-chou and Wei-chou, two little-frequented islands that flanked the peninsula and gave them easy access to both the salt fleets of T'ien-pai and the vessels passing through the narrow strait of Hainan.[36] From there they moved east along the coast to establish a second headquarters on Lantao Island, which stretched from Victoria Harbor (Hong Kong) to the mouth of the Pearl River, and provided access to the major seaways of Kwangtung province. From Lantao, the pirates soon extended their operations into the small unfortified islands along the coast as well as the two major passages of the Pearl River itself.[37]

After joining forces, a major consideration in the allocation of territory to confederation leaders seems to have been the fleet leader's native place. The leaders of the Blue, Yellow, and Green Flag fleets, who were natives of western Kwangtung, made their headquarters in the Lei-chou peninsula; while the leaders of the Red, Black, and White fleets operated farther east, nearer Canton.[38]

Not only was the territorial sphere of professional pirates more extensive than that of petty pirates, but so, too, were their supply networks. Instead of relying solely on one city or base, these professional pirates had accomplices throughout Kwangtung. From agents they obtained iron, cannons, and ammunition. So pervasive was this network that the arrest of five hundred suppliers in 1805 scarcely affected their operations at all.[39]

Junks and Weapons

Undergirding their enterprise were a variety of craft and armaments. Pirate vessels included everything from oceangoing junks to rowboats. In 1809, at the peak of its strength, two hundred of the confederation's craft were ocean junks (*yang-chu'an*), capable of carrying between three hundred and four hundred men and mounting twenty to thirty cannons. These were comparable in size to the British ships that sailed between India

Left: *Chui Apoo, a Hong Kong barber who joined up with Shap-'ng-tsai and became his lieutenant and commander of a pirate fleet. He was based at Bias Bay, a pirate stronghold near Hong Kong. There, in 1849, he was cornered by a Royal Navy force led by Commander Dalrymple Hay. Chui Apoo's fleet was destroyed and four hundred of his men killed. Chui himself was wounded and escaped, but was later betrayed and imprisoned. Sentenced to be banished, he committed suicide before this could be carried out.*

ARMED JUNK, 1800

THIS IS AN example of the smaller type of seagoing junk that was used by pirates operating on the southeast coast of China. Such a vessel would have been built originally for carrying cargo, but after being captured by the pirates she would have been converted into an armed war junk by the insertion of gun ports for the mounted guns on deck and by the fitting of swivel guns on the rails.

The pirate confederation on the South China coast at the beginning of the nineteenth century had between six hundred and eight hundred junks similar to this. To western eyes the simple sail plan and rounded hull form may appear primitive, but the junk rig is extremely effective and these vessels were fast and seaworthy. With a large crew of heavily armed pirates she would have been a formidable threat to an unarmed merchant ship, and when a fleet of pirate junks went into action they carried all before them. It was not until the introduction of Dutch and British steam-powered gunboats in the region that the pirate junks met their match.

Key

1 Bamboo battens to strengthen and support the shape of the sail.
2 Stern davits for the junk's tender.
3 Windlass for raising the rudder.
4 Extended rudder post.
5 Large rudder, held in position by grass ropes,

so that it acts like a drop-keel to prevent leeway or sideways drift.
6 Galley with charcoal stove.
7 Swivel gun mounted on the rail.
8 Six-pounder gun mounted on a carriage.

9 Stone ballast.
10 Four-pounder gun.
11 Water barrels.
12 Treasure chest containing looted valuables.
13 Anchor cable.
14 Anchor windlass.
15 Bow gallows.
16 Main or bower anchor.

and China. More numerous than the ocean junks were the seagoing craft (*hai-ch'uan*) that allowed pirates to carry out operations in coastal waters. Most vessels in this category consisted of captured merchant junks approximately forty feet (12m) long and fourteen feet (4.2m) wide that carried at most two hundred men and between twelve and twenty-five cannons. Altogether the confederation boasted between six hundred and eight hundred of these vessels, which would have been most comparable to the American schooners or Portuguese brigs (two-masted ships of less than two hundred tons displacement) then on the scene.[40]

The pirates' fleets were completed by a host of river junks capable of plying the empire's "inner waters." Foremost among them were the small rowboats with one or two sails, fourteen to twenty oars, and crews of eighteen to thirty men. They were armed with six to ten wall-pieces and were well-stocked with boarding pikes and swords. Such vessels were used for communicating between ships and for going ashore at night to destroy villages that were delinquent in the payment of protection fees.[41]

The pirates protected their fleets with an impressive array of arms. In 1806 the flagship of the Red Flag Fleet mounted ten cannons: two long eighteen-pounders and eight small six-pounders, but by 1809 the number of cannons had been increased to thirty-eight on one deck alone. Two fired twenty-four-pound (11kg) shot while eight fired eighteen-pound (8kg) shot.[42] Pirate cannons generally weighed between sixty and three thousand *catties* (a typical *catty* being 1¾ pounds or 0.8kg). Some were wooden, with an iron bore, but the majority were smelted from varying grades of raw and scrap iron.[43]

Their stocks of arms included crudely built wall-pieces commonly known as *gingalls* or Chinese blunderbusses. With a barrel seven feet (2.1m) long and with a weight of twelve pounds (5.5kg), the *gingall* resembled the European swivel gun of the early eighteenth century or the elephant gun of the nineteenth

Below: Nemesis destroying junks in Ansons Bay in 1841. The Nemesis was a steam-driven paddleship owned by the East India Company and she took part in several of the Royal Navy's antipiracy operations. The superior firepower of the steamships and their ability to outmaneuver the sailing junks enabled the British commanders to wreak havoc when they cornered the pirate fleets along the South China Sea coast.

century.[44] Besides *gingalls*, the pirates possessed a miscellany of old matchlocks and fowling pieces. Many of these, however, were of doubtful value since their owners knew little about their care and operation.[45]

The pirates' most deadly weapon was a bamboo pike with a sharp, saberlike blade used in the hand-to-hand combat at which they so excelled. The majority of the pikes were fourteen to eighteen feet (4.2-5.5m) long and were hurled like javelins. The pirates also had shorter pikes with shafts of wood and slightly curved blades that were sometimes sharpened on both edges. In addition, they wielded knives of all sorts and rounded out their arsenal with bows and arrows.[46] The pirates were also well supplied with gunpowder and shot. Their ammunition was usually obtained from captured ships or stolen from government forts and smuggled to them by agents in Canton or Macao.

With no shortage of weapons, well-armed fleets looked like floating fortresses. In 1805, an eleven-junk squadron of 310 men possessed an arsenal of sixty-two cannons, forty lead shells, two fowling pieces, thirty-six *catties* (sixty-three pounds/29kg) of gunpowder, twenty-seven *catties* (forty-seven pounds/21kg) of iron bullets, 216 knives, 180 bamboo spears, 134 short knives, twenty-three rattan shields, and ten iron chains.[47]

Such was the infrastructure of a potentially powerful pirate organization, but leadership was still required to make it work, and Cheng I was not destined to sail at its head for long. He died suddenly in Vietnam on November 16, 1807, at age forty-two. According to one account he was blown overboard and drowned in a gale; according to

another, he was struck by a cannonball while fighting in an attempt to recapture Vietnam on behalf of his former Tay-son allies.[48]

Mrs. Cheng the Pirate

Though some of Cheng I's cofounders must have aspired to command the confederation's largest fleet, power passed virtually uncontested into the hands of his widow, Cheng I Sao (also known as Mrs. Cheng, or Mrs. Ching). Upon the death of her husband, Cheng I Sao, who had participated fully in her husband's piracy, moved to create personal relationships that would legitimize her status and allow her to exercise authority.

But what ultimately secured her position at the top of the pirate hierarchy was the creation of a new leader to replace her husband as the commander of the most powerful Red Flag Fleet. For this position she needed a man to whom she could entrust considerable authority in the day-to-day operation of the entire fleet and in giving orders to the other pirate leaders. She also needed a person who could win the acceptance and engage the cooperation of prospective subordinates and, at the same time, one who, in owing to the Cheng family his entire status within the hierarchy, would be absolute in his loyalty.

There was only one person to fill this position: the young captive Chang Pao. Chang Pao, a fisherman's son, had joined the pirates at fifteen, after having been captured by Cheng I. Cheng I first initiated Chang Pao into the pirate order by means of a homosexual liaison and then entrusted him with the command of a junk. Ultimately, he adopted Chang Pao as a son. Thus, for five years Chang Pao, as an extension of the leader's

Above: *The handle of a kris, or dagger, dating from the seventeenth century, which was recovered from a shipwrecked Chinese pirate junk off Malaysia. Made of gold and encrusted with precious stones, the weapon to which this was attached presumably belonged to a pirate chief.*

family, had functioned as a junior member of the confederation. At some point Chang Pao was further invested by the Tay-son as "Great Generalissimo."[49]

Consequently in 1807, when Cheng I Sao needed a lieutenant, the twenty-one-year-old Chang Pao was a natural choice. Having come into the confederation as an outsider, Chang Pao had developed no prior loyalties to other leaders, but at the same time had demonstrated qualities of leadership. Once her decision had been made, Cheng I Sao acted boldly and decisively to further the alliance with Chang Pao through a sexual relationship of her own. Within weeks the two became lovers and, at some later point, husband and wife.[50]

The Pirate Code

Upon becoming leader of the confederation, Cheng I Sao issued a code of laws that further helped to transform the personal patron-client relationships that undergirded the confederation into more formal power relations, but whether or not these regulations were written down is impossible to determine. The code was short and severe. Anyone caught giving commands on his own or disobeying those of a superior was to be decapitated. Pilfering from the common treasury or public fund as well as stealing from the villagers who regularly supplied the pirates were also capital offenses. Desertion or absence without leave were to result in a man's ear being cut off and his being paraded through his squadron. Raping female captives was also a capital offense, and if there was fornication by mutual consent, the pirate was to be beheaded and the female captive cast overboard with a weight on her legs.[51]

On more than one occasion, Westerners saw pirates who had violated the code flogged, put in irons, or quartered. According to one Western captive, the pirates' code was strictly enforced and transgressions punished with an efficiency that seemed "almost incredible." Such severity, he concluded, gave rise to a force that was intrepid in attack, desperate in defense, and unyielding when outnumbered.[52]

Cheng I Sao demonstrated even more far-reaching power by taking responsibility for the creation of financial and military structures that were indispensable to the pirates' survival. In contrast to the petty pirates, for whom piracy was an economic survival strategy, piracy for the confederation members was a form of economic entrepreneurship characterized by sophisticated financial operations. While petty pirates were entirely dependent on the chance seizure of vessels at sea, with the creation of the confederation piracy became a business within which the heist was but one dimension. Even then, in contrast to the uncoordinated assaults of petty pirates, attacks by the professionals were planned in advance and systematically executed. Confederation made it possible for professional pirates to overpower even large oceangoing junks by force and to operate freely in the inshore waters of South China. It also made possible attacks on the shore whose objects were the plunder of villages, markets, rice fields, and small forts.[53]

With confederation, the ransoming of captives, vessels, and even villages became systematic and professional, and extended even to foreigners who were no longer exempt from attack. Vessels of no use to the pirates were ransomed at standard rates of fifty silver yuan for fishing junks and 130 yuan for cargo carriers. Human captives were seldom released for less than ninety taels

Above: *Mrs. Cheng (Cheng I Sao) in action, the famous woman pirate chief who took over command of the confederation on the South China Sea coast in 1807 and thus leadership of a community of fifty thousand pirates. This fanciful depiction is from the* History of the Pirates of all Nations *published in 1836.*

each, while for foreigners the sum might go as high as seven thousand Spanish dollars.[54]

Paying for Protection

It was in the sale of protection, however, that the pirates most successfully regularized their financial operations. With the help of secret societies, the pirates first turned their attention to the salt trade, whose merchants soon found it more expedient to negotiate directly or to hand over large sums for the safe passage of their junks than to pay high prices after a strike. By 1805, so forcefully did pirates dominate the salt trade that nearly every vessel setting out for Canton found it necessary to purchase protection at such standard rates as fifty yuan of silver for each 100 *pao* (packages) of salt. Sometimes the pirates even provided escort service, as in 1805 when a fleet of salt junks paid two hundred Spanish dollars apiece for a pirate convoy to Canton.[55]

Through the collection of set fees, the pirates established a system that yielded predictable profits from season to season. They reached the pinnacle of their power when they were able to extend their enterprise to all vessels afloat and a significant number of villages on land. In return for specified sums, merchants, junk owners, pilots, and fishermen received documents signed by the pirate leaders. Usually these fees were collected annually, although temporary certificates could be purchased for specified periods. In some areas, merchant junks were assessed by the value of their cargoes at rates ranging from fifty to five hundred yuan of silver per trip. In other areas the price for an oceangoing merchant junk was four hundred Spanish dollars upon leaving port and eight hundred upon return.[56]

Protection documents were widely available from pirate leaders aboard ship and from their agents onshore. As their activities expanded, members of the confederation established financial outposts along the coast and even set up a tax office in Canton as a collection point for fees. The overall headquarters of their operation, however, appear to have been at Macao, where assistants sold protection and supplied the pirates with weapons and ammunition. Pirate leaders were scrupulous in abiding by the terms of their protection documents, which were universally respected throughout the confedera-

Left: *A pair of Chinese dirks from the mid–nineteenth century. They have tapering grips capped with brass, brass semicircular guards, and fretted brass wrapping at the shoulders of the blades. The blades are slightly curved and the back edge is sharpened on the outer surface. They are made flat enough to fit into a single scabbard and appear as one weapon.*

聖母 天后

Left: *Shap-'ng-tsai's silk pirate flag captured in October 1849 from his flagship. Elaborately decorated, it shows the mythical empress of heaven T'ien Hou, calmer of storms and protector of merchant ships. Each squadron had a flag and the flag carrier led the attack when pirates boarded a ship. Shap-'ng-tsai survived the battles that saw him lose fifty-eight junks and nearly two thousand men in the face of a British onslaught. Not only did he escape but he was later pardoned and given a minor appointment by the Chinese authorities.*

tion. On being intercepted, vessels had merely to produce their documents as proof of payment and were then allowed to proceed.[57] Thanks to success in these endeavors, the confederation had little want of money, and its flagships often carried sums of between fifty thousand and 100,000 dollars in cash.[58]

The pirates' ability to regularize their finances enabled their transformation into true professionals. Moreover, piracy within the confederation meant long-term, full-time employment for both leaders and followers to the point where, by 1807, leaders refused to admit individuals who did not agree to stay for at least eight or nine months.[59] Like petty pirates, many confederation members were fishermen, who joined "by the hundreds," but in addition there were others, who in hoping to escape the tyranny and executions of Ch'ing officials onshore may have had somewhat more political reasons for signing up.

More than anything else, what probably allowed the pirate confederation to survive unpatronized and unprotected in the very heart of one of China's richest trading areas was the military prowess it wielded. As a capable military strategist, Cheng I Sao deployed her forces up and down the coast, planning and coordinating her offensives well in advance so that her designs usually succeeded. She was able, as a result, not only to enforce compliance with her protection system, but also to overpower the provincial navy and challenge fortresses on land.

As early as 1804, pirates occupied the Taipa anchorage of Macao, and by April had reduced the city to a two-day supply of rice.[60] A few months later, pirates had so terrorized the provincial naval forces that Chinese admirals, fearing a confrontation, spent most of their time ashore waiting for favorable winds. Patrol squadrons, not wanting to do battle, simply fired their guns upon the approach of pirates so that the latter, upon hearing the shots, could evade contact. By the end of the decade, the situation had deteriorated to the extent that military personnel, afraid to go to sea at all, were sabotaging their own vessels.[61] Confident pirates boasted that one of their junks was equal to four of the navy's.

Plundering the Coast

With little to stop them at sea, pirates were soon able to mass their forces for assaults on land. Favorite targets were the coastal garrisons, rich with stores and provisions. It was not uncommon for three hundred pirates to come sweeping into a harbor and overpower all the officers on duty. On such occasions, pirates, who excelled in hand-to-hand combat, would use their larger vessels to provide a cover of fire while the smaller ones moved in for the direct assault. In time the pirates extended their activities to the coastal habitations as well. There they plundered villages, markets, and rice fields.

By 1808 the pirates held the military initiative along the coast and had demonstrated their power by killing the provincial commander-in-chief of Chekiang province, who had sailed into Kwangtung on a special assignment.[62] Six months later, the pirates had destroyed most of the vessels allocated for the defense of Canton and had so reduced the government's forces that the navy had to bolster its ranks by the temporary hiring of thirty private fishing vessels. As pirates swarmed into the tributaries of the interior, official policy was in trouble. The governor-general's attempt to confront the pirates at sea had failed. The provincial fleet had been reduced by half. More junks awaited repair in the dockyards than sailed the sea, and Canton was left with little protection. Provincial resources were at an all-time low.[63]

As "sea-war" policies proved of little avail, the government repeatedly tried "pacification" in hopes of wooing the pirates ashore without a fight to the finish. Among the leaders their overtures initially fell on deaf ears, while among the rank and file there ensued a game of individuals accepting resettlement fees only to return to the water a short time later. In 1809 government hopes raised with the advent of the new Provincial Governor-General Pai Ling. While replenishing the navy, he tried to accompany a renewed policy of sea-war with an embargo that prevented or drastically curtailed coastal intercourse, but did not result in an actual evacuation or resettlement of coastal

Below: *The destruction of Chui Apoo's pirate fleet in Bias Bay on October 1, 1849. This picture is after a watercolor by Edward Cree who witnessed the action. After defeating the pirate fleet, the British commander Dalrymple Hay sent parties ashore to destroy the shipyard and vessels on the stocks.*

inhabitants. The implementation of this policy left the pirates with severely reduced sources of succor and revenue, but instead of starving them out, it seems only to have pushed them farther inland.

Pirates moving into the heart of the province threw the city of Canton into a real panic when in August 1809 they posted notices of their intention to attack. A few weeks later, within the space of a day the pirates forced five American schooners to run for safety within gunshot range of Macao. They also captured a brig belonging to the

Portuguese governor of Timor, and blockaded the mouth of the Pearl River against a tribute mission newly arrived from Siam.[64]

Imperial Negotiations with Europeans

With these actions the pirates forced Chinese officials to play their last card—alliances with foreigners. But the government did so in the traditional mode of trying to keep the outsiders at a distance while availing themselves of their services. After nearly a decade of refusing assistance from both the British and Portuguese, the Chinese

Below: *The British paddle gunboat* Medea *taking thirteen junks in action against pirates at Kut-O near Hong Kong on March 5, 1850. As depicted here, the armed paddle steamer, belching black smoke from her funnel, has tracked down the pirate base and is in the process of systematically destroying the enemy junks drawn up along the waterfront.*

authorities, unable to suppress the pirates themselves, had to look to the "barbarians." In early September 1809 they called upon the British, making overtures to hire a ship to free the tribute vessels from Siam. After two weeks of complex discussions, the East India Company supercargoes gave their reluctant consent and on September 15 the *Mercury*, equipped with twenty cannons and fifty American volunteers, set sail.[65] At the same time, the Chinese signed an agreement with the Portuguese for the lease of six men-o'-war to sail with the Cantonese navy for six months.[66]

Action began in earnest on November 19 when the pirates awoke to find themselves surrounded in a bay off the north shore of Lantao Island. The barrage continued for two hours. Thereafter, combined government and Portuguese forces maintained a blockade meant to spell the end of the pirates. Reports flew back to Canton and rumors of the pirates' imminent destruction spread far and wide. On November 28, all the conditions were in place. With great anticipation the government's fire ships were launched. Just at that moment the wind changed, and the denouement was that the fire ships ignited two of the junks that had originally launched them.[67]

The End of the Confederation

Westerners as well as Chinese had proved unable to destroy the confederation. Ultimately, however, discord between the Red and Black Flag fleets resulted in a "return to allegiance" of all but the most diehard. As a result of skillful negotiation on the part of Cheng I Sao and the other women in the confederation, the pirates were allowed to retain the bulk of their spoils. The rank and file who so desired were allowed to join the army, and a number of pirate leaders were rewarded with official rank. But, once again, these pirates were not used to colonizing some far-removed outpost of civilization or exploring new worlds in the hope of hitherto undiscovered sources of profit and power. Instead, they were employed close at hand, under the arm of the state, to patrol nearby shores.

Yet, for all their idle boasts about being able to overthrow the state, the pirates did not come close. In the end, they were unable to win over any significant number of the

Right: *This is a tabular element from Captain Lockyer's report of the* Medea*'s action of March 5, 1850, during which no British casualties were sustained. The report is in the Public Record Office as part of* China Station Records Vol. 4, Piracy at & In The Neighborhood of Hong Kong 1835–1852.

gentry élite, whose support was essential to the successful establishment of Chinese political power. Nor were they able to create truly impersonal, self-perpetuating organizations. Thus, when its leaders retired, the confederation folded. With its demise came the end of what may well have been the world's most significant instance of piracy *qua* piracy: piracy without some other overarching political, economic, or social reason for its existence. So far as I can tell, the pirates of the Six Flag fleets had no other reason for existence than the sheer force of strong leaders who, for nearly a decade, outperformed the state's own officials in extracting resources from the local economy and enforcing their "right" to do so with military power.

Twenty years later, in the 1830s, the pendulum swung back to the point where once again economics held out to the sons and grandsons of these pirates a new raison d'être in the form of opium.

CHAPTER ELEVEN

PIRACY
TODAY

~

__P__iracy today is simply robbery or banditry made distinctive
only by the fact that it occurs on water.

J. VAGG[1]

ANY MEANINGFUL discussion on modern-day piracy is complicated by two main factors: the lack of a comprehensive definition of the term "piracy"; and the lack of available information about the acts committed by "pirates." The United Nations Conventions on the High Seas (1958) and Convention on the Law of the Sea (1982) define piracy as an attack mounted for private ends on a ship on the high seas that involves violence, illegal detention of persons or property, or the theft or destruction of goods.[2]

However, the definition includes two provisos that make for subsequent difficulty. The first of these points is that the attack must be mounted for private gain. This can cause problems because, very often, the identity of the attackers is in doubt and their motives unclear. The second area of difficulty with the definition concerns the location of attacks. Both conventions relate to incidents on the high seas. This stroke of the legislative pen immediately puts the vast majority of current attacks out of the legal definition of piracy unless the littoral state concerned has created the offense within its own waters.

Because piracy is a real crime with real victims, the International Chamber of Commerce (ICC) and its International Maritime Bureau (IMB) have sought to find a more practical definition. They define piracy as "an act of boarding any vessel with the intent to commit theft or other crime and with the capability to use force in the furtherance of the act." The IMB deliberately left any mention of an assaulting vessel out of its definition, because many of today's attacks on merchant vessels come from the land when the vessel is in dock.

The problems of modern piracy are complicated by its diversity in terms of modus operandi and geography. There are few incentives, and many problems, for victims wishing to report attacks to the relevant authorities, even assuming a vessel is within national waters. Many shipping companies still do not report incidents of piracy because of the risk (and cost) of the vessel being detained while the crew is interviewed, and the suspicion that in some cases the local law enforcement agencies are involved.

An example that illustrates this point is the case of the *Kafu Maru*, which was boarded by officers from the Philippines Coast Guard shortly after she left Subic Bay on January 7, 1995. The officials said they were looking for firearms and ended up confiscating the vessel's cargo of cigarettes and liquor worth 4,500,000 pesos. They did not report their seizure, which was later recovered from their homes.

Any analysis of modern piracy highlights the fact that most attacks take place in the waters of developing countries, close to shore, and with theft the main motive. The history of piracy further suggests that it can only prosper when and where it is allowed to do so by the authorities, either in furtherance of their national interests or because of local corruption.

Turning a Blind Eye to the Pirates

Most modern pirates are land-based. They need somewhere to operate from, somewhere to hide, and a means of converting their "treasure" into hard currency. To be successful, they need a degree of cooperation from others, or at least for the local authorities to turn a blind eye. Today, the many countries involved have different laws, a different level of commitment to the problem, and varying degrees of competence to take effective action. Pirates know that their pursuit into territorial waters, without the consent of the

Left: *A pirate of today in the South China Sea. A masked man nicknamed "Tony" wearing a baseball cap and holding an automatic weapon provides a stark contrast with the traditional image of the pirate.*

Below: *Two rounds of 7.62mm ammunition: the longer, rimmed round is suitable for a Soviet support machine gun, the other is unrimmed and would be suitable for a Kalashnikov, the favored assault weapon of insurgents worldwide.*

Above: *A Filipino pirate crouches on the outrigger of a vessel with his gun at the ready. For many years piracy has been a major problem for shipping using the waters around the Philippines and Indonesia. The pirates hide in the creeks and waterways of the innumerable islands and make hit-and-run raids on the slow-moving merchant ships, which, with their small crews, are often easy targets.*

coastal state concerned, is an invasion of sovereignty.

On the high seas, however, the legal situation at least is more clear. A country that has granted a ship the right to sail under its flag has the right to pass and enforce legislation over its ships on the high seas, with the exception of unauthorized broadcasting and piracy.[3] Any ship suspected of piracy may be boarded. Pirate ships on the high seas can be seized by warships or official government vessels and the pirates arrested. Pirates can be tried before any court in any country and are subject to its laws and penalties.

Many governments are getting increasingly nervous about the use of the term "piracy," which they feel is too emotive and dramatic. Indonesia for example, one of the countries most affected by the modern crime, told the International Maritime Organization (IMO) in 1994 that it thought "robbery at sea" was a more appropriate term. But if the problem of piracy is to be dealt with effectively, there must be no shirking of the issue or its impact on commerce. To get the full picture, it is necessary to examine the history of piracy in recent times.

Piracy in the 1980s

The phenomenon that is now called modern piracy first came to world attention in the early 1980s with the escalating number of attacks reported on Vietnam's fleeing boat people. With the reports came the realization that the Gulf of Thailand and the South China Sea had a regional piracy problem. The "boat people" were an easy target for local fishermen, and such preventative measures as were taken to stop the attacks were clearly not working. Thailand's subsequent actions did much to subdue that particular problem. But, in the first six months of 1990, there were still thirty-three attacks against Vietnamese boat people reported, and twenty-four of these were classified as severe, resulting in nine deaths, 266 people missing, and thirty-five rape victims.

For the region, it appeared the die was now cast, and by 1990 commercial shipping began to wake up to the fact that piracy posed a serious problem. The Philip Strait, lying between Indonesia and Singapore, became the new focus of activity, as up to two hundred ships each day made their way through its two-mile (3km) wide channel. Early attacks there were largely non-violent and most took the form of intruders boarding the vessels at night from high-speed craft, before taking possession of cash and valuables.

Such attacks were a nuisance and led many shipping companies to increase their security precautions. Both the shipowners and the authorities (of the two sovereign states in whose waters the attacks were taking place) reasoned that the cost of prevention should not exceed the cost of the problem; and so it was given a low degree of priority. After all, this form of piracy attack, although grabbing the headlines, was only the maritime equivalent of the robberies that people ashore considered a part of everyday life.

Other forms of attack, however, could not be dealt with in such a matter-of-fact way. For example, piracy off the coast of West Africa at around the same time was an entirely different matter. These pirates used a high degree of violence during their attacks and, in addition to seeking cash and valuables, also sought to steal items from the ship's equipment and cargo.

The nature of piracy in Southeast Asia then began to take on a more menacing face. In August 1990 the *Martha*, a Cypriot-registered cargo vessel, was boarded by armed men while on passage from Bangkok to Busan. The crew were quickly overpowered and locked up. The pirates took over the vessel, changed course, and steamed to a new location where they dropped anchor. They made contact with accomplices ashore and, in an operation that lasted two days, discharged her cargo of tin-plate into a barge that had been brought alongside. When the operation was complete, the vessel was sailed to another location and the crew released as the pirates fled.

The attack was very well planned and executed with precision. Another, on the *Hai Hui 1* in Vietnamese waters, soon followed. Organized crime had entered the arena. Then, in late 1992, came the attack on the *Baltimar Zephyr*, during which the master and first officer were shot and killed. By now, reports of attacks by pirates in the region were coming in on almost a daily basis. And more worrying, 27 percent of the 115 attacks reported in Southeast Asia during 1991 involved fully laden tankers—an easy target due to their low freeboard.[4]

Suddenly, there was a very real fear about the environmental and commercial consequences of such a vessel grounding in a narrow channel as a result of loss of command during an attack by pirates. For instance, the Philip Strait could be closed and the port of Singapore effectively immobilized. After one attack, a fully laden tanker reported she had been out of command for seventy minutes. In another, pirates threw explosives onto the poop deck of the *World Bridge*, loaded with gas, oil, and kerosene, when she would not stop; and then peppered the hull with automatic weapons fire. With visions of the devastations caused by the spill from the *Exxon Valdez* in Alaska still fresh in people's minds, the world began to focus more closely on piracy.

The IMB was one of the first agencies to issue warnings about the consequences of vessels being left "not under command" during such incidents, and its fears were later amplified in a report by the U.S. Department of Energy that assessed the threat to Southeast Asia in detail.

Although the situation is constantly changing, modern piracy is concentrated in certain regions of the world, each characterized by different opportunities, different kinds of people involved, different levels of organization, and different types of attack targeting different types of vessel.

The Malacca Strait

The Malacca Strait region still experiences the highest rate of piracy in the world today. But the fears expressed in the early 1990s that piracy could spiral out of control have proved to be unfounded. An antipiracy initiative by Singapore, Indonesia, and Malaysia resulted in a dramatic decline in attacks in 1992, 1993, and 1994.

A high concentration of shipping, leading to congestion and the need for vessels to reduce speed, especially when transiting the narrow Philip Strait, still provides a temptation for coastal dwellers seeking to supplement their income from fishing with takings from passing ships. Attacks are generally conducted on an opportunity basis, and the pirates favor vessels with low freeboard, as only basic climbing equipment is needed.

South and East China Seas

Piracy in this region is a complex phenomenon involving many countries, including China, Russia, Hong Kong, and a number of local criminal syndicates. The area of highest risk lies within a triangle drawn to link Hong Kong, Luzon (Philippines), and Hainan island (China). Between 1991 and 1993, piracy here accounted for half of all the incidents reported worldwide, according to IMO figures. The year 1994 saw attacks in the South China Sea increase dramatically as the reports flooded in about vessels being boarded and hijacked by "officials" in Chinese uniforms from boats with evident Chinese markings. Several, including the *Alicia Star*, were seized in international waters and taken to ports along the south China coast, where their cargoes were confiscated and their crews held until payment of a fine, supposedly as part of a drive against smuggling.

Other attacks, such as those on the 16,960–ton *Jui Ho* and *Peder Most*, were apparently motivated by theft, and were reported to have been carried out by uniformed and armed men whose boat flew a red flag and was painted with Chinese-style signs. Responsibility for most of the attacks was ultimately attributed to officers from China's Border Patrol Bureau, who were working for

Below: *Pirates have always gone into the attack armed to the teeth, but instead of cutlasses and muskets the modern pirate will usually be armed with a powerful rifle or automatic weapon plus modern communications equipment. The folding butt on this AK 47 makes it a compact, easily concealed weapon. It is strongly made and its operation is quickly mastered by those with little firearms experience.*

profit without the authority of their government. After publicity given by the IMB and following representation from the IMO, the Chinese authorities acknowledged the problem and introduced regulations to curb the attacks. These were successful for a time, but reports received during 1995 suggest their reemergence. It is believed that some of the other attacks by men in Chinese uniforms during this period were the work of pirates using withdrawn naval cutters and impersonating Chinese government forces.

The area has also been the scene of several vessel hijacks. Evidence suggests these were the work of well-connected Chinese and Japanese criminal gangs, whose motive was to secure suitable transport to deliver cargoes of illegal aliens to North America. This has proved to be a highly lucrative business in recent years. Hundreds of immigrants are forced to pay up to $15,000 for their passage, which lasts several weeks in cramped and inhuman conditions. Reports have also intimated that there have been cases where such ships have been scuttled and their passengers drowned to avoid detection by American authorities.

The Philippines

The Philippines is the one Southeast Asian nation to buck the otherwise downward trend of piracy attacks in the region in recent years. Figures released by Manila almost certainly underplay the full extent of the problem when they record a total of 1,065 incidents during the period 1983–94, an average of nine attacks or attempted attacks a month. More particularly, the figures show an upswing: the 1994 monthly average was 50 percent higher than that given for 1984.

However, most incidents are confined to waters off the island of Mindanao, where government forces are in conflict with local Muslim separatists and so maintain only tenuous control. Here, the pirates mostly target fishermen operating out of General Santos City, stealing their fish, equipment, and, occasionally, the boats themselves. The most violent attacks have generally been in the far southwest of the Sulu Sea, between Basilan, Sulu, and Tawi-Tawi islands. Several people were killed in the sixteen incidents reported to the police in the first five months of 1995. However, attacks on oceangoing vessels have been rare and largely unsuccessful.

Explanations for the growth of piracy in the Philippines include poverty, the displacement of traditional fishing communities as a result of unsound environmental policies, and simple greed. Suppression is hindered by the enormous areas to be policed (the waters around the several thousand islands are six times larger than the land), and inadequate law enforcement equipment and facilities. The coast guard has only seven boats to control all the southern islands. Not only that, but the boats are large, slow, and have a limited range, so that pirate vessels are easily able to outrun them. Added to this is the fact that corruption and complacency appear to be firmly rooted in government, and these combine to temper official efforts and compromise antipiracy operations. The authorities admit that members of law enforcement agencies and the military are sometimes in league with the pirates.

Africa

Today, piracy in West Africa makes little impact. Twenty years ago this region boasted the highest number of incidents in the world, and in 1981 Nigeria's coastline was declared the world's most dangerous by the IMO. The new focus of activity on the continent is Somalia, where the civil war and resultant breakdown in government have led to something of a free-for-all. Most worrisome about the attacks taking place in this region is the increased use of heavy weapons such as mortars and grenades against vessels, both in port and while transiting the coastline.

The pirates often present themselves as coast guard officials, and in some cases are believed to actually be corrupt law enforcement officials. It is known that the reason behind some attacks is the desire to hijack a vessel to replace existing attack craft that are too small or not fast enough to be fully effective.

In 1994, the vessel *Bonsella* was hijacked by twenty-four armed men on a dhow and held for five days, being repeatedly used to try and attack other ships in the area during this time, before both ship and crew were released, frightened but unharmed. In 1995, an attack on the British-registered yacht *Longo Barda* was only foiled by the intervention of a Canadian vessel in the area. The *Nourberg Mofarrij* came under heavy machine-gun fire near Djibouti, and the *Tropical Sun* was the

Below: *A Colt Commando, a version of the Armalite AR-15 to which it is identical save for the fact that it has a barrel half the length of the one used in the rifle. The butt is telescopic.*

victim of a mortar attack while in the port of Mogadishu.

The regional administration of northeast Somalia has reacted angrily to press reports concerning piracy along the coastline in their control, which they refute. Yet, the Somali Salvation Democratic Front, the political voice for the administration, has previously admitted that it sent heavily armed militiamen in speedboats to capture foreign vessels on several occasions. The vessels were accused of illegal fishing in Somali waters.

South and Central America

Piracy in South and Central America is particularly prevalent in Colombia, Costa Rica, and Ecuador. But it is the situation in Brazil, and in particular at the key ports of Santos and Rio de Janeiro, that gives rise to most concern. In the early 1990s, these were listed among the world's most dangerous ports by the International Shipping Federation. More recently, in 1995, a report on Brazilian ports and their state security problems, compiled and sent to Washington by the U.S. ambassador to Brazil, was cited as a potential major impediment to the renewal of the maritime treaty between the two countries.

Attacks by armed gangs on ships in port was highlighted as the major problem. But this was further compounded by cumbersome bureaucratic procedures and slow port clearances. The U.S. has now joined with the U.K., Germany, Norway, and Greece in protesting to the Brazilian government about the secu-

rity problems. Threats of a boycott of Brazilian ports by shipowners have also been voiced. In June 1995, President Cardoso of Brazil responded with a decree ordering state and federal bodies to cooperate in the introduction of countermeasures to stop the attacks on commercial vessels, and promised a tough crackdown on criminal activity.

The Caribbean

The presence of a great deal of drug-related crime makes piracy in the Caribbean very difficult to gauge. Of the twenty-five attacks recorded between 1981 and 1987, half were against yachts. The U.S. estimates for the same period are much higher than that and suggest the disappearance of around two hundred people.

Reaction and Response

By the 1990s there was substantial international concern about the rise in incidents of piracy. But what was still missing was accurate statistical information. The response of the shipping community has, at best, been noisy but feeble. The incompleteness of the figures can be attributed to the reluctance of shipowners to report crimes where losses are small or negligible and where the bureaucratic procedures for doing so are protracted and costly. Other explanations put forward have included the fear of higher insurance premiums, concerns over increased payments to crews, the absence of established reporting structures in underdeveloped parts of the

Above: *Pirates in the Philippines in June 1991. The long, narrow craft shown here is typical of the vessels used for pirate attacks. Of traditional local design with outriggers, they are usually powered by a powerful inboard or outboard engine that enables the pirates to approach—and depart—their victims at high speed. The pirates board merchant ships by shinnying up bamboo poles or throwing up ropes or grappling hooks.*

Above: *Indonesian coast guards on antipirate patrol. Since many pirate attacks take no longer than ten to twenty minutes, it is impossible for even the fastest patrol vessels to come to the aid of a ship under attack. There is, of course, the added difficulty of tracking down the pirate lairs among the hundreds of Indonesian islands. The Indonesians possess a range of vessels for antipiracy purposes that formerly belonged to East Germany.*

world, and even, in some cases, because there have been no survivors to tell the tale.

In December 1992, ten badly burned human skeletons were found in the refrigerator of the vessel *Hai Sin*, formerly *Erria Inge*, when she arrived in a Chinese breaker's yard. The vessel had been "missing" for some months before the discovery, and the mystery of the bodies has never been solved.

At the same time, the physical suppression of piracy is now strictly a matter for those states affected, and many of these simply do not appear to have an interest in its suppression. The scale of effort that an affected nation devotes to antipiracy operations largely reflects the resources at its disposal and the priorities of those in power.

When Nigeria was threatened with the loss of control of its ports in the 1980s, it reacted by executing pirates and administering curfews. The then Soviet Union is reported to have had a naval unit tow a group of captured African pirates out to sea before shooting them in 1982. In 1994 China, under pressure from the IMO to respond to international protests, gave pirates the chance to surrender in return for leniency. Other lesser but still partially effective measures have been taken by Thailand to combat attacks on the Vietnamese boat people, and by the littoral states of Singapore, Indonesia, and Malaysia to jointly police the Malacca Strait.

Because piracy is versatile, occurs in different regions, and varies widely in character, many observers have been moved to suggest bilateral agreements to deal with it, similar to those used against drug traffickers. Certainly, any response to the problem lends itself to international cooperation. But the absence, so far, of an international policing organization leads to inaction and the involvement of wider political concerns.

International Efforts

In the meantime, it has fallen to international bodies like the United Nations and IMO to try and find a way forward. The United Nations Conference on Trade and Development (UNCTAD) has stressed its support for international cooperation between countries and agencies, which may include an umbrella organization, perhaps with investigative powers.

In 1993 the IMO stated its intention to create a task force to deal with piracy in the Malacca Strait and, in June of that year, published the report of its findings. These included: recommended measures to be taken by vessels to protect themselves from attack; actions by port authorities to be taken in the event of a hazardous spill following a grounding as the result of a pirate attack; creation of the means to warn other shipping in the area; and the creation of a central agency to record and analyze attack reports. The IMO also suggested that police forces and governments should maintain a close liaison with neighboring states to facilitate the apprehension and conviction of pirates.

Many experts consider the most realistic solution to the piracy problem is the creation of a series of specialist-manned, regionally based intelligence centers. But, as ever, there is a difference between the idea as a concept and its translation into a reality. The differences between countries, their laws, resources, commitment to the cause, and culture, all stand in the way. Cooperation can manifest itself in many ways and a blanket agreement between governments can neatly disguise the real differences on the ground. Effective collaboration, meanwhile, is a skilled process requiring skilled personnel.

Today, it is the IMB that has so far gone the farthest down the route toward this optimal solution. It opened the world's first Regional Piracy Center in October 1992 in Kuala Lumpur, Malaysia. Principally created to monitor and report on the piracy situation in Southeast Asia, the center nevertheless collates and publishes piracy warnings around the world. The center is manned twenty-four hours a day. It provides advice for shipping in the area about pirate activity, collects reports on attacks, and acts to alert the relevant law enforcement about suspicious craft movements. The data collected is analyzed and passed on to all interested parties. In the three years it has been in operation, the center has been able to witness the effect it has had on piracy. Worldwide numbers of reported piracy attacks have fallen steadily from 115 in 1992 to ninety in 1994.

Looking to the Future

But can piracy ever be eradicated? The nature of modern piracy, with its many different forms of attack, geographic spread, and the occasional connivance of state forces, all ensure that piracy cannot and never will be dealt with in a swift and simple manner. There will always remain an element of conflict between the priorities of the different parties. Law enforcement agencies see reporting the crime and recording the details as of paramount importance. The shipping industry views the speedy delivery of cargo as its main priority.

In an ideal world, the suppression of piracy would best be handled by a multinational force with the power to enter territorial waters when required, seize and detain suspects, together with the subsequent authority to imprison those found guilty. Being realistic, the necessary political will to make this happen is extremely unlikely. But the steps taken so far have at least focused world attention on piracy and made people see that it is no longer simply the pursuit of the "gutsy buccaneer."

Today, people know piracy for what it really is—an often brutal crime with the potential to damage economies, endanger the environment, and provoke conflict between states. Defeating piracy will never be easy and probably never be completely successful. But the lead taken by international and some national bodies has already resulted in its partial containment. It is therefore realistic to expect that continuing inroads into the problem can be made in the future.

The key to success must surely be a more positive approach to defeating piracy by the world's shipping companies. They are among the main victims. They, and their insurers, often have the most to lose. They ultimately can shape the solution by supporting the measures already in place, and by lending their weight to the growing body of international opinion that truly believes anything is possible if you want it badly enough.

Left: *The notorious Filipino pirate, Emilio Changco, in a maximum security prison in Manila where he is seving a life sentence with his brother Cecilio and three other pirates. Changco was involved in the seizure of the oil tanker* Tabangao *off Mindanao in 1991, as well as in the operation of phantom ship syndicates and numerous hijackings where ships were simply stolen and sold to order.*

BIBLIOGRAPHY

INTRODUCTION

Books

Calendar of State Papers, Colonial Series, American and West Indies 1574–1733. 27 vols. London: Public Record Office, 1862–1939.

Cordingly, D. *Life Among the Pirates: The Romance and the Reality.* London, 1995.

Gosse, P. *The History of Piracy.* London, 1932.

Marley, D. *Pirates and Privateers of the Americas.* London, 1994.

Mitchell. D. *Pirates.* London, 1976.

Ritchie, R. C. *Captain Kidd and the War against the Pirates.* Cambridge, Mass.: Harvard University Press, 1987.

Senior, C. *A Nation of Pirates.* London, 1976.

Other

Records of the High Court of Admiralty (HCA). London: Public Record Office.

THE LURE OF SPANISH GOLD

Books

Alsedo y Herrara, D. *Piraterías y agresiones de los ingleses y otros pueblos de Europa a la América española desde el siglo XVI al XVIII.* Madrid: Justo Zaragoza, 1883.

Andrews, K. R. *Drake's Voyages: A Re-Assessment of Their Place in Elizabethan Maritime Expansion.* London: Weidenfeld & Nicolson, 1967.

——. *Elizabethan Privateering: English Privateering during the Spanish War, 1585–1603.* Oxford: Oxford University Press, 1964.

——. *The Last Voyage of Drake and Hawkins.* Cambridge: Cambridge University Press [and Hakluyt Society], 1972.

——. *The Spanish Caribbean: Trade and Plunder, 1530–1630.* New Haven: Yale University Press, 1978.

Azcárraga y Bustamante, J. L. de. *El corso marítimo.* Madrid: Consejo Superior de Investigaciones Científicas, 1959.

Bradley, P. T. *The Lure of Peru: Maritime Intrusion into the South Sea, 1598–1701.* New York: St. Martin's Press, 1990.

Calendar of State Papers: Venetian. vol. 8 (1581–1591). London: Her Majesty's Stationery Office (HMSO), 1894.

Chaunu, H. and P. *Séville et l'Atlantique.* 9 vols. Paris: Colin, 1955.

Colección de documentos inéditos relativos al descubrimiento, conquista y colonizacion de las posesiones españolas en América y Oceanía. 42 vols. Madrid: Imprenta de Manuel B. de Quirós, 1864–84.

Colección de documentos inéditos relativos al descubrimiento, conquista y organización de las antiguas posesiones españolas de ultramar. 25 vols. Madrid: Estudio Tipográfico "Sucesores de Rivadeneyra," 1885–1932.

Corbett, Sir J. S. *Drake and the Tudor Navy, with a History of the Rise of England as a Maritime Power.* 2 vols. London: Longmans Green, 1898.

——. *Papers Relating to the Navy during the Spanish War, 1585–1587.* London: Navy Records Society, 1898.

——. *The Successors of Drake.* London: Longmans Green, 1900.

Fernández Asis, V. *Epistolario de Felipe II sobre asuntos de mar.* Madrid: Editora Nacional, 1943.

Fernández Duro, C. *Armada española desde la unión de los reinos de Castilla y de Aragón.* Vols. 1-4 of 9. Madrid: Rivadeneyra, 1896. Reprinted, Museo Naval, 1972–73.

Goslinga, C. C. *The Dutch in the Caribbean and on the Wild Coast, 1580–1680.* Gainesville: University of Florida Press, 1971.

Hakluyt, R. *The Principall Navigations Voyages Traffiques & Discoveries of the English Nation.* Glasgow: James MacLehose, 1903–5. Hakluyt Society, Extra Series (vols. 1-12).

Hampden, J. and J., eds. *Sir Francis Drake's Raid on the Treasure Trains: Being the Memorable Relation of his Voyage to the West Indies in 1572.* London: Folio Society, 1954.

Hampden, J. *Francis Drake, Privateer: Contemporary Narratives and Documents.* London: Eyre Methuen, 1972.

Israel, J. I. *The Dutch Republic and the Hispanic World, 1606–1661.* Oxford: Clarendon Press, 1986.

——. *Dutch Primacy in World Trade, 1585–1740.* Oxford: Oxford University Press, 1989.

Jármy Chapa, M. *Un eslabón perdido en la Historia: Piratería en el Caribe, siglos XVI y XVII.* Mexico, 1983.

Kraus, H. P. *Sir Francis Drake: A Pictorial Biography.* Amsterdam: N. Israel, 1970.

Landaeta Rosales, M. *Los piratas y escuadras extranjeras en las aguas y costas de Venezuela desde 1528 hasta 1903.* Caracas: Empresa Washington, 1903.

Lang, M. F. *El monopolio estatal del mercurio en el México colonial (1550–1710).* Mexico City: Fondo de Cultura Económica, 1977.

Lucena Salmoral, M. *Piratas, bucaneros, filibusteros y corsarios en América: perros, mendigos y otros malditos del mar.* Caracas: Grijalbo, 1994.

Marcel, G-A. *Les corsaires français au XVIe siècle dans les Antilles.* Paris: Ernest Leroux, 1902.

Markham, C. R. *The Hawkins' Voyages during the Reigns of Henry VIII, Queen Elizabeth, and James I.* London: Hakluyt Society, 1878.

Marx, R. F. *The Treasure Fleets of the Spanish Main.* Cleveland and New York: World Publishing, 1968.

Masiá de Ros, A. *Historia general de la piratería.* Barcelona, 1959.

Maynarde, T. *Sir Francis Drake his Voyage, 1595.* London: Hakluyt Society, 1849.

Menes Llaguno, J. M. *Bartolomé de Medina: Un Sevillano Pachuqueño.* Pachuca, Hidalgo, Mexico: Universidad Autonoma del Estado de Hidalgo, 1989.

Olson, J. S., ed. *Historical Dictionary of the Spanish Empire, 1402–1975.* New York: Greenwood Press, 1991.

Oppenheim, M. M., ed. *The Naval Tracts of Sir William Monson in Six Books.* 5 vols. London: Navy Records Society, 1902–14.

Parker, G. *The Dutch Revolt,* London: Allen Lane, 1977.

Peralta, M. M. de. *Costa Rica, Nicaragua y Panamá en el siglo XVI.* Madrid: Murillo, 1883.

"Piracy and Privateering": Catalogue 4, National Maritime Museum Library. London: HMSO, 1972.

Postma, J. M. *The Dutch in the Atlantic Slave Trade, 1600–1815.* Cambridge: Cambridge University Press, 1990.

Rahn Phillips, C. *Six Galleons for the King of Spain: Imperial Defense in the Early Seventeenth Century.* Baltimore and London: Johns Hopkins University Press, 1986.

Rowse, A. L. *Sir Richard Grenville of the Revenge.* London: Jonathan Cape, 1940.

Rumeú de Armas, A. *Piraterias y ataques navales contra las Islas Canarias.* 5 vols. Madrid: Consejo Superior de Investigaciones Científicas, 1947.

——. *Los viajes de John Hawkins a América (1562–1595).* Seville: Escuela de Estudios Hispanoamericanos, 1964.

Sáiz Cidoncha, C. *Historia de la piratería en América Española.* Madrid: Editorial San Martin.

Tenison, E. M. *Elizabethan England: Being the History of this Country "In Relation to all Foreign Princes," from Original Manuscripts.* 13 vols. Leamington Spa: privately printed, 1933–61.

Thomas, H. *Conquest: Montezuma, Cortés, and the Fall of Old Mexico.* New York: Simon & Schuster, 1993.

Unwin, R. *The Defeat of Sir John Hawkins: A Biography of his Third Slaving Voyage.* London: Allen & Unwin, 1960.

Williams, N. *The Sea Dogs: Privateers, Plunder and Piracy in the Elizabethan Age.* New York: Macmillan, 1975.

Williamson, G. C. *George, Third Earl of Cumberland (1558–1605): His Life and Voyages. A Study from Original Documents.* Cambridge: Cambridge University Press, 1920.

Williamson, J. A. *The Age of Drake.* London: A. & C. Black, 1938.

——. *Hawkins of Plymouth: A New History of Sir John Hawkins and of Other Members of his Family Prominent in Tudor England.* London: A. & C. Black, 1969.

Wright, I. A., ed. *Spanish Documents Concerning English Voyages to the Caribbean, 1527–1568; Selected from the Archives at Seville.* London: Hakluyt Society, 1929.

——. *Documents Concerning English Voyages to the Spanish Main, 1569–1580.* London: Hakluyt Society, 1932.

——. *Further English Voyages to Spanish America, 1583–1594.* London: Hakluyt Society, 1949.

Other

Harris, S. "The Tragic Dream of Jean Ribaut." *American Heritage* 14, no. 6 (October 1963): p. 8–15 and 88–90.

Hewitt, G. R. "Drake at San Juan de Puerto Rico." *The Mariner's Mirror* 50 (August 1964): p. 199–204.

Jameson, A. K. "Some New Spanish Documents Dealing with Drake." *English Historical Review* 49 (July 1934): p. 14–31.

Lewis, M. "The Guns of the *Jesus of Lubeck.*" *The Mariner's Mirror* 22 (July 1936): p. 324–25.

——. "Fresh Light on San Juan de Ulúa." *The Mariner's Mirror* 23 (July 1937): p. 295–315.

Perea, J. A. and S. "La catástrofe dramatica de Drake en Puerto Rico." *Ateneo Puertorriqueño* 4 (July–September 1940): p. 214–23.

Sluiter, E. "Dutch-Spanish Rivalry in the Caribbean Area, 1594–1609." *Hispanic American Historical Review* 28, no. 2 (May 1948): p. 165–96.

BRETHREN OF THE COAST

Books

Acts of the Privy Council of England, Colonial Series, 1630–80. 6 vols. London: Public Record Office.

Acts of the Privy Council of England, Colonial Series, 1691–1783. 6 vols. London: Public Record Office.

Andrews, K. R., ed. *The Spanish Caribbean, Trade and Plunder 1530–1630.* New Haven & London, 1978.

Arber, E., ed. *The True Travels and Adventures of Captaine John Smith 1608–1631.* Birmingham (England), 1884.

Archenholz, J. W. von. *The History of the Pirates, Freebooters and Buccaneers of America.* London, 1807.

Arciniegas, G. *The Caribbean.* Translated by Harriet de Onis. New York, 1954.

Bell, H. C. *Guide to British West Indian Archive Materials.* Washington, D.C., 1926.

Blond, G. *Histoire de la Filibuste.* Paris, 1969.

Boxer, C. R. *The Dutch Seaborne Empire 1600–1800.* New York, 1965.

Bridges, G. W. *The Annals of Jamaica.* London, 1837.

Burchett, J. *A Complete History of the Most Remarkable Transactions at Sea.* London, 1720.

Charlevoix, P. F. X. de. *Histoire de l'Isle Espagnole.* Paris, 1730.

Crouse, N. M. *French Pioneers in the West Indies 1624–1664.* New York, 1940.

——. *The French Struggle for the West Indies 1665–1713.* New York, 1943.

Dampier, W. *A New Voyage Round the World.* London, 1697. Reprinted 1927.

Defoe, D. *The Life and Strange Surprizing Adventures of Robinson Crusoe of York.* London, 1719.

Esquemelin (Exquemeling), A. O. *The Buccaneers of America.* London, 1684 (first edition in English), 1685.

Golif, L. le. *Memoirs of a Buccaneer.* New York, 1954.

Gosse, P. *The Pirates' Who's Who.* London & Boston, 1924. Reprinted, Glorieta, New Mexico: 1988.

——. *The History of Piracy.* London, 1932.

Haring, C. H. *The Buccaneers in the West Indies in the Seventeenth Century.* New York, 1910.

——. *Trade and Navigation between Spain and the Indies.* Cambridge, Massachusetts, 1918.

Howse, D., and Thrower, N., eds. *A Buccaneer's Atlas: Basil Ringrose's South Sea Wagoner.* Berkeley, Los Angeles, and Oxford, 1992.

Labat, J. *Memoirs 1693–1705.* London, 1734. Reprinted, 1971.

Lindsay, P. *The Great Buccaneer.* New York, 1951.

Lussan, R. de. *Raveneau de Lussan, Buccaneer of the Spanish Main.* Edited by M. E. Wilbur, Cleveland, Ohio, 1930.

Marx, J. *Pirates and Privateers of the Caribbean.* Malabar, Florida, 1992.

Marx, R. F. *Pirate Port,* New York, 1967.

——. *The Treasure Fleets of the Spanish Main.* New York, 1968.

——. *Port Royal Rediscovered.* New York, 1973.

——. *The Capture of the Treasure Fleet.* New York, 1977.

Newton, A. P. *European Nations in the West Indies, 1493–1688.* London, 1933.

Parry, J. H. *The Spanish Seaborne Empire.* London, 1966.

Pope, D. *Harry Morgan's Way.* London, 1977.

Rankin, H. F. *The Golden Age of Piracy.* New York, 1969.

Sloane, Sir H. *A Voyage to the Islands.* London, vol. 1, 1707; vol. 2, 1725.

Wafer, L. *A New Voyage and Description of the Isthmus of America.* London, 1699. Reprinted, Oxford, 1934.

Williams, N. *Captains Outrageous.* New York, 1962.

BUCCANEER EXPLORERS

Books

Dampier, W. *The Voyages of Captain William Dampier*. Edited by J. Masefield. London, 1906.

Esquemelin, A. O. *De Americaaensche Zee-Rovers*. Amsterdam, 1678. Trans. as *The Bucaniers of America*, London, 1684; the edition cited in this chapter was published in London and New York in 1923 (Edited by W. S. Stallybrass) and entitled *Esquemeling, The Buccaneers of America*.

Fernandez-Armesto, F., ed. *The Times Atlas of World Exploration*. London, 1991.

Howse, D., and Thrower, N., eds. *A Buccaneer's Atlas: Basil Ringrose's South Sea Wagoner*. Berkeley, Los Angeles, and Oxford, 1992.

Norris, G. ed., *William Dampier, Buccaneer Explorer*. London, 1994.

Rogers, W. *A Cruising Voyage Round the World*. Edited by G. E. Mainwaring. London, 1928.

Wafer, L. *A New Voyage & Description of the Isthmus of America*. Edited by Elliott Joyce, L. E. Oxford, 1934.

Williams, N. *The Sea Dogs: Privateers, Plunder and Piracy in the Elizabethan Age*. London, 1975.

CORSAIRS OF THE MEDITERRANEAN

Books

Blouet, B. *The Story of Malta*. London: Faber & Faber, 1967.

Bradford, E. *The Great Siege: Malta 1565*. London, 1962.

Brown, H. P. and Hopkins, S. V., *A Perspective of Wages and Prices*. London, 1981.

Currey, E. H. *Sea Wolves of the Mediterranean*. London, 1910.

Earle, P. *Corsairs of Malta and Barbary*. London, 1970.

Fage, J. D., *History of Africa*. London, 1988.

Fisher, G. *Barbary Legend*. Oxford, 1957.

Hough, R. *Fighting Ships*. London, 1969.

Lane-Poole, S. *The Barbary Corsairs*. London, 1880.

Lloyd, C. *English Corsairs on the Barbary Coast*. 1981.

Lucie-Smith, E. *Outcasts of the Sea*. London, 1978.

Luke, Sir H. *An Account and Appreciation of Malta*. London, 1960.

Morgan, J. *Several Voyages to Barbary*. London, 1736.

Sire, H. J. A. *The Knights of Malta*. London, 1994.

Thrower, R. *The Pirate Picture*, New York, 1980.

Other

Cavaliero, R. E. "The decline of the Maltese corso in the XVIIIth century." *Melita Historica* (Valletta) 2, no. 4: 1959.

Wettinger, G. "The galley-convicts and *buonavoglie* in Malta during the rule of the Order." *Journal of the Faculty of Arts, University of Malta* (Valletta) 3, no. 1: 1965.

THE GOLDEN AGE OF PIRACY

Books

Acts of the Privy Council of England, Colonial Series, 1691–1783. 6 vols. London: Public Record Office.

An Account of the Pirates with Divers of their Speeches, Letter and a Poem (26 executed July 19, 1723 at Newport) (pamphlet). Reprinted, 1769.

Arciniegas, G. *The Caribbean*. Translated by Harriet de Onis. New York, 1954.

Bell, H. C. *Guide to British West Indian Archive Materials*. Washington, D.C., 1926.

Boswell, J. *The Life of Samuel Johnson*. London, 1791.

Bradlee, F. *Piracy in the West Indies and Its Suppression*. Salem, 1923.

Bridges, G. W. *The Annals of Jamaica*. London, 1837.

Burns, A. C. *History of the British West Indies*. London, 1954.

Calendar of State Papers, Colonial Series, American and West Indies 1574–1733. 27 vols. London: Public Record Office, 1862–1939.

Carse, R. *The Age of Piracy*. New York, 1957.

Edwards, B. *The History, Civil and Commercial, of the British Colonies in the West Indies*. London, 1801.

Ellms, C. *The Pirates' Own Book*, Boston, 1837. Reprinted Salem, 1924.

The Autobiography of Benjamin Franklin. Edited by Larabee, L. W. New Haven, Conn., 1964.

Gosse, P. *The Pirates' Who's Who*. London & Boston, 1924. Reprinted, Glorieta, New Mexico: 1988.

———. *The History of Piracy*. London, 1932. Reprinted, Glorieta, New Mexico, 1988.

Jameson, J. G. *Privateering and Piracy in the Colonial Period: Illustrative Documents*. New York, 1923.

Johnson, Capt. C. *A General History of the Robberies and Murders of the Most Notorious Pirates*. London, 1724; enlarged

editions 1724, 1725, and 1726.

Lee, R. E. *Blackbeard the Pirate*. Winston-Salem, N. C. 1974.

Mahan, A. T. *The Influence of Sea Power Upon History 1660–1783*. New York, 1968.

Marx, J. *Pirates and Privateers of the Caribbean*. Malabar, Florida, 1992.

Marx, R. F. and J. *The Search For Sunken Treasure*. Toronto and New York, 1993.

Philips, J. (printer), *A Compleat Coll. of Remarkable Tryals of the Most Notorious Malefactors etc.*, 2 vols. London, 1718.

Rankin, H. F. *The Golden Age of Piracy*. New York, 1969.

Rediker, M. *Between the Devil and the Deep Blue Sea*. London, 1987.

Smith, A. *The Atrocities of the Pirates*. London, 1824.

Spotswood, A. *The Official Letters of Alexander Spotswood, Lieutenant Governor of the Colony of Virginia, 1710–22*. 2 vols. Edited by R. A. Brock. Richmond, Virginia, 1882–85.

State Trials and Proceedings (trials of Major Stede Bonnet and thirty-three others), vol. 8. London: Public Record Office, 1731.

Tryals of Captain John Rackham and other Pyrates (pamphlet). London, 1721.

Westergaard, W. *The Danish West Indies under Company Rule, 1671–1754*. New York, 1917.

Woodbury, G. *The Great Days of Piracy in the West Indies*. New York, 1951.

LIBERTALIA: THE PIRATE'S UTOPIA

Books

Alexander, J. K. "Forton Prison During the American Revolution: a Case Study of the British Prisoner of War Policy and the American Prisoner Response to that Policy." *Essex Institute Historical Collections* CII, 1967.

An Account of the Conduct and Proceedings of the Late John Gow, alias Smith, Captain of the Late Pirates. London, 1725. Reprinted, Edinburgh: Gordon Wright Publishing, 1978.

Atkins, J. *A Voyage to Guinea, Brazil, & the West Indies*. London, 1735. Reprinted, London: Frank Cass, 1970.

Baer, J. H. "Piracy Examined: A Study of Daniel Defoe's *General History of the Pyrates* and its Milieu." Ph.D. diss. Princeton University, 1970.

Baynham, H. *From the Lower Deck: The Royal Navy, 1780–1840*. Barre, Mass.: Barre Publishers, 1970.

Bellamy, R. R., ed. *Ramblin' Jack: The Journal of Captain John Cremer*. London, 1936.

Betagh, W. *A Voyage Round the World*. London, 1728.

Boswell, J. *The Life of Samuel Johnson*. London, 1791.

Bowman, L. G. *Captive Americans: Prisoners during the American Revolution*. Athens, Ohio: Ohio University Press, 1976.

Bridenbaugh, C. and R. *No Peace Beyond the Line: The English in the Caribbean, 1624–1690*. New York: Oxford University Press, 1972.

Cooke, E. *A Voyage to the South Sea*. London, 1712.

Course, A. G. *The Merchant Navy: A Social History*. London, 1963.

Creighton, M., and Norling, L., eds. *Iron Men, Wooden Women: Gender and Atlantic Seafaring, 1700–1920*. Baltimore: John Hopkins University Press, 1995.

Davis, R. *The Rise of the English Shipping Industries in the Seventeenth and Eighteenth Centuries*. London, 1962.

Deschamps, H. *Les Pirates à Madagascar aux XVIIe et XVIIIe siècles*. Paris: Editions Berger-Levrault, 1972.

Dugaw, D. *Warrior Women and Popular Balladry 1650–1850*. Cambridge: Cambridge University Press, 1989.

Furbank, P. N., and Owens, W. R. *The Canonization of Daniel Defoe*. New Haven: Yale University Press, 1988.

Gilbert, A. N. "The Nature of Mutiny in the British Navy in the Eighteenth Century." In *Naval History: The Sixth Symposium of the U.S. Naval Academy*. Wilmington, Del.: Scholarly Resources, Inc., 1987, p. 111-21.

Haring, C. H. *The Buccaneers in the West Indies in the XVII Century*. London, 1910, reprinted Hamden, Conn.: Archon Books, 1966.

Hayward, A. L., ed. *Lives of the Most Remarkable Criminals*. London, 1735, p. 37.

Hill, C. "Pottage for Freeborn Englishmen: Attitudes to Wage Labour." In his *Change and Continuity in Seventeenth-Century England*. Cambridge, Mass., 1975, p. 219-38.

———. "Radical Pirates?" In *The Origins of Anglo-American Radicalism*. London: George Allen & Unwin, 1984, p. 17-32.

Howell, C., and Twomey, R., eds. *Jack Tar in History: Essays in the History of Maritime Life and Labour*. Fredericton, New Brunswick: Acadiensis Press, 1991.

Jacob, M. and J., eds. *The Origins of Anglo-American Radicalism*.

London: George Allen & Unwin, 1984.

Jameson, J. F., ed. *Privateering and Piracy in the Colonial Period: Illustrative Documents*. New York: Macmillan, 1923.

Johnson, Capt. C. *A General History of the Pyrates*, Edited by Schonhorn, M. 1724, 1728. Reprinted, Columbia, S.C.: University of South Carolina Press, 1972.

Kemp, P. *The British Sailor: A Social History of the Lower Deck*. London, 1970.

Kemp, P. K., and Lloyd, C. *Brethren of the Coast: Buccaneers of the South Seas*. New York: St. Martins Press, 1960.

Krantz, F., ed. *History From Below: Studies in Popular Protest and Popular Ideology in Honour of George Rudé*. Montreal: Concordia University, 1985.

Lloyd, C. *The British Seaman, 1200–1860: A Social Survey*. Rutherford, N.J., 1970.

Lyte, M. H. C., ed. *Journal of the Commissioners for Trade and Plantations*. vol. 3, London, 1924.

Mainwaring, G. E., and Dobree, B. *Mutiny: The Floating Republic: The Mutinies at Spithead and Nore, 1797*. London, 1935. Reprinted, 1987.

Masterson, D., ed. *Naval History: The Sixth Symposium of the U.S. Naval Academy*. Wilmington, Del.: Scholarly Resources, Inc., 1987.

Mather, C. *Instructions to the Living, From the Condition of the Dead: a Brief Relation of Remarkables in the Shipwreck of above One Hundred Pirates*. Boston, 1717.

McFee, W. *The Law of the Sea*. Philadelphia, 1951.

Merriman, R. D., ed. *Queen Anne's Navy: Documents Concerning the Administration of the Navy of Queen Anne, 1702–1714*. London, 1961.

Moore, J. R. *Defoe in the Pillory and Other Studies*. Bloomington: Indiana University Press, 1939.

Morris, R. B. *Government and Labor in Early America*. New York, 1946.

Morton, A. L. *The English Utopia*. London: Lawrence & Wishart, 1952.

Price, R. *Maroon Societies: Rebel Slave Communities in the Americas*. 2nd ed. Baltimore: John Hopkins University Press, 1979.

Rankin, H. *The Golden Age of Piracy*. New York, 1969.

Rediker, M. *Between the Devil and the Deep Blue Sea: Merchant Seamen, Pirates, and the Anglo-American Maritime World, 1700–1750*. Cambridge: Cambridge University Press, 1987.

Ritchie, R. C. *Captain Kidd and the War against the Pirates*. Cambridge, Mass.: Harvard University Press, 1987.

Rogers, W. *A Cruising Voyage Round the World*, Edited by G. E. Mainwaring. 1712. Reprinted, New York, 1928.

Sainsbury, W. N., et al., eds. *Calendar of State Papers, Colonial Series, America and the West Indies*. Vol. 39, p. 350. London, 1860–.

Shelvocke, G. *A Voyage Round the World*. London, 1726.

Snelgrave, W. *A New Account of Some Parts of Guinea and the Slave Trade*. London, 1734. Reprinted, London: Frank Cass, 1971.

Stanley, J. *Bold in her Breeches: Women Pirates Across the Ages*. London: HarperCollins, 1995.

Stock, F. L. *Proceedings and Debates of the British Parliaments respecting North America*. Vol. 3. Washington, D.C.: Carnegie Institute, 1930.

The Trials of Eight Persons Indited for Piracy. Boston, 1718.

The Trials of Five Persons for Piracy, Felony, and Robbery. Boston, 1726.

The Tryals of Major Stede Bonnet and Other Pirates. London, 1719.

Thomson, J. E. *Mercenaries, Pirates and Sovereigns: State-Building and Extraterritorial Violence in Early Modern Europe*. Princeton: Princeton University Press, 1994.

Tracy, J. D., ed. *The Political Economy of Merchant Empires*. Cambridge: Cambridge University Press, 1991.

Other

American Weekly Mercury

Boston Gazette

Boston News-Letter

Bromley, J. S. "Outlaws at Sea, 1660–1720: Liberty, Equality, and Fraternity among the Caribbean Freebooters." In *History From Below: Studies in Popular Protest and Popular Ideology in Honour of George Rudé*, pp. 301–20. Montreal: Concordia University, 1985.

Graus, F. "Social Utopias in the Middle Ages." *Past and Present* 38. (1967): p. 3-19.

High Court of Admiralty Papers (HCA). London: Public Record Office.

Laughton, L. G. C. "Shantying and Shanties," *Mariner's Mirror* 9 (1923): p. 48-50.

Lemisch, J. "Jack Tar in the Streets: Merchant Seamen in the Politics of Revolutionary America." *William and Mary Quarterly* 25 (1968): p. 375-376, 379, 406.

———. "Listening to the 'Inarticulate.' William Widger's Dream and the Loyalties of American Revolutionary Seamen in British Prisons." *Journal of Social History* 3 (1969-70): p. 1–29.

May, W. E. "The Mutiny of the *Chesterfield*." *Mariner's Mirror* 47 (1961): p. 178-87.

Moore, J. P. III. "'The Greatest Enormity that Prevails': Direct Democracy and Workers' Self-Management in the British Naval Mutinies of 1797." In *Jack Tar in History: Essays in the History of Maritime Life and Labour*. p. 76–104. Fredericton, New Brunswick: Acadiensis Press, 1991.

Pérotin-Dumon, A. "The Pirate and the Emperor: Power and the Law on the Seas, 1450–1850." In *The Political Economy of Merchant Empires*. Cambridge: Cambridge University Press, 1991.

Rediker, M. "'Under the Banner of King Death': The Social World of Anglo-American Pirates, 1716 to 1726." *William and Mary Quarterly*, 3rd ser. 38 (1981): p. 203-27.

———. "The Common Seaman in the Histories of Capitalism and the Working Class." *International Journal of Maritime History* 1 (1989): p. 352-53.

———. "Liberty beneath the Jolly Roger: The Lives of Anne Bonny and Mary Read, Pirates." In *Iron Men, Wooden Women: Gender and Atlantic Seafaring, 1700–1920.* Baltimore: Johns Hopkins University Press, 1995.

Ross, H. "Some Notes on the Pirates and Slavers around Sierra Leone and the West Coast of Africa, 1680–1723." *Sierra Leone Studies* 11 (1928): p. 16-53.

Spencer, T. "Pigs Meat." In *The Marine Republic.* Vol. 2. 2nd ed. London, 1794: p. 68-72.

THE PIRATE ROUND

Books

Arciniegas, G. *The Caribbean.* Translated by Harriet de Onis. New York, 1954.

Acts of the Privy Council of England, Colonial Series, 1691–1783. 6 vols. London: Public Record Office.

Bell, H. C. *Guide to British West Indian Archive Materials.* Washington, D.C. 1926.

Bradlee, F. *Piracy in the West Indies and Its Suppression.* Salem, 1923.

Bridges, G. W. *The Annals of Jamaica.* London, 1837.

Burns, A. C. *History of the British West Indies.* London, 1954.

Calendar of State Papers, Colonial Series, American and West Indies 1574–1733. 27 vols. London: Public Record Office, 1862–1939.

Cambridge History of the British Empire. Vol. 1. Cambridge, 1960.

Carse, R. *The Age of Piracy.* New York, 1957.

Casson, L. *The Ancient Mariners.* New York, 1959.

Cochran, H. *Freebooters of the Red Sea.* New York, 1965.

Crouse, N. M. *The French Struggle for the West Indies 1665–1713.* New York, 1943.

Documents Relative to the Colonial History of the State of New York. Vols. 1 and 3. Albany, New York, 1853–54.

Drury, R. *Madagascar: Or, Robert Drury's Journal.* 1890. Reprinted, Westport, Conn., 1960.

Duro, F. C. de. *La Armada Española.* 9 vols. Madrid, 1895–1903.

Dutertre, J. B. *Histoire Générale des Antilles.* Paris, 1667–71.

Edwards, B. *The History, Civil and Commercial, of the British Colonies in the West Indies.* London, 1801.

Ellms, C. *The Pirates' Own Book.* Boston, 1837. Reprinted, Salem, Mass., 1924.

Gosse, P. *The History of Piracy.* London, 1932.

Grey, C. *Pirates of the Eastern Seas.* London, 1933.

Hanson, E. P., ed. *South from the Spanish Main.* New York, 1967.

Haring, C. H. *Trade and Navigation between Spain and the Indies.* Cambridge, 1918.

Jameson, J. G. *Privateering and Piracy in the Colonial Period: Illustrative Documents.* New York, 1923.

Johnson, Capt. C. *A General History of the Robberies and Murders of the Most Notorious Pirates.* London 1724; enlarged eds. 1724, 1725, and 1726.

Kidd, W. *A Full Account of the Proceedings in Relation to Capt. Kidd* (pamphlet). London, 1701.

Labat, J. B. *Memoirs 1693–1705.* London, 1734. Reprinted, 1971.

Larabee, L. W., ed. *The Autobiography of Benjamin Franklin.* New Haven, Conn., 1964.

Lucie-Smith, E. *Outcasts of the Seas.* New York and London, 1978.

Lee, R. E. *Blackbeard the Pirate.* Winston-Salem, N.C., 1974.

Mahan, A. T. *The Influence of Sea Power upon History 1660–1783.* New York, 1968.

Mannix, D. and Crowley, M. *Black Cargoes: A History of the Atlantic Slave Trade, 1518–1865.* New York, 1962.

Martin-Nieto, A. *Piratas del Pacifico.* Bilbao, 1968.

Marx, J. *Pirates and Privateers of the Caribbean.* Malabar, Florida, 1992.

Marx, R. F. *The Treasure Fleets of the Spanish Main.* New York, 1968.

Parry, J. H. *Trade and Dominion.* London, 1971.

Rankin, H. *The Golden Age of Piracy.* New York, 1969.

Rediker, M. *Between the Devil and the Deep Blue Sea.* London, 1987.

Ritchie, R. C. *Captain Kidd and the War Against the Pirates.* Cambridge, Mass. and London, 1986.

Snelgrave, W. *A New Account of Some Parts of Guinea and the Slave-Trade.* London, 1734. Reprinted, Portland, Ore., 1972.

Ward, R. T. *Pirates in History.* Baltimore, 1974.

Williams, E. *From Columbus to Castro.* New York, 1971.

FRENCH AND AMERICAN PRIVATEERS

Books

Albion, R., and Pope, J. B. *Sea Lanes in Wartime.* New York, 1942, p. 41–42.

Allen, G. W. *A Naval History of the American Revolution.* 2 vols. 1913. Reprinted, Williamstown, Mass., 1970.

———. *Massachusetts Privateers of the Revolution.* Cambridge, Mass., 1927.

———. *Our Navy and the West Indian Pirates.* Salem: Corner House, 1929.

Auger, H. *The Secret War of Independence.* New York, 1955.

Bonnel, U. *La France, Les Etats-Unis et la Guerre de Course, 1797–1815.* Paris, 1961.

Chapin, H. M. *Privateering Ships and Sailors, the First Century of American Colonial Privateering, 1625–1725.* Toulon, France, 1926.

———. *Privateering in King George's War, 1739–48.* Providence, R.I., 1928.

Clark, W. B. *Ben Franklin's Privateers.* Baton Rouge, Louisiana. 1956.

Clark, W. B., and Morgan, W. J., eds. *Naval Documents of the American Revolution.* 9 vols. to date. Washington, D.C. 1964–.

Coggeshall, G. *History of American Privateers and Letters-of-Marque During Our War with England in the Years 1812, '13, and '14.* New York, 1856.

Dudley, W. S., et al., eds. *The Naval War of 1812: A Documentary History.* 2 vols. Washington, D.C. 1985–.

Falconer, W. *An Universal Dictionary of the Marine: or, Copious Explanation of the Technical Terms and Phrases Employed in the Construction, Equipment, Furniture, Machinery, Movements, and Military Operations of a Ship.* New edition, corrected. London: Cadell, 1780.

Ford, W. C., et al., eds. *Journals of the Continental Congress.* Washington, D.C., 1904–37.

Grummond, J. L. de. *The Baratarians and the Battle of New Orleans.* Baton Rouge, Louisiana, 1961, p. 3015.

Garitee, J. R. *The Republic's Private Navy: The American Privateering Business as Practiced by Baltimore during the War of 1812.* Middletown, Conn.: Wesleyan University Press, 1977.

Hagan, K. J., ed. *In Peace and War.* Westport, 1978.

Howard, M., Andreopoulos, G. J., and Shulman, M. R., eds. *The Laws of War.* New Haven, Conn., 1995.

Jackson, M. H. *Privateers in Charleston, 1793–1796.* Washington, 1969.

Jameson, J. F., ed. *Privateering and Piracy in the Colonial Period: Illustrative Documents.* New York, 1923.

Jenkins, E. H. *A History of the French Navy.* Annapolis, Md., 1973.

Knox, D. W., ed. *Naval Documents Related to the Quazi-War with France.* 7 vols. Washington, D.C., 1935–8.

Laing, C. H. *A Seafaring America.* New York, 1974.

Lincoln, C. H. "Naval Records of the American Revolution [calendar]." Manuscript Division, Library of Congress, Washington.

Love, R. *A History of the U.S. Navy.* 2 vols. Harrisburg, Pa.: Stackpole Books, 1992.

Maclay, E. S. *A History of American Privateering.* New York, 1924.

Marsden, R., ed. *Select Pleas in the Court of Admiralty.* 2 vols. London, 1894–7.

Morse, S. G. "New England Privateering in the American Revolution." Ph.D. diss., Harvard University, 1941.

Paullin, C. O. *The Navy of the American Revolution.* Cleveland, Ohio, 1906.

Reilly, R. *The British at the Gates: The New Orleans Campaign in the War of 1812.* New York, 1974.

Rhode Island Colonial Records. 10 vols. Providence, R.I., 1856–65.

Roberts, A., and Guelff, R., eds. *Documents of the Laws of War.* Oxford, 1989.

Robinson, W. M., Jr. *The Confederate Privateers.* New York, 1928.

Stark, F. R. *The Abolition of Privateering and the Declaration of Paris.* New York, 1897.

Swanson, C. E. *Predators and Prizes: American Privateering and Imperial Warfare, 1739–1748.* Columbia, S.C.: University of South Carolina Press, 1991.

Symox, G. *The Crisis of French Sea Power, 1688–1697: From Guerre d'Escadre to Guerre de Course.* The Hague, 1974.

Syrett, D. "Defeat at Sea: The Impact of American Naval Operations upon the British, 1775–1778." In *Maritime Dimensions of the American Revolution.* Washington, D.C., 1977.

Tatum, E. H., Jr., ed. *The American Journal of Ambrose Serle, Secretary to Lord Howe, 1776–1778.* San Marino, 1940.

Wharton, F., ed. *The Revolutionary Diplomatic Correspondence of the United States.* 6 vols. Washington, D.C.,1889.

Wheeler, R. *In Pirate Waters.* New York, 1969.

Other

Boston Independent Chronicle, April 8 and 22, 1779, and March 9, 1780.

Bradford, C. J. "Navies of the American Revolution." In *In Peace and War.* Westport, 1978. p. 3–26.

Clark, G. "The English Practice with Regard to Reprisals by Private Persons." *American Journal of International Law* 27 (1933), p. 694–723.

The Gentleman's Magazine 82, Part 2 (September 1812).

Hattendorff, J. B. "Maritime Conflict." In *The Laws of War.* p. 98-115. New Haven, Conn., 1995.

Jamieson, A. G. "American Privateers in the Leeward Islands, 1776–1778." *American Neptune* 43 (1983) p. 24–25.

"Letters of Oliver Pollock." Papers of the Continental Congress, National Archives, Washington, D.C.

London Public Advertiser, December 14, 1778, and May 24, 1779.

Morgan, W. J. "American Privateering in America's War for Independence, 1775–1783." *American Neptune* 36 (1976).

Niles' National Register, (Baltimore), April 19, 1823.

THE EASTERN SEAS

Books

Abdullah bin Adbul Kadir. *The Hikayat Abdullah, the Autobiography of Abdullah bin Abdul Kadir.* Annotated translation by A. H. Hill. London, 1969.

Baring-Gould, S., and Bampfylde. *A History of Sarawak under its Two White Rajahs.* London, 1909.

Belcher, E. *Narrative of the Voyage of H.M.S.* Samarang *During the Years 1843–46.* 2 vols. London, 1848.

Brooke, J. *A Letter from Borneo . . . addressed to James Gardner, Esq.* London, 1842.

Buckley, C. B. *An Anecdotal History of Old Times in Singapore.* Singapore, 1902.

Burrows, M. *Memoir of Admiral Sir Henry Ducie Chads, G. C. B.* Portsea, 1869.

Dampier, W. *A New Voyage Round the World.* London, 1697. Reprint, with an introduction by Sir Albert Gray, 1937.

Hill, S. C. *Notes on Piracy in Eastern Waters.* Bombay, 1923.

Keppel, H. *The Expedition to Borneo of H.M.S.* Dido. 2 vols. London, 1846 and 1853.

Mackenzie, H. *Storms and Sunshine of a Soldier's Life: Lt. General Colin Mackenzie, C. B. 1825–1881.* Edinburgh, 1884.

Osborn, S. *Quedah: or Stray Leaves from a Journal in Malayan Waters.* London, 1857.

Marryat, F. S. *Borneo and the Indian Archipelago.* London, 1848.

Mundy, G. R. *Narrative of events in Borneo and Celebes.* 2 vols. London, 1848.

Rutter, O. *The Pirate Wind.* London, 1930.

St. John, S. *Life in the Forests of the Far East.* 2 vols. London, 1862.

Tarling, N. *Piracy and Politics in the Malay World.* Melbourne, 1963.

Tarling, N. *The Burthen, the Risk, and the Glory. A Biography of*

Sir James Brooke. Kuala Lumpur, 1982.

Templar, J. C., ed. *The Private Letters of Sir James Brooke*. 3 vols. London, 1853.

Thomson, J. T. *Some Glimpse of Life in the Far East*. London, 1864.

Trocki, C. A. *Prince of Pirates: the Temenggongs and the Development of Johore and Singapore 1784–1885*. Singapore, 1979.

Turnbull, M. *The Straits Settlements 1826–67*. London, 1972.

Warren, J. F. *The Sulu Zone 1768–1898*. Singapore, 1981.

Wurtzburg, C. E. *Raffles of the Eastern Isles*. London, 1954.

Other

India Office Records, Board's Collections, IOR/F/4/714 (19495)

India Office Records, Board's Collections, IOR/F/4/1330 (52554)

India Office Records, Board's Collections, IOR/F/4/1331 (52585)

India Office Records, Board's Collections, IOR/F/4/1474 (57847)

India Office Records, Board's Collections, IOR/F/4/1724 (69433)

India Office Records, Board's Collections, IOR/F/4/1978 (86974)

India Office Records, Board's Collections, IOR/F/4/52588

Journal of the Indian Archipelago, vol. 4, 1850.

The Times, July 16, 1862.

CHINESE PIRATES

Books

Andrade, J. *Memoria dos feitos macaenses contra los piratas da China: e da entrada violenta dos inglezes na cidade de Macáo*. 2 eds. Lisbon, 1835.

Brown, E. *Cochin-China, and My Experience of It; A Seaman's Narrative of His Adventures and Sufferings During a Captivity Among Chinese Pirates, on the Coast of Cochin-China, and Afterwards During a Journey on Foot Across That Country, in the Years 1857–58*. London, 1861. Reprinted, Taipei, 1971.

Chan Hok-lam, "The Chien-wen, Yung-lo, Hung-hsi and Hsüan-te reigns, 1399–1435." In *The Cambridge History of China: The Ming Dynasty, 1368–1644*. Vol. 7: part 1. p. 182-304. Cambridge: Cambridge University Press, 1988.

Chang Pin-tsun, "Maritime trade and local economy in late Ming Fukien." In *Development and Decline of Fukien Province in the 17th and 18th centuries*. Leiden: E. J. Brill, 1990. p. 63–81.

Dalrymple, A. *Further Statement of the Ladrones on the Coast of China Intended as a Contribution of the Accounts Published by Mr. Dalrymple*. London, 1812.

Deveria, G. *Histoire des relations de la Chine avec l'Annam-Vietnam du XVIe au XICe siècle*. Paris, 1880.

Downing, C. T. *The Fan-Oui in China in 1836–7*. 3 vols. London, 1838.

Elisonas, J. "The inseparable trinity: Japan's relations with China and Korea." In *The Cambridge History of Japan: Early Modern Japan. Vol. 4*. Cambridge: Cambridge University Press, 1991. p. 235-300.

Fox, G. *British Admirals and Chinese Pirates 1832–69*. London, 1940.

Glasspoole, R. "Glasspoole's letter to the president of the East India Company's factory. December 8th, 1809." In *Further Statement of the Ladrones on the Coast of China Intended as a Contribution of the Accounts Published by Mr. Dalrymple*. London, 1812, p. 33–39.

———. "Substance of Mr. Glasspoole's relation, upon his return to England respecting the Ladrones." In *Further Statement of the Ladrones on the Coast of China Intended as a Contribution of the Accounts Published by Mr. Dalrymple*. London, 1812, p. 40-45.

———. "A brief narrative of my captivity and treatment amongst the Ladrones." In *History of the Pirates Who Infested the China Sea from 1807 to 1810*. Translated by K. F. Neumann, London, 1831, p. 97-128.

Gomes, A. L. *Esboço da historia de Macau, 1511 a 1849*. Macau, 1957.

Gomes, L. G. *Páginas da historia de Macau*. Macau, 1966.

Ho, C. *Huang-ch'ao Ching-shih wen-pien* [Statecraft writings of the Ch'ing period], 1827.

Hsiao Wan-om (Hsiao Yun-han), "Research in the History of the Pirates on the China Sea, 1140–1950." Unpublished manuscript in Chinese, September 1976.

Hsü Chien-ping (Hui Kim-bing), "Shih-tzu-ling yü Ch'ing-ch'u Hsiang-kang Chiu-lung, Hsin-chieh ch'ien-hai yü fu-chieh." [The Lion Rock and the Abandonment of the Coastal Strip and its Subsequent Reoccupation During Early Manchu Rule]. In *I-pa-ssu erh nien i-ch'ien chih Hisang-kang chi ch'i-tui wai-chiao-t'ung*. [Hong Kong and its external communications before 1842.] Hong Kong, 1959, p. 129–50.

Hsü Immanuel C.Y. *The Rise of Modern China*. 3rd ed. Oxford: Oxford University Press, 1983.

Hu Chieh-yü (Woo Kit-yü) "Hsi-Ying-p'an yü Chang Pao-tsai huo-luan chih p'ing-ting" [Hsi Ying-P'an and the end of the ravages of the pirate Chang Pao-tsai]. In *I-pa-ssu erh nien i-ch'ien chih Hisang-kang chi ch'i-tui wai-chiao-t'ung*. [Hong Kong and its external communications before 1842.] Hong Kong, 1959, p. 151–70.

Kani, H. *A General Survey of the Boat People in Hong Kong*. Hong Kong, 1967.

Kawazoe, S. "Japan and East Asia." Translated by Hurst, G. C., III. In *The Cambridge History of Japan: Medieval Japan*. Vol. 3. Cambridge: Cambridge University Press, 1990, p. 396–446.

Lin, R. "Fukien's Private Sea Trade in the 16th and 17th Centuries." In *Development and Decline of Fukien Province in the 17th and 18th centuries*. Leiden: E. J. Brill, 1990, p. 163–215.

Lo, H., ed. *I-pa-ssu erh nien i-ch'ien chih Hisang-kang chi ch'i-tui wai-chiao-t'ung*. [Hong Kong and its external communications before 1842.] Hong Kong, 1959.

Maughan, P. "An Account of the Ladrones Who Infested the Coast of China." In *Further Statement of the Ladrones on the Coast of China Intended as a Contribution of the Accounts Published by Mr. Dalrymple*. London, 1812, p. 7–32.

Maybon, C. B., *Histoire moderne du pays d'Annam, 1592–1820*. Paris, 1919.

Montalto de Jesus, C.A., *Historic Macao: International Traits in China Old and New*. Macao. 2nd ed. 1926.

Mote, F. W., and Twitchett, D., eds. *The Cambridge History of China: The Ming Dynasty, 1368–1644*. Vol. 7, part 1. Cambridge: Cambridge University Press, 1988.

Murray, D. *Pirates of the South China Coast 1790–1810*. Stanford: Stanford University Press, 1987.

Naquin, S. *Shantung Rebellion: The Wang Lun Uprising of 1774*. New Haven: Yale University Press, 1976.

Neumann, K. F., trans. *History of the Pirates Who Infested the China Sea from 1807 to 1810*. London, 1831.

Renouard de Sainte-Croix, C. L. F. F. *Voyage commercial et politique aux Indes Orientales, aux iles Philippines, à la Chine, avec des notions sûr la Cochinchine et le Tonquin, pendant les années 1803–1804*. 2 vols. Paris, 1810.

Scott, B. *An Account of the Destruction of the Fleets of the Celebrated Pirate Chieftains Chui-apoo and Shap-ng Tsai, on the Coast of China, in September and October 1849*. London, n.d.

So, K. *Japanese Piracy in Ming China During the 16th Century*. East Lansing: Michigan State University Press, 1975.

Spence, J. D., and Wills, J. E., Jr., eds. *From Ming to Ch'ing: Conquest, Region and Continuity in Seventeenth-century China*. New Haven: Yale University Press, 1879.

Trinh Hoai Duc. *Can trai thi tap*. [Collected poems of Can Trai.] Hong Kong, 1962.

Turner, J., "Account of the Captivity of J. Turner, Chief Mate of the ship *Tay*, Amongst the Ladrones; Accompanied by Some Observations Respecting Those Pirates." In *Further Statement of the Ladrones on the Coast of China Intended as a Contribution of the Accounts Published by Mr Dalrymple*. London, 1812, p. 46–73.

Vermeer, E. B., ed. *Development and Decline of Fukien Province in the 17th and 18th centuries*. Leiden: E.J. Brill, 1990.

Von Krusenstern, A. J. *Voyage Round the World in the Years 1803, 1804, 1805 and 1806 by Order of His Imperial Majesty Alexander the First, on Board the Ships* Nadeshda *and* Neva. 2 vols. Translated by A. B. Hoppner, London, 1813.

Wang, C. "I hai-k'ou Ch'ing-hsing shu." [Discussion of the seaport situation.] In *Huang-ch'ao Ching-shih wen-pien* [Statecraft writings of the Ch'ing period]. Compiled by Ho Ch'ang-ling. 120 chüan, 1827, 85:33-36b.

Wei Yüan, *Sheng-wu-chi* [Record of the Ch'ing military exploits]. 14 chüan, 1846. Reprinted, 1849.

Whitney Hall, J., ed. *The Cambridge History of Japan: Early Modern Japan*. Vol. 4. Cambridge: Cambridge University Press, 1991.

Wills, J. E., Jr. "Maritime China from Wang Chih to Shih Lang: Themes in Peripheral History." In *From Ming to Ch'ing: Conquest, Region and Continuity in Seventeenth-century China*. New Haven: Yale University Press, 1879, p. 203-38.

———. *Pepper, Guns and Parleys: the Dutch East India Company and China, 1662-1681*. Cambridge, Mass.: Harvard University Press, 1974.

Worcester, G. R. G. *Sail and Sweep in China: The History and Development of the Chinese Junk as Illustrated by the Collection of Junk Models in the Science Museum*. London, 1966.

Yamamura, K., ed. *The Cambridge History of Japan: Medieval Japan*. Vol. 3. Cambridge: Cambridge University Press, 1990.

Yeh, L. *Cheng Pao-tsai ti ch'uan-shuo ho chen-hsiang*. [The legends and facts about Chang Pao-tsai.] Hong Kong, 1970.

Other

CHFC Yüan Yung-lun. *Ching hai-fen chi* [Record of the pacification of the pirates]. 2 chüan. Canton, 1830.

CP Chu-p'i tsou-che [Rescripted memorial collection], First Historical Archives, Peking.

CLS Ta Ch'ing li-ch'ao shih-lu [Veritable records of the successive reigns of the Ch'ing dynasty], 4,485 chüan Peking. 1927–28. Reprint, Mukden, 1937.

DNYL Dai Nam yhuc luc [Veritable records of Imperial Vietnam (the Nguyen dynasty)]. 20 vols. Tokyo, 1961.

HFHC Hai-feng hsien-chih [Gazetteer of Hai-feng county]. Compiled by Ts'ai Feng-en, 1873.

HNHC Hsin-ning hsien-chih [Gazetteer of Hsin-ning county], 20 chüan. Compiled by Lin Kuo-keng, 1893.

KCFC Kuang-chou fu-chih [Gazetteer of Kuang-chou prefecture: 1879]. Compiled by Tai Chao-ch'en. 163 chüan, Taipei, 1966.

KCFC (2) Kao-chou fu-chih [Gazetteer of Kuang-chou prefecture]. Compiled by Huang An-t'ao, 1827.

KCT Kung-chung tang [Palace memorial archive]. National Palace Museum, Taipei.

KTHFHL Kuang-tung hai-fang hui-lan [An Examination of Kwangtung's sea defense]. Compiled by Lu K'un and Ch'eng Hung-ch-ih, 42 chüan, n.d.

LF Chün-ch'i-ch'u tsou-che lu-fu [Grand Council reference file]. First Historical Archives, Peking.

NHHC Nan-hai hsien-chih [Gazetteer of Nan-hai county]. Compiled by Cheng Meng-yü, 26 chüan, 1872. Reprinted, Taipei, 1971.

NYC (Na-yen-ch'eng) Na-wen i-kung tsou-i [The collected memorials of Na-yen-ch'eng]. 1834. Reprinted, Taipei, 1968.

TKHC Tung-kuan hsien-chih [Gazetteer of Tung-kuan county]. Compiled by Yeh Chüeh-mai, 102 chüan, 1921. Reprinted, Taipei, 1969.

STHC Shun-te hsien-chih [Gazetteer of Shun-te county]. Compiled by Kuo Ju-ch'eng, 32 chüan, 1853. Reprinted, Taipei, 1974.

WCHC Wu-ch'uan hsien-chih [Gazetteer of Wu-ch'uan county]. Compiled by Li Kao-k'uei, 1825.

YCHC Yang-chiang hsien-chih [Gazetteer of Yang-chiang county]. Compiled by Li Yün, 8 chüan, 1822. Reprinted, Taipei, 1974.

Canton Consultations, Consultations and Transactions of the Select Committee of Resident Supercargoes appointed by the Honourable Court of Directors of the United East India Company to Manage Their Affairs in China Together with the Letters Written and Occurrences. Factory Records C/12/100–G/12/174, March 1791 to January 1811.

"Chinese Pirates: Ching Chelung; His Son Ching-kung; Combination of Gangs in 1806; Narratives of J. Turner and Mr. Glasspoole; Chinese and Portuguese Join Their Forces Against the Pirates; Divisions Among Them, and Their Submission to the Government." In *Chinese Repository* 3 (June 1834): p. 62-83.

Skinner, G. W. "Presidential Address: The Structure of Chinese History." *The Journal of Asian Studies* 44.2:271 92 (February 1985).

PIRACY TODAY

Other

Vagg, J. "Rough Seas." In *British Journal of Criminology*. Winter, 1995.

U. S. Department of Energy Report, 1993.

ENDNOTES

INTRODUCTION
Notes
1. *Records of the High Court of Admiralty* (HCA), HCA 1/99.3, Public Record Office (PRO).
2. *Calendar of State Papers: Colonial Series, America and West Indies* (CSPC), vol. 1724-5, no. 338, p. 208.
3. CSPC, vol. 1719-20, no. 578.
4 C. Senior, *A Nation of Pirates* (1976), p. 10.
5. Ibid., p. 13.
6. In 1703 the Royal Navy enlisted 53,785 men and after demobilization in 1715 there were only 13,430 men. These figures are taken from the Admiralty records and quoted in R. Ritchie, *Captain Kidd* (1986), p. 234.
7. CSPC, vol. 1720-21, no. 213, p. 128.
8. See D. Cordingly, *Life Among the Pirates* (1995) and D. Marley, *Pirates and Privateers* (1994).
9. Accounts of piracy in the Persian Gulf and the Red Sea can be found in D. Mitchell, *Pirates* (1976), pp. 24-25 and 173-74; and in P. Gosse, *The History of Piracy* (1932, reprinted 1990) in his chapter "The Pirate Coast."
10. There is an excellent survey of the early history of piracy and in particular the pirates of Cilicia in R. Ritchie, *Captain Kidd*, pp. 2-19.
11. Quoted by P. Gosse in *The History*, p. 317.

THE LURE OF SPANISH GOLD
Notes
1. R. Unwin, *The Defeat of Sir John Hawkins* (1960), p. 152.
2. H. Thomas, *Conquest* (1993), p. 565.
3. Ibid., pp. 568-9. See also C. Fernández Duro, *Armada española* (1896), vol. I, pp. 202-3.
4. H. Thomas, *Conquest* (1993), p. 569.
5. C. Sáiz Cidoncha, *Historia de la pirateria* (1985), p. 22.
6. See H. and P. Chaunu, *Séville et l'Atlantique* (1955), vol. II, "Le trafic de 1504 à 1560": pp. 130-73; and A. Rumeú de Armas, *Piraterias y ataques navales* (1947), vol. I.
7. C. Fernández Duro, *Armada española* (1896), vol. I, p. 204.
8. Ibid., p. 208.
9. Ibid., pp. 360-64; C. Sáiz Cidoncha, *Historia de la pirateria* (1985), p. 28.
10. H. and P. Chaunu, *Séville et l'Atlantique* (1955), vol. II, p. 354; C. Fernández Duro, *Armada española* (1896), vol. I, p. 210; C. Sáiz Cidoncha, *Historia de la pirateria* (1985), pp. 28-9.
11. C. Sáiz Cidoncha, *Historia de la pirateria* (1985), pp. 24-5.
12. H. and P. Chaunu, *Séville et l'Atlantique* (1955), vol. II, p. 418; C. Sáiz Cidoncha, *Historia de la pirateria* (1985), pp. 43-50.
13. C. Sáiz Cidoncha, *Historia de la pirateria* (1985), pp. 25-6.
14. Ibid., p. 29
15. C. Fernández Duro, *Armada española* (1896), vol. I, pp. 212-13; C. Sáiz Cidoncha, *Historia de la pirateria* (1985), pp. 29-30.
16. C. Sáiz Cidoncha, *Historia de la pirateria* (1985), pp. 30-31.
17. Ibid., p 31
18. H. and P. Chaunu, *Séville et l'Atlantique* (1955), vol. III, "Le trafic de 1561 à 1595", pp. 18-20.
19. Harris, S. "The Tragic Dream of Jean Ribaut," *American Heritage*, vol. XIV, no. 6 (October 1963): pp. 8–15 and 88–90.
20. Ibid.
21. Ibid.; also C. Sáiz Cidoncha, *Historia de la pirateria* (1985), pp 32-40.
22. Ibid.
23. Ibid.
24. Ibid.
25. M. F. Lang, *El monopolio estatal del mercurio* (1977); J. M. Menes Llaguno, *Bartolomé de Medina* (1986).
26. R. Unwin, *The Defeat of Sir John Hawkins* (1960).
27. Ibid.
28. Ibid.
29. Ibid.
30. Ibid.
31. Ibid.
32. Ibid.
33. Ibid; also H. and P. Chaunu, *Séville et l'Atlantique* (1955), vol. III, pp 116-121; C. Sáiz Cidoncha, *Historia de la pirateria* (1985), pp 57-62.
34. Ibid.
35. Ibid.

36. K. R. Andrews, *Drake's Voyages* (1967).
37. Ibid.
38. C. Sáiz Cidoncha, *Historia de la pirateria* (1985), p. 41.
39. J. and J. Hampden, eds., *Sir Francis Drake's Raid on the Treasure Trains* (1954).
40. C. Sáiz Cidoncha, *Historia de la pirateria* (1985), pp. 72-9.
41. Ibid.
42. K. R. Andrews, *The Spanish Caribbean* (1978).
43. J. I. Israel, *The Dutch Republic* (1986); also G. Parker, *The Dutch Revolt* (1977).
44. C. C. Goslinga, *The Dutch in the Caribbean* (1971); J. I. Israel, *Dutch Primacy in World Trade* (1989); J. M. Postma, *The Dutch in the Atlantic Slave Trade* (1990); E. Sluiter, "Dutch-Spanish Rivalry in the Caribbean Area, 1594–1609," *Hispanic American Historical Review*, vol. 28, no. 2 (May 1948): pp. 165–96.
45. C. Sáiz Cidoncha, *Historia de la pirateria* (1985), pp. 143-52.

BRETHREN OF THE COAST
Notes
1. P. Labat, *Memoirs 1693–1705* (1734, reprinted 1971), p. 35.
2. J. Marx, *Pirates and Privateers* (1992), p. 8.
3. A. O. Esquemelin, *The Buccaneers* (1684), part I, chapter VII.
4. A. O. Esquemelin, *The Buccaneers* (1685), part II, chapter III.
5. P. F. X. Charlevoix, de, *Histoire de l'Isle Espagnole* (1730).
6. R. F. Marx, *Pirate Port* (1967) in R. F. Marx, *Port Royal Rediscovered* (1973), p. 3.
7. A. O. Esquemelin, *The Buccaneers* (1684), part I, chapter VI.
8. Sir H. Sloane, *A Voyage to the Islands* (1707), vol. I, pp. xcviii-cxix.
9. The author had this verse recited to her by an old Jamaican man in 1966.

BUCCANEER EXPLORERS
Notes
1. William Funnell, describing Dampier's attack on the Manila galleon in 1704. See G. Norris, ed., *William Dampier* (1994), p. 240.
2. See A. O. Esquemeling, *The Buccaneers* (edn. published in 1923, W. S. Stallybrass, ed.), pp. 257–83. Dick is identified as the author of the anonymous piece in Esquemeling's book by D. Howse and N. Thrower, eds., *A Buccaneer's Atlas* (1992), p. 261.
3. This quote is from John Welbe, who was Dampier's midshipman on the *St. George*, quoted in G. Norris, ed., *William Dampier* (1994), p.00
4. A. O. Esquemeling, *The Buccaneers* (1923 edn.), p. 257.
5. J. Masefield, ed., *The Voyages of Captain William Dampier*, (1906), vol. 1, p.31.
6. Ibid., vol. 1, p. 98 and vol. 2, p. 283.
7. Later in life he was appointed governor of the Bahamas and was instrumental in ridding those islands of a notorious colony of pirates.
8. Capt. W. Rogers, *A Cruising Voyage Round the World* (G. E. Mainwaring, ed., 1928), p. 94.
9. Ibid., p. 314.
10. According to figures issued by the Bank of England, £1 in 1700 was the equivalent of £66.35 in 1996.
11. Quoted by D. Howse and N. Thrower, eds., *A Buccaneer's Atlas* (1992) p. 29; and A. O. Esquemeling, *The Buccaneers* (1923 edn.), p.276.
12. A. O. Esquemeling, *The Buccaneers* (1923 edn.), p. 381
13. Ibid., p. 456.
14. See D. Howse and N. Thrower, eds., *A Buccaneer's Atlas* (1992), p. 24.
15. A. O. Esquemeling, *The Buccaneers* (1923 edn.), p. 473
16. See D. Howse and N. Thrower, eds., *A Buccaneer's Atlas* (1992), pp. 27–28.
17. Ibid., p. 30; and J. Masefield, ed., *The Voyages of Captain William Dampier* (1906), vol. 1, p. 286.
18. See L. Wafer, *A New Voyage* (L. E. Elliott Joyce, ed., 1934).
19. D. Howse and N. Thrower, eds., *A Buccaneer's Atlas* (1992), pp. 32–33.
20. L. Wafer, *A New Voyage*, (L. E. Elliott Joyce, ed., 1934), p. 128.

CORSAIRS OF THE MEDITERRANEAN
Notes
1. Jean Martelleille de Bergerac's description of life on board Kust Aly's galley is quoted by E. Bradford, *The Great Siege: Malta 1565* (1961), p. 35.
2. R. Thrower, *The Pirate Picture* (1980), p. 3.
3. J. D. Fage, *History of Africa* (1988), p. 154.
4. After P. Earle, *Corsairs of Malta and Barbary* (1970), p. 138. Peter Earle's scholarly yet readable book is undoubtedly the best description of this episode in maritime history.
5. Jean Martelleille de Bergerac's description of life on board Kust Aly's galley is quoted by E. Bradford, *The Great Siege: Malta 1565* (1961), p. 35.
6. P. Earle, *Corsairs of Malta and Barbary* (1970), p. 49.
7. R. Hough, *Fighting Ships* (1969), p. 33.
8. J. Morgan, *Several Voyages to Barbary* (1736), p. 17.
9. P. Earle, *Corsairs of Malta and Barbary* (1970), p. 64.
10. Ibid., p. 59.
11. J. Morgan, *Several Voyages to Barbary* (1736), p. 43.
12. Ibid., p. 44.
13. Ibid., p. 42.
14. The word "debauchery" is used here in its older sense, meaning corruption or seduction from religious duty rather than indulgence in pleasures of the flesh.
15. J. Morgan, *Several Voyages to Barbary* (1736), p. 42.
16. Sieur de Brèves, quoted by E. Lucie-Smith, *Outcasts of the Sea* (1978).
17. i.e., to go whoring.
18. C. Lloyd, *English Corsairs on the Barbary Coast* (1981), p. 49.
19. H. P. Brown and S. V. Hopkins, *A Perspective of Wages and Prices*, London, 1981.
20. Sir H. Luke, *An Account and Appreciation of Malta* (1960), p. 72.
21. Barras de la Penne, an officer of the French navy, quoted by E. Bradford, *The Great Siege: Malta 1565* (1961), p. 36.
22. Quoted by P. Earle, *Corsairs of Malta and Barbary* (1970), p. 151.
23. G. Wettinger, "Coron Captives in Malta," *Melita Historica* (vol. II), 1959.
24. P. Earle, *Corsairs of Malta and Barbary* (1970), p. 122.
25. B. Blouet, *The Story of Malta* (1967), p. 106.
26. Ibid., p. 88.
27. Ibid., p. 156.
28. P. Earle, *Corsairs of Malta and Barbary* (1970), p 16.

THE GOLDEN AGE OF PIRACY
Notes
1. Capt. C. Johnson, *A General History of the Robberies and Murders of the Most Notorious Pirates* (1724), chapter x.[references to Johnson's work will be by chapter since there are countless editions].
2. Ibid., pp. 160–61.
3. John Graves, collector of the Customs, Bahamas, 1706.
4. P. Gosse, *The Pirates' Who's Who* (1924; reprinted 1988), p. 230.
5. M. Rediker, *Between the Devil and the Deep Blue Sea* (1987), p. 259.
6. Capt. C. Johnson, *A General History of the Robberies and Murders of the Most Notorious Pirates* (1724), chapter x.
The Roberts' articles quoted in Johnson are as follows:
I. Every man has a vote in affairs of moment; has equal title to the fresh provisions or strong liquors at any time seized, and may use them at pleasure unless a scarcity (no uncommon thing among them) make it necessary for the good of all to vote a retrenchment.
II. Every man to be called fairly in turn, by list, on board of prizes, because over and above their proper share, they are allowed a shift of clothes. But if they defrauded the Company to the value of a dollar, in plate, jewels or money, Marooning was the punishment. (This was a barbarous custom of putting the offender on shore on some desolate or uninhabited cape or island, with a gun, a few shot, a bottle of water and a bottle of powder, to subsist with or starve.) If the robbery was only between one another they contented themselves with slitting the ears and nose of him that was guilty, and set him on shore, not in an uninhabited place, but somewhere where he was sure to encounter hardships.
III. No person to game at cards or dice for money.
IV. The lights and candles to be put out at eight o'clock at

night. If any of the crew at that hour remained inclined to drinking, they were to do it on the open deck (which Roberts believed would give a check to their debauches, for he was a sober man himself; but he found that all his endeavours to put an end to this debauch proved ineffectual).

V. To keep their piece, pistols, and cutlass clean and fit for service. (In this they were extravagantly nice, endeavouring to outdo one another in the beauty and richness of their arms, giving sometimes at an auction at the mast, thirty or forty pieces of eight for a pair of pistols. These were slung in time of service with different coloured ribbons over their shoulders in a way peculiar to those fellows, in which they took great delight.)

VI. No boy or woman to be allowed among men. If any man be found seducing any of the latter sex, and carried her to sea disguised, he was to suffer Death. (So that when any fell into their hands, as it chanced on the *Onslow*, they put a sentinel immediately over her to prevent ill consequences from so dangerous an instrument of division and quarrel. But then here lies the roguery; they contend who shall be sentinel, which happens generally to be one of the greatest bullies who, to secure the lady's virtue, will let none lie with her but himself.)

VII. To desert their ship or their quarters in battle was punished with Death or Marooning.

VIII. No striking one another on board, but every man's quarrels to be ended on shore, at sword and pistol. (Thus, the quartermaster of the ship, when the parties will not come to any reconciliation, accompanies them on shore with what assistance he thinks proper, and turns the disputants back to back at so many paces distant. At the word of command they turn and fire immediately or else the piece is knocked out of their hands. If both miss they come to their cutlasses and then he is declared victor who draws the first blood.)

IX. No man to talk of breaking up their way of living till each had a share of 1,000 pieces of eight. If, in order to do this, any man lost a limb or became a cripple in their service, he was to have 800 dollars [each Spanish dollar was a piece of eight] out of the public stock, and for lesser hurts proportionately.

X. The Captain and the Quartermaster to receive two shares of a prize; the master, boatswain and gunner, one share and a half, and the other officers one and a quarter.

XI. The musicians to have rest on the Sabbath day, but the other six days and nights none, without special favour.

7. M. Rediker, *Between the Devil and the Deep Blue Sea* (1987), p. 47.

8. Capt. C. Johnson, *A General History of the Robberies and Murders of the Most Notorious Pirates* (1724), chapter xiv.

9. R. A. Brock, ed., *The Official Letters of Alexander Spotswood*, 2 vols. (1932-35), p. 168, 351ff.

10. R. F. and J. Marx, *The Search for Sunken Treasure* (1993), p. 86.

11. Capt. C. Johnson, *A General History of the Robberies and Murders of the Most Notorious Pirates* (1724), chapter xxviii.

12. Ibid., chapter iv.

13. Ibid. chapter x.

14. Ibid.

LIBERTALIA: THE PIRATE'S UTOPIA

Notes

1. Capt. C. Johnson, *A General History of the Pyrates* (1724, reprinted 1972, M. Schonhorn, ed.), p. 244.

2. Ibid., pp. 392, 425. On Misson, see H. Deschamps, *Les Pirates à Madagascar* (1972), ch. 9, and J. H. Baer, "Piracy Examined," (1970), ch. 5.

3. Capt. C. Johnson, *A General History of the Pyrates* (1724, reprinted 1972, M. Schonhorn, ed.), pp. 432, 391, 393, 392, 403, 433, 434.

4. Ibid., pp. 389, 392, 390. The essential background here is C. Hill, "C. Hill, "Pottage for Freeborn Englishmen," in *Change and Continuity* (1975), pp. 219–38.

5. Capt. C. Johnson, *A General History of the Pyrates* (1724, reprinted 1972, M. Schonhorn, ed.), pp. 427, 432, 394, 415, 423, 435. Individual plots of land were to be permitted in Libertalia; see pp. 432-3, 434.

6. Ibid., pp. 392, 425, 417, 403, 427. Libertalia was, in Johnson's account, eventually destroyed by natives of Madagascar who apparently feared that the new settlement would upset the balance of tribal power on the island. The end came "without the least Provocation given, in the Dead of Night, [when] the Natives came down upon them in two great Bodies, and made a great Slaughter, without Distinction of Age or Sex, before they could put themselves in a Posture of Defence." (See p. 437.)

7. The case for Defoe's authorship was made by J. R. Moore, *Defoe in the Pillory* (1939), pp. 129-88, but this argument has recently been challenged, convincingly in my estimation, by P. N. Furbank and W. R. Owens, *The Canonization of Daniel Defoe* (1988), pp. 100-121. It should be noted that the overall reliability of *A General History of the Pyrates* has been established, regardless of specific authorship.

8. Information of Clement Downing (1724), High Court of Admiralty Papers (hereafter HCA) 1/55, fo. 79, Public Record Office, London. Ranter Bay is also mentioned in Information of Charles Collins (1724), HCA, 1/55, fo. 77. See C. Hill, "Radical Pirates?" in M. and J. Jacob, eds., *The Origins of Anglo-American Radicalism* (1984), pp. 17-32.

9. Hill was the first to note the "survival of Utopian and radical ideas" among pirates; see his "Radical Pirates?", p.18. Other important works on the social history of pirates in this era are J. S. Bromley, "Outlaws at Sea, 1660-1720" in F. Krantz, ed., *History From Below* (1985), and R. C. Ritchie, *Captain Kidd and the War against the Pirates* (1987).

10. A. L. Hayward, ed., *Lives of the Most Remarkable Criminals* (1735), p. 37.

11. R. C. Ritchie, *Captain Kidd and the War against the Pirates* (1987), pp. 147-51. Piracy was colored less by religious and national antagonism in the eighteenth than in the seventeenth century, when hatred for Catholic Spain had energized a great many buccaneers.

12. See A. L. Morton, *The English Utopia* (1952), ch.1; F. Graus, "Social Utopias in the Middle Ages," *Past and Present*, 38 (1967), pp. 3-19; W. McFee, *The Law of the Sea* (1951), pp. 50, 54, 59, 72; J. S. Bromley, "Outlaws at Sea, 1660-1720," p. 5. See also the discussion below, pp. 12-17.

13. P. K. Kemp and C. Lloyd, *Brethren of the Coast* (1960); C. and R. Bridenbaugh, *No Peace Beyond the Line* (1972); C. H. Haring, *The Buccaneers in the West Indies in the XVII Century* (1910, reprinted 1966), pp. 71, 73; J. S. Bromley, "Outlaws at Sea, 1660-1720," p. 3.

14. P. K. Kemp and C. Lloyd, *Brethren of the Coast* (1960) p. 3; C. and R. Bridenbaugh, *No Peace Beyond the Line* (1972), pp. 62, 176; J. S. Bromley, "Outlaws at Sea, 1660-1720," p. 7 (quotation), 8.

15. J. S. Bromley, "Outlaws at Sea, 1660-1720," p. 15. See also the useful collection of essays edited by R. Price, *Maroon Societies* (1979, 2nd ed.).

16. C. Hill, "Radical Pirates?" pp. 20, 25; P. K. Kemp and C. Lloyd, *Brethren of the Coast* (1960), p. 17 (quotation); J. S. Bromley, "Outlaws at Sea, 1660-1720," p. 6.

17. Ibid., pp. 8, 9.

18. J. Boswell, *The Life of Samuel Johnson* (1791), p. 86; J. Lemisch, "Jack Tar in the Streets," *William and Mary Quarterly* 25 (1968), pp. 379, 375-6, 406; R. B. Morris, *Government and Labor in Early America* (1946), pp. 246-7, 257, 262-8; Capt. C. Johnson, *A General History of the Pyrates* (1724, reprinted 1972, M. Schonhorn, ed.), pp. 244, 359; A. G. Course, *The Merchant Navy* (1963), p. 61; R. Davis, *The Rise of the English Shipping Industries in the Seventeenth and Eighteenth Centuries* (1962), pp. 144, 154-5.

19. Gov. Lowther to Council of Trade, in *Calendar of State Papers, Colonial Series, America and the West Indies* (W. N. Sainsbury et al., eds.), vol. 39, p. 350; R. D. Merriman, ed., *Queen Anne's Navy* (1961), pp. 170-72, 174, 221-2, 250; C. Lloyd, *The British Seaman* (1970), pp. 44-6 (for estimates that half of all men pressed between 1600 and 1800 died at sea), pp. 124-49; P. Kemp, *The British Sailor* (1970), chaps. 4, 5.

20. A. G. Course, *The Merchant Navy* (1963), p. 84; C. Lloyd, *The British Seaman* (1970), p. 57. For examples of early eighteenth century privateering voyages, see E. Cooke, *A Voyage to the South Sea* (1712), pp. v-vi, 14-16; W. Rogers, *A Cruising Voyage Round the World* (1712, reprinted 1928, G. E. Mainwaring, ed.), pp. xiv, xxv; G. Shelvocke, *A Voyage Round the World* (1726), pp. 34-6, 38, 46, 157, 214, 217; W. Betagh, *A Voyage Round the World* (1728), p.4.

21. Many of the arguments below draw on evidence presented in my earlier work, "'Under the Banner of King Death': The Social World of Anglo-American Pirates, 1716 to 1726," *William and Mary Quarterly*, ser. 3, 38, (1981), pp. 203-27; and *Between the Devil and the Deep Blue Sea* (1987), ch. 6. My principal (though not exclusive) subject here will be the pirates of the Anglophone Atlantic World.

22. Capt. C. Johnson, *A General History of the Pyrates* (1724, reprinted 1972, M. Schonhorn, ed.), p. 213.

23. Examination of John Brown (1717) in J. F. Jameson, ed., *Privateering and Piracy in the Colonial Period* (1923), p. 294; W. Snelgrave, *A New Account of Some Parts of Guinea and the Slave Trade* (1734, reprinted 1971), p. 199.

24. A. L. Hayward, ed., *Lives of the Most Remarkable Criminals* (1735), p. 37; Capt. C. Johnson, *A General History of the Pyrates* (1724, reprinted 1972, M. Schonhorn, ed.), pp. 42, 296, 337.

25. Capt. C. Johnson, *A General History of the Pyrates* (1724, reprinted 1972, M. Schonhorn, ed.), p. 423.

26. The pirates' emphasis on equality did not sit well with the merchant captains whose place in the world depended upon maritime hierarchy and privilege. To such people it was galling that "there is so little Government and Subordination among [pirates], that they are, on Occasion, all Captains, all Leaders." See *An Account of the Conduct and Proceedings of the Late John Gow, alias Smith, Captain of the Late Pirates* (1725, reprinted 1978).

27. Capt. C. Johnson, *A General History of the Pyrates* (1724, reprinted 1972, M. Schonhorn, ed.), pp. 338, 582.

28. Proceedings of the Court held on the Coast of Africa, HCA 1/99, fo. 101; *Boston Gazette*, October 24-31, 1720; *Boston Gazette*, March 21-28, 1726.

29. W. Snelgrave, *A New Account* (1734; reprinted 1971), p. 225.

30. *Boston News-Letter*, November 14-21, 1720; W. Snelgrave, *A New Account* (1734; reprinted 1971), p. 241.

31. Testimony of Thomas Checkley (1717) in J. F. Jameson, ed., *Privateering and Piracy* (1923), p. 304; *The Trials of Eight Persons Indited for Piracy*, Boston, 1718, p. 11.

32. *An Account of . . . the Late John Gow*, p. 3. Immediately after the mutiny, the pirates sought a prize vessel "with Wine, if possible, for that they wanted Extreamly" (p. 13). See also Capt. C. Johnson, *A General History of the Pyrates* (1724, reprinted 1972, M. Schonhorn, ed.), pp. 307, 319.

33. Ibid., pp. 244, 224. Bartholomew Roberts's crew was taken in 1722 because many of the men were drunk when the time came for an engagement. See p. 243, and J. Atkins, *A Voyage to Guinea, Brazil, & the West Indies* (1735, reprinted 1970), p.192. It would have been for such reasons that drunkenness was banned in Libertalia.

34. Capt. C. Johnson, *A General History of the Pyrates* (1724, reprinted 1972, M. Schonhorn, ed.), pp. 129, 135, 167, 211, 222, 280, 205. See also pp. 209, 312, 353, 620; *American Weekly Mercury*, March 17, 1720; W. Snelgrave, *A New Account* (1734; reprinted 1971), pp. 233-8.

35. Capt. C. Johnson, *A General History of the Pyrates* (1724, reprinted 1972, M. Schonhorn, ed.), pp. 212, 308, 343.

36. Rankin, *Golden Age*, p. 34, has noted that some free blacks who signed pirates' articles were taken to the West Indies and sold as slaves, but I have found no evidence of such a practice.

37. *American Weekly Mercury*, March 17, 1720. Such hangings were rare, for the British state preferred to sell captured black pirates as slaves to stock its New World plantations.

38. Capt. C. Johnson, *A General History of the Pyrates* (1724, reprinted 1972, M. Schonhorn, ed.), p. 82. Information of Joseph Smith and Information of John Webley (1721), HCA 1/18, fo. 35; Information of William Voisy (1721) HCA 1/55, fo. 12. Native Americans also manned pirate ships, though in much smaller numbers. See *The Trials of Five Persons for Piracy, Felony and Robbery*, Boston, 1726.

39. One of the references to slaves came in the legal efforts of a group of merchants to recover property taken by a pirate crew; see Masters vs. *Revenge*, Minutes of the Vice-Admiralty Courts of Charleston, South Carolina (1718), Manuscript Division, Library of Congress, folio 308. See also J. F. Jameson, ed., *Privateering and Piracy* (1923), p. 344.

40. *Boston News-Letter*, June 17-24, 1717; *The Tryals of Major Stede Bonnet and Other Pirates* (1719), pp. 46; Capt. C. Johnson, *A General History of the Pyrates* (1724, reprinted 1972, M. Schonhorn, ed.), pp. 173, 427, 595. Rankin notes that a "surprising number of Negroes and mulattoes were listed among the members of pirate crews" but that one captain, Edward Low, seems to have refused to allow African-Americans to serve aboard his vessel (*Golden Age*, pp. 24-5, 148). See also *Boston News-Letter*, April 29-May 6, 1717.

41. *Boston News-Letter*, April 4-11, 1723.

42. R. R. Bellamy, ed., *Ramblin' Jack*, (1936), p. 144; Rankin, *Golden Age*, p. 82. Just before the events in Antigua, Virginia's rulers had worried about the connection between the "Ravage of Pyrates" and "an Insurrection of the Negroes." See Virginia Council to the Board of Trade, August 11, 1715, Colonial Office (CO) 5/1317, Public Record Office, London.

43. Capt. C. Johnson, *A General History of the Pyrates* (1724, reprinted 1972, M. Schonhorn, ed.), p. 273.

44. H. Ross, "Some Notes on the Pirates and Slavers around Sierra Leone." *Sierra Leone Studies* 11, 1928, pp. 16–53. Some of these were probably men from Roberts's crew who escaped into the woods when attacked by the Royal Navy in 1722. See *American Weekly Mercury*, May 31-June 7, 1722.
45. Capt. C. Johnson, *A General History of the Pyrates* (1724, reprinted 1972, M. Schonhorn, ed.), p. 131.
46. L. G. C. Laughton, "Shantying and Shanties," *Mariner's Mirror* 9, 1923, pp. 48–50.
47. Trial of John McPherson and others, Proceedings of the Court of Admiralty, Philadelphia, 1731, HCA 1/99, fo. 3; Information of Henry Hull (1729) HCA 1/56, fos. 29-30.
48. Lawes to Council of Trade and Plantations, January 31, 1719, in *Calendar of State Papers, Colonial Series*, vol. 41, p. 19; Walter Hamilton to Council of Trade and Plantations, January 6, 1717, CO 152/12, fo. 211; Representation from several merchants trading to Virginia to Board of Trade, April 15, 1717, CO 5/1318, fos. 12-13; Capt. C. Johnson, *A General History of the Pyrates* (1724, reprinted 1972, M. Schonhorn, ed.), pp. 359, 468, 474; *Boston Gazette*, July 6-13, 1725; Proceedings of the Court held on the Coast of Africa, HCA 1/00, fo. 139; A Discovery of an Horrid Plot aboard the *Antelope*, CO 323/3, fos. 92-3.
49. See my "Liberty beneath the Jolly Roger," in M. Creighton and L. Norling, eds., *Iron Men, Wooden Women* (1996). See also the fine books by D. Dugaw, *Warrior Women and Popular Balladry* (1989) and J. Stanley, *Bold in her Breeches* (1995).
50. C. Mather, *Instructions to the Living* (1717), p. 4; meeting of April 1, 1717, in M. H. C. Lyte, ed., *Journal of the Commissioners for Trade and Plantations* (1924), vol. III, p. 359; Capt. C. Johnson, *A General History of the Pyrates* (1724, reprinted 1972, M. Schonhorn, ed.), p. 7; *American Weekly Mercury*, November 24, 1720; *New England Courant*, March 19–26, 1722.
51. Capt. C. Johnson, *A General History of the Pyrates* (1724, reprinted 1972, M. Schonhorn, ed.), pp. 115-6; W. Snelgrave, *A New Account* (1734; reprinted 1971), p. 203.
52. Capt. C. Johnson, *A General History of the Pyrates* (1724, reprinted 1972, M. Schonhorn, ed.), p. 43 (quotation); L. F. Stock, *Proceedings and Debates of the British Parliaments respecting North America*, Washington, D.C: Carnegie Institute, 1930, vol. III, pp. 364, 433, 453, 454; R. Ritchie, *Captain Kidd* (1987), pp. 235-7. Walpole's direct involvement can be seen in Treasury Warrant to Capt. Knott, T52/32 (August 10, 1722), PRO, and in *American Weekly Mercury*, July 1-8, 1725. On the new imperial consensus against piracy, see A. Pérotin-Dumon, "The Pirate and the Emperor," in J. D. Tracy, ed., *The Political Economy of Merchant Empires*, (1991), pp. 196-227, and J. E. Thomson, *Mercenaries, Pirates and Sovereigns* (1994).
53. J. S. Bromley, "Outlaws at Sea," p. 17; M. Rediker, "The Common Seaman in the Histories of Capitalism and the Working Class," *International Journal of Maritime History* 1 (1989), pp. 352-3.
54. W. E. May, "The Mutiny of the *Chesterfield*," *Mariners' Mirror* 47 (1961), pp. 178-87. For a similar example see Information of William Omara (1737), HCA 1/57, fos. 8-9. In planning a mutiny in 1736, Nicholas Williams announced to his fellow conspirators, "I have brought in Johnson, who is a special good fellow for this purpose and has several times been upon the Account."
55. J. Lemisch, "Listening to the 'Inarticulate,'" *Journal of Social History* 3 (1969-70), pp. 1-29, quotations at pp. 21, 23, 24, 27; L. G. Bowman, *Captive Americans* (1976), pp. 40-67; J. K. Alexander, "Forton Prison during the American Revolution," *Essex Institute Historical Collections 102* (1967), p. 369.
56. See T. Spencer, "Pigs' Meat," *The Marine Republic*, vol. II, pp. 68-72, 2nd edn., London, 1794; A. L. Morton, *The English Utopia* (1952), pp. 164, 165 (quotation).
57. H. Baynham, *From the Lower Deck* (1970), p. 9; A. N. Gilbert, "The Nature of Mutiny in the British Navy in the Eighteenth Century," in D. Masterson, ed., *Naval History: the Sixth Symposium of the US Naval Academy* (1987), pp. 111-21; G. E. Mainwaring and B. Dobree, *Mutiny: the Floating Republic* (1935, reprinted 1987); J. P. Moore, III, "'The Greatest Enormity that Prevails,'" in C. Howell and R. Twomey, eds., *Jack Tar in History* (1991), pp. 76-104.

THE PIRATE ROUND

Notes

1. Capt. C. Johnson, *A General History of the Robberies and Murders of the Most Notorious Pirates* (1724, enlarged edns. 1724, 1725 and 1726), chapter XXIII. References to Johnson's work will be by chapter since there are countless editions.
2. *Records of the High Court of Admiralty* (HCA), HCA 1/98 fos. 98–101.
3. See Ward, 1974 and L. Casson, *The Ancient Mariners* (1959) for a fuller account.
4. See P. Gosse, *The History of Piracy* (1932) for a fuller account.
5. *Calendar of State Papers, Colonial Series, American and West Indies 1574–1733*, June 6, 1699, no. 495.
6. Phips's tomb is at St. Mary Woolnoth, London. In the 1970s American treasure hunter Burt Webber recovered a significant amount of additional treasure from the Silver Shoals shipwreck.
7. Capt. C. Johnson, *A General History of the Robberies and Murders of the Most Notorious Pirates* (1726), chapter xxiii.
8. Ibid.
9. Ibid.
10. C. Ellms, *The Pirates' Own Book* (1837, reprinted 1924), chapter II.
11. Capt. C. Johnson, *A General History of the Robberies and Murders of the Most Notorious Pirates* (1726), chapter i.
12. R. C. Ritchie, *Captain Kidd and the War Against the Pirates* (1986), pp. 112–16.
13. Ibid., a wealth of well-documented information on Kidd.
14. Capt. C. Johnson, *A General History of the Robberies and Murders of the Most Notorious Pirates* (1726), chapter V.

FRENCH AND AMERICAN PRIVATEERS

Notes

1. W. Falconer, *An Universal Dictionary of the Marine* (1780), p. 175. According to the *Oxford English Dictionary*, 1989, the term "privateer" was first used in the Calendars of State Papers in 1651 and in papers issued to individuals and ships *c.* 1664. It probably arose as a colloquial contraction of "private" and "volunteer" and replaced the earlier term "private man-of-war." Prior to the 19th century, the term "letter of marque" was often rendered "letter-of-mart" (W. Falconer, *Universal Dictionary*, p. 175).
2. R. de Kerchove, *International Maritime Dictionary* (1961, 2nd edn.), p. 447; G. Clark, "The English Practice with Regards to Reprisals by Private Persons," *American Journal of International Law*, 27 (1933): pp. 694–723.
3. G. Symcox, *The Crisis of French Sea Power* (1974), pp. 221–233.
4. For the careers of Bart and DuGuay-Trouin see E. H. Jenkins, *A History of the French Navy* (1973), pp. 63, 72–5, 89–92, 101–4.
5. Quoted in H. M. Chapin, *Privateering in King George's War* (1928), pp. 5–6. For American privateering prior to the eighteenth century see H. M. Chapin, *Privateering Ships and Sailors* (1926), and J. F. Jameson, ed., *Privateering and Piracy in the Colonial Period* (1923).
6. C. E. Swanson, *Predators and Prizes* (1991), p. 140.
7. W. C. Ford, et al., eds., *Journals of the Continental Congress* (1904–37), 25 November 1775, 23 March and 2 April 1776, vol. 3: pp. 371–5; vol. 4: pp. 203–31, 247–8, 251.
8. For such embargoes see Rhode Island Colonial Records (10 vols.) (Providence, 1856–65), vol. 8: p. 53; and Acts of Connecticut, May 1780, cited in C. O. Paullin, *The Navy of the American Revolution* (1906), pp. 146 & 365.
9. *Journals of the Continental Congress* (1904–37), vol. 4: p. 254.
10. E. H. Tatum, Jr., ed., *The American Journal of Ambrose Serle* (1940), p. 102.
11. Vice-Admiral Molyneux Shuldham to Philip Stevens, February 26, 1776, Hyde Parker, Jr. to Shuldham, April 29, 1776, in W. B. Clark and W. J. Morgan, eds., *Naval Documents of the American Revolution* (9 vols. to date, 1964–), vol. 4: pp 38 & 1312.
12. J. C. Bradford, "Navies of the American Revolution" in K. J. Hagan, ed., *In Peace and War* (1978), p. 18.
13. C. H. Lincoln, "Naval Records of the American Revolution [Calendar]," Manuscript Division, Library of Congress, quoted in G. W. Allen, *A Naval History of the American Revolution* (2 vols.) (1970 [1913], vol. 1: pp. 46, 181, 288, 363, 486–7, 544 & 613.
14. G.W. Allen, *Massachusetts Privateers of the Revolution* (1927), p. 53
15. S. G. Morse, "New England Privateering in the American Revolution" (Ph.D. dissertation, Harvard University, 1941) cited in W. J. Morgan, "American Privateering in America's War for Independence, 1775–1783," *American Neptune*, 36 (1976), pp. 84–5.
16. G. W. Allen, *Naval History*, vol. I: pp. 254–5, 270–72 & 279. Passage from the *Annual Register*, vol. XXI (1778), p. 36 quoted on p. 272.
17. Stopford-Sackville Mss, vol. II, folio 73, quoted in D. Syrett, "Defeat at Sea: The Impact of American Naval Operations upon the British, 1775–1778," in *Maritime Dimensions of the American Revolution* (1977), p. 19.
18. These three were probably the only American privateers operating in British waters in early 1779. London *Public Advertiser*, December 14, 1778 and May 24, 1779; Boston *Independent Chronicle*, April 18 and 22, 1779.
19. Quoted in R. Love, *History of the U. S. Navy* (2 vols., 1992), vol. 1: p. 17 (note 14).
20. G. W. Allen, *Naval History*, vol II: pp. 598–9.
21. Franklin explained his motives, summarized the cruises of the privateers, and described his links to the individuals granted the letters of marque in a letter to French foreign minister, Count Vergennes, 18 June 1780, F. Wharton, ed., *The Revolutionary Diplomatic Correspondence of the United States* (6 vols., 1889), vol. 3: pp. 801–3. Marchant published an account of the voyages in the Boston *Independent Chronicle*, March 9, 1780. All of Franklin's dealings with privateers are described in detail in W. B. Clark, *Ben Franklin's Privateers* (1956).
22. H. Auger, *The Secret War of Independence* (1955), pp. 202–7.
23. Macartney to Lord Germain, April 2, 1777, CO 101/20, Colonial Office Papers, Public Record Office quoted in A. G. Jamieson, "American Privateers in the Leeward Islands, 1776–1778," in *American Neptune* 43 (1983), pp. 24–5.
24. Deposition of Josiah Durham, December 13, 1777 quoted in Ibid., p. 28.
25. An account of the American Privateers and Armed Vessels Taken by the King's Ships under Admiral Young at Barbados and the Leeward Islands, November 24, 1775 to July 20, 1778, ADM 1/310, Admiralty Papers, Public Record Office, quoted ibid., pp. 26–7.
26. R. Albion and J. B Pope, *Sea Lanes in Wartime* (1942), pp. 41–2.
27. M. H. Jackson, *Privateers in Charleston, 1793–1796* (1969); Thomas Jefferson to France, September 7, 1793, J. Boyd, et al., eds., *The Papers of Thomas Jefferson*, (26 vols. to date, 1950-), vol. 27.
28. D. W. Knox, ed., *Naval Documents Related to the Quazi-War with France* (7 vols., 1935–8), vol. 1: pp. 67–8, 116–18, 141–2, 149–50 & 175–9.
29. U. Bonnel, *La France, Les Etats-Unis et la Guerre de Course, 1797–1815* (1961), p. 367.
30. Ibid., pp. 74–8, 87, 116–18, 142–3, 146–9 & 193–4.
31. W. S. Dudley, et al., eds., *The Naval War of 1812* (2 vols. to date, 1985–), vol. 1: pp. 167–70.
32. E. S. Maclay, *A History of American Privateering* (1924), pp. 225-6.
33. Ibid., pp. 228–31.
34. "A List of American Privateers Taken and Destroyed [July 1 to August 25, 1812]," in W. S. Dudley, et al., eds., *The Naval War of 1812* (2 vols to date, 1985–), vol. 1: 225–6.
35. Maclay, *American Privateering*, pp. 329–35.
36. Ibid., pp. 265–74.
37. William Jones to Commodore William Bainbridge, 11 October 1812, W. S. Dudley, et al., eds., *The Naval War of 1812* (2 vols. to date, 1985–), vol. 1: pp. 513.
38. Secretary of the Navy William Jones to Commanders of Ships Now in Port Refitting, February 22, 1813. Ibid., vol. 2: p. 48.
39. J. R. Garitee, *The Republic's Private Navy* (1977), provides the most comprehensive analysis of privateering for any port during any period.
40. Captain Reid's report of the action and that of John B. Dabney, U. S. consul at Fayal, are printed in G. Coggeshall, *History of American Privateers and letters of marque* (1856), pp. 371–83.
41. J. L. de Grummond, *The Baratarians and the Battle of New Orleans* (1961), pp. 3–15.
42. The *Spy* captured Spanish property worth $1,000,000. Maclay, *American Privateers*, p. 322.
43. de Grummond, *Baratarians*, pp. 19–21.
44. Ibid., pp. 37–48.
45. Proclamation of Andrew Jackson to the People of New Orleans, quoted in R. Reilly, *The British at the Gates* (1974), p. 205.
46. de Grummond, *Baratarians*, p. 278.
47. Reilly, *British at the Gates*, pp. 331–2.
48. *Niles' National Register*, April 19, 1823.
49. Quoted in R. G. Albion and J. B. Pope, *Sea Lanes in*

Wartime (1968, 2nd edn.), p. 146.
50. G. W. Allen, *Our Navy and the West Indian Pirates* (1929) and R. Wheeler, *In Pirate Waters* (1969).
51. "1856 Paris Declaration Respecting Maritime Law" in A. Roberts and R. Guelff, eds., *Documents on the Laws of War* (1989), pp. 23–7; F. R. Stark, *The Abolition of Privateering and the Declaration of Paris* (1897).
52. Garitee, *The Republic's Private Navy*, p. 243.
53. J. D. Richardson, *Compilation of the Messages and Papers of the Confederacy* (1906), pp. 60–62.
54. Lincoln's proclamation is quoted in W. M. Robinson, Jr., *The Confederate Privateers* (1928), p. 13, which also summarizes the legal actions taken by both sides (pp. 13–24).
55. Ibid., pp. 35–42.
56. Ibid., pp. 154–8 & 166–8.
57. Ibid., pp. 104–7 & 110–13.
58. Ibid., pp. 291–301.
59. "1907 Hague Convention VII Relating to the Conversion of Merchant Ships into Warships" in Roberts and Guelff (eds), *Laws of War*, pp. 79–84. C. D. Davis, *The United States and the Second Hague Peace Conference* (1975).

THE EASTERN SEAS

Notes
1. E. Presgrave to K. Murchison, Resident Councillor at Singapore. Report on Piracy in the Straits Settlements, December 5, 1828. India Office Records, Board's Collections, (IOR), IOR/F/4/1724 (69433).
2. S. Raffles to J. Crawford, Singapore, June 7, 1823, reproduced in full in C. B. Buckley, *An Anecdotal History of Old Times in Singapore,* 1902, pp. 116-19.
3. Abdullah bin Adbul Kadir. *The Hikayat Abdullah,* 1969, p. 163.
4. *Journal of the Indian Archipelago*, vol. 4, 1850, p. 47.
5. The Straits Settlements government, however, had to administer an active policy of piracy suppression without exceeding its authority as an appendage of the Indian government. Until 1867, when the Straits Settlements (comprising Singapore, Penang, and Malacca) were transferred to Colonial Office Administration, they were governed from India, and the Calcutta authorities had to weigh its responsibilities to protect British subjects and British trade in the East against the demands of international relations. The shifting relationships of these groups were in large measure to define the varying degrees of success in the fight against piracy over the next forty years.
6. *Journal of the Indian Archipelago*, vol. 4, 1850, p. 47.
7. C. Malcolm, Superintendent of Marine, Bombay, to Sir J. Malcolm, May 29, 1829, IOR/F/4/1330 (52554).
8. Owen to Pridham, July 31, 1830, IOR/F/4/1331 (52585).
9. IOR/F/4/52588, p. 73, 101.
10. "Complaint of the native merchants of Singapore...," 1833. IOR/F/4/1474 (57847).
11. Quoted by Governor Ibbetson in a letter to Fort William, Calcutta, May 4, 1833. IOR/F/4/1474 (57847).
12. H. Mackenzie, *Storms and Sunshine*, 1884, p. 57.
13. M. Burrows, *Memoir of Admiral Sir Henry,* 1869, p. 23.
14. H. Mackenzie, *Storms and Sunshine*, 1884, pp. 64-5.
15. M. Burrows, *Memoir of Admiral Sir Henry,* 1869, p. 22.
16. Account of the attack on Galang by Captain H. D. Chads, June 29, 1836. IOR/F/4/1724 (69433).
17. Captain H. D. Chads to Rear-Admiral Capel, Account of the affair off Point Romania, June 15, 1836. IOR/F/4/1724 (69433).
18. H. Keppel, *The Expedition to Borneo,* 1846.
19. H. Keppel, *The Expedition to Borneo,* 1853, vol. I, pp. 128-29.
20. H. Keppel, *The Expedition to Borneo,* 1846, vol. II, p. 89.
21. Ibid., p. 111.
22. H. Keppel, *The Expedition to Borneo,* 1846, vol. I, p. 158.
23. G. R. Mundy, *Narrative of Events*, 1848, vol. II, p. 17.
24. W. Dampier, *A New Voyage,* 1697 (1937 edn.), pp. 227-28.
25. IOR/F/4/1724 (69433). A more detailed account of Ilanun piracy was written by Captain Edward Belcher. His report was prepared with the help of firsthand information supplied by a Spanish naval officer who had been active in antipiracy in the Philippines in the late 1830s. (Belcher also repeats much of a report made by Captain Blake of HM sloop *Larne*, sent to gather information on the Ilanuns during a voyage to Manila in 1838.)
26. E. Belcher, *Narrative of the Voyage,* 1848, vol. I, p. 264. This seemingly magical disappearance was achieved by an efficiently organized system of lookouts in the trees. On the alarm being given, ropes were quickly led to the boats' point of entry into the mangrove and the proas hauled in over slips made from intersecting wooden stakes which formed a V-shaped bed extending into deep water, so that the impetus of the boats carried them up and almost out of the water. The ropes were then attached and the boats pulled through the mangrove deep into the forest.
27. H. Keppel, *The Expedition to Borneo,* 1846, vol. I, pp. 195-96.
28. Ibid., p. 195.
29. Report on piracy in the Sulu Sea by Captain Blake of the *Larne*, August 13, 1838. IOR/F/4/1978 (86974).
30. E. Belcher, *Narrative of the Voyage,* 1848, vol. I, p. 270.
31. Mundy, 1848, vol. II, p. 16.
32. E. Belcher, *Narrative of the Voyage,* 1848, vol. I, p. 270.
33. The *Seaflower* affair is described in IOR/F/4/714 (19495).
34. S. St. John, *Life in the Forests of the Far East,* 1862, vol. II, p. 214.
35. Unfortunately this victory was turned into a public relations disaster by Bishop McDougall of Labuan who took part in the fight and wrote a stirring account of the action in a letter to *The Times*. For a man of the cloth, he displayed a questionable enthusiasm for the slaughter to which he had been a willing party. While offering due thanks to God for allowing them to "punish these bloodthirsty foes of the human race," he reserved particular praise for his own breech-loader which "proved itself a most deadly weapon" and never failed once in eighty rounds. *The Times*, July 16, 1862, p. 5.
36. Brooke to Burdett Coutts, quoted in N. Tarling, *Piracy and Politics in the Malay World*, 1963, p. 179.
37. S. St. John, *Life in the Forests of the Far East,* 1862, vol. II, p. 212.

CHINESE PIRATES

Notes
Some material is quoted from *Pirates of the South China Coast, 1790 to 1910*, Copyright 1987 by the Board of Trustees of the Leland Stanford Junior University. Reproduced by permission of Stanford University Press.

CHINESE CURRENCY:
All references to dollars in the text are to Spanish dollars.

10 *cash* (*li* or *wen*)	= 1 candareen (*fen*)
10 candareen	= 1 mace (*ch'ien*)
10 mace	= 1 tael (*liang*)
1 tael	= approx. 1.33 Spanish dollars

1 dollar of foreign or Spanish silver (yuan) = 720-750 Chinese *cash*.
These equivalents cannot be accepted as firm, for there was considerable regional and local variation. For example, in 1805, twenty yuan of foreign silver equaled fourteen taels, one mace. In sycee or pure silver, the same amount equaled thirteen taels, one mace, four candareens, eight *cash*.
CHINESE DATES AND CITATIONS:
Citations from documentary collections are followed by a date of reign year, lunar month, and day according to the Chinese calendar. The Ch'ien-lung reign (1736–95) is abbreviated CL; The Chia-ch'ing reign (1796–1820) is abbreviated CC. "CL 58/8/11" is thus to be read Ch'ien-lung 58th year, eighth month, eleventh day. An asterisk(*) next to the month indicates the intercalary month that followed it. An "E" indicates an enclosure to the original document. Full titles of all works cited are given in the bibliography
1. J. Dryden, *Aenius*, VIII.
2. J. E. Wills, Jr., 1974: pp. 208, 211.
3. Ibid., p. 211.
4. Chan Hok-lam, "The Chien-wen, Yung-lo, Hung-hsi and Hsüan-te reigns, 1399–1435." in *The Cambridge History of China* (1988), vol. 7: part 1., p 236.
5. J. E. Wills, Jr., *Pepper, Guns and Parley* (1974), p. 206.
6. For more information see D. Murray, *Pirates of the South China Coast 1790–1810* (1987), p. 6.
7. For examples of fishermen's poverty see C. T. Downing, *The Fan-Oui in China in 1836–7* (1838, 3 vols.), vol. 1: pp. 106, 144, 210 and vol. 2: pp. 222, 223.
8. H. Kani, *A General Survey of the Boat People in Hong Kong* (1967), p. 70.
9. ***KTHFHL***, 2: 17-17b, also 23: 30 and 25: 7; Wang, C. "I hai-k'ou Ch'ing-hsing shu." [Discussion of the seaport situation.] in *Huang-ch'ao Ching-shih wen-pien* [Statecraft writings of the Ch'ing period], (comp. Ho Ch'ang-ling), 120 *chüan*, 1827, 85:36.
10. D. Murray, *Pirates of the South China Coast 1790–1810* (1987), pp. 24-26.
11. Ibid., pp. 26, 27.
12. Later, during the nineteenth century, as the Chinese control of the coast weakened and the British presence in Hong Kong complicated the jurisdictional situation even more, Hong Kong supplanted Chiang-p'ing as the premier headquarters of petty piracy.
13. The Navigation Acts were imposed by the British to interdict Dutch shipping to the American colonies in 1651.
14. In 1371 the first in a series of decrees forbidding coastal traders from voyaging overseas for private purposes was promulgated.
15. "Tribute system" is the term used by Westerners to describe the foreign relations of imperial China.
16. Chang Pin-tsun, "Maritime trade and local economy in late Ming Fukien," in *Development and Decline of Fukien* (1990), pp. 67-8; R. Lin, "Fukien's Private Sea Trade in the 16th and 17th Centuries." in *Development and Decline of Fukien* (1990). pp. 177-8.
17. J. Elisonas, "The inseparable trinity: Japan's relations with China and Korea." in *The Cambridge History of Japan* (1991), *vol. 4.*, pp. 249, 257. The destroyer of the bases was Chu Wan.
18. K. So, *Japanese Piracy in Ming China* (1975), p. 66; Chang Pin-tsun, "Maritime trade and local economy in late Ming Fukien," in *Development and Decline of Fukien* (1990), p. 69.
19. *Daimyo* literally means "great names" and referred to the powerful military families that controlled Japan's territory and functioned as local rulers from the Sengoku period (1467-1568) until the end of the Tokugawa shogunate in 1867.
20. Li Tan, the heir to Wang Chih's base in Hirado, negotiated with the Dutch for their removal from the Pescadores, which they had occupied in 1622, to Taiwan, which was accomplished in 1625. Cheng, Chih-lung was his agent and heir apparent.
21. J. E. Wills, Jr., *Pepper, Guns and Parley* (1974), p. 218.
22. These were of a different family from the Nguyen at Hue.
23. For more on the Tay-son Rebellion see C. B. Maybon, *Histoire moderne du pays d'Annam, 1592–1820* (1919), pp. 150-350 and D. Murray, *Pirates of the South China Coast 1790–1810* (1987), pp. 32-40.
24. G. Deveria, *Histoire des relations de la Chine avec l'Annam-Vietnam du XVIe au XICe siècle* (1880), p. 48; Wei Yüan, *Sheng-wu-chi* [Record of Ch'ing military exploits], 14 *chüan*, (1846, reprinted 1849), 8: 24b-25; ***TKHC*** 26: 5b; ***TKHC*** 33: 21b-22; ***DNTL***, 6: 5b.
25. D. Murray, *Pirates of the South China Coast 1790–1810* (1987), p. 65.
26. Hsiao Wan-om (Hsiao Yun-han), "Research in the History of the Pirates on the China Sea, 1140–1950." unpublished manuscript in Chinese (1976), fos. 23, 27; Hu Chieh-yü (Woo Kit-yü) "Hsi Ying-P'an and the end of the ravages of the pirate Chang Pao-tsai" in *Hong Kong and its external communications before 1842* (1959), p. 161; ***YCFC***, 8: 18b; ***KCT*** 008517, CC7/7/14.
27. For an account of this mission, see Trinh Hoai Duc, *Collected Poems of Can Trai* (1962), pp. 129-31.
28. Canton Consultations, March 24, 1804.
29. A translation of the entire agreement can be found in D. Murray, *Pirates of the South China Coast 1790–1810* (1987), pp. 57-9.
30. ***CHFC*** 1: 3, 10b; ***CP*** 1121/17, CC1/7/12.
31. ***KTHFHL*** 42: 31b-32, CC15/1; ***NHHC***, 14: 20-20b; Hsiao Wan-om (Hsiao Yun-han), "Research in the History of the Pirates on the China Sea, 1140–1950." unpublished manuscript in Chinese (1976), fo. 20; Hu Chieh-yü (Woo Kit-yü) "Hsi Ying-P'an and the end of the ravages of the pirate Chang Pao-tsai" in *Hong Kong and its external communications before 1842* (1959), p. 164; ***CHFC*** 1: 3; ***NYC*** 13: 60, CC10/11/6; ***CP*** 1139/5, CC11/4/30; and ***CP*** 1121/08, CC12/11/11.
32. ***NYC*** 13: 57, CC10/11/6.
33. D. Murray, *Pirates of the South China Coast 1790–1810* (1987), p. 61.
34. ***CSL*** 137: 176, CC9/11/24.
35. ***CHFC*** 1: 5b, 6b, and P. Maughan, "An Account of the Ladrones Who Infested the Coast of China." in *Further Statement of the Ladrones* (1812), p 29.
36. ***CHFC*** 1: 4b; ***KTHFHL*** 42: 32-3; P. Maughan, "An Account of the Ladrones Who Infested the Coast of China." in *Further Statement of the Ladrones* (1812), p 12.
37. D. Murray, *Pirates of the South China Coast 1790–1810* (1987), pp. 68-9.

38. *CHFC* 1: 14-14b; J. Turner, "Account of the Captivity of J. Turner" in *Further Statement of the Ladrones* (1812), p. 67; *NYC* 13: 1b, CC10/9/4.
39. *NYC* 12: 51-52b, CC10/7/1; *NYC* 12: 67b-68a, CC10/7/25.
40. C. A. Montalto de Jesus, *Historic Macao* (1926, 2nd. edn.), p. 231; p. 63, 65; Maughan (1812), pp. 24, 25.
41. J. Turner, "Account of the Captivity of J. Turner" in *Further Statement of the Ladrones* (1812), p. 65.
42. Ibid., p. 49, and R. Glasspoole, "Glasspoole's letter to the president of the East India Company's factory" in *Further Statement of the Ladrones* (1812), p. 33.
43. *NYC* 12: 81b, C10/8/28 and C. L. F. F. Renouard de Sainte-Croix, *Voyage commercial et politique aux Indes Orientales* (1810, 2 vols.), vol. 2, p. 56.
44. J. Turner, "Account of the Captivity of J. Turner" in *Further Statement of the Ladrones* (1812), p. 63; G. R. G. Worcester, *Sail and Sweep in China* (1966), 1966: p. 44; E. Brown, *Cochin-China, and My Experience of It* (1861, reprinted Taipei 1971), p. 79.
45. R. Glasspoole, *History of the Pirates Who Infested the China Sea from 1807 to 1810* (1831, trans. Neumann, K. F.), p. 112.
46. J. Turner, "Account of the Captivity of J. Turner" in *Further Statement of the Ladrones* (1812), pp. 63, 64; Maughan, 1812; p. 25; C. L. F. F. Renouard de Sainte-Croix, *Voyage commercial et politique aux Indes Orientales* (1810, 2 vols.), vol. 2, p. 56; *NYC* 12: 53, CC10/7/1.
47. *NYC* 12: 81b-82, CC10/8/28; *NYC* 13: 35b-36, CC10/10/2.
48. *CHFC* 1: 15; *KCT* 010976, CC13/5*/19; *NHHC* 25: 20b.
49. *KTHFHL* 42: 26b; *CHFC* 1:5a; Hsiao Wan-om (Hsiao Yun-han), "Research in the History of the Pirates on the China Sea, 1140–1950." unpublished manuscript in Chinese (1976), fo. 28.
50. *CHFC* 1: 5a-b; Hsiao Wan-om (Hsiao Yun-han), "Research in the History of the Pirates on the China Sea, 1140–1950." unpublished manuscript in Chinese (1976), fo.

28.; *NHHC*, 14: 20b; Lin Tse-hsu, memorial of TK 20/5/15 (July 14th, 1840), reproduced in L. Yeh, *The legends and facts about Chang Pao-tsai* (1970), p. 69.
51. *CHFC* 1: 5b-6b; J. Turner, "Account of the Captivity of J. Turner" in *Further Statement of the Ladrones* (1812), p. 71, and P. Maughan, "An Account of the Ladrones Who Infested the Coast of China." in *Further Statement of the Ladrones* (1812), p. 29.
52. R. Glasspoole, "Substance of Mr. Glasspoole's relation" in *Further Statement of the Ladrones* (1812), pp. 44-5.
53. D. Murray, *Pirates of the South China Coast 1790–1810* (1987), pp. 80, 81.
54. *KCT* 000981, CC1/7/29; *NYC* 12: 41, CC10/7/1; Renouard de Sainte-Croix, 1810, vol. 2, p. 54; *NYC* 14: 23, CC10/4/20; and J. Turner" in *Further Statement of the Ladrones* (1812), pp. 49-61.
55. *NYC* 12: 31b-32, CC10/6/15; April 4, 1805.
56. P. Maughan, "An Account of the Ladrones Who Infested the Coast of China." in *Further Statement of the Ladrones* (1812), pp. 30, 69; A. J. Von Krusenstern, *Voyage Round the World* (1813), 2 vols., trans. A. B. Hoppner), vol. 2, p. 310; *NYC* 12: 32, CC10/6/15.
57. J. Turner, "Account of the Captivity of J. Turner" in *Further Statement of the Ladrones* (1812), p. 69. A. J. Von Krusenstern, *Voyage Round the World* (1813), vol. 2, p. 310.
58. P. Maughan, "An Account of the Ladrones Who Infested the Coast of China." in *Further Statement of the Ladrones* (1812), p. 30; J. Turner "Account of the Captivity of J. Turner" in *Further Statement of the Ladrones* (1812), p. 72.
59. Ibid., p. 66.
60. Canton Consultations, April 3, 1804.
61. *CSL* 137: 16b, CC9/11/24.
62. *KCT* 009666, CC13/1/6; *KCT* 09669, CC13/1/7; *KCT* 009676, CC13/1/8.
63. P. Maughan, "An Account of the Ladrones Who Infested the Coast of China." in *Further Statement of the Ladrones* (1812), p 19; *KCT* 013354, CC14/2/16.

64. *CHFC* 1: 7b; Canton Consultations, September 1st/2nd/5th, 1809; *KCT* 015184, CC14/8/23; L. G. Gomes, *Páginas da historia de Macau*, (1966), pp. 140, 141; J. Andrade, *Memoria dos feitos macaenses* (1835), p. 34.
65. Canton Consultations, September, 1809.
66. A. L. Gomes, *Esboço da historia de Macau, 1511 a 1849* (1957), p. 309; J. Andrade, *Memoria dos feitos macaenses* (1835), pp. 44-5; L. G. Gomes, *Páginas da historia de Macau*, (1966), p. 160.
67. R. Glasspoole, *History of the Pirates Who Infested the China Sea from 1807 to 1810* (1831, trans. Neumann, K. F.), p. 123. Chinese accounts of the siege can be found in *KTHFHL* 42: 216-22 and *CP* 1120/01, CC14/10/29.

PIRACY TODAY
Notes
1. J. Vagg, "Rough Seas," British Journal of Criminology, Winter 1995.
2. Article 101 of the U.N. Convention of the Law of the Sea defines piracy as:
(a) any illegal acts of violence or detention, or any act of depredation committed for private ends by the crew or the passengers of a private ship or a private aircraft and directed
    (i) on the high seas, against another ship or aircraft, or against persons or property on board such ship or aircraft
    (ii) against a ship, aircraft, persons or property in a place outside the jurisdiction of any State;
(b) any act of voluntary participation in the operation of a ship or of an aircraft with knowledge of facts making it a pirate ship or aircraft;
(c) any act of inciting or intentionally facilitating an act described in para. (a) or (b).
3. Interview with Dr. Martin Gill, Centre for the Study of Public Order, Leicester University.
4. U. S. Department of Energy Report 1993.

GLOSSARY OF SEA TERMS

aft Situated at the back or stern part of a vessel.
bangkong A shallow Dyak craft up to 100 feet long (30m) with a long overhanging stem and stern.
bark or barque A vessel with fore-and-aft sails on the mizzen or aftermost mast, and square-rigged sails on the other two (or sometimes three) masts.
bow The front or forward part of a ship or boat.
brig A two-masted vessel, fully square-rigged on both masts, with a fore-and-aft sail on the lower part of the mainmast.
brigantine A two-masted vessel having a fully square-rigged foremast and a fore-and-aft rigged mainmast with square sails on the main topmast.
canoe A boat without a keel, propelled by paddles. The native canoes of Central and South America were dug-outs carved out of solid tree trunks.
caravel Sailing vessel used by the Portuguese and Spanish for coastal work as well as ocean voyages. Early caravels carried lateen sails on two or three masts.
careen An operation that involved beaching a ship, heeling her over, and cleaning the weed and barnacles from her bottom.
carrack A large, heavily built vessel, usually three-masted, developed in the Mediterranean and used as a warship and for trading voyages from the fourteenth to the seventeenth centuries.
consort A vessel sailing in company with a pirate ship; a companion vessel.
cruiser A warship sent on detached operations alone or in company with one or two others.
cutter A small one-masted vessel rigged with a fore-and-aft mainsail, foresail, and jib. In the eighteenth century a cutter usually had a square topsail as well.
dhow A sailing vessel of Arabian origin with one or two lateen sails, particularly associated with the Red Sea and the shores of the Indian Ocean.
East Indiaman A large, armed merchant ship owned and operated by the East India companies for trading with India and the East.

fellucca A small coasting vessel with a lateen sail, used in the Mediterranean.
fore Situated in front; the front part of a vessel at the bow.
frigate A fast warship, usually armed with between twenty and thirty guns, that was too small for the line of battle but powerful enough for independent action and often used against pirates.
galeass A formidable fighting vessel developed in the Mediterranean around 1500 that combined the speed of the oar-powered galley with the seaworthiness of the galleon.
galleon A large square-rigged warship developed around 1570. Most of the Spanish treasure ships were galleons, but they were also used by the navies of England, France, and Holland.
galleot A small galley (a galliot was a Dutch coasting vessel).
galley A swift oar-powered vessel that was the principal fighting ship of the Mediterranean from Ancient Greece to the sixteenth century. It carried sails in addition to oars.
gig A light, narrow ship's boat.
grab An Indian sailing vessel used for carrying cargo and usually rigged with three masts.
guineaman A large, armed merchant ship used by the maritime countries of Europe for trading with the Guinea coast of Africa.
jolly boat The smallest of a ship's boats.
junk The general term for the flat-bottomed, ligsail-rigged vessels used for centuries in the China Seas. There were a variety of local types adapted for coastal work and ocean voyages.
lateen-rig Triangular sail or sails set from a longyard at an angle of forty-five degrees to the mast.
man-o'-war An armed warship used by the navy of a country.
paddleship (or paddle steamer) A vessel propelled by paddle-wheels that were usually powered by a steam engine.
pinnace A small, fast vessel decked like a ship that could be rowed and sailed; the term was also used to describe one

of the larger boats used by naval ships for ferrying men ashore.
pirogue A large dug-out canoe propelled by paddles or oars, and sometimes fitted with a single sail, that was used by the natives of Central and South America.
proa A Malayan boat with a large triangular sail and an outrigger.
sampan A small Far Eastern boat propelled by a single scull over the stern and having a roofing of matting.
schooner A two-masted vessel, fore-and-aft rigged on both masts. Some vessels had square topsails on the foremast or on both topmasts.
shallop In the sixteenth century this was a large, seaworthy vessel, but the term was later used to describe a light open boat.
ship of the line A warship large enough to take her place in the line of battle; in the early eighteenth century this ranged from fourth-rate ships of fifty guns up to first-rate ships of 100 guns.
sloop A vessel having one fore-and-aft rigged mast with mainsail and a single foresail. In the eighteenth century the term also applied to a small vessel armed with four to twelve guns on her upper deck and rigged with one, two, or three masts.
sloop-of-war A small warship. In the Royal Navy the term was used to describe a cruising vessel smaller than a sixth-rate that was commanded by a master and commander.
square-rigged The principal sails set at right angles to the length of the ship and extended by horizontal yards slung to the mast (as opposed to fore-and-aft rigged).
steam tender A small vessel powered by a steam engine.
tartan A single-masted lateen-rigged vessel that originated in the Mediterranean.
trireme Ancient Greek warship with three banks of oars.
xebec A fast Mediterranean sailing vessel, originally lateen-rigged but later fitted with square sails.
yacht Now generally refers to vessels used for sport and pleasure, but in the seventeenth century royal and naval yachts were armed and accompanied fleets into battle.

PICTURE CREDITS

The publishers are grateful to the institutions and individuals that helped to illustrate the book. Particular thanks go to John Batchelor for his outstanding artwork and professionalism; Janos Marffy for his reliable mapwork; Christopher Gray at the Customer Services division of the National Maritime Museum for his help over the time it took to bring everything together; Trudy Apple at the Delaware Art Museum for her patience; John R. Schoonover; David Edge at the Wallace Collection; and last, but by no means least, Anita Pensar, librarian at Stiftelsen Ålands Sjöfartsmuseum, Mariehamn, Finland, for the work put in with Rita Jokiranta in order to provide us with a transparency of a pirate flag.

All the sources that supplied photographs, paintings and/or artifacts are credited here by page number and position, with any reference numbers where known. For reasons of space, some references have had to be abbreviated. The principal photographic source is the National Maritime Museum (NMM), Greenwich, England.

Front cover: Ålands Sjöfartsmuseum, photo ©Rita Jokiranta; **Back cover:** National Maritime Museum (NMM), Greenwich, photograph by Peter Robinson; **1:** Reproduced by permission of the Trustees of the Wallace Collection OA 1633; **2:** Delaware Art Museum, Museum Purchase 1912: *The Buccaneer Was A Picturesque Fellow*, by Howard Pyle; **3:** NMM D5470; **4/5:** Reproduced by permission of the Trustees of the Wallace Collection OA 2087; **6:** NMM BHC 0360; **7:** NMM A1763; **8:** The Board of Trustees of the Royal Armouries, TR 603, object XXVIS–58; **9:** (left) Hulton Deutsch Collection 04177114, (right) The Science Museum/Science & Society Picture Library SCM/ORM/100067; **10/11:** NMM BHC 0354; **12:** NMM PW 4548; **13:** NMM D7565; **14:** courtesy John R. Schoonover; **15:** Public Record Office, HCA 1/99, photographed by Jonathan Pollock for Salamander Books, Crown copyright reproduced with the permission of the Controller of Her Majesty's Stationery Office; **16:** Christie's Images KSSIL290592; **17:** Ancient Art & Architecture Collection PE15DC5; **18:** NMM D5269-26; **19:** NMM BHC 0320; **20:** (top) Salamander Books Ltd., (bottom) NMM C9690; **21:** NMM BHC 0262; **22:** Mary Evans Picture Library; **23:** Robert F. Marx; **24-25:** Reproduced by permission of the Trustees of the Wallace Collection A596; **25:** Ancient Art & Architecture Collection F12TB216; **26:** The Masters and Fellows, Magdalene College, Cambridge; **27:** NMM BHC 2603; **28:** NMM 2673; **29:** Mary Evans Picture Library; **30:** Mary Evans Picture Library; **31:** NMM BHC 2662; **32:** NMM A6820; **33:** NMM A6821; **34:** (both) Robert F. Marx; **35:** NMM BHC0801; **36:** NMM D6170-1; **37:** Robert F. Marx; **38:** Christie's Images KS1SIL280592158F; **39:** map by Janos Marffy, © Salamander Books Ltd; **40:** Hulton Deutsch Collection 02861844; **41:** Delaware Art Museum, Museum Purchase, 1912 *An Attack on a Galleon*, by Howard Pyle; **42-43:** John Batchelor artwork, © Salamander Books Ltd; **44:** NMM D6004-E; **45:** Delaware Art Museum, *Marooned*, by Howard Pyle; **46:** Delaware Art Museum, Gift of Dr. James Stillman, *Which Shall be Captain?*, by Howard Pyle; **48:** NMM D6170-5; **49:** NMM D7336-H; **50:** NMM D6004-D; **51:** NMM BHC 1841; **52:** NMM A1275; **53:** Collection of Mr. and Mrs. E. Douglas Allen, Photograph courtesy of the Brandywine River Museum;

54-55: Mary Evans Picture Library; **56:** NMM 752; **57:** (top) Hulton Deutsch Collection 02888491, (bottom) NMM BHC 2874; **58:** NMM D4447A; **59:** NMM 8450; **60:** NMM BHC 0315; **61:** map by Janos Marffy, © Salamander Books Ltd; **62:** By Courtesy of the National Portrait Gallery, London; **63:** NMM D7512; **64:** NMM D7490-A; **65:** courtesy John R. Schoonover; **66:** NMM D5219; **67:** NMM C9775; **68:** Hulton Deutsch Collection 04172925; **69:** NMM C4563; **70:** NMM C4563; **71:** Hulton Deutsch Collection; **72:** NMM C4563; **73:** NMM D5215; **74:** NMM D4791; **75:** NMM no ref; **76:** NMM BHC 0747; **77:** Ålands Sjöfartsmuseum, photo ©Rita Jokiranta; **78:** Ancient Art & Architecture Collection; **79:** map by Janos Marffy, © Salamander Books Ltd; **80:** (top) NMM D6170-4, (bottom) NMM D6045-C; **81:** NMM PU229; **82-83:** John Batchelor artwork, © Salamander Books Ltd; **84-85:** Reproduced by permission of the Trustees of the Wallace Collection, OA 1787; **85:** NMM B4863; **86-87:** NMM BHC0893; **88:** NMM BHC 1945; **89:** NMM BHC0849; **90:** NMM D6045; **91:** NMM D6045-B; **92:** NMM BHC0617; **93:** NMM A1607; **94:** NMM D7703; **95:** NMM BHC 0256; **96:** Reproduced by permission of the Trustees of the Wallace Collection, A 493; **97:** (both) Mary Evans Picture Library; **98:** NMM S5964; **99:** Reproduced by permission of the Trustees of the Wallace Collection, OA 2157; **100:** courtesy John R. Schoonover; **101:** NMM D7566; **102:** NMM D5970; **103:** Delaware Art Museum, courtesy John Falconer, *Extorting Tribute from the Citizens*, by Howard Pyle; **104-105:** NMM BHC 0348; **106:** Richard Platt; **107:** NMM BHC 1109; **108:** NMM D7491-F; **109:** NMM D7491-E; **110-111:** NMM 436; **112:** NMM 6569; **113:** courtesy John R. Schoonover/Millport Conservancy, Lititz, PA; **115:** Delaware Art Museum, Gift of Willard S. Moore, 1922: Acc 1878, *Blackbeard's Last Fight*, by Howard Pyle; **116:** NMM 6588; **117:** NMM D6170-3; **118:** NMM 7750; **119:** NMM D6038; **120:** NMM A497; **121:** NMM BHC 2917; **122:** NMM D7526; **123:** Public Record Office, photographed by Jonathan Pollock for Salamander Books, Crown copyright reproduced with the permission of the Controller of Her Majesty's Stationery Office; **124:** Mary Evans Collection; **125:** NMM D4001; **126:** NMM 774; **127:** NMM 3945; **128-129:** NMM BHC 1118; **130:** NMM 7301; **131:** NMM PU 0157; **132-133:** Delaware Art Museum, Acc no 904, Museum Purchase 1912: *So the Treasure was Divided*, by Howard Pyle; **134:** NMM D3864-10; **135:** NMM D7531-N; **136:** NMM D3920; **137:** Mansell Collection no 961; **138:** Mansell Collection no 974; **139:** Mutiny by Howard Pyle, Permanent Collection of the University of Delaware; **140:** NMM BHC 1011; **141:** Robert F. Marx; **142:** map by Janos Marffy, © Salamander Books Ltd; **142-143:** NMM BHC 0748; **144:** Hulton Deutsch Collection 02032780; **145:** NMM PU 1834; **146:** NMM D7543-D; **147:** Public Record Office, ref HCA 1/98 Pt.1 85B, photographed by Jonathan Pollock for Salamander Books; **148:** Mary Evans Picture Library; **149:** Peabody Essex Museum, Salem, Mass., photo by Mark Sexton, E72016; **150:** NMM 829; **151:** NMM D5988; **153:** Delaware Art Museum, Museum Purchase, 1912: *Kidd on the deck of the Adventure Galley*, by Howard Pyle; **154:** NMM BHC 2993; **155:** Public Record Office, ref HCA 1/15 Pt.2 F.108, Crown copyright reproduced with the permission of the Controller of Her Majesty's Stationery Office; **156-157:** John Batchelor artwork, © Salamander Books Ltd; **158:** Mary Evans Picture Library; **159:** Mary Evans Picture Library;

160: (left) NMM A8392, (right) NMM D3864-15; **161:** courtesy John R. Schoonover; **162:** NMM BHC 1873; **163:** NMM D7491-D; **164:** *Privateers of '76* by Frank Schoonover, Permanent Collection of the University of Delaware; **165:** NMM D6033; **166:** NMM PW 3284; **167:** Public Record Office, Prize Office document 4 May 1703 ADM1/3662, photographed by Jonathan Pollock for Salamander Books, Crown copyright reproduced with the permission of the Controller of Her Majesty's Stationery Office; **168/169:** NMM A4217; **170:** NMM BHC 1038; **171:** map by Janos Marffy, © Salamander Books Ltd; **172:** NMM 9694; **173:** NMM D7490-B; **174:** NMM PW3477; **175:** NMM D4739; **176:** NMM D8260; **177:** NMM BHC 0425; **178:** NMM A2413; **179:** courtesy John R. Schoonover; **180/181:** (top) Peabody Essex Museum, Salem, Mass., photograph by Mark Sexton, ref M3459; **181:** Salamander books Ltd; **182:** NMM D7531-K; **183:** courtesy John R. Schoonover; **185:** Gift of Samuel B. Bird, The Herbert F. Johnson Museum of Art, Cornell University, Ithaca, NY; **186/187:** NMM A103; **188:** John Falconer; **189:** NMM D6096; **191:** NMM A3968; **192/193:** Sotheby's Transparency Library, ref JL3112; **194:** NMM PW 4801; **195:** John Falconer; **196:** John Falconer; **197:** NMM B3836; **198:** (both) John Falconer; **199:** The Mansell Collection no 948; **200/201:** NMM D6035; **201:** John Falconer; **202:** Reproduced by permission of the Trustees of the Wallace Collection, OA 1700; **203:** John Falconer; **204:** Liverpool University via John Falconer; **205:** John Falconer; **206:** John Falconer; **207:** NMM D5978-A; **208:** John Falconer; **209:** Reproduced by permission of the Trustees of the Wallace Collection, OA 1634; **210:** Public Record Office: China Station Records: Piracy in the Straits of Malacca 1873-74, ADM 125/148, folio 296, photographed by Jonathan Pollock for Salamander Books; **211:** John Falconer; **212:** NMM D7497; **213:** NMM D5470; **214:** NMM X2905; **215:** map by Janos Marffy, © Salamander Books Ltd; **216:** NMM BHC 4214; **217:** The Board of Trustees of the Royal Armouries, TR 614, object XXVIS-191; **218:** NMM C7829; **219:** Sotheby's Transparency Library JL 3648; **220:** Peabody Essex Museum, Salem, Mass., by Mark Sexton, ref 124, 724; **221:** NMM X2894; **222:** NMM D5977-A; **223:** NMM D7615; **224:** (top) NMM D5488, (below) NMM D3865-10; **225:** NMM D8106; **226/227:** John Batchelor artwork, © Salamander Books Ltd; **228:** NMM 792; **229:** Robert F. Marx; **230:** NMM D7119-A; **231:** The Board of Trustees of the Royal Armouries, TR 588, object XXVID-35; **232:** NMM D5453; **233:** NMM A7548; **234:** NMM A7547; **235:** Public Record Office, China Station Records Vol. 4, Piracy at & In The Neighborhood of Hong Kong 1835-1852, photographed by Jonathan Pollock for Salamander Books; **236:** Mike Goldwater/Network F00303-E1-01-004; **237:** Salamander Books Ltd; **238:** Eric Pasquier/SYGMA 267995; **239:** Salamander Books Ltd; **240:** Salamander Books Ltd; **241:** Eric Pasquier/SYGMA 267995; **242:** Mike Goldwater/ Network F00303-E1-060; **243:** Mike Goldwater/Network F00303-E1-019.

Editor's Note

Every effort has been made to contact original sources, where known, for permissions. The selection and captioning of all illustrations in this book have been the responsibility of Salamander Books Ltd and not of the individual contributors.

INDEX